Multidisciplinary Approaches to the Discourses of Extremism

This collection highlights multidisciplinary approaches toward better understanding the discourses of extremism, exploring the ways in which insights from linguistics and other disciplines might inform each other in enacting meaningful reforms in policy, social media, and education.

The volume is divided into three sections, bridging different disciplinary perspectives in examining different dimensions of the language of extremism in case studies from around the world. The first section features contributions on extremist language from a political lens, such as in election campaigns and media discourse. The second section looks at religious extremism and language used for the purposes of jihadist radicalisation and recruitment. A final section reflects on policy development, peace education, and conflict resolution, toward discussing ways to subvert radicalised discourses and future research building on these efforts.

This book will be of interest to students and scholars in discourse analysis, language and communication, and language education, as well as related fields such as psychology, political science, and sociology.

Katie Jane Patterson obtained her PhD in 2016 from the University of Liverpool. She has held full-time teaching positions at the University of Eastern Finland, University Austral de Chile, and the University of Roehampton in London. She now works at the University of Granada. Her research interests include metaphor, lexical priming and discourse analysis.

Encarnación Hidalgo-Tenorio is a Full Professor in English Linguistics at the University of Granada. Since obtaining her PhD, her work has combined her interest in the relationship between language and gender, language and politics, Critical Discourse Analysis, Corpus Linguistics, Forensic Linguistics and Systemic Functional Linguistics.

Routledge Research in Language and Communication

Revisiting Trustworthiness in Social Interaction
Mie Femø Nielsen and Ann Merrit Rikke Nielsen

Communicative Spaces and Media in Bilingual Contexts
Discourses, Synergies and Counterflows in Spanish and English
Edited by Ana Sánchez-Muñoz and Jessica Retis

The Impact of Plain Language on Legal English in the United Kingdom
Christopher Williams

Political Myth-making, Populist Performance and Nationalist Resistance
Examining Kwame Nkrumah's Construction of the African Unity Dream
Mark Nartey

Metaphor and Argumentation in Climate Crisis Discourse
Anaïs Augé

Perspectives on Teaching Workplace English in the 21st Century
Mable Chan

The Discursive Construction of Place in the Digital Age
Edited by Alejandro Parini and Francisco Yus

Perspectives on Knowledge Communications
Concepts and Settings
Edited by Jan Engberg, Antoinette Fage-Butler, and Peter Kastberg

Multidisciplinary Approaches to the Discourses of Extremism
Edited by Katie Jane Patterson and Encarnación Hidalgo-Tenorio

For more information about this series, please visit: https://www.routledge.com/Routledge-Research-in-Language-and-Communication/book-series/RRLC

Multidisciplinary Approaches to the Discourses of Extremism

Edited by Katie Jane Patterson and Encarnación Hidalgo-Tenorio

Routledge
Taylor & Francis Group
NEW YORK AND LONDON

First published 2025
by Routledge
605 Third Avenue, New York, NY 10158

and by Routledge
4 Park Square, Milton Park, Abingdon, Oxon, OX14 4RN

Routledge is an imprint of the Taylor & Francis Group, an informa business

Library of Congress Cataloging-in-Publication Data
Names: Patterson, Katie J., editor. | Hidalgo Tenorio, Encarnación, 1968– editor.
Title: Multidisciplinary approaches to the discourses of extremism / edited by Katie Jane Patterson and Encarnación Hidalgo-Tenorio.
Description: New York: Routledge, 2024. |
Series: Routledge research in language and communication |
Includes bibliographical references and index. |
Identifiers: LCCN 2024014958 | ISBN 9781032600680 (hbk) | ISBN 9781032600697 (pbk) | ISBN 9781003457381 (ebk)
Subjects: LCSH: Language and languages—Political aspects. | Language and languages—Religious aspects. | Radicalization. | Radicalism. | LCGFT: Essays.
Classification: LCC P119.3 .M84 2024 | DDC 306.44/9—dc23/eng/20240418
LC record available at https://lccn.loc.gov/2024014958

ISBN: 9781032600680 (hbk)
ISBN: 9781032600697 (pbk)
ISBN: 9781003457381 (ebk)

DOI: 10.4324/9781003457381

Typeset in Sabon
by codeMantra

Contents

Contributors

Ruth Breeze is a Full Professor of English at the University of Navarra, Spain, and combines teaching with research as a member of the GradUN Research Group in the Instituto Cultura y Sociedad. Her research interests include corpus linguistics, legal discourse and media discourse.

Jocelyn J. Bélanger is an Associate Professor at Carnegie Mellon University in Qatar. Dr. Bélanger's research focuses on the process of radicalization and interventions to bring about deradicalization.

Enrique Clari is a "la Caixa" INPhINIT predoctoral researcher and a PhD candidate at the Autonomous University of Madrid (UAM). He researches Europeans' attitudes towards democracy and the declining support for liberal principles among the citizenship.

Andrea Cocchini lectures in Public International Law and European Union Law at the University of Navarra. He holds a doctoral degree in Public International Law and International Relations from the University of Navarra and read Law at the University of Milan.

Jordi Collet Social educator and sociologist, is an associate professor of sociology of education at the University of Vic-UCC (Barcelona), as well as a Visiting Fellow at University College London and the University of Cambridge. His research interests are education policy; family-school-community relations; equity and inclusion in education; and educations for the common (good).

Federico Aznar Fernández-Montesinos is Principal Analyst of the Spanish Institute for Strategic Studies, Commander of the Navy, Graduate (UNED) and Doctor (UCM) in Political Science. He has written three books and more than 200 articles with three books on topics related to Theory of War, geopolitics, Terrorism and Sociology.

Javier García-Marín is a professor of political science at the University of Granada. He focuses on new methodologies and machine learning in the study of political communication.

Saqlain Hassan currently works as an Assistant Professor of English Linguistics and corpus linguistics at the Riphah International University, Pakistan. His interests lie in the sentiment analysis of social media (such as X), discourse and corpus-assisted discourse analysis of media and refugee discourses.

Encarnación Hidalgo-Tenorio is a Full Professor in English Linguistics at the University of Granada. Since obtaining her PhD, her work has combined her interest in the relationship between language and gender, Corpus-Assisted Critical Discourse Analysis, Forensic Linguistics, and Systemic Functional Grammar.

Jonatan Morillo Losada is a Doctoral candidate in the doctoral program in Social and Legal Sciences at the University of Córdoba (Spain). Engaged in the Psychosocial Research, Clinical, and Applied Psychology research line. His primary concerns revolve around violent radicalization and violent Islamist extremism.

Djallil Lounnas is an Associate professor of International Relations at Al AKhawayn University and the coordinator of Alakhwayn research team part of the H2020 European Union consortium Preventing Violent Extremism (PREVEX) project. He is a specialist of Jihadism a topic over which he has published numerous papers as well as the book Le Djihadism en Afrique du Nord et au Sahel (2019).

Michele Martini is a Postdoctoral Fellow at the Institute of Media and Journalism (Università della Svizzera Italiana), and works at the intersection of Sociology of Communication, Critical Discourse Analysis and Computational Social Science. His work focuses on the relationship between digital media and education, with a specific emphasis on global institutions.

Tony McEnery is a Distinguished Professor of Linguistics and English Language at Lancaster University and holds the Changjiang Chair at Xi'an Jiaotong University. He has worked since the late 1980s on studying language using corpus data. He has published widely on a range of languages, topics and methods, with notable publications including Corpus Linguistics: Method, Theory and Practice (Cambridge University Press, 2011, with Hardie).

José Javier Olivas Osuna is a senior Talento Programme Researcher at the National Distance Education University (UNED) in Madrid and a Research Associate at LSE IDEAS. His areas of expertise include populism, borders, civil-military relations and democratisation.

Michael T. L. Pace-Sigge is a Senior Lecturer at the University of Eastern Finland, Finland. His key areas of research are spoken English, corpus linguistics and lexical priming. Formerly of the University of Liverpool, he is a specialist in the Scouse accent. He is the author of Lexical Priming in Spoken English Usage (2013), Spreading Activation, Lexical Priming and the Semantic Web (2018) and Linked Noun Groups (2020) as well as co-editor of Lexical Priming: Advances and Applications (2017).

Katie Jane Patterson is a researcher at the University of Granada. Her main research areas are metaphor, discourse analysis and lexical priming.

Pascual Pérez-Paredes is a Professor of Applied Linguistics and Linguistics, U. Murcia, and a former Lecturer in Research in Second Language Education at the University of Cambridge. His main research interests are the use of corpus linguistics methods in applied linguistics, corpus-assisted discourse analysis and corpora and digital resources in language education.

Massimo Ramaioli is an Assistant Professor of International Relations at Al Akhawayn University and Coordinator at the School of Human and Social Sciences (SHSS). Specialist of Salafism jihadism, he has authored several academic papers and book chapters with a focus on Salafism in Jordan.

Lynn Revell is a Professor of Religion and Education at Canterbury Christ Church University where she is Director of Research for the Faculty of Arts, Humanities and Education. She has published widely in the areas of extremism, the representation of Islam in Education and the place of Religions in schools as well as notions of free speech and academic freedom in schools and universities.

Ignacio-Jesús Serrano-Contreras is a lecturer in political science at the University of Granada. He is also a research collaborator at the Robert Zajonc Institute of the University of Warsaw. He specialises in natural language processing and the development of multidisciplinary techniques.

Francisco José Sánchez-García is an Associate Professor of Linguistics at the Department of Spanish Language of Universidad de Granada. His main line of research focuses on the pragmatics of discourse, namely political language and journalistic manipulation, populist discourse and the language of social networks, presently combined with an interest in multimedia communication and transmedia narratives.

Francesc Torras is a social educator and anthropologist. He is the coordinator of different community projects in the county of Osona (Barcelona). He is a specialist in the anthropological approach and research-action at the service of community processes and development.

Teun A. van Dijk is a professor of discourse studies at Pompeu Fabra University and founding Director of the Centre of Discourse Studies, Barcelona. After earlier research on text grammar and the psychology of discourse in the 1970s, his work since the 1980s is in the field of Critical Discourse Studies, with publications on racist discourse, news analysis, ideology, context, knowledge and antiracism.

Polina Zavershinskaia is a doctoral researcher at the Institute of Political Science, Leipzig University and a research investigator of Mapping the Far-Right Truth Industry (MAFTI) international research group. In her research, she examines national memory narratives of various German and Russian conservative populist actors and their symbolic affective potential.

Acknowledgements

We heartily thank Jasmine Erice-Harling and Elysse Preposi, from Routledge, for their helpful comments; as well as Miguel-Ángel Benítez-Castro, from the University of Zaragoza, Juan-Luis Castro-Peña, from the University of Granada, and David J. Carter, from Cambridge University, for encouraging exciting academic discussion on extremism and its consequences. The synthesis of serendipity, unwavering persistence and fervent enthusiasm has harmoniously converged to bring forth this precious edited volume. Its preparation was facilitated by a Marie Curie Postdoctoral Fellowship (Reference: H2020-MSCA-IF-2019), and a research project funded by the Spanish Ministry of Science and Innovation (Reference: PID2021-125788OB-I00).

Pushing Radical Agendas to the Extreme

How an Extremist Ideology Takes Root (and How It Is Spread amongst the Masses)

Katie Jane Patterson and Encarnación Hidalgo-Tenorio

1. Background

On the morning of the 6th of January 2021, over a period of several hours, hundreds of Trump supporters breached police perimeters of the US Capitol, ransacking, and vandalising the government building, and violently attacking police officers. The mob gathered there to protest the results of the 2020 general elections. Many people were injured, and the scene turned deadly when one of the rioters, 35-year-old Ashli Babbitt, was fatally shot, after having attempted to climb through one of the doors of the building; two more individuals died from heart conditions and another from amphetamine intoxication; furthermore, the following day, Police Officer Brian Sicknick passed away, after suffering two strokes, having been physically attacked during the riot.

Just some hours before the most severe assault on the Capitol since the British sacked the building in 1814, the same Trump allies had attended the Save America Rally at the Ellipse. There a number of incendiary speeches were delivered, one of these given by the President himself; Trump urged the crowd to "stop the steal" of the election which incited rioters into action with hostile, inflammatory, deceitful directives(such as "fight like hell"), and threats such as "if you don't fight like hell, you're not going to have a country anymore!".[1] Whilst the speech was still being delivered, Capitol Police had responded to reports of individuals overrunning the perimeter of the US Congress, and an explosive device (later confirmed as a pipe bomb) was also found. What is obvious is that, whether Trump's message was intended to be taken figuratively or not, the rioters thought that it had been used with its most simple (or basic) meaning and had come prepared for the carnage that was to ensue.

That day, the US (and the rest of the world, too) witnessed with terror a (probably pre-meditated) act of extremism unfold at the seat of US

DOI: 10.4324/9781003457381-1

democracy. It was a clear sign that, through those violent actions, largely led by QAnon,[2] extremism had become embedded in the home-turf politics of a well-established democratic, civilised nation. The preparation had been taking place not only in the days before the riot, but through social media platforms and news feeds in the months, and even years, leading up to it. What is perhaps not surprising is that the turmoil took root from seemingly innocuous conspiracy theories and fake news. In times of global crises like the current situation in Gaza, the Syrian and the Afghan-Taliban wars, the Brexit referendum, the Covid pandemic, and the Russian invasion of Ukraine, to name but a few, disinformation feeds into human deepest-seated emotions, creating polarisation, and an environment of anger, hatred, and scepticism, which can finally be translated into extremist behaviour (Mason et al., 2022).

Backed by the anonymity of online content-sharing platforms, unchecked facts, misinformed beliefs, and hypothetical speculation create a collective sense of distrust and fear. This can be exacerbated through potent algorithms and a lack of content moderation, leading to deeply disquieting narratives becoming both widespread and normalised. The concern is that these singular views (or distorted news stories) have the potential to develop collectively into radical ideologies, something far more challenging for a society to deal with, as is seen the world over. Research has shown how social media has been used as a very efficient platform for both left-wing populist, and far-right, neo-fascist discourses, and the kinds of social practices that are shaped by them (García-Marín & Luengo, 2019; Hidalgo-Tenorio et al., 2019; Gounari, 2021). Likewise, Islamic terrorists have been demonstrated to be adept at mobilising individuals via online methods (Europol, 2022). In many ways, the 2019 Capitol riots, just like the tension following the 2019 Catalan illegal independence referendum (Vakarchuk, 2020), or the 2023 Bolsonarist threat to democratic rule in Brazil and the anti-LGBTQ Ugandan bill, can be seen as a symptom of the prevailing times; it is largely through the spread of disinformation (by local or international agencies), together with economic and social instability, and disenchantment in mainstream politics, that global populist movements have flourished. The radicalisation of such a population (whether small or large, organised or seemingly random) has paved the way to more dangerous acts of extremism.

2. Defining Extremism

When we think of extremism as an act, together with 9/11, a number of other major terrorist attacks are brought to mind: (a) chemical terrorism (e.g., by LTTE in Sri Lanka in 1986, by Saddam Hussein's regime in 1988 against his civilian Kurdish population, or by Aum Shinrikyo in Japan in

1995); (b) mail bombs like Kaczynski's from the late 1970s to 1990s in the US; (c) train bombings like those in Madrid in 2004; (d) mass shootings such as the ones in Christchurch (2019) or the Norwegian Island of Utoya (2011); (e) the suicide bombings that shocked Sri Lanka in 2019 or Kabul in 2021; (f) vehicle ramming in Nice and Berlin (2016), and Barcelona and Stockholm (2017); (g) sieges on schools (e.g., Beslan in 2004) or shopping malls (e.g., Westgate, Kenya, in 2017); and (h) cyberattacks like 2015 Russia's Ukraine power grid hack. Whilst some of these were carried out by (mentally unstable and socially isolated) lone wolves (Lazzari, Nusair & Rabottini, 2021), others were orchestrated by (well-organised) cells, sometimes led by supremacists or fundamentalists, or even sponsored by governments or political organisations.[3] Irrespective of motive and justification, such atrocity is generally driven by a common desire to right a (perceived) wrong, and subsequently to inflict harm on those who are claimed to cause it or whose views are not in line with those of the (alleged) victim. More often than not, victimisers tend to otherise and dehumanise those people conceived of as their enemies (Scrimin & Rubaltelli, 2019), construing them as animals, or things, and depriving them of individuality or even human attributes. Consequently, such people are rendered expendable, standing in for a problem in the behaviour of society at large.

Acts of terror such as those above are often the ultimate manifestation of a complex web of persuasion, manipulation, cognitive radicalisation and, finally, violent radicalisation (Wolfowicz et al., 2021). They are the physical representation of a pervasive extremist ideology; a set of extreme beliefs or values, whose expression requires an extreme act to gain a platform for attention. In a literal and de-contextualised sense, the term *extremism* carries the meaning of pushing a value, or a set of values, to the limit. In a social context, extremism refers to the radical views and actions against prevailing social norms and rules that are globally recognised, accepted, and endorsed by most actors in a certain environment, for instance, in an ideological, religious, or political domain (Mölder, 2011). According to Kilp (2011, p. 16), the term refers primarily to the nature of commitment to (rather than content of) the cause or goal of an extremist individual or group. This commitment can be realised as much in words as in (violent) actions. Whilst religion and politics have traditionally been seen as the backdrop to many forms of extremism (through fundamentalist doctrines, far-right or far-left political parties, or government regimes), the expression and realisation of extreme and militant ideologies is manifest in a number and wide variety of settings: Even abolitionism, veganism, nationalism, feminism, or climate change activism may also be regarded as examples of extremism, if their supporters draw on civil unrest and armed insurrection, interfering with institutionalised power and police action, and turning violent against citizens and property.

The propagation and proliferation of disinformation are linked directly in some cases to this phenomenon, and, as shown by the European Commission's Radicalisation Awareness Group (RAN),[4] have become an ongoing and systemic risk in current societies. In recent years, extremist and terrorist groups have increasingly utilised conspiracy narratives as a tool for the recruitment, indoctrination, and radicalisation of vulnerable individuals; exploiting their angst, fears, uncertainties, and doubts.[5] They provide extremist narratives with black- and- white, or seemingly orderly, explanations of events and cause-and-effect relationships, eroding the trust between people, institutions, and governments; spreading hate speech, sexism, racism, xenophobia, and the like, far and wide; and, in some cases, inciting and encouraging the use of brute force.[6]

Not all radical narratives result in violence or terror, though. Pickets and sit-ins, marching, rallies, and protests can be peaceful and managed without disruption. Some extremist content is never realised physically, other than the act of communication itself, which, however, is not something trivial. When we read our Twitter newsfeed, whose algorithms are reported to be manipulative,[7] it is easy to see how this online social media, a "sewer of disinformation",[8] has become the very locus for the public spilling of hatred,[9] where (very democratically) both minorities and celebrities are lynched indistinctly by (almost always) anonymous users.

We are aware that discourse can have the power to distort an individual's sense of reality and spread beyond the computer screen. Polarisation and otherisation do naturally divide society, encourage revenge, hamper critical thinking, and stop public debate (even in a democratic setting), compromising the very foundation of democracy. According to RAN,[10] the latter can provide an enabling environment for the rise of extremist ideologies and movements; the reason is that extremism propagates a system of beliefs based on the (moral) superiority of the "in-group" over an "out-group" that lacks all the positive traits of the former.[11] We are beginning to witness such discourse in more mundane channels, not least through social networking sites. The digital transformation that we are currently undergoing has instigated an algorithmic accelerationism which has made it possible for extremist narratives to reach a global audience online, with violence never far behind.

3. The Discourse Structure of Extremism

Once we understand discourse as a social practice, it is easy to view language as both a product of our values and belief systems (collectively and individually), and a tool for legitimating, communicating, disseminating, and reinforcing those beliefs and values within society (van Leeuwen,

2016), through education and power. As such, discourse analysis as a very flexible and comprehensive approach provides us with various frameworks to study the relationship between language usage and our environment, conceptually and relationally. Through these frameworks (Fairclough, 2001; van Dijk, 2009; van Leeuwen, 2016), we can investigate exhaustively how mental representations are socially shared and articulated, through what we say as well as how we say it; paying special attention to the discursive manifestation of all sorts of ideologies, including, for instance, extreme ideologies (Gounari, 2021), on the one hand, and counter terrorist narratives, on the other (MacDonald & Hunter, 2013). This makes the abovementioned frameworks valuable for exploring not only the language extremists employ to instil a needed sense of belonging in the community they are addressing, but the bigger societal consequences of their mental constructs becoming action.

Our language choices can serve to unite people around social, cultural, or political values, and, naturally, our moral code (O'Regan & Betzel, 2015). These help to create an "us" versus "them" dichotomy, a sense of safety, which is construed around what we believe to be right or wrong, true or false, normal or abnormal, legal or illegal, natural or alien. Unexpectedly, governments and other power centres in many parts of the world can decide what is allowed to think and what has to be censored, playing thus a significant role in this sense. The media, whether mainstream or small-scale, can be seen as a (sometimes critical) part of the information cycle, largely responsible for framing all sorts of issues, by not only informing the general public about key events, but also shaping their understanding of those events (O'Keeffe, 2013; Viola & Musolff, 2019).

Pushing an extremist agenda requires astute acts of linguistic persuasion and manipulation. Propaganda, in its varying forms, is capable of disrupting public opinion, and creating a cognitive dissonance, "influencing the thoughts, emotions, and behaviours – that is, the psychology" of their readership (Aggarwal, 2019, p. 6). This has been explored in a number of settings, through a host of discourse strategies. Research has shown, for instance, that authors of extremist material often focus their rhetoric on "themes of morality, social proof, inspiration and appeals to religion" (Prentice, Rayson, & Taylor, 2012, p. 260). Furthermore, exploiting religious imagery through metaphor allows jihadist recruiters to justify evil acts of violence as religiously sanctioned end goals (Matusitz & Olufowote, 2016; Patterson, 2022). Narratives of personal wrong (see Benítez-Castro & Hidalgo Tenorio, 2022), or the glorified accounts of suicide bombers as martyrs and heroes (Aggarwal, 2019) are yet other strategies which have been shown to successfully incite individuals emotionally towards extreme beliefs. By creating a shared discourse community, a group (or an individual) can construe a coherent identity which will justify any act of terror, if on behalf of the very existence of that identity. Our motivation to research extremist discourse ultimately lies in the desire to reveal the innermost working of this coherent mental identity, and subsequently reflect on how to cope with the threat of extremist narratives.

Discourse analysis can also provide an abundant toolbox in the challenge to de-escalate, de-radicalise, and even prevent radical action from taking place. Narratives can offer us insight into the various forces behind extremism taking root. These may be deeply personal motivations, but collectively they paint a picture of a number of prominent driving factors, related to our particular sense of justice and a sense of community, and the societal and cultural pressures that conflict with this (Benítez-Castro et al., 2023). In addition, language also plays a prominent role in the laws criminalising terrorism or hate speech and equally defines how we construe what constitutes extremist content in the first place. It is important to consider that creating guidelines for how extremism is both defined and dealt with is a task not only for governmental policy makers; it should also be informed by the knowledge of linguists, psychologists, and political scientists, amongst other specialists. The legal and official discourse surrounding extremism propagates society's attitudes towards it, having the power to instil, challenge, or promote certain beliefs.

Additionally, findings support the idea that preventing individuals with extremist ideals from becoming violently radicalised necessitates tailored, rather than broad or generalised policies. Consequently, if multiple trajectories into violent extremism exist, so too should there be multiple policies to encourage prevention. We believe in a multitrajectory approach in our research, too. Whilst the main aims of this volume are centred on discourse, the contributions do not approach their data from the same methods or frameworks, but instead draw on a variety of techniques to analyse extremism. The collection of papers brings together some of the latest studies at the forefront of their respective areas including psychology, political science, education, and discourse analysis, to explore a number of diverse text types and contexts. It is our hope that they can offer a multifaceted, multidiscipline outlook to extremism, with the aims of detecting it, challenging its momentum, and ultimately preventing it.

4. Reasons for Writing This Book

The idea of this book germinated when organising an international workshop at the University of Granada in May 2022, entitled *Discourse, Politics and Extreme Ideologies*. On that occasion, we explored current research in extremism, to determine what and how we could learn from each other. The event was successful in bringing together a number of both scholars and practitioners working in a wide range of disciplines and fields. Thus, clinical psychologists, social and political scientists, linguists, government strategy analysts and members of the Spanish Police Forces came together to present cutting-edge investigation in their fields. From here, we understood that it would be more than interesting to publish a volume where to showcase the relevance between individual and often parallel strands of research.

At the time, the editors were leading two projects: "Nutcracker: System for the detection, tracking, monitoring and analysis of terrorist discourse on the Internet", funded by the Spanish Ministry of Research (FFI2016-79748-R); and "ISCID: Exploring the linguistic identity construction of Islamic State members in online discourse", funded by the European Commission (H2020 MSCA-IF-2019-ID:882556). In ISCID and Nutcracker, we combined our common interest in spotting the discursive strategies employed by radical Islamic terrorist organisations to recruit and indoctrinate all sorts of individuals from anywhere via the Internet. Whilst analysing the language of jihadists in online propaganda, we could observe that current findings from our research offered insights that can be of significance beyond the context of Islamic extremism, beyond linguistics, more generally; and that they even potentially extend beyond a scholarly setting. For instance, in the Computer Science Department at the University of Granada, colleagues led by Juan-Luis Castro-Peña have been working on groundbreaking work in the area of radical profile detection through machine learning, and have concluded that their semi-supervised algorithm improves current systems on offer (see Francisco et al., 2022). On their part, the linguists in the team were able to offer support in the design of the algorithm, the ontologies it draws on, as well as the categorisation and manual tagging of Tweets in several languages, paying special attention to features such as gender, speech act category, pragmatic function, document sentiment, and finally, the radical nature of the text (or not). In the lens of psychology (see Panksepp 1998; Plutchik 2003; Power & Dalgleish 2008; Fontaine, Scherer & Soriano 2013; Barrett 2017) and along the lines of Reilly and Seibert (2003), there is a conviction that a model explaining the way emotion works can be of use for the construction of another whose goal is to describe the operational principle of the act of persuading in the context of jihadism. Terrorism is not only performance, but also an act of communication (De Graaf, 2020), where the speaker seeks to convince any listener logically and, in particular, emotionally. At the other end of the scale, language plays an important role post-event, allowing us to make sense of acts of terror or why radicalisation may have occurred. To be able to discover the patterns of such a type of communicative act is not only a challenge for the academe, but also a necessity for society as a whole. The final outcome of this research has the potential to be adopted by border forces and counter-terrorism practitioners as a tool to detect and monitor extremist content with the aim of prevention. Additionally, and in parallel, the Psychology Department in the University of Cordoba were focusing on the terrorist cell that committed a terrorist attack in Barcelona in 2017; their contention is that their analyses of the materials the terrorists produced and the spoken interviews with those close to them can help determine the specific social frictions and identity conflict factors that led to those young men's radicalisation and endorsement of violence (González et al., 2022).

The coming together of multidisciplinary teams epitomises the many benefits of joining efforts with scholars from various areas to reach a more thorough understanding of such a non-monolithic phenomenon in our current globalised and fractured societies. Nevertheless, it is important to acknowledge here that we are not making the over-ambitious claim that our contributions can be directly applied to the numerous fields of expertise mentioned. Instead, the intention is that our findings and discussions can filter through to clinicians working with de-radicalising youths, to policy makers, or to social media companies, through further research in the respective areas. Thus, the aim of this volume is to open a dialogue between disciplines in which extremism infiltrates. With this in mind, the first section of this volume focuses on extremist narratives in a number of settings, including populism, the far right and religious fundamentalism. The second one presents a case study on Islamic extremism; and the third section discusses policies, measures, and strategies to detect, prevent and deal with extremism in its various forms.

5. Structure of the Book

Section 1 is entitled **Extremism as a mainstream narrative: Politics and religion**. Its seven contributors explore how this phenomenon is articulated in its more mainstream forms (such as politics, religion and media discourse) and in very different geographical contexts (from Europe through Brazil to the US). **Teun van Dijk**'s paper on far-right political parties examines the relationships between socio-political and discourse structures in terms of personal and social cognition. The author contends that the far right does not constitute a group defined by a specific ideology, as is the case with (anti)racists, feminists, or socialists; instead, it represents a political stance drawing on different attitudes of different ideologies. Van Dijk provides examples such as racism, nationalism, neoliberalism, and anti-feminism, each of which relies on the socio-political context of each country. Thus, an ideology can emerge merely as a response to an existing ideological threat.

Similarly, Utilising data from an original survey conducted in the USA, along with a newly developed scale of populist attitudes, José Javier Olivas

Osuna, Enrique Clari, and Jocelyn J. Bélanger analyse the connection between populist sentiments, nativism, right-wing ideology, radicalised networks, and the inclination towards both peaceful and radical activism. Their findings indicate that, while individuals with nativist views are more inclined to adopt populist beliefs, they do not demonstrate a greater propensity for engaging in either peaceful or violent activism. However, personal connections with advocates of violence significantly predict radicalisation, whereas alignment with left or right ideologies does not. Ultimately, their paper suggests that populist beliefs may not necessarily lead to radical behaviour. Conversely, pluralist perspectives may not only help prevent radicalism but also encourage political participation.

Francisco José Sánchez García investigates the radicalisation facilitated by the populist far right in the Spanish context. He argues that, in our current global climate, marked by the emergence of new parties in response to disillusionment and a lack of trust in the status quo, it is imperative to attend to the radical messages disseminated through the social media. Through an analysis of the strategies employed by the extreme right to coalesce its followers on Twitter, this research identifies their most frequent conceptual frameworks; it also raises concerns about this platform, which can have the capacity to globally influence the younger generation at an unprecedented pace.

By employing automated image classification analysis, **Ignacio-Jesús Serrano-Contreras and Javier García-Marín** scrutinise political leaders of the radical populist right, including Donald Trump, Giorgia Meloni, and Javier Milei. The researchers illustrate the existence of visual patterns in emotion, characteristic of a certain populist ideology, and assert that their study lays the groundwork for a multidisciplinary approach in which the audiovisual format plays a significant role in large-scale reviews. Their findings contribute to the use of algorithms in the examination of extensive image datasets. Once perfected, this capability will offer immense benefits in the analysis of propaganda videos and various other datasets.

In its analysis of Russian and German conservative populism in relation to the ongoing war in Ukraine, **Polina Zavershinskaia**'s paper combines Civil Sphere Theory and Multilayered Narrative Analysis. This shows how German and Russian conservative actors utilise discourses of liberty and repression in their efforts to portray Russian military actions as a purportedly legitimate struggle to protect their territory and culture against the collective West and NATO.

Extremism, in this context, is not only a political manoeuvre to advance radical policies or justify acts of war; it also manifests at the individual level. For instance, in the realm of religious ideology, extremist discourse plays a fundamental role in recruiting vulnerable individuals into fundamentalist sects. In his chapter on the Universal Church of the Kingdom of God, **Michele Martini** uses Network Text Analysis to see the effects of the post-Covid rise of alternative online forms of communication and new devotional figures, such as religious webmasters. This approach allows for a comprehensive understanding of how these figures reach, indoctrinate and radicalise members. While these online communities create a sense of togetherness, there is also the potential to incite division and polarisation.

In a similar vein, the concluding chapter of this section by **Ruth Breeze and Saqlain Hassan** delves into the role of social media in fostering division of opinions and driving the dynamics of extremist language. Drawing on corpus-assisted sentiment analysis on Twitter, the authors examine how, in the aftermath of Mahsa Amini's death during her incarceration by the Iranian Morality Police, interactions concerning the use of the hijab, and other related topics in that network, became increasingly polarised and polarising. However, amidst this polarisation, there also emerged a distinct space for a certain discourse of contestation.

Section 2, entitled **Extremism as a fundamentalist ideology: The case of jihadism,** brings together research from various collective projects exploring Islamic extremism as a religious ideology. In contrast to mere political affiliation, religious fundamentalism taps into something more profound within the individual. Religion can serve as a lens through which people perceive the world and dictate their actions; it can be wielded as a tool to provide the necessary justification for extreme beliefs and behaviours, including violence and terror. Unlike the recent rise of populism, religious ideology tends to resonate with a community's sense of tradition through historical literature and sacred books. Actions promoted or supported by a fundamentalist group carry a divine authority, warranting an all-or-nothing ultimatum with the additional promise of reward or punishment in the next life. This section focuses on the ways in which language is manipulated and exploited for the purposes of jihadist radicalisation and recruitment. It begins with a purely theoretical paper by **Federico Aznar Montesinos and Katie Patterson,** outlining how, at the extreme end, the nature of terrorism as a theoretical concept crucially depends on the media, and gains its power from the media and the State's framing of it.

Djallil Lounnas and Massimo Ramaioli posit the thesis that multiple myths associated with jihad exert a compelling influence on individuals, irrespective of their backgrounds. Through insights gleaned from interviews with jihadi returnees and psychologists engaged in de-radicalisation programmes, three key magnets were identified, namely, the idealisation of the Muslim community, redemption through jihad, and Manichaean reasoning. The authors argue that these three myths should be differentiated from more personally experienced grievances.

The paper by **Pascual Pérez-Paredes and Tony McEnery** explores the term "Muslim" within a collection of jihadist magazines. Using corpus linguistic methods, and informed by representation theory, and keyword and colligational analyses, their findings suggest that representation strategies in their dataset are driven by recruitment and indoctrination purposes. The authors explain that these texts contribute to the overarching narrative of violent jihad (Matusitz, 2020), by constructing reality through framing and perspectivation strategies, wherein Muslims are portrayed as instruments and facilitators of jihad.

Drawing on the same corpus, **Michael Pace-Sigge's** chapter applies Michael Hoey's lexical priming theory to elucidate how primings create and reinforce a closed discourse instilling a mental framework of group-belonging. He concentrates on lexical items conveying power relations and contends that, within the community of readers, the collocation, colligation, and semantic association divergence of such items form a distinctive lexical set of characteristics. These forced primings affiliate members and readers with the aims and philosophy of grievances employed by the Islamic State, simultaneously fostering a clear idea of, and stance against, a perceived other.

Jonatan Morillo Losada underscores that Islamic extremism and the resulting radicalisation have not only evolved but continue to adapt to changing contexts. This chapter illustrates how radicalisation can take root through subcultures such as rap music. The author observes the recurring presence of violent rap in the daily lives of the individuals responsible for some major terror attacks in Europe. And concludes the following: Considering that the latest wave of jihadists consists of youths raised amidst Western traditions, and acknowledging that a culture of violence is already established in rap music, it is apparent that individuals who regularly interact with such music could be at a higher risk of radicalisation. This is particularly true for those already familiar with narratives that justify violence, as they may be more prone to recruitment by extremist groups.

The concluding section, titled **Extremism as an act: Detection and prevention strategies**, reflects on policy development, peace education, and conflict resolution, aiming to discuss ways to undermine radicalisation and to explore future research that builds upon these efforts. One of its central goals is to demonstrate the feasibility of subverting and even eradicating radicalised discourses. The section begins with **Andrea Coccini**'s chapter, which documents the existing international legal framework addressing a frequent act of extremism, namely, hate speech. This paper elucidates that, whilst hate speech against certain groups is frequently recognised as a precursor to crimes against humanity, such as genocide and terrorism, there is still no clear, legal definition, due to concerns about its potential infringement on free speech. Freedom of opinion and expression constitutes a fundamental element of International Human Rights Law, and is a cornerstone of every liberal democratic society, as it reinforces other basic rights, such as freedom of thought. Coccini's primary objective is to precisely delineate the (thin) line between legitimate and prohibited opinion.

The focus of the paper by **Francesc Torras and Jordi Collet** is on a specific region in Spain, Catalonia, where, prior to the pandemic, de-radicalisation programmes were actively promoted (and achieved some success) in various local Muslim communities. The authors present one specific grassroots prevention model that engaged various stakeholders, across formal, non-formal and informal education spaces; it also addressed the challenges of the 3N model of analysis for radicalisation (Kruglanski et al., 2019), with an emphasis on identifying and eliminating different types of barriers and inequalities – social, legal, institutional, familial, and personal. Its final goal was to co-construct conditions for the successful integration of those at risk and foster a sense of belonging.

In her chapter, **Lynn Revell** examines the UK's approach to preventing extremism in education through various policies, including the Prevent Duty, the 2015 Counter Terrorism Act, and the requirement for schools to promote fundamental British values. The Prevent strategy has garnered attention in the UK, being successfully integrated into all areas of education since its inception in 2011. Internationally, it is recognised as one of the most successful soft power initiatives addressing extremism. As research indicates, designing and implementing processes of de-radicalisation is complex (Horgan & Braddock, 2010; Dugdale, 2017; Walanda, 2020); therefore, prevention emerges as one of the most important tools to mitigate and avoid extremism.

It is hoped that the collective academic effort in this edited volume will be relevant to other researchers and practitioners in the field. In particular, we are convinced that, through further research and collaboration, education experts can leverage this material to design programmes of de-radicalisation, disengagement, and reintegration. The hope is that these experts will empower young, vulnerable individuals to fact-check questionable assertions about topics such as Islam, the West, democracy, and gender equality, just to name a few, and critically assess acts of violence. As a consequence, these experts will be well-equipped to formulate counter-narratives for deconstructing jihadist discourse both in substance and in form (Miravitllas, 2015), ultimately leaving room for alternative approaches to addressing extremism in both its discursive and physical manifestations.

Notes

1 See https://www.bbc.co.uk/news/world-us-canada-55640437
2 See https://apnews.com/article/twitter-blocks-70k-qanon-accounts-171a5c9062be1c293169d764d3d0d9c8

3 See https://www.visionofhumanity.org/wp-content/uploads/2023/03/GTI-2023-web-170423.pdf
4 Seehttps://home-affairs.ec.europa.eu/system/files/2021-12/spotlight_on_conspiracy_narratives_disinformation_122021_en.pdf
5 See https://www.theguardian.com/uk-news/2021/nov/19/extremists-using-online-gaming-and-covid-conspiracies-to-recruit-youngsters
6 See https://unicri.it/news/article/hate_crime_speech_violent_extremism
7 See https://businessinsider.mx/musk-and-dorsey-argue-over-manipulative-twitter-algorithms-2022-5/
8 See https://foreignpolicy.com/2023/07/15/elon-musk-twitter-blue-checks-verification-disinformation-propaganda-russia-china-trust-safety/
9 See https://www.nytimes.com/2022/12/02/technology/twitter-hate-speech.html
10 See https://home-affairs.ec.europa.eu/system/files/2022-04/ran_spotlight_polarisation_en.pdf
11 See https://home-affairs.ec.europa.eu/whats-new/publications/media-and-polarisation-europe-strategies-local-practitioners-address-problematic-reporting-may-2023_en

References

Aggarwal, N. K. (2019). *Media persuasion in the Islamic State*. New York: Columbia University Press.

Barrett, L. F. (2017). The theory of constructed emotion: An active inference account of interoception and categorization. *Social Cognitive and Affective Neuroscience*, *12*(1), 1–23. https://doi.org/10.1093/scan/nsw154

Benítez-Castro, M. Á., & Hidalgo-Tenorio, E. (2022). I am proud to be a traitor: The emotion/opinion interplay in jihadist magazines. *Pragmatics and Society*, *13*, 3, 501-531. https://doi.org/10.1075/ps.21029.ben

Benítez-Castro, M. Á., Hidalgo-Tenorio, E., Patterson, K. J., Moyano, M., & González, I. (2023). They were not radical, even when they committed that: An appraisal-driven discourse analysis of feelings and attitudes towards the 17-A terrorist cell in Barcelona. *Journal of Language Aggression and Conflict*. https://doi.org/10.1075/jlac.00084.ben

De Graaf, B. (2020 [2011]). Why communication and performance are key in countering terrorism. *The International Centre for Counter-Terrorism Journal*, *1*, 1–10.

Dugdale, W. (2017). Prison de-radicalisation: To rehabilitate or merely isolate? *Rivista Antigone*, *1*, 201–221.

Europol. (2022). *Online Jihadist Propaganda 2021 in review*. Publications Office of the European Union, Luxembourg. https://www.europol.europa.eu/publications-events/publications/online-jihadist-propaganda-2021-in-review

Fairclough, N. (2001). The dialectics of discourse. *Textus*, *14*(2), 231–242.

Fontaine, J. J., Scherer, K. R., & Soriano, C. (Eds.). (2013). *Components of emotional meaning: A sourcebook*. Oxford: Oxford University Press.

Francisco, M., Benítez-Castro, M. Á., Hidalgo-Tenorio, E., & Castro, J. L. (2022). A semi-supervised algorithm for detecting extremism propaganda diffusion on social media. *Pragmatics and Society*, *13*(3), 532–554. https://doi.org/10.1075/ps.21009.fra

García-Marín, J., & Luengo, Ó. G. (2019). Populist discourse in the 21st century. The definition of otherness in Twitter in the cases of Spain, Bolivia and Venezuela. In E. Hidalgo-Tenorio , M. A. Benítez-Castro , & F. De Cesare (Eds.), *Populist Discourse* (pp. 81–99). London: Routledge.

Gidron, N., Adams, J., & Horne, W. (2020). *American affective polarization in comparative perspective*. Cambridge: Cambridge University Press.

González, I., Moyano, M., Lobato, R. M., & Trujillo, H. M. (2022). Evidence of psychological manipulation in the process of violent radicalization: An investigation of the 17-A cell. *Frontiers in Psychiatry*, *13*, 789051. https://doi.org/10.3389/fpsyt.2022.789051

Gounari, P. (2021). From Twitter to Capitol Hill: One-dimensional discursive extremism and the language of digital aggressiveness. In *From Twitter to Capitol Hill. Far-right authoritarian populist discourses, social media and critical pedagogy* (pp. 66–99). Leiden & Boston: Brill.

Hidalgo-Tenorio, E., Benítez-Castro, M. Á., & De Cesare, F. (Eds.). (2019). *Populist discourse: Critical approaches to contemporary politics*. London: Routledge.

Horgan, J., & Braddock, K. (2010). Rehabilitating the terrorists? Challenges in assessing the effectiveness of de-radicalization programs. *Terrorism and Political Violence*, *22*(2), 267–291. https://doi.org/10.1080/09546551003594748

Kilp, A. (2011). The ontology and epistemology of extremism. *Estonian National Defence College Proceedings*, *14*(2), 9–25.

Kruglanski, A. W., Bélanger, J. J., & Gunaratna, R. (2019). *The three pillars of radicalization: Needs, narratives, and networks*. Oxford: Oxford University Press.

Lazzari, C., Nusair, A., & Rabottini, M. (2021). Phenomenology and social psychology of lone wolf radicalization and terrorism. In C. Lazzari (Ed.), *Psychological assessment and interventions for individuals linked to radicalization and lone wolf terrorism* (pp. 70–80). Potomac, MD: Bentham Science Publishers.

MacDonald, M., & Hunter, D. (2013). Security, population and governmentality: UK counter-terrorism discourse (2007–2011). *Critical Approaches to Discourse Analysis Across Disciplines*, *7*(1), 123–140.

Mason, C. B., Winter, D. A., Schmeer, S., & Berrington, B. T. J. S. L. (2022). The Radicalization of Brexit Activists. *Front Psychol*, *9*(12), 798232. https://doi.org/10.3389/fpsyg.2021.798232.

Matusitz, J. (2020). Islamic terrorist radicalization through online jihadist magazines. *Journal of Communication & Religion*, *43*(1), 26–39.

Matusitz, J., & Olufowote, J. O. (2016). Visual motifs in Islamist terrorism: Applying conceptual metaphor theory. *Journal of Applied Security Research*, *11*(1), 18–32. https://doi.org/10.1080/19361610.2016.1104276

Miravitllas, E. (2015). *Hacia una tipología de contranarrativas frente al extremismo violento*. Universidad de Barcelona.
https://aecpa.es/es-es/hacia-una-tipologia-de-contranarrativas- frente- al-extremismo-violento/congress-papers/1228/

Mölder, H. (2011). The culture of fear in international politics. A western-dominated international system and its extremist challenges. *Estonian National Defence College Proceedings*, *14*(2), 241–263.

O'Keeffe, A. (2013). Media and discourse analysis. In *The Routledge handbook of discourse analysis* (pp. 441–454). London: Routledge.
O'Regan, J. P., & Betzel, A. (2015). Critical discourse analysis: A sample study of extremism. In *Research methods in intercultural communication: A practical guide* (pp. 281–296). Oxford: John Wiley & Sons Inc.
Panksepp, J. (1998). *Affective neuroscience: The foundations of human and animal emotions*. Oxford: Oxford University Press.
Patterson, K. J. (2022). Under the shadow of swords: The rhetoric of jihad: A corpus-based critical analysis of religious metaphors in jihadist magazines. *Pragmatics and Society*, *13*(3), 477–500. https://doi.org/10.1075/ps.21017.pat
Plutchik, R. (2003). *Emotions and life: Perspectives from psychology, biology, and evolution*. Washington: American Psychological Association.
Power, M. J., & Dalgleish, T. (2008). *Cognition and emotion: From order to disorder*. Hove: Psychology Press.
Prentice, S., Rayson, P., & Taylor, P. J. (2012). The language of Islamic extremism: Towards an automated identification of beliefs, motivations, and justifications. *International Journal of Corpus Linguistics*, *17*(2), 259–286. https://doi.org/10.1075/ijcl.17.2.05pre
Reilly, J., & Seibert, L. (2003). Language and emotion. In R. J. Davidson, K. R. Scherer, & H. H. Goldsmith (Eds.), Handbook of affective sciences (pp. 535–559). Oxford: Oxford University Press.
Scrimin, S., & Rubaltelli, E. (2019). Dehumanization after terrorism: The role of psychophysiological emotion regulation and trait emotional intelligence. *Current Psychology*, *40*(6), 2707–2714. https://link.springer.com/article/10.1007/s12144-019-00189-x
Vakarchuk, K. (2020). The impact of the media on the Catalonia referendum. *Rhetoric and Communications*, *43*, 83–95.
Van Dijk, T. A. (2009). News, discourse, and ideology. In *The handbook of journalism studies* (pp. 191–204). London: Routledge.
Van Leeuwen, T. (2016). Discourse as the recontextualization of social practice —a guide. In *Methods of critical discourse studies* (pp. 137–153). Oxford: Oxford University Press.
Viola, L., & Musolff, A. (Eds.). (2019). *Migration and media: Discourses about identities in crisis*. Amsterdam: John Benjamins Publishing Company.
Walanda, G. (2020). The path to sustainable deradicalization program. *Journal of Terrorism Studies*, *2*(1). https://doi.org/10.7454/jts.v2i1.1017
Wolfowicz, M., Litmanovitz, Y., Weisburd, D., & Hasisi, B. (2021). Cognitive and behavioral radicalization: A systematic review of the putative risk and protective factors. *Campbell Systematic Reviews* 17(3), e1174. https://doi.org/10.1002/cl2.1174

1 Ideology and Populism of the Reactionary Right

Teun A. van Dijk

1. Introduction

Most studies of the Far Right have been carried out in political science. This is obvious because the phenomenon as well as the very label suggests that we deal with a political trend, although with important social conditions and consequences (Husbands, 2020; Mudde, 2019).

In this paper, we focus on one aspect of the Far Right that has received less attention in the literature: ideology. There are many studies, also in political science, that mention the discourse of the Far Right, but do not engage in detailed and systematic discourse analysis, as is the case in critical discourse studies of the Far Right (Wodak, KhosraviNik, & Mral, 2013; Forchtner, 2020; Wodak, 2021). The same is true for ideology, also often associated with the Far Right (e.g., Mudde, 2000), but not in terms of detailed sociocognitive analysis.

This paper presents a more detailed analysis of the ideological structures of Far-Right political parties within the framework of a sociocognitive paradigm, in which the relationships between sociopolitical structures and discourse structures are examined in terms of personal and social cognition.

The main thesis of this paper is that the Far Right is not an ideological group, defined by an ideology, as is the case for (anti) racists, feminists, socialists or pacifists, but a political position using different attitudes of different ideologies, such as racism, (ultra)nationalism, neoliberalism, antifeminism, etc. depending on the sociopolitical context of a country.

There has been much debate about how to call the political parties at the right of conservative parties. Mudde (2019) has proposed to call most of these parties the "Radical Right" (such as Vox in Spain, the PVV in the Netherlands and Sweden Democrats in Sweden), and only the parties that do not accept democratic principles (such as elections) the "Extreme Right" (as was the case for the NSDAP in Germany) both categorized as the "Far Right". In this paper, I will provide some arguments to call these parties the "Reactionary Right" (henceforth RR), because their discourse and

DOI: 10.4324/9781003457381-2

ideology are generally a reaction against liberal discourses and ideologies, rather than independent original ideas.

2. Theory of Ideology: A Summary

Ideologies have been studied in several disciplines in the social sciences and humanities since the notion of "ideology" as a discipline was introduced at the end of the 18th century by Destutt de Tracy. The main paradigm was set by the study of ideology by Marx Engels as a form of "false consciousness", a vague cognitive notion that has influenced Marxist approaches until today, especially in philosophy and the social sciences. In political science also other theories of ideologies have been developed in the last decades, more in terms of systems of ideas (see, e.g., Freeden, 1996). Ignored in most of these studies is a detailed sociocognitive definition of ideology and how ideologies are related to actual social practices, in general, and discourse, in particular. Our theory of ideology is multidisciplinary and is not only based on theories of ideological social practices, but also develops a cognitive theory and its relations to discourse. This theory can be summarized as follows (for detail, see Van Dijk, 1998):

- Ideologies are forms of social cognition, stored in Long Term Memory. They are based on, and presuppose, socioculturally shared knowledge, as the basis of all social cognition, shared by the members of an epistemic community.
- No detailed cognitive organization of ideologies has ever been proposed, but systematic discourse analysis of ideological text and talk suggests the following main categories.
    - Identity (Who are we? Who belong to us?)
    - Action (What do we do?)
    - Goals (What do we want?)
    - Norms and Values (What is good vs. bad for us?)
    - Group Relations (Who are our allies vs. our enemies?)
    - Resources (What are our weaknesses vs. our strengths?)
- Ideologies are gradually acquired and shared by the members of ideological groups, such as feminists, (anti) racists, pacifists, etc.
- Individual social actors can be members of various ideological groups: A woman can be a feminist, a socialist, a pacifist, etc. But in each context one of these ideological identities will be dominant.
- Ideologies are the organizational basis of more specific (ideological) socially shared attitudes, i.e., ideas about such issues as immigration, capital punishment, abortion, climate change, etc. It is at this, more

specific level of social cognition that ideologies are acquired, developed, changed, and debated. Ideological "struggle" takes place at this level.
- Ideological attitudes influence the personal experiences of individual group members (e.g., as personal opinions of their personal mental models of situations, actions and interactions). These mental models may be influenced by several ideologies, and be more or less detailed and developed, depending on the ideological learning and sophistication of a person.
- A combination of socially shared attitudes and personal mental models influence the structures of ideological discourse and other social practices. Because of the polarized structures of ideologies (Ingroup vs. Outgroup) and attitudes (For or Against an issue), also discourse structures at all levels are polarized by the ideological square:
    - Emphasize our good things
    - Emphasize their bad things
    - De-emphasize our bad things
    - De-emphasize their good things
- Besides these polarized structures of ideological discourse, discourse structures are also controlled by the communicative situation, as it is represented in the mental "context models" of individual group members. These define the appropriateness of a discourse and control its (formal, popular, etc) style. Finally, the (de) emphatical structures of ideological discourse may be shaped by rhetorical structures and strategies (such as hyperboles and euphemisms) and organized by context-dependent genre structures (such as those of every conversation, narrative, news reports, scholarly articles, manifestos, and many more).

3. Ideologies in Political Psychology

Political ideologies of the Far Right have been studied in a large number of (mostly experimental) studies in political psychology, only briefly mentioned here (see especially, Jost, 2021). These studies are largely about the psychological conditions of political attitudes, e.g., on the continuous Left/Progressive-Right/Conservative-Right scale, in terms of various personality dimensions or predispositions, such as authoritarianism, sensibility to various kinds of threat or anxiety, social domination orientation, need for closure, etc. For instance, in a meta-analysis of a vast number of studies on the role of perceived fear as a condition of (more) conservative ideology, Jost et al. (2017, p. 324) concluded that "[p]sychological reactions to fear and threat thus convey a small-to-moderate political advantage for conservative leaders, parties, policies, and ideas". Obviously, such fears not only exist on the Right, but also on the Left, for instance about climate change or police brutality (Jost et al., 2017, p. 344). See also, the papers in the same issue of *Social Cognition*: Choma and Hodson (2017), Crawford (2017), Morgan and Wisneski (2017), Proulx and Brandt (2017).

Also in social psychology, recent studies of populism have focused on "the tribal challenge to liberal democracy", with studies of anger, grievances, authoritarianism, status-seeking, self-uncertainty, leadership and values (Forgas, Crano, & Fiedler, 2021). However, exclusive psychological explanations, ignoring social and political analysis, may tend to explain political extremism of the Left and the Right in the same way, e.g., as overconfidence in one's own beliefs (Van Prooijen, 2019, p. 148), possibly confounding prejudice of the Right (e.g., about minorities or feminists) with justified beliefs (knowledge) of the Left on some social issues, such as the reality of racism or sexism. Ideologies as forms of social cognition are by definition shared by a collectivity of social actors, which we simply call "ideological groups", as is the case for the knowledge shared by an epistemic community. For the same reason that there are no individual languages, there are no individual ideologies, only individual, subjective uses or applications of shared ideologies at the basis of specific (inter) action or discourse, and always modified (or even remaining implicit) in the interactive or communicative context.

We assume that the personal acquisition or use of ideologies depends on a complex sociocognitive process of accumulated personal experiences, social interaction, conversation, many types of public discourse and probably the personality variables studied in political psychology. Indeed, whether as a function of relatively stable personality characteristics or of an already formed ideology, language users as social actors may select and focus on discourses, media and other sources for their personal opinions – such as the use of Fox media by the Right in the USA, or the tabloids in the UK or Germany (for a study of the use of Twitter, see Barberá et al., 2015).

As forms of social cognition, ideologies do not develop, change or spread overnight, also because they may control many specific attitudes and the personal experiences and interactions of many people. However, depending on the context, individual changes in the use of ideologies may be much more common, for instance, as a consequence of argumentation, manipulation, a movie or dramatic experiences, such as terrorist attacks or a severe economic recession (for detail, see Bar-Tal & Magal, 2021). Repeated similar experiences of many social actors (e.g., violence, hunger or unemployment) may thus also lead to the formation or change of shared ideologies. Moreover, this requires communication and hence discourse about these experiences before a shared ideology can develop.

3.1 Political Ideologies

Within the framework of the theory of ideology summarized above, we need to make necessary distinctions between ideologies and other forms of social cognition and other phenomena. Although political psychology examines ideologies on a continuous scale of political positioning of (Far) Left and (Far) Right, according to our theory, these are not ideologies, but higher-level, summarizing concepts of political positioning. The identification of the "Left" presupposes adherence to (fragments of) ideologies such as Socialism, Feminism, Antiracism, etc., and the "Right" with ideologies such as Neoliberalism, Sexism, Racism, Nationalism, etc. The same is true for political concepts such as Illiberalism and Conservatism: They are political positions, not ideologies, and their discourses, actions and policies are based on fragments or attitudes of different ideologies.

An analysis of party programs in Spain, the Netherlands and Sweden shows that the Far Right does not have "a" Far-Right ideology, but a politically strategic selection of attitudes borrowed from several ideologies usually summarized in terms of "radical right", "populist" or "conservative", such as nationalism, racism or xenophobia, depending on the (variable) sociopolitical situation in a city, region/state or country. For instance, in countries such as the Netherlands and Sweden, it hardly makes electoral sense to include limitation of the right to abortion in Far-Right political programs because this attitude is dominant and hence would yield few votes (for the role of gender issues in the Far Right, see De Lange & Mugge, 2015; Kováts, 2018). Hence, our analysis of the programs of Far-Right parties in Spain, the Netherlands and Sweden, needs to examine how their ideologically based attitudes, and hence their discursive expression, are adapted to mainstream attitudes in these countries.

There are other isms that often are treated and analyzed as ideologies, but need to be analyzed in other terms, as is the case for authoritarianism, which is a form of government, associated with extremist forms of Left or Right ideology clusters. And such political structures need to be distinguished from personality structures such as an authoritarian personality, and its actions and interactions. Similarly, very relevant for this paper, populism will here be defined as a discursive political strategy, and not as an ideology ("thin" or otherwise) (see Aslanidis, 2016). Indeed, this also allows populism to occur not only at the Right, but also at the Left.

4. Reactionary Ideas of the Far Right

The general theory of ideology, summarized above, applied to the study of the Far Right, implies that there is no ideology of the Far Right, but rather a strategic political position on attitudes based on various ideologies already extant in society, especially racism (including xenophobia, antisemitism, islamophobia) and nationalism (usually called "nativism"). These ideologically based attitudes did not develop as original ideas of the Far Right, but as a reaction to the growing acceptance of ideologically based liberal attitudes that have developed in large parts of the world, but especially in Europe and the USA, since the 1960s (Norris & Inglehart, 2019). The broader these attitudes were accepted and even became dominant in some countries (or in their intellectual centers and cities, among younger generations, the better educated and women), the more Far-Right parties and organizations became more radical in the formulation and propagation of reactionary attitudes. This growing backlash spreading among (older, male, provincial, less educated, economically threatened) conservative voters, emphasized by their symbolic elites (those who have preferential access to public discourse such as conservative politicians, journalists and scholars) are among the main causes of the generalized move to the Right, and hence the increased support of authoritarian Far-Right parties in many countries. In sum, the backlash is a reaction of those losing cultural power in the increase of liberal values. Depending on each country, these reactionary attitudes are often the negative mirror image of the very corresponding liberal attitudes (see Table 1.1).

Reactionary Far-Right ideas and policies, as shown in Table 1.1, are based on relevant fragments of existing ideologies, such as racism, nationalism, sexism, militarism, and the attitudes they dominate, e.g., on immigration, abortion, gay marriage, law and order, language policies, etc.

Table 1.1 The reactionary dimension of the Far Right

Sociopolitical and cultural changes since the 1960s	*Far-Right/populist reactions and radical conservatism*
Dominant values: Equality, diversity, pluralism, solidarity, collectivism	**Dominant values:** Inequality, supremacy, homogeneity, individualism
NATION	
• United Nations, Internationalism • European Union • Globalization • Immigration • Anti-colonialism • Human Rights • Progressive parties • Politics of hope and solidarity	• Anti-internationalism, anti-UN • Anti-EU • Nationalism, nativism, patriotism • Anti-immigration • Neo-colonialism • Revisionism • Conservative, populist parties • Politics of paranoid fear

(*Continued*)

Table 1.1 (Continued)

Sociopolitical and cultural changes since the 1960s	*Far-Right/populist reactions and radical conservatism*
RACE/ETHNICITY	
• Civil Rights Movement • Black Power, Black Lives Matter (BLM) • Antiracism, Critical Race Theory (CRT) • Diversity • Increased immigration • Multiculturalism • Critical history (of slavery)	• White priority/supremacy • Continued racism/ethnicism • Xenophobia • Anti-BLM, Anti-CRT • Anti-immigration • Anti-multiculturalism • Homogeneity • Anti-Islam • Revisionism
GENDER/SEXUALITY/FAMILY	
Feminism(s) *Abortion laws* *Gay marriage* *LGBT+* *Diverse families*	*Antifeminism* *Anti-abortion laws and practices* *Against gay marriage* *Anti-LGBT+* *Traditional families, family values*
CULTURE	
• Multiculturalism • Multilingualism • Religious diversity, agnosticism	• Anti-multiculturalism • Our language first • Our religion (Christianity), anti-Islam
STATE/POWER	
• Liberalism • Democracy • Antiauthoritarian • No/anti death penalty • Antimilitary • Critical of police power abuse • Anti-imperialism • Socialism	• Illiberalism, populism • Authoritarianism • Law and order • Death penalty • Militarism • Police powers • Imperialism • Anticommunism

More specifically, some of the reactionary attitudes of the Far Right are strategically less relevant as part of political propaganda or manipulation, such as anti-abortion attitudes in the Netherlands and Sweden, where such policies have become mainstream. This is not the case for attitudes based on racism, because anti-racism is not mainstream in the same countries. Indeed, racist attitudes (prejudice), especially on immigration are prevalent in "white" populations, in Europe and the Americas. Hence, we may expect that on most Far-Right attitudes this will have a major influence, as we see in Table 1.2, where attitudes in different domains (nation, gender, culture, etc.) all are somehow related to racist attitudes.

The ideologies and attitudes of the Far Right, as summarized above, have gradually become more influential since 2000, together with the

Table 1.2 The ethnicist/racist dimensions of the Far Right

PRO	*Contra*
Nationalism/Nativism	
• Homogeneous (white) nation • Our country first • Our own people first • Exclusion • Patriotism • Revisionism	• Immigration of non-whites • Inclusion • Internationalism, globalism
Racism/Xenophobia	
• Discrimination of (ethnic) others • Racism, antisemitism • Racism denial • Deportation of ethnic criminals	• Priority of (ethnic) others • Jewish conspiracy • Anti-racist textbooks and programs • Quotas for ethnic minorities
Culture	
• Our values • Our own language first • Cultural imperialism, neo-colonialism • Our glorious past, heroes • Holocaust denial/mitigation, revisionism • National symbols • Our/Christian culture	• Multiculturalism • Foreign customs and values • Multilingualism • Black Studies, Critical Race Theory • Black Lives Matter • Islam, Mosques
Security	
• Strengthening borders • Strong state, law and order • Policing of blacks, immigrants, Arabs, gypsies, etc.	• Illegal aliens • Soft on "ethnic" crime, terrorism • Minority drug users
Gender/Sexuality	
• White male dominance	• Black, immigrant men • Hijab of Muslim women • Drop of (white) birth-rate • Multicultural marriages
Economy	
• Welfare chauvinism	• Subsidies to immigrants • International cooperation

growth of Far-Right parties in many countries. This does not mean that reactionary ideas and parties are new. Indeed, many of the fascist ideas of pre-war parties have maintained their influence in underground or marginal groups or organizations. This important historical influence will not be studied here (for the continuity of Far-Right discourse see, e.g., Feldman & Jackson, 2014).

An exclusive psychological explanation of the increase of Far-Right attitudes in many countries would tend to explain such changes in terms of one or more motivational variables (e.g., uncertainty) rather than in terms of sociopolitical conditions (such as social cultural challenges to privileges, power and domination). The "cultural revolution" (such as increased rights of female, non-white, homosexual, non-religious (or Muslim) and lower-class citizens) challenges the traditional privileges or domination of white, male, heterosexual, religious (Christian), middle-class citizens. In that sense, the increased power of the Far Right is indeed a backlash against these cultural and sociopolitical changes (Norris & Inglehart, 2019), even when such changes may also partly be explained in terms of the psychological aspects of losing influence or importance, such as collective narcissism (Golec de Zavala, Lantos, & Keenan, 2019).

4. Studies of Far-Right Ideologies

Although there is no such thing as "a" Far-Right Ideology, much of the literature on the Far Right does assume such ideological identification. We have seen above that there is today a vast literature on the Far Right. Many of these studies also deal with Far-Right ideology, but few are specialized in detailed ideological analysis. Let us review a few of these studies, including studies on populism. It should however be stressed from the outset that, in our conception, populism and the Far Right are very different notions. Many studies of populism, although recognizing that populism exists at the Left and the Right, provide most examples of contemporary populism(s) of the (Far) Right, thus confusing populism as various moves of a discursive-political strategy with a characterization of Far-Right political parties or positions.

4.1 Theories of Populism

Although Far-Right ideologies are not the same as populism, much of the literature deals with them as being closely related. The most prominent scholar of the Far Right, Cas Mudde, has also extensively written on Far Right and populist ideology (see especially Mudde, 2000). Although his specialized book on the ideology of the Far Right is already more than 20 years old, and many studies have been published since, Mudde (2000,

p. 18) also observes that few studies are specifically on ideology. He defines party ideology in a broad sense as "a party's body of normative(-related) ideas about the nature of man and society as well as the organisation and purposes of society" (Mudde 2000, p. 19). Based on a study of the Republikaner and the Volkunion in Germany, the Vlaams Blok in Belgium, and the Centrum Partij in the Netherlands, among others, Mudde identifies the (more or less) presence or absence of ideologies such as (Ethnic) Nationalism, Exclusionism, Xenophobia, Revisionism, Patriotism, Antisemitism, and Welfare Chauvinism; and prominent Values, such as traditional family and Christian values (e.g., on abortion), a strong state and a Law-and-Order focus on crime.

These are indeed ideological positions, variably adhered to the Far Right, but analytically it makes sense, as we have done above, to distinguish between ideologies (and their categories, including identities, actions, goals norms and values) and more specific attitudes. Indeed, not all isms are ideologies: For instance, Welfare Chauvinism, is not a general ideology of an ideological group (We the Chauvinists?) with general application in many social and political domains, but a more specific attitude controlled by Nationalism and/or Racism (together defined as "Nativism"), according to which social services should be given only or primarily to members of the own (ethnic, national) group. Similarly, Revisionism is not an ideology, but an (historical) aspect of Nationalism, and Patriotism is rather an attitude or even personal feeling or value, or a mode of Nationalism, not a complex ideology controlling different attitudes. And Exclusionism is an aspect (Action) of Racism, Xenophobia or Nationalism.

In later studies, Mudde defines populism as a "thin ideology" (Mudde, 2014), organized by the perceived relations between We the People and Them the (ruling) Elite. This polarization is also found in other studies of populism. Yet, populism does not seem to have the internal organization of ideologies, nor its sociopolitical basis. Indeed, there are populists on the Left and on the Right, hence associated with different ideologies. There is no shared identity (We the populists?), no general Action, no shared Values and Norms. Rather, populism is a political strategy, e.g., in elections, and expressed in political discourse, pretending to fight for ordinary people (in that sense right wing populism is rather a form of pseudo-socialism), and exploiting broadly shared social attitudes against the (political) powers that be.

Against general definitions of populism in terms of the opposition of the (good) People vs. the (bad, corrupt, etc.) Elites (Rooduijn, 2014b), it should first be stressed that in Far-Right discourse, ordinary people (or The People) are Our (white) people, and the elites the other politicians (especially at the Left) and never the Far-Right politicians themselves. This is confirmed by studies of Far-Right parties in power, for instance in Hungary and the Balkans, whose discourse (at the supply side) and popular support (at the demand side) is barely articulated in terms of this opposition (Krekó, 2019). In other words, Far-Right populist polarization is primarily discursive and political, not ideological, in the sense of strategic and legitimating moves to get (more) power, and once acquired to maintain power, in terms of pseudo-democratic values. Indeed, our research on racist discourse in politics (e.g., Van Dijk, 1993) has shown that already in the 1980s conservative British politicians (in power) legitimated anti-immigration policies in terms of their constituents, and hence in terms of popular support. In other words, the illiberal, anti-democratic ideas and policies of the Far Right need a "democratic" mask to be politically acceptable for the people as well as the other (political) elites, whether at home or abroad.

If the opposition between the (good) People vs. the (bad) Elites is characteristic of populist discourse (and not of ideology), such a strategy may indeed be found at the Right and the Left and should be defined by the political position of a party. Thus, Rooduijn and Akkerman (2017), in their analysis of the 32 parties in 5 European countries, show that the populist opposition characterizes radical parties both at the Left and the Right. Such an analysis still leaves the possibility that other discursive (but non-ideological) aspects of populism may differentiate Radical Left and Radical Right populism. Although this paper does not examine Radical Left political discourse, we surmise that the polarization between the People vs. the Elite in such discourse is closely related to an ideologically based (e.g., socialist) political analysis about power relations in society, with a focus on various forms of socioeconomic power abuse and its victims, whether or not formulated in terms of "elites" and "the people". In radical right-wing discourse, the opposition is rather rhetorical, and as a strategy to legitimate its democratic credentials and only to get power through votes, and not as a critical analysis of unequal power relations in society. Moreover, the mythical celebration of the People (as Our Volk) in radical right-wing discourse is a rhetorically enhanced expression of nativist ideology consistent with radical conservatism, not a form of popular resistance against injustice. In other words, it is crucial to distinguish between Left and Right populism. Indeed, the polarization between the people and the elites (as those who abuse their power) in radical left-wing political discourse may not be populist at all if we examine other aspects of discourse examined below.

Aslanidis (2016) also refutes Mudde's concept of populism as a "thin-centered ideology", comparable with e.g., liberalism and socialism. Indeed, unlike fully fledged ideologies, populism lacks coherence, and may be associated with vastly different ideological groups at the left and the right, as is the case for Podemos and Vox in Spain. Indeed, as Aslanidis holds, there is no "Populist International". He shows that Mudde's conception has been borrowed from Freeden (1996, p. 485), who considers nationalism, feminism and ecologism "as ephemeral 'groupings of political thought' displaying a 'decreased internal integration'", a characterization that hardly applies to the ideologies of feminism and nationalism as movements of more than 200 years and the widespread movement of contemporary ecologism. Unlike the adherence to ideologies, Aslanidis further argues that much research has shown that populism comes in degrees. He cites Weyland (1996), who defines populism as a "political strategy" to seek the support of large groups of followers. Rather, he defines populism as a discursive strategy "invoking the supremacy of popular sovereignty to claim that corrupt elites are defrauding 'the People' of their rightful political authority. It becomes an anti-elite discourse in the name of the sovereign People" (Aslanidis, 2016, p. 96). He refers to Laclau's (2005) approach to populism, although not assuming all its aspects. Correctly so, because Laclau hardly provides detailed insight in discursive strategies. Instead, Aslanidis proposes "frame theory" of social movement research (Benford & Snow, 2000) as an alternative, although frame theory hardly provides detailed discourse analysis either (see Van Dijk, 2023a).

In sum, we agree with Aslanidis criticism of Mudde's definition of populism and his proposal to define it as a political discourse strategy, but he does not provide details on these strategies and hardly provides references to contemporary discourse studies outside of political science. This is generally the case for studies on ideology in political science.

5. Far-Right Discourse and Ideology

Assuming that populism is a discursive political strategy, studies of Far-Right discourse may provide more detailed insight into such strategies and another approach to the study of Far-Right attitudes and ideologies. Our thesis, formulated above, is not only that populism is not an ideology (thin or thick), but that there is no Far-Right ideology either. Rather, the Far Right is a political (party) position of the political spectrum, strategically using attitudes of various ideologies so as to manipulate voters, depending on the sociopolitical situation of a country.

Harrison and Bruter (2011) propose an "empirical geography" of the ideology of "extreme right" political parties in Europe. They define "a model of the extreme right as a multidimensional ideology based on two strategic-discursive dimensions (negative identity and authoritarianism), and four resulting ideological pillars (xenophobic, populist, reactionary, and repressive)" (Harrison & Bruter, 2011, p. xiii). Like Mudde (2000) before them, these authors also observe that few studies of the extreme right have taken an ideological approach (Harrison & Bruter, 2011, p. 32), which they attribute to the difficulty to analyze the discourse and ideology of a political party. They also use Mudde's definition of an ideology as a "set of normative ideas on how society or man are versus how they ought to be" (Mudde, 2000). Based on various kinds of party discourse, they propose a "conceptual map" of the ideological dimensions of extremist right parties. This map can be summarized as follows:

- An Authoritarian Dimension (Repressive vs. Reactionary)
- Negative Identity Dimension (Xenophobic vs. Populist)

These dimensions allow for each party four combinations ("pillars") such as "xenophobic repressive" or "populist reactionary", with variations of style. For instance, the repressive form of the authoritarian dimension consists of a form of social control and strict obedience to the authority of the State (the principle of Law and Order), although different parties may be more or less radical as to the proposed forms of control. On the other hand, the "cultural" aspects of the Negative Identity dimension deal with the Volk (or Nation), as ingroup, and define the racism, xenophobia or antisemitism of a party.

The schema proposed by Harrison and Bruter, based on various discourses of extreme right parties in Europe, features several heterogeneous dimensions, as is often the case of political approaches to ideology. Authoritarianism and Repression are types of governance or control, while Reaction is a form of conservatism. (Negative) Identity is a basic category of all ideologies (Us vs. Them), and Xenophobia and Racism are fully fledged ideologies. Populism is a political, discursive strategy. These different levels, dimensions and aspects of Far-Right parties are no doubt relevant, but do not define an ideology, also because they are based on, or presuppose, existing ideologies. So, also this conceptual analysis suggests that the Far Right should not be defined in terms of an ideology but as a complex political position, featuring fragments or categories of various ideologies, styles of governance, discursive strategies, norms and values, etc.

Importantly, at the end of his edited volume on the Radical Right, Mudde (2017) concludes that many of the ideological positions of Far-Right parties, e.g., on immigration, were already widely shared by mainstream parties (see also my earlier analyses of elite racism and discourse in Van Dijk, 1993).

Also, in other recent studies of the Far Right, whatever labels are used to identify it, a large variation of ideological isms have been used. For instance, the authors of the chapters of an edited book on the Far Right in the Americas (Bar-On, and Molas, 2022), identify the following isms as ideologies: Corporatism (like the New State in Brazil), Fascism, Catholic Nationalism and the Justicialista doctrine (in Argentina), Neoliberalism (of the Chicago boys in Chile during and after the dictatorship of Pinochet), and alt-right White-Supremacism in the USA, especially since Trump.

In his study of the radical right party Vox in Spain, Ferreira (2019) concludes that its ideology is similar to that of other radical right parties in Europe, a combination of nationalism and xenophobia ("nativism"), and a non-violent authoritarian "vision" of society (Law and Order), with a non-populist rhetoric, and a neoliberal economic perspective. Crucial in Vox meetings are its antifeminism, and antiabortism, defense of the family and a traditionalist conception of society. In our study of the Vox program (Van Dijk, in preparation), we will pay more detailed attention to the underlying ideological structures of this party.

Most of the political studies of the Far Right that also pay attention to ideology list more or less the same ideological properties, but without detailed analysis of these ideologies, and hardly ever on the basis of cognitive psychological or discursive analysis. Political psychology explains ideological variation in terms of personality, also without the cognitive aspects of ideologies, nor of the detailed cognitive structures and processes of how many types of "needs" or "motivation" (grievances, frustration, uncertainty, etc.) are related to either the support of populist ideas or voting for the Far Right.

6. Conclusion

From the literature in various disciplines, especially in political science and social and political psychology, it is obvious that multidisciplinary research on such complex topics as the Far Right and populism is crucial – and that not always research in one area is known in others (Rooduijn, 2019). From a perspective of the discipline of discourse studies, for instance, it is relevant to observe that many studies on the discourse of the Far Right (e.g., Wodak, KhosraviNik, & Mral, 2013) are hardly used in political science, despite the fact that many of the characteristics of populism are discursive. On the other hand, in political science, the notion of ideology is widely used, also to characterize the Far Right and populism, but without detailed ideological analysis and theorizing. In the many studies in social and political psychology, many aspects of motivation or personality are related to adherence to the Far Right, or populist ideas, but without much cognitive and political analysis about the differences between Left or Right radicalism.

References

Aslanidis, P. (2016). Is populism an ideology? A refutation and a new perspective. *Political Studies, 64*, 88–104.

Bar-On, T., & Molas, B. (Eds.). (2022). *The right and radical right in the Americas. Ideological currents from interwar Canada to contemporary Chile*. Lanham: Lexington Books.

Barberá, P., Jost, J. T., Nagler, J., Tucker, J. A., & Bonneau, R. (2015). Tweeting from left to right: Is online political communication more than an echo chamber? *Psychological Science, 26*(10), 1531–1542.

Bar-Tal, D., & Magal, T. (2021). Socio-psychological analysis of the deterioration of democracy and the rise of authoritarianism: The role of needs, values, and context. In J. P. Forgas, W. D. Crano, & K. Fiedler (Eds.), *The psychology of populism* (pp. 42–61). London: Routledge.

Benford, R. D., & Snow, D. A. (2000). Framing processes and social movements: An overview and assessment. *Annual Review of Sociology, 26*, 611–639.

Choma, B.L., & Hodson, G. (2017). Right-wing ideology: Positive (and negative) relations to threat. *Social Cognition, 35*(4), 415–432.

Crawford, J. T. (2017). Are conservatives more sensitive to threat than liberals? It depends on how we define threat and conservatism. *Social Cognition, 35*(4), 354–373.

De Lange, S., & Mugge, L. (2015). Gender and right-wing populism in the low Countries: Ideological variations across parties and time. *Patterns of Prejudice, 49*(1–2), 61–80.

Elgenius, G., & Rydgren, J. (2019). Frames of nostalgia and belonging: The resurgence of ethno-nationalism in Sweden. *European Societies, 21*(4), 583–602.

Feldman, M., & Jackson, P. (Eds.). (2014). *Doublespeak. The rhetoric of the Far Right since 1945*. Stuttgart: Ibidem-Verlag.

Ferreira, C. (2019). Vox como representante de la derecha radical en España: Un estudio sobre su ideología. *Revista Española de Ciencia Política, 51*, 73–98.

Forchtner, B. (Ed.). (2020). *The Far Right and the environment. Politics, discourse and communication*. London/New York: Routledge, Taylor & Francis Group.

Forgas, J. P., Crano, W. D., & Fiedler, K. (Eds.). (2021). *The psychology of populism. The tribal challenge to liberal democracy*. New York: Routledge.

Freeden, M. (1996). *Ideologies and political theory: A conceptual approach*. Oxford: Oxford University Press.

Harrison, S., & Bruter, M. (2011). *Mapping extreme right ideology. An empirical geography of the European extreme right*. Houndmills, Basingstoke, Hampshire, New York: Palgrave Macmillan.

Husbands, C. T. (2020). *Reflections on the extreme right in Western Europe, 1990–2008*. London: Routledge.

Jost, J. T. (2021). *Left and right. The psychological significance of a political distinction*. New York: Oxford University Press.

Jost, J., Stern, C., Rule, N., & Sterling, J. (2017). The politics of fear: Is there an ideological asymmetry in existential motivation? *Social Cognition, 35*(4), 324–353.

Kováts, E. (2018). Questioning consensuses: Right-wing populism, anti-populism, and the threat of 'gender ideology'. *Sociological Research Online, 23*(2), 528–538.

Krekó, P. (2019). Populism in power. In J. P. Forgas, W. D. Crano, & K. Fiedler (Eds.), *The psychology of populism. The tribal challenge to liberal democracy* (pp. 240–257). London: Routledge.

Laclau, E. (2005) Populism: What's in a name? In F. Panizza (Ed.), *Populism and the mirror of democracy* (pp. 32–49). London: Verso.

Morgan, G. S., & Wisneski, D. C. (2017). The structure of political ideology varies between and within people: Implications for theories about ideology's causes. *Social Cognition, 35*(4), 395–414.
Mudde, C. (2000). *Ideology of the extreme right.* Manchester: Manchester University Press.
Mudde, C. (2014). Fighting the system? Populist radical right parties and party system change. *Party Politics*, 20(2), 217–226.
Mudde, C. (Ed.). (2017). *The populist radical right. A reader.* London/New York: Routledge, Taylor & Francis Group.
Mudde, C. (2019). *The far right today.* Cambridge: Polity.
Norris, P., & Inglehart, R. (2019). *Cultural backlash. Trump, Brexit, and the rise of authoritarian-populism.* New York: Cambridge University Press.
Proulx, T., & Brandt, M. (2017). Beyond threat and uncertainty: The underpinnings of conservatism. *Social Cognition, 35*(4), 313–323.
Rooduijn, M. (2014b). Vox populismus: A populist radical right attitude among the public? *Nations and Nationalism, 20*(1), 80–92.
Rooduijn, M. (2019). State of the field: How to study populism and adjacent topics? A plea for both more and less focus. *European Journal of Political Research, 58*, 362–372.
Rooduijn, M., & Akkerman, T. (2017). Flank attacks: Populism and left-right radicalism in Western Europe. *Party Politics, 23*(3), 193–204.
Teun A van Dijk (2023) Discourse and Ideologies of the Radical Right.
Van Dijk, T. A. (1993). *Elite discourse and racism.* Newbury Park, CA: Sage Publications.
Van Dijk, T. A. (1998). Ideology: A multidisciplinary approach. Ideology, 1–384
Van Prooijen, J.-W. (2019). Overconfidence in radical politics. In J. P. Forgas, W. D. Crano, & K. Fiedler (Eds.), *The psychology of populism. The tribal challenge to liberal democracy* (pp. 143–157). London: Routledge.
Weyland, K. (1996) Neopopulism and neoliberalism in Latin America: Unexpected affinities. *Studies in Comparative International Development, 31*(3), 3–31.
Wodak, R. (2021). *The politics of fear: The shameless normalization of Far Right discourse* (2nd ed.). London: Sage.
Wodak, R., KhosraviNik, M., & Mral, B. (Eds.). (2013). *Right wing populism in Europe. Politics and discourse.* London: Bloomsbury Academic.

2 Populist Atitudes and Radical Activism in the USA

José Javier Olivas Osuna, Enrique Clari and Jocelyn J. Bélanger

1. Introduction

Populist discourses, performances, and ideas are used to mobilize citizens by harnessing their grievances and fears and getting them more involved in political action against a specific "other" (Weyland, 2001; Canovan, 2002; Laclau, 2005). This political impetus is typically directed against those on the top, "the elites", but also sometimes against those at the bottom, "deviants" and the "underserving" (Brubaker, 2020, p. 54). Sometimes populist mobilization is expressed in a peaceful manner as was largely the case of the *Indignados*, Occupy Wall Street, and *Movimento 5 Stelle* movements that emerged as a reaction to the Great Recession (Kyriakidou & Olivas Osuna, 2017; Pirro, 2018; Gerbaudo, 2023). However, there are many examples in which populist mobilizations become violent. Political leaders such as Jair Bolsonaro, Nicolás Maduro, Evo Morales, Daniel Ortega, and Donald Trump have been accused of fueling episodes of radical activism incompatible with a pluralist conception of democracy (De la Torre, 2016; Borba, 2021; Corrales, 2020; Arceneaux & Truex, 2022). Several of the *yellow vest* protests in France in 2018 and 2019, the 2019 riots triggered by Catalan secessionists in Barcelona, the assault on the Capitol building by Trump supporters in January 2021, and the *bolsonaristas* attack on the Brazilian Congress in January 2023 are recent examples of populist activism turning violent and threatening the stability of democratic governments.

Although many analysts have connected the aggressive speeches, performances, and policy proposals of certain leaders to the radicalization of their supporters, who are the supply-side of this phenomenon, studies have rarely, if ever, tried to establish a potential link between the citizens' populist attitudes (i.e., the demand-side) and their propensity to engage in radical activism. This chapter provides an insightful exploration of the relationship between populist attitudes (Akkerman et al., 2014) and two types of political activism displayed by individuals who defend a political cause:

DOI: 10.4324/9781003457381-3

peaceful (or mainstream) activism and radical activism (Gousse-Lessard et al., 2013). The findings are derived from an original survey conducted in the USA through Amazon Mechanical Turk (MTurk) with a sample of 861 individuals. These participants self-declared their involvement with either a political party (Democratic or Republican Party) or an advocacy group, encompassing gun rights groups, anti-racism groups, anti-abortion groups, and LGBTQ-rights groups.

A populist worldview may shape how individuals make sense of political events and make them more susceptible to radicalizing discourses by politicians and media outlets. In this chapter, we provide a concise overview of the theoretical connections between populism, activism, and radicalization. Moreover, we emphasize the importance of delving into individuals' attitudes. Then we explain the dataset and measures used in our statistical analysis and discuss the main results. Our findings challenge common perceptions and some previous analyses (Neiwert, 2017; Perry et al., 2019; Campani et al., 2022). Contrary to conventional wisdom, we discovered that populist attitudes are positively correlated with a higher degree of peaceful activism but show no significant association with radical activism. Likewise, we detect no statistically significant relationship between activism and right-wing ideology and nativist views (Young et al., 2019). Low levels of religiosity, younger age, and, especially, belonging to a radicalized network (Moyano, 2011) emerge as predictors of a more extreme understanding of political activism among citizens. This preliminary study suggests the need to further analyze the political and psychological attitudinal traits that may facilitate or amplify radicalized activism.

2. From Populist Ideas to Political Activism and Violent Behavior?

Populism can be perceived as a form of democratic illiberalism (Pappas, 2019) characterized by a moral and antagonistic view of society. It constructs a narrative in which "the people" are perceived as under threat from an external "other" who aims to strip them of their sovereignty, rights, and way of life (Mudde, 2004; Albertazzi & McDonnell, 2008). The populist outlook is based on the discursive articulation of chains of equivalent grievances and demands (Laclau, 2005, pp. 77–83), and the selective highlighting of boundaries to (re)construct antithetical collective political identities (Olivas Osuna, 2022). Populism entails processes of social inclusion and exclusion that are justified by (and usually exacerbate) prejudice and fear vis-à-vis out-groups (Olivas Osuna, 2021). Populist movements rely on mass mobilization to challenge the political establishment and dominant socioeconomic paradigms. Sometimes these mobilizations turn violent and threaten pluralism.

The interdisciplinary literature on activism and radicalization provides some insights to better understand this process. Political values and beliefs lead individuals to develop a sense of obligation and personal norms that can induce several types of behaviors, like activism (Stern, 2000). Activism has been usually conceptualized as a mainstream behavior, such as joining a demonstration, backing popular petitions, and exercising advocacy activities (Gousse-Lessard et al., 2013, pp. 18–19). However, some activists may participate in radical non-normative behaviors, such as engaging in physical attacks, harassment, or other illicit actions. The process of radicalization has been linked to different factors, such as the development of an obsessive passion for a cause (Gousse-Lessard et al., 2013; Bélanger et al., 2020), a psychological need to feel meaningful (Kruglanski et al. 2013; Bélanger et al., 2019) and to criminogenic factors such as radical peers and networks (Wolfowicz et al., 2021). A radical behavior is defined as engaging in illegal acts and resorting to violence, driven by a cause or ideology, a quest for significance or moral disengagement (McCauley & Moskalenko, 2017). It is usually judged as immoral or socially unacceptable because, while instrumental to achieve a (political or non-political) goal, it is detrimental to other goals or interests (including those of the person who engages in that behavior) (Gousse-Lessard et al., 2013, p. 20).

The study of radical activism grew considerably after the 9/11 attacks in New York and the subsequent waves of terrorism. One theoretical perspective that links activism with radicalism (referred to as the "conveyor belt") argues that alienated people may radicalize via the manipulation of their grievances (Moskalenko & McCauley, 2009). This argument has problematic implications, as it assumes that political activists may eventually embrace violence and even turn into terrorists. It therefore legitimizes preventive police monitoring of non-violent activists. Meanwhile, an alternative scholarly perspective argues that non-violent activist groups compete and detract followers from violent ones and that the transition from mainstream activism to radicalism is far from an unescapable path (Moskalenko & McCauley, 2009, pp. 240–242, 255–257). Currently, radicalization research is addressing a wide variety of pathways to violence, looking into individual-level psychological factors (such as cognitive and emotional vulnerabilities, identity-seeking behavior, and personal significance) and into group-level factors (such as community grievances, group polarization, groupthink, in-group/out-group bias, recruitment models, and incentives to violent outcomes) (Jensen et al., 2020; Bélanger, 2021). There are also efforts that combine both types of factors such as the 3N model of radicalization which assesses needs, narratives, and networks (Webber & Kruglanski 2017; González et al., 2022).

Framing theory (Entman, 1993; Chong & Druckman, 2007) helps explain the interaction between "supply" and "demand-side" factors in radicalization. Influential members of a group or movement disseminate frames regarding group norms, injustices, grievances, and the attribution of blame to shape identity, perceptions, and preferences. Through a process of cognitive frame alignment some individuals develop values, interests, and beliefs congruent with those of the movement (Snow et al., 1986). Dynamic intersubjective and communicative processes of framing an issue involving peer pressure, manipulation of pre-existing sentiments, and social networks appear to be better predictors of violent extremism and terrorism recruitment than inherent psychological traits and socioeconomic deprivation (Dalgaard-Nielsen, 2010).

In the second decade of the 21st century, whilst the so-called "War on Terror" has dwindled (both at the policy and communication levels) and Islamist terrorism has lost relative centrality in the public sphere, other forms of extremist behavior have gained prominence as a source of concern and attracted considerable academic attention. Many of these have been connected to right-wing populist movements that have broadened the boundaries of what is considered legitimate violence, such as American "gun populism" (Carlson, 2019), vigilantism in Asia (Jaffrey, 2021) and xenophobic populists in Europe (Ruzza, 2018). However, it is worth reminding that populism is not only considered a peril to our societies; scholars such as Grattan (2016) and Mouffe (2018) have defended that some populist movements exhibit a democratizing aspiration, fight for civil rights, and act as a counter-hegemonic offensive against corporate and government abuse. From this angle, populism can be considered as an empowering ideal that gives voice to the ordinary people and brings them closer to politics (Canovan, 2002).

Having said this, can we consider populism as a decisive factor in the emergence of new violent groups? The literature on populism historically prioritized the analysis of the discourses, political ideas and electoral success of populist leaders and parties (Berlin, 1968; Rovira-Kaltwasser et al., 2017); this is on the "supply-side" of this phenomenon. Populism was conceptualized as a "flexible mode of persuasion" (Kazin, 1998), an appeal to "the people" (Canovan, 1999), or as a "political strategy" (Weyland, 2001) seeking to mobilize ordinary people against the elites and the institutions and ideals on which their power is sustained. Several techniques were designed to assess the degree of populism in political communications such as speeches (Hawkins et al., 2009), press releases (Bernhard & Kriesi, 2019), manifestos (Rooduijn & Pauwels, 2011) and social media exchanges (García-Marín & Luengo, 2019). This type of approach can be useful to understand radicalization because communication frames shape the definition of social problems, the diagnosis of causes, moral judgments, and the choice of solutions (Entman, 1993, p. 52). "Frames in communication" can activate specific "frames in thought" and steer an individual's assessment and actions in an intended direction (Chong & Druckman, 2007, pp. 105–106). Looking into what populist parties say helps understand when and why their supporters are mobilized.

After the emergence of the "ideational approach" to populism, which considers it as a "thin-centered" ideology (Mudde, 2004; Hawkins & Rovira-Kaltwasser, 2017), many populism scholars turned their attention to measuring the "demand-side". Thus, a variety of scales of populist attitudes were applied in empirical comparative work (e.g., Akkerman et al., 2014; Elchardus & Spruyt, 2016; Schulz et al., 2018). Populism scales consist of questionnaires that present users with specific statements that try to capture a somewhat populist interpretation of reality. Respondents rate them according to their level of agreement. This approach relies on the assumption that different versions of reality can be encoded in written or oral communication via different linguistic choices and that the acceptance or rejection of a statement would reflect a specific ideological positioning (Halliday & Matthiessen, 2014, p. 217; Bartley & Hidalgo-Tenorio, 2015).

However, the relationship between the supply- and demand-side of populism is complex, and comparative data show that support for "populist" parties is not always significantly correlated with voters' underlying populist attitudes (Olivas Osuna & Rama, 2022). The presence of populist parties does not always contribute to a heightened mobilization and elections turnout (Leininger & Meijers, 2021). Attitudes toward populist communication style and some components of the "host" or "thick" ideology may outweigh voters' own populist views regarding the endorsement of populist candidates or parties (Kefford et al., 2021; Castanho Silva et al., 2022). Moreover, some populist attributes such as anti-immigration discourses or people-centrism tend to mobilize voters more than anti-elitism and anti-globalization sentiments (Neuner & Wratil, 2021), and, therefore, populism scales may not display the same capacity to predict support for right- and left-leaning populist movements (Marcos-Marne, 2021).

This complex relationship between populist discourses and political behavior means that we cannot explain the successful activation of peaceful and/or radical type activism by simply analyzing populist leaders' ideas and communications. The understanding of why citizens adopt extremist political behavior requires the analysis of mediating sociodemographic and attitudinal factors that could make them more prone to justify the use of violence to advance a social or political cause. Populist attitudes among citizens may reflect an ongoing process of framing alignment conducive to populist activism. This chapter aims to shed some light on this area of research by drawing from political science and psychology literatures, and exploring, for the first time, the link between citizens' populist views and activist behaviors. We test whether peaceful and radical activisms are associated with sociodemographic features, nativism, right-wing ideology, radicalized network, and populist attitudes. We include in our models one of the most widely used populist attitudes indexes (Akkerman et al., 2014) and a new populism attitudes scale that distinguishes two types of populisms and a set of pluralist features.

3. Methodology

3.1 Participants and Procedure

Social psychology research has shown that attitudes and intentions can be used as proxy to predict behavior (Fishbein & Ajzen, 1975). This research is based on an original online survey conducted among US residents ($N = 861$) recruited via the crowdsourcing platform Amazon's Mechanical Turk (Mturk) in August 2021. The USA was chosen as the case study due to its growing polarization, frequent clashes among its political elites over immigration and identity-related issues (Gidron et al., 2020), and the regular outbursts of far-right and Islamist violence (Jasko et al., 2022). The rise of Donald Trump to power in 2016 can be considered a milestone in an international populist wave. His, often-imitated, rhetorical strategy is based on hyperbolic and simplistic accounts that seek to fuel grievances by spectacularizing politics and establishing an emotional connection with the public (Wahl-Jorgensen, 2018; Hidalgo-Tenorio & Benítez-Castro, 2022). The violent assault on the Capitol by radicalized supporters in 2021 exemplifies the worrisome potential connections between populism and political extremism that risk destabilizing democracies. Interestingly, the USA is also home to many civil society groups that adopt populist discourse but a peaceful and constructive demeanor in their efforts to shape society.

Assuming small-to-medium effect sizes (f_2 =.085) and power set at .80, a minimal sample of 185 people was suggested by G*power (Faul et al., 2009). Participants were invited to take part in this study because they either self-identified as Democrats or Republicans in an independent pre-screening survey posted on Amazon Mechanical Turk. We used TurkPrime (Litman et al., 2017) to ensure data quality (e.g., high approval ratings, no duplicate IP addresses). The final sample, once missing values and responses that failed attention checks were eliminated, consisted of 861 participants (48.43% *male*, 50.87% *female*, and 6.97% *non-binary*), aged from 20 to 85 (M=41.26, SD=12.31). Of them, 78.39% completed higher education whereas 21.61% did not attend university. Regarding their ethnicity, 76.07% of the participants were *white*, 9.87% were *black*, 6.97% were *Asian*, 3.48% were *Hispanic*, and the rest belonged to other ethnic groups. In terms of participants' *household annual income*, 53.77% earned $69,000 or less, 41.58% earned between $70,000 and $200,000, and 4.65% earned more than $200,000. Regarding religion, 56.10% of the participants were *Christian*, 35.77% had *no religion*, and 8.13% followed *other religions*. Finally, 45.52% declared to be strongly involved in the

Democratic Party, 29.50% in the *Republican Party*, 5.46% in *anti-racism groups*, 4.76% in *LGBTQ rights groups*, 2.79% in *anti-abortion groups*, and 2.32% in *gun-rights groups* – put differently, 55.74% supported *liberal movements* whereas 34.61% *conservative groups* (and 9.65% supported other advocacy organizations).

3.2 *Measures*

The questionnaire was designed by an interdisciplinary team of psychologists and political scientists and included several sociopolitical attitudinal scales, as well as a set of sociodemographic items. Following the logic applied by most studies measuring populist and other psychosocial attitudes (e.g., Akkerman et al., 2014; Elchardus & Spruyt, 2016; Bélanger et al., 2020), we present items as Likert scales and ask respondents to rate their level of agreement with statements (7-point Likert) and build compensatory additive indexes. Before analyzing the correlations among these scales, we measure their internal consistency via factor analysis. Model fit is assessed using a combination of fit indices, with values of the comparative fit index (CFI) and the Tucker–Lewis index (TLI), root mean squared error by approximation (RMSEA), and values of the standardized root mean residual (SRMR) (Hu & Bentler, 1999).

Populist Attitudes: For our first study, we use the populist attitudes scale initially developed by Hawkins et al. (2012) and further expanded by Akkerman et al. (2014) (Table 2.1). This scale was conceived to reflect a minimal definition of populism and to capture three basic attributes: (1) Popular sovereignty, (2) anti-elitism, and (3) Manichean outlook.

Table 2.1 Populist attitudes

Item	*Wording*	*Mean*	*Loading*
pop1	The politicians in the Capitol need to follow the will of the people	5.46	0.659
pop2	The people, and not politicians, should make our most important policy decisions	4.71	0.761
pop3	The political differences between the elite and the people are larger than the differences among the people	4.56	0.637
pop4	I would rather be represented by a citizen than by a specialized politician	4.43	0.783
pop5	Elected officials talk too much and take too little action	5.30	0.731
pop6	What people call "compromise" in politics is really just selling out on one's principles	3.30	0.439

Note: ML estimator, CFI = 0.929, TLI = 0.881, RMSEA = 0.129, SRMR = 0.047, $\omega = 0.82$. Items measured on a 1–7 scale.

It is currently the most popular instrument to analyze the demand-side of populism and one that has been favorably compared to other alternative scales (Castanho Silva et al., 2019; Van Hauwaert et al., 2020).

To test the robustness of the relationship found between populist attitudes and activism in our second study we use the New Populist Attitudes Scale (NPAS) (Olivas Osuna et al. forthcoming). The NPAS items were selected in a process combining deductive and inductive phases, and several validation rounds by experts in populism and psychology. The NPAS distinguishes three different types of attitudes (according to the loading of its items). The first factor captures aspirational/subversive (populist) attitudes (Table 2.2), the second factor (that correlates inversely with the other factors) reflects pluralist (anti-populist) views (Table 2.3), and the third one with an identitarian/protective (populist) outlook (Table 2.4).

Table 2.2 NPAS aspirational-subversive populist attitudes

Item	*Wording*	*Mean*	*Loading*
asp]	The elites are enemies of the people	3.25	0.872
asp2	The current system is broken and it must be radically replaced	3.84	0.676
asp3	The powerful will never be on the side of the people	3.96	0.787
asp4	The people must remain united against the elites	3.56	0.880
asp5	Politicians are immoral and unfair	4.22	0.710

Table 2.3 NPAS pluralist attitudes

Item	*Wording*	*Mean*	*Loading*
plul	Making compromises and agreements with political opponents is worthy	4.37	0.696
plu2	Society is not divided into opposing blocs and therefore politics requires moderation and consensus building	3.91	0.627
plu3	It is important to recognize the legitimacy of our political opponents and listen to them	4.48	0.841
plu4	Moderation and consensus building are key to the success of democracy	4.72	0.843
plu5	A good political leader should always listen to other politicians, even if they belong to other parties	5.34	0.745
plu6	Leaders who defend ideas that are opposed to mine can be also right	4.80	0.686

Note: ML estimator, CFI = 0.962, TLI = 0.937, RMSEA = 0.111, SRMR = 0.038, w = 0.88. Items measured on a 1–7 scale.

Note: ML estimator, CFI = 0.984, TLI = 0.967, RMSEA = 0.097, SRMR = 0.022, w = 0.89. Items measured on a 1–7 scale.

Table 2.4 NPAS identitarian-protective populist attitudes

Item	*Wording*	*Mean*	*Loading*
idenl	A strong leader is more important than political parties	4.47	0.530
iden2	The people must remain united against those who threaten our values and way of life	4.67	0.839
iden3	Our singular identity and way of life must be preserved at all costs	3.68	0.736
iden4	The people must remain united and speak with a single voice	4.04	0.430

Note: ML estimator, CFI = 0.998, TLI = 0.994, RMSEA = 0.029, SRMR = 0.011, w = 0.73. Items measured on a 1–7 scale.

Nativist Attitudes: The border has been instrumentalized by far-right populist leaders to unite "the people" (in-group) against an undeserving "other", or out-group, that was accused of causing some of the problems that affected the former (Wodak, 2021; Olivas Osuna, 2022). In the USA, anti-immigration attitudes, spurred by the collective trauma of the 9/11, the terrorist waves that followed worldwide, and the Great Recession, have been identified as a factor for political radicalism (Campani et al., 2022). Hence, we include Young et al.'s (2019) nativist attitudes scale with five items (Table 2.5) as a control factor between populist attitudes and activism.

Radicalized network: Previous studies have found belonging to a radicalized network as a determinant of support for political violence (Bélanger et al., 2020). We include in our study a three-item additive scale (Moyano, 2011) to act as control variable in our analysis of the relationship between populist attitudes and political activism (Table 2.6).

Peaceful and Radical Activism: The scale we use to measure the type of activism (i.e., peaceful or radical) is an adaptation of the scale employed by Gousse-Lessard et al. (2013) in their analysis of mainstream and radical activist behavior. Activism for a cause was measured separately through 13 items. For that, we created two different scales, one with seven items for peaceful activism (Table 2.7) and one with six items for radical activism (Table 2.8).

4. Results

Our statistical analysis confirms a significant correlation between peaceful activism and radical activism (Table 2.9). This seems in line with previous studies (Moskalenko & McCauley, 2009). Many of those who are willing to undertake violent action to defend a cause or a party are also willing

Table 2.5 Nativism

Item	*Wording*	*Mean*	*Loading*
natl	USA would be stronger if we stopped immigration	2.47	0.845
nat2	USA would be better off if we let in all immigrants who wanted to come here	2.50	−0.293
nat3	When jobs are scarce, people should prioritize hiring people of this country over immigrants	3.63	0.796
nat4	Immigrants take jobs away from real Americans	2.68	0.928
nat5	Immigrants take important social services away from real Americans	2.95	0.936

Note: ML estimator, CFI = 0.990, TLI = 0.979, RMSEA = 0.085, SRMR = 0.021, w = 0.87. Items measured on a 1–7 scale.

Table 2.6 Radicalized network

Item	*Wording*	*Mean*	*Loading*
rad]	People around me say it is appropriate to use violence for an ideology	1.98	0.802
rad2	The people that I know would fight for a cause that is dear to them	3.37	0.520
rad3	I personally know someone that supports violence for political change	2.03	0.759

Note: ML estimator, CFI = 1.000, TLI = 1.000, RMSEA = 0.000, SRMR = 0.000, w = 0.73. Items measured on a 1–7 scale.

Table 2.7 Peaceful activism

Item	*Wording*	*Mean*	*Loading*
pal	Sending news about [group] to my friends	3.60	0.808
pa2	Organizing fundraising activities for [group]	2.90	0.890
pa3	Raising public awareness about [group]	3.60	0.844
pa4	Sensitizing close relatives or colleagues about the importance of [group]	3.13	0.753
pa5	Organizing social activities to increase people awareness about [group]	3.06	0.888
pa6	Financially supporting people that works for [group]	3.15	0.832
pa 7	Posting signs reminding people to [support group]	3.30	0.848

Note: ML estimator, CFI = 0.949, TLI = 0.923, RMSEA = 0.149, SRMR = 0.034, w = 0.94. Items measured on a 1–7 scale.

Table 2.8 Radical activism

Item	*Wording*	*Mean*	*Loading*
ral	Doing risky or illegal actions to help [group]	1.34	0.811
ra2	Harassing supporters of [rival group]	1.37	0.848
ra3	Physically attacking [members of rival group]	1.25	0.846
ra4	Destroying signs that support [rival group]	1.45	0.823
ra5	Put an end to my friendship with anyone who supports [rival group]	1.97	0.595
ra6	Using any means, even violent ones, to undermine [rival group]	1.35	0.842

Note: ML estimator, CFI = 0.930, TLI = 0.883, RMSEA = 0.179, SRMR = 0.044, ω = 0.89. Items measured on a 1–7 scale.

to engage in mainstream advocacy activities. Activism is not correlated either with the left-right ideological standpoint of participants or anti-immigration view. Radicalized network (that is, having personal ties with people willing to employ violence to advance their political goals) is associated to right-wing ideas and nativism, and the best predictor of radical activism and the second best of peaceful activism. Populist attitudes, as defined by Akkerman et al. (2014), are positively correlated in our sample with peaceful activism and right-wing ideology, but not with violent ones. We also confirm that the NPAS populism aspirational-subversive and identitarian-protective subscales display a significant positive association with Akkerman et al.'s populism index.

4.1 *Study 1*

In our first study, we run three linear regression models using peaceful activism as a dependent variable and the other three using radical activism. In all of them we include sociodemographic variables such as age, gender, education, income, and religiosity level. The first model for each type of activism (Gousse-Lessard et al., 2013) assesses its relationship with populist attitudes (Akkerman et al., 2014), the second excludes populist attitudes and includes ideology, radicalized network, nativism, and the type of activism, which does not act as a dependent variable. The third model includes all these scales. We find a significant positive correlation between populist views and peaceful activism, also controlling for other indexes and sociodemographic factors. Nativism and ideology show no impact on either type of activism. Radical activism is negatively correlated with populist attitudes in our sample when controlling for peaceful activism, radicalized network, nativism, and ideology. Radicalized network appears as the strongest predictor of radical activism, but not correlated to peaceful activism. Age is the only sociodemographic variable

Table 2.9 Correlation matrix

			Right-			*Aspirational*		*Identitarian*
	Peaceful Activism	Radical Activism	wing. ideology	Nativism	Radicalized Network	Populism (NPAS)	Pluralism (NPAS)	Populism (NPAS)
Radical Activism	0.39***							
Right-wing ideology	0.03	0.01						
Nativism	0.07	0.05	0.60***					
Radicalized Network	0.20***	0.41***	0.16***	0.18***				
Aspirational populism NPAS	0.14***	0.22***	–0.07	0.12***	0.28***			
Pluralism NPAS	–0.02	–0.17***	–0.11**	–0.15***	–0.08*	–0.21***		
Identitarian populism NPAS	0.03	0.01	0.34***	0.40***	0.24***	0.31***	0.06	
Populism (Akkerman et al., 2014)	0.14***	0.06	0.17***	0.31***	0.23***	0.57***	–0.07*	0.48***

Note: Pearson correlation coefficients (*** $p < 0.001$, **$p < 0.01$, *$p < 0.05$).

that impacts mainstream activism. Older people tend to engage more into peaceful activism and disapprove radicalism. Religiosity seems to reduce the likelihood of exhibiting radical behavior in our sample (Table 2.10).

Table 2.10: Regression results Study 1

	Peaceful activism			*Radical activism*		
	(1)	*(2)*	*(3)*	*(1)*	*(2)*	*(3)*
Sociodemographics						
Age	0.03	0.16*	0.17**	−0.18***	−0.12	−0.13**
	(0.07)	(0.06)	(0.06)	(0.03)	(0.03)	(0.03)
Male	−0.06	−0.13	−0.14	0.11	0.11	0.11
	(0.13)	(0.12)	(0.12)	(0.07)	(0.06)	(0.06)
University	−0.19	−0.22	−0.20	O.Ql	0.05	0.05
	(0.16)	(0.15)	(0.15)	(0.09)	(0.07)	(0.07)
Income	−0.01	0.02	0.03	−0.06	−0.05	−0.05
	(0.07)	(0.06)	(0.06)	(0.04)	(0.03)	(0.03)
Religious	−0.08	0.00	O.Ql	−0.14	−0.18	−0.19**
	(0.14)	(0.13)	(0.13)	(0.07)	(0.06)	(0.06)
Political variables	0.03	−0.01	−0.00	0.05	−0.02	−0.02
Right-wing ideology						
	(0.07)	(0.08)	(0.08)	(0.04)	(0.04)	(0.04)
Radicalized network		0.10	0.06		0.31***	0.32***
		(0.07)	(0.07)		(0.03)	(0.03)
Nativism		0.05	−0.02		0.02	0.04
		(0.07)	(0.08)		(0.04)	(0.04)
Radical activism		0.69***	0.70			
		(0.07)	(0.07)			
Peaceful activism					0.31***	0.32*
					(0.03)	(0.03)
Populism (Akkerman et al., 2014)	0.24***		0.21***	0.04		−0.08*
	(0.06)		(0.06)	(0.03)		(0.03)
(Intercept)	3.48***	3.48***	3.47**	1.48***	1.48***	1.49***
	(0.18)	(0.17)	(0.17)	(0.09)	(0.08)	(0.08)
R^2	0.02	0.17	0.18	0.05	0.30	0.31
Adj. R^2	0.01	0.16	0.17	0.05	0.29	0.30
Num. obs.	782	782	782	782	782	782

Note: ***$p < 0.001$; **$p < 0.01$; *$p < 0.05$. Standardized regression coefficients (standard errors in parentheses).

4.2 *Study 2*

As a robustness test, in our second study, we replace Akkerman et al.'s populism scale with the three NPAS subscales and run four regression

Table 2.11: Regression results Study 2

	Peaceful		*Activism*			*Radical*	*Activism*	
	(1)	(2)	*(3)*	*(4)*	*(1)*	*(2)*	*(3)*	*(4)*
Sociodemographics								
Age	0.18	0.14	0.16	0.17	–0.11	–0.10	–0.13	–0.10
	(0.06)	(0.06)	(0.06)	(0.06)	(0.03)	(0.03)	(0.03)	(0.03)
Male	–0.15	–0.13	–0.13	–0.16	0.11	0.11	0.11	0.10
	(0.12)	(0.12)	(0.12)	(0.12)	(0.06)	(0.06)	(0.06)	(0.06)
University	–0.20	–0.22	–0.22	–0.20	0.06	0.05	0.04	0.04
	(0.15)	(0.15)	(0.15)	(0.15)	(0.07)	(0.07)	(0.07)	(0.07)
Income	0.03	0.01	0.02	0.02	–0.05	–0.04	–0.06	–0.04
	(0.06)	(0.06)	(0.06)	(0.06)	(0.03)	(0.03)	(0.03)	{0.03)
Religious	0.02	–0.00	0.00	0.03	–0.18**	–0.1T*	–0.17**	–0.15*
	(0.13)	(0.13)	(0.13)	(0.13)	(0.06)	(0.06)	(0.06)	{0.06)
Political variables								
Right-wing ideology	0.02	0.00	–0.01	0.04	–0.01	–0.03	–0.01	–0.01
	(0.08)	(0.08)	(0.08)	(0.08)	(0.04)	(0.04)	(0.04)	(0.04)
Radicalized network	0.07	0.10	0.10	0.07	0.30***	0.31**	0.32***	0.31*
	(0.07)	(0.07)	(0.07)	(0.07)	(0.03)	(0.03)	(0.03)	{0.03)
Nativism	0.02	0.06	0.05	0.04	0.01	0.00	0.04	0.02
	(0.08)	(0.07)	(0.08)	(0.08)	(0.04)	(0.04)	(0.04)	{0.04)
Radical activism	0.68***	0.70	0.69*'*	0.69***				

(*Continued*)

Table 2.11 (Continued)

	Peaceful		*Activism*		*Radical*	*Activism*		
	(1)	(2)	*(3)*	*(4)*	*(1)*	*(2)*	*(3)*	*(4)*
Peaceful activism	(0.07)	(0.07)	(0.07)	(0.07)				
			0.31***			0.31	0.31***	0.31
			(0.03)			(0.03)	(0.03)	(0.03)
Aspirational populism NPAS	0.12		0.16*	0.04				0.04
	(0.07)		(0.07)	(0.03)	0.13*			(0.03)
Pluralism NPAS	0.09					–0.12*		–0.11***
	{0.06)		(0.06)			(0.03)		{0.03)
Identitarian populism NPAS			–0.00	–0.07			–0.08*	–0.07
			(0.07)	(0.07)			(0.03)	{0.03)
(Intercept)	3.46***	3.49**	3.48	3.46**	1.48***	1.47*	1.48***	1.47**
	(0.17)	(0.17)	(0.17)	(0.17)	(0.08)	(0.08)	(0.08)	(0.08)
R^2	0.17	0.17	0.17	0.18	0.30	0.32	0.31	0.32
Adj. R^2	0.16	0.16	0.16	0.16	0.29	0.31	0.30	0.31
Num. obs.	782	782	782	782	782	782	782	782

Note: $^{***}p < 0.001$; $^{**}p < 0.01$; $^{*}p < 0.05$. Standardized regression coefficients (standard errors in parentheses).

models for each type of activism (peaceful and radical). The first, second, and third models assess the impact of each of these NPAS subscales (controlled by the same sociodemographic variables as well as by ideology, radicalized network, nativism, and the other type of activism), and the fourth model compounds the effect of all scales, subscales, and sociodemographics on that specific type of activism. The impact of most variables included in the model remain the same. Radicalized network and peaceful activism continue to be the factors with the strongest impact on radical activism. Sociodemographic factors keep the same, mostly non-statistically significant relationship with activism. However, our analysis shows a different pattern between the two types of populisms. Aspirational-subversive populist attitudes are positively correlated with peaceful activism and identitarian-protective populist attitudes display a small negative association with violent activism. Pluralist views are positively associated with peaceful activism and negatively with radical activism (Table 2.11).

5. Discussion and Conclusion

Although populist leaders are often blamed for the outburst of violent behavior among their supporters (the investigation into Donald Trump's responsibility in the assault on the Capitol building exemplifies it), our analyses suggest the need for a slightly more ambitious research agenda to explain the radicalization phenomenon. The literature has identified multiple pathways to extremism. For instance, violent attitudes can be facilitated or activated by group-level factors such as a collective sense of victimization and injustice, group norms, grievances, biases, and polarization, as well as by underlying individual-level attitudes and beliefs (Jensen et al., 2020). Indeed, populists tend to instrumentalize and amplify many of these sentiments and collective interpretations in their allocutions and performances (Moffitt, 2015; Olivas Osuna, 2022). However, the relationship between populism ideas and radicalization remains understudied. To our knowledge, this is the first time the Gousse-Lessard et al.'s (2013) scales of activism have been used in conjunction with any populist attitudes index. Our statistical analysis shows that, in our USA sample, individuals holding populist attitudes (Akkerman et al., 2014) are more supportive of peaceful activism and less prone to radical activism than the average citizen.

We confirm a strong positive correlation between both types of activism anticipated in previous research (Moskalenko & McCauley, 2009). Those holding anti-immigration views seem to be prone to exhibit populist ideas, but they do not display a higher than average propensity to engage in (peaceful or violent) activism. Likewise, there is no correlation between any specific ideological self-placement and radicalism. Older and more religious people tend to disagree with the use of violence and other illicit means in the defense of cause. The rest of the sociodemographic variables, such as gender, education, and income level, do not explain radical or peaceful activism. These results indicate that populist discourses and right-wing nativist ideas may not be the cause of increased levels of radical behavior in the USA, as some authors have argued (Neiwert, 2017; Perry et al., 2019; Campani et al., 2022).

We observe that belonging to a radicalized network (i.e., personal ties with people who support the use of violence) is a better predictor of political radical activism. This is consistent with studies that highlight the importance of social networks in radicalization (Dalgaard-Nielsen, 2010; Moyano, 2011; Bélanger et al., 2020). Extant radical organizations may be acting as confounders in the perceived relationship between individuals' right-wing and anti-immigration views, and their adoption of violent political attitudes. Further research is required to test what other social and psychological factors underpin radical activism and the relative weight of ideological and interpersonal components.

This chapter also contributes to the literature on populism and pluralism. Firstly, our results resonate with the theoretical arguments that emphasize the value of populism as a mechanism to promote peaceful political engagement (Canovan, 1999; Grattan, 2016; Mouffe, 2018). Akkerman et al.'s index of populism attitudes and NPAS aspirational-subversive attitudes are positively associated with mainstream activism, and an identitarian-protective outlook is negatively correlated with radicalism.

Secondly, our analysis shows that individuals scoring higher in the NPAS pluralist attitudes subscale are less prone to participate in or approve of violent activism and display a propensity for peaceful activism. The items in the pluralism subscale were designed to capture views opposed to those theoretically held by populist individuals, such as the rejection of a Manichean interpretation of society and preference for a more consensual approach to politics (Olivas Osuna, 2021; Olivas Osuna et al. forthcoming). Thus, populist ideas may not be conducive to radical behavior, but pluralist views may be useful to prevent it (stronger negative correlation), and similarly useful to stimulate political engagement.

Thirdly, this chapter offers some methodological insights. Akkerman et al.'s (2014) scale is arguably the most frequently used comparative studies. However, this scale focuses mostly on the anti-elite and people-centric component of populism, and does not fully capture the moral and identitarian dimensions of this latent construct. New multidimensional instruments to measure the demand-side of populism, such as the NPAS, may potentially reveal hidden relationships between specific types of populist and pluralist individuals, and other psychosocial variables.

There are also some caveats to our analysis. Our relatively small sample (861 participants) does not allow us to provide a representative picture of populism and activism in the USA. Yet, it is sufficient to test the internal validity and identify some relevant correlations among the scales and sociodemographic variables included in our survey. Although no causal inference can be extracted from this exploratory analysis of the attitudinal determinants of activism, due to the correlational nature of the data, our findings indicate that further research (using either experimental design or longitudinal data) could shed light on the complex relationship between populism, pluralism, and political activism. This chapter may be considered as a first step and an invitation to other researchers to investigate potential pathways leading from populist and/or pluralist ideas to political activism and radicalization and vice versa.

References

Funding

This study was supported by the Spanish Agencia Estatal de Investigación [Grant PID2020-113182RA-I00/AEI/10.13039/501100011033] and Comunidad de Madrid [Grant 2022-5A/SOC-24238]

Akkerman, A., Mudde, C., & Zaslove, A. (2014). How populist are the people? Measuring populist attitudes in voters. *Comparative Political Studies*, *47*(9), 1324–1353.

Albertazzi, D., & McDonnell, D. (2008). Introduction: The sceptre and the spectre. In *Twenty-first century populism: The spectre of Western European democracy* (pp. 1–11). London: Palgrave Macmillan.

Arceneaux, K., & Truex, R. (2022). Donald Trump and the lie. *Perspectives on Politics*, 1–17. https://doi.org/10.1017/S1537592722000901

Bartley, L., & Hidalgo-Tenorio, E. (2015). Constructing perceptions of sexual orientation: A corpus-based critical discourse analysis of transitivity in the Irish press. *Estudios Irlandeses, 10*(10), 14–34.

Bélanger, J. J. (2021). The sociocognitive processes of ideological obsession: Review and policy implications. *Philosophical Transactions of the Royal Society B*, *376*(1822). https://doi.org/10.1098/rstb.2020.0144

Bélanger, J. J., Moyano, M., Hayat, M., Richardson, L., Lafrenieère, M. A., McCaffery, P., Framand, K., & Nociti, P. (2019). Radicalization leading to violence: A test of the 3N model. *Frontiers in Psychiatry, 10*. https://www.frontiersin.org/articles/10.3389/fpsyt.2019.00042/full

Bélanger, J. J., Robbins, B. G., Muhammad, H., Moyano, M., Nisa, C. F., Schumpe, B. M., & Blaya-Burgo, M. (2020). Supporting political violence: The role of ideological passion and social network. *Group Processes & Intergroup Relations*, *23*(8), 1187–1203.

Berlin, I. (1968). To define populism. *Government and Opposition*, *3*(2), 137–79.

Bernhard, L., & Kriesi, H. (2019). Populism in election times: A comparative analysis of 11 countries in Western Europe. *West European Politics*, *42*(6), 1188–1208.

Borba, R. (2021). Disgusting politics: Circuits of affects and the making of Bolsonaro. *Social Semiotics*, *31*(5), 677–694.

Brubaker, R. (2020). Populism and nationalism. *Nations and Nationalism*, *26*(1), 44–66.

Campani, G., Fabelo Concepción, S., Rodriguez Soler, A., & Sánchez Savín, C. (2022). The rise of Donald Trump right-wing populism in the United States: Middle American Radicalism and anti-immigration discourse. *Societies*, *12*(6), 154. https://doi.org/10.3390/soc12060154

Canovan, M. (1999). Trust the people! Populism and the two faces of democracy. *Political Studies*, *47*(1), 2–16.

Canovan, M. (2002). Taking politics to the people: Populism as the ideology of democracy. In Y. Mény & Y. Surel (Eds.), *Democracies and the populist challenge* (pp. 25–44). Basingstoke: Palgrave Macmillan.

Carlson, J. (2019). Revisiting the Weberian presumption: Gun militarism, gun populism, and the racial politics of legitimate violence in policing. *American Journal of Sociology*, *125*(3), 633–682.

Castanho Silva, B., Jungkunz, S., Helbling, M., & Littvay, L. (2019). An empirical comparison of seven populist attitudes scales. *Political Research Quarterly*, *73*(2), 409–424.

Castanho Silva, B., Fuks, M., & Tamaki, E. R. (2022). So thin it's almost invisible: Populist attitudes and voting behavior in Brazil. *Electoral Studies*, *75*. https://doi.org/10.1016/j.electstud.2021.102434

Chong, D., & Druckman, J. N. (2007). Framing theory. *Annual Review of Political Science*, *10*, 103–126.

Corrales, J. (2020). Why Maduro hasn't fallen. *Journal of Democracy*, *31*, 39–53.

Dalgaard-Nielsen, A. (2010). Violent radicalization in Europe: What we know and what we do not know. *Studies in Conflict & Terrorism*, *33*(9), 797–814.

De La Torre, C. (2016). Left-wing populism: Inclusion and authoritarianism in Venezuela, Bolivia, and Ecuador. *Brown Journal of World Affairs*, *23*, 61–76.

Elchardus M., & Spruyt, B. (2016), Populism, persistent republicanism and declinism: An empirical analysis of populism as a thin ideology. *Government and Opposition*, *51*(1), 111–33.

Entman, R. M. (1993). Framing: Toward clarification of a fractured paradigm. *Journal of Communication*, *43*, 51–58.

Faul, F., Erdfelder, E., Buchner, A., & Lang, A. G. (2009). Statistical power analyses using G* Power 3.1: Tests for correlation and regression analyses. *Behavior Research Methods*, *41*(4), 1149–1160.

Fishbein, M., & Ajzen, I. (1975). *Belief attitude, intention, and behavior: An introduction to theory and research*. Reading, MA: Addison-Wesley.

García-Marín, J., & Luengo, Ó. G. (2019). Populist Discourse in the 21st Century: the definition of otherness on Twitter in the cases of Spain, Bolivia and Venezuela. In E. Hidalgo-Tenorio, M.A. Benítez-Castro & F. De Cesare (Eds.) *Populist Discourse* (pp. 81–100). London: Routledge.

Gerbaudo, P. (2023). From Occupy Wall Street to the Gilets Jaunes: On the populist turn in the protest movements of the 2010s. *Capital & Class*, *47*(1), 107–124.

González, I., Moyano, M., Lobato, R. M., & Trujillo, H. M. (2022). Analysis of the radicalization of the 17-A terrorist cell: An empirical approach using the 3N model. *International Journal of Social Psychology*, *37*(3), 529–553.

Gousse-Lessard, A. S., Vallerand, R. J., Carbonneau, N., & Lafrenière, M. A. K. (2013). The role of passion in mainstream and radical behaviors: A look at environmental activism. *Journal of Environmental Psychology*, *35*, 18–29.

Gidron, N., Adams, J., & Horne, W. (2020). *American affective polarization in comparative perspective*. Cambridge: Cambridge University Press.

Grattan, L. (2016). *Populism's power: Radical grassroots democracy in America*. Oxford: Oxford University Press.

Halliday, M., & Matthiessen, M. (2014). *An introduction to functional grammar*. London: Routledge.

Hawkins, K. A., Riding, S., & Mudde, C. (2012). Measuring populist attitudes. *Political Concepts Committee on Concepts and Methods Working Paper Series*, *55*, 1–35.

Hawkins, K. A., & Rovira-Kaltwasser, C. (2017). The ideational approach to populism. *Latin American Research Review*, *52*(4), 513–528.

Hidalgo-Tenorio, E., & Benítez-Castro, M. Á. (2022). Trump's populist discourse and affective politics, or on how to move 'the People' through emotion. *Globalisation, Societies and Education*, *20*(2), 86–109.

Hu, L. T., & Bentler, P. M. (1999). Cutoff criteria for fit indexes in covariance structure analysis: Conventional criteria versus new alternatives. *Structural Equation Modeling: A Multidisciplinary Journal*, *6*(1). https://doi.org/10.1080/107055199095401

Jaffrey, S. (2021). Right-wing populism and vigilante violence in Asia. *Studies in Comparative International Development*, *56*(2), 223–249.

Jasko, K., LaFree, G., Piazza, J., & Becker, M. H. (2022). A comparison of political violence by left-wing, right-wing, and Islamist extremists in the United States and the world. *Proceedings of the National Academy of Sciences*, *119*(30), 1–9.

Jensen, M. A., Atwell Seate, A., & James, P. A. (2020). Radicalization to violence: A pathway approach to studying extremism. *Terrorism and Political Violence*, *32*(5), 1067–1090.

Kazin, M. (1998). *The populist persuasion: An American history*. Ithaca, NY: Cornell University Press.

Kefford, G., Moffitt, B., & Werner, A. (2021). Populist attitudes: Bringing together ideational and communicative approaches. *Political Studies*, *70*(4), 1006–1027.

Kruglanski, A. W., Bélanger, J. J., Gelfand, M., Gunaratna, R., Hettiarachchi, M., Reinares, F., Orehek, E., Sasota, J., & Sharvit, K. (2013). Terrorism-A (self) love story: Redirecting the significance quest can end violence. *American Psychologist*, *68*, 559–575.

Kyriakidou, M., & Olivas Osuna, J. J. (2017). The indignados protests in the Spanish and Greek press: Moving beyond the 'protest paradigm'? *European Journal of Communication*, *32*(5), 457–472.

Laclau, E. (2005). *On populist reason*. London: Verso.

Leininger, A., & Meijers, M. J. (2021). Do populist parties increase voter turnout? Evidence from over 40 years of electoral history in 31 European democracies. *Political Studies*, *69*(3), 665–685.

Litman, L., Robinson, J., & Abberbock, T. (2017). TurkPrime.com: A versatile crowdsourcing data acquisition platform for the behavioral sciences. *Behavior Research Methods*, *49*(2), 433–442.

Marcos-Marne, H. (2021). A tale of populism? The determinants of voting for left-wing populist parties in Spain. *Political Studies*, *69*(4), 1053–1071.
McCauley, C., & Moskalenko, S. (2017). Understanding political radicalization: The two-pyramids model. *American Psychologist*, *72*(3), 415–433.
Moffitt, B. (2015). How to perform crisis: A model for understanding the key role of crisis in contemporary populism. *Government and Opposition*, *50*(2), 189–217.
Moskalenko, S., & McCauley, C. (2009). Measuring political mobilization: The distinction between activism and radicalism. *Terrorism and Political Violence*, *21*(2), 239–260.
Mouffe, C. (2018). *For a left populism*. London: Verso Books.
Moyano, M. (2011). Factores psicosociales contribuyentes a la radicalización islamista de jóvenes en España. Construcción de un instrumento de evaluación. Doctoral Thesis. Universidad de Granada. https://digibug.ugr.es/handle/10481/18403
Mudde, C. (2004). The populist zeitgeist. *Government and Opposition*, *39*(3), 541–563.
Neiwert, D. (2017). *Alt-America: The rise of the radical right in the age of Trump*. London: Verso Books.
Neuner, F. G., & Wratil, C. (2021). The populist marketplace: Unpacking the role of "thin" and "thick" ideology. *Political Behavior, 44*, 551–574.
Olivas Osuna, J. J. (2021). From chasing populists to deconstructing populism: A new multidimensional approach to understanding and comparing populism. *European Journal of Political Research*, *60*(4), 829–853.
Olivas Osuna, J. J. (2022). Populism and borders: Tools for constructing "The People" and legitimizing exclusion. *Journal of Borderline Studies*, 1–24. https://doi.org/10.1080/08865655.2022.2085140
Olivas Osuna, J. J., & Rama, J. (2022). Recalibrating populism measurement tools: Methodological inconsistencies and challenges to our understanding of the relationship between the supply-and demand-side of populism. *Frontiers in Sociology*, *7*. https://doi.org/10.3389/fsoc.2022.970043
Olivas Osuna, J. J., Martín-Fernández, M., Barrada, J. R., Moyano, M., & Clarí, E. (forthcoming). Varieties of populist attitudes in Brexit Britain: Socio-political and psychological correlates of a new multidimensional scale.
Pappas, T. S. (2019). *Populism and liberal democracy: A comparative and theoretical analysis*. Oxford: Oxford University Press.
Perry, B., Scrivens, R., Perry, B., & Scrivens, R. (2019). Epilogue: The Trump effect on right-wing extremism in Canada. In B. Perry & R. Scrivens (Eds.), *Right-wing extremism in Canada* (pp. 143–172). London: Palgrave.
Pirro, A. L. (2018). The polyvalent populism of the 5 Star Movement. *Journal of Contemporary European Studies, 26*(4), 443–458.
Rooduijn, M., & Pauwels, T. (2011). Measuring populism: Comparing two methods of content analysis. *West European Politics*, *34*(6), 1272–1283.
Rovira-Kaltwasser, C., Taggart, P. Ochoa-Espejo, P., & Ostiguy, P. (2017). Populism: The state of the art. In C. Rovira-Kaltwasser, P. Taggart, P. Ochoa-Espejo, & P. Ostiguy (Eds.), *The Oxford handbook of populism* (pp. 1–24). Oxford: Oxford University Press.

Ruzza, C. (2018). Populism, migration, and xenophobia in Europe. In C. De la Torre (Ed.), *Routledge handbook of global populism* (pp. 201–215). London: Routledge.

Schulz, A., Müller, P., Schemer, C., Wirz, D. S., Wettstein, M., & Wirth, W. (2018). Measuring populist attitudes on three dimensions. *International Journal of Public Opinion Research, 30*(2), 316–326.

Snow, D., Rochford, E. B., Worden, S., & Benford, R. (1986). Frame alignment processes, micromobilization, and movement participation. *American Sociological Review, 51*, 464–481.

Stern, P. (2000). Toward a coherent theory of environmentally significant behavior. *Journal of Social Issues, 56*, 407–424.

Van Hauwaert, S. M., Schimpf, C. H., & Azevedo, F. (2020). The measurement of populist attitudes: Testing cross-national scales using item response theory. *Politics, 40*(1), 3–21.

Wahl-Jorgensen, K. (2018). Media coverage of shifting emotional regimes: Donald Trump's angry populism. *Media, Culture and Society, 40*(5), 766–778.

Webber, D., & Kruglanski, A. W. (2017). Psychological factors in radicalization: A "3N" approach. In G. LaFree & J. Freilic (Eds.), *The handbook of the criminology of terrorism* (pp. 33–46). Hoboken, NJ: Wiley Blackwell.

Weyland, K. (2001). Clarifying a contested concept: Populism in the study of Latin American politics. *Comparative Politics, 34*(1), 1–22.

Wodak, R. (2021) *The politics of fear: The shameless normalization of far-right discourse* (2nd ed.). London: Sage.

Wolfowicz, M., Litmanovitz, Y., Weisburd, D., & Hasisi, B. (2021). Cognitive and behavioral radicalization: A systematic review of the putative risk and protective factors. *Campbell Systematic Reviews, 17*(3), e1174. https://doi.org/10.1002/cl2.1174

Young, C., Ziemer, K., & Jackson, C. (2019). Explaining Trump's popular support: Validation of a nativism index. *Social Science Quarterly, 100*(2), 412–418.

3 Against the Civil Society's Centre

Mimetic Crises by the German Populist Right

Polina Zavershinskaia

1. Introduction

Nowadays, populism can be considered a prominent attribute of contemporary civil societies. As one of the civil actors participating in the symbolic design of civil society, populist parties and social movements divide the discursive space of civil society to their allies (i.e., the 'people') and their opponents (i.e., 'corrupt elites') (Mudde, 2004), who allegedly abuse civil power and act in their private interest rather than in the interest of civil society. Scholarly research (e.g., Wodak, 1998/2015; Moffitt, 2016; Alexander, Kivisto, & Sciortino, 2021) evidenced that such Manichean narration is especially compelling when it is supported by the populist construction and/or amplification of crises aftermath of alleged fatal failures of those in power. Such populist discursive strategies can facilitate civil repair revealing the mistakes and abuses of public offices and other civil institutions by their holders, and be a corrective for democracy in their demand for expansion of civil solidarity, for instance, by voicing the demands of minorities (on which, see Kaltwasser, 2012; Mudde & Rovira Kaltwasser, 2017; Alexander, 2021).

Nevertheless, this is not the case for the populist Right. Compared to the populist Left, instead of opting for the expansion of civil solidarity in the form of multiculturalism, this type of populism targets the very centre of democratic civil society (on which, see Mudde, 2007, 2017; Wodak, 1998/2015; Alexander, 2021; Zavershinskaia, 2023a). For instance, it attacks liberal centrist and left-wing parties, office holders and civil institutions as corrupt and autocratic. Furthermore, it attempts to reduce civil solidarity discourses by constructing the exclusive floating concepts of the so-called 'native people' and 'native people's democracy' at the same time rejecting the Other's presence in civil society and representing the Other as allegedly not corresponding to primordial features of a given society (e.g., different in skin colour, gender, ethnicity ideological direction, etc.) and therefore polluting the 'people's' solidarity. Second, the populist

DOI: 10.4324/9781003457381-4

Right also antagonises civil institutions such as media, civil associations and public offices, claiming their 'selfish' intentions and, at times, allowing violence against their holders as an alleged 'civilising' measure and civil repair (Alexander, 2006; Zavershinskaia, 2023a). This inverts the civil agonism inherent in civil society to uncompromising antagonism (Mouffe, 2000, 2005; Alexander, 2021), leading to discrimination of chosen opponents. Consequently, the populist Right can be considered harmful to democratic civil societies since it targets the civil society centre and can facilitate the reduction of inclusive solidarity at the core of democratic civil society (Alexander, 2019, 2021; Zavershinskaia, 2023a).

This chapter illustrates the right-wing populist activity in German civil society through the example of the populist construction of mimetic crises connected to the most recent traumatic events sparking social and economic discontent in German civil society: The Covid-19 pandemic and the Russian invasion of Ukraine. Three prominent German right-wing populist actors (Zavershinskaia, 2023a, p. 3) were chosen for this analysis, namely, the right-wing populist party Alternative for Germany (*Alternative für Deutschland*, AfD; on which, see Havertz, 2021) and two protest movements which utilise right-wing populist discourse (on which, see Volk, 2020; Havertz, 2021; Zavershinskaia, 2023a): Patriotic Europeans Against the Islamisation of the West (*Patriotische Europäer gegen die Islamisierung des Abendlandes*, PEGIDA) and Identitarian Movement Germany (*Identitäre Bewegung [Deutschland]*, IBD). By examining the populist discourses of these actors regarding the two traumatic events mentioned above, this chapter investigates whether and how, while constructing mimetic crises, the populist Right antagonises the centre of civil society by targeting the Other and civil institutions (elites) such as public offices, media, civil associations, research institutes, etc.

The synthesis of the civil sphere theory (CST) and Mimetic Theory (Girard, 1972/2013, 1978/2016; regarding the synthesis, see Zavershinskaia, 2023a) was implemented in this chapter for analysing the right-wing populist activity in German civil society. The CST developed by Jeffrey C. Alexander (2006) and elaborated on by other cultural sociologists (e.g., Smith, 2005; Khosrokhavar, 2019; Ostertag, 2019; Binder, 2021; Luengo & Kolankowska, 2021; Mast, 2021) suggests a new conceptualisation of civil society as the civil sphere which allows analysing cultural aspects of civil society and the influence of symbolic representations (e.g., cultural codes, narratives, discourses) on preferences and choices of civil society's actors (e.g., Olick, 2016; Simko & Olick, 2021). It is complementary to the Mimetic Theory of Rene Girard (1972/1979), described below in this chapter. Mimetic Theory permeates analysing the symbolic construction of mimetic crises with an outcome of either civil repair or an outbreak of violence. Drawing on this theoretical framework, this study attempts to answer the following questions:

- Whether and how does the populist Right target the civil centre?
- What are the discursive features of the right-wing populist construction of mimetic crises regarding the Covid-19 pandemic and the Russian invasion of Ukraine? And, in particular, how close is the antagonisation of civil institutions by the German populist Right to those observed in Kremin's discourses?
- Does the populist Right stimulated violent actions in the German civil sphere?

This chapter is divided into two parts. The first part explains the synthesis of the CST and Mimetic Theory and details civil society's components relying on the CST and its conception of the civil sphere. Additionally, the phenomenon of the populist Right in civil society will be detailed from a theoretical perspective. On the example of right-wing populist construction of crises, the second part illustrates the right-wing populist destructive activity in German civil society during the Covid-19 pandemic and the Russian invasion of Ukraine. Briefly, it also describes the general reaction of German civil society to such traumatic events, which contrasts with their right-wing populist representations. Finally, the study's outcomes are summarised, followed by suggestions for future research.

2. Theoretical Framework: Synthesis of the CST and Mimetic Theory

Over the centuries, scholarship suggested different conceptualisations of civil society. The foundations of civil relations date back to the theories of, e.g., Ferguson (1767/1996) and de Tocqueville (1835/2002). Further, in contemporary social science, researchers defined civil society as the sphere of private interests (on which, see Alexander, 2006, 2014) and public actions (Habermas, 1962/2015). Similarly, the CST suggests the interpretation of civil society as a particular sphere of moral solidaristic existence of individuals and associations, different from the economic and political subsystems, which is also typical for Habermasian (1962/2015) and his supporters' (e.g., Cohen & Arato, 1992) 'society-centric' conceptualisation of civil society. However, despite these similarities, Alexander (2006) still contrasts his CST to previous civil society theories arguing that the disadvantage of the former is that they closely link the civil society's dynamics to market processes, which, in turn, were suggested to be determined by the State apparatus. According to Alexander, such conceptualisations left only a secondary role to culture and, therefore, minimised its importance for civil society's functioning. Furthermore, Alexander suggests that civil society should be symbolically delimited from noncivil expressions, not only in terms of institutional or organisational parameters of dependence and independence from the state. It also should be differentiated from nominally civil social and economic organisations and other public structures if they rely on principles of reciprocity and competitiveness different from the ideals of civil solidarity.

Relying on the CST, this chapter suggests considering culture as having agency (Alexander & Smith, 2003). This means that culture is not only manipulated by various social actors but can also influence their decisions determining their actions (Olick, 2016; Simko & Olick, 2021). By bringing culture to the forefront, cultural sociologists offer their reformed understanding of civil society as the civil sphere (e.g., Alexander, 2006; Alexander, Giesen, & Mast, 2006; Alexander, Stack, & Khosrokhavar, 2019; Alexander, Kivisto, & Sciortino, 2021; Smith, 2005). In their opinion, the core of the civil sphere is constituted by various discourses, which are institutionally enforced. Therefore, the CST emphasises the importance of studying the structures of feelings and experiences of civil society's members, which arise under the everyday influence of civil discourses as well as the specifics of civil solidarity's cultural coding and its sacralisation and desacralisation.

2.1 *Civil Sphere's Structures*

Drawing on the importance of cultural attributes in the formation of civil society, Alexander suggests defining it as the civil sphere:

> a world of values and institutions that generates the capacity for social criticism and democratic integration at the same time. Such a sphere relies on solidarity, on feelings for others whom we do not know but whom we respect out of principle, not experience, because of our putative commitment to a common secular faith.
>
> (Alexander, 2006, p. 4)

The discursive foundation of the civil sphere is construed by binary cultural codes that determine the central discourses of the civil sphere. These codes are constituted by the relation of 'us versus them' (Eisenstadt & Giesen, 1995), which is defined by the elementary binary bifurcations to 'good' and 'bad', 'sacred' and 'profane' and 'civil' and 'anticivil'. These binaries, however, are floating signifiers (Lévi-Strauss, 1987/2001): They receive a particular meaning depending on society's symbolic *milieu* and are ordered to narratives and discourses which illustrate the specific character of a particular society (see Smith, 2005; Koschorke, 2012; Zavershinskaia,

2023a). Such binaries of 'civil' and 'anticivil' are the 'skeletal structures' of the central discourses of the civil sphere (Alexander, 2006, p. 60), coined by Alexander as discourses of liberty and repression. Consequently, the discourse of liberty reinforces the symbolic solidarity between society's members, sacralising society's foundations and underpinning society's 'civil' characteristics by, e.g., creating heroic figures (Giesen, 2004) as an embodiment of the 'civil' in society. Usually, these are the stories about society's origin and territory, where its unique character was formed (see Smith, 1991; Wodak et al., 2009), and about its 'sacred' traditions, rules and duties that every 'civil' member should follow. In contrast to the discourse of liberty, the discourse of repression illustrates the 'anticivil' that attempts to destroy solidarity. In national communities, the discourse of repression often focuses on the antagonisation of the Other as dangerous for civil solidarity (e.g., Eisenstadt & Giesen, 1995; Alexander, 2006; Karolewski, 2012; Khosrokhavar, 2019). The Other is illustrated as a 'profane' perpetrator who does not comply with the characteristics of a given community (Giesen, 2004). For instance, the Other is not familiar with, or does not follow, society's rules, or (especially according to the nativist discourses) does not possess certain primordial qualities such as race or gender (see Heins & Unrau, 2019; Khosrokhavar, 2019; Ostertag, 2019).

Finally, the discourses of liberty and repression mentioned above are not self-sustaining in the civil sphere. They are constructed (e.g., the normative definition of what is 'civil' and 'anticivil' through, for instance, fiction literature), transmitted (e.g., discursive remediation in mass media) and regulated (e.g., punishment for 'anticivil' actions enforced by law) by civil institutions. Alexander (2006) defines two types of civil institutions: Communicative institutions (such as fiction, mass media, associations and public polls); and regulative institutions (such as voting, office, political parties and law). According to Alexander, apart from constructing and transmitting the representations of 'civil' and 'anticivil', civil institutions also execute civil power and society's self-governing by regulating how the incumbent complies with office duties, and revealing and punishing the 'polluted' by, e.g., publicly announcing power abuses in the form of scandals and taking disciplinary actions against deviants backed by laws.

Acknowledging the multifacetedness of the civil sphere's discourses and institutions that enforce them, this chapter, however, focuses only on one of the civil sphere's components, namely, the social construction of the Sacred and actions against the Other in the framework of the discourses of liberty and repression. Girard's (1972/2013, 1978/2016) Mimetic Theory is complementary to the CST in this regard and allows for further detailing the symbolic actions of various social actors and explaining the sacralisation of violence in the civil sphere.

In his Mimetic Theory, Girard suggested a connection between mimetic crisis, violence, the sacred and power in society. Constructing an imitative model of the Other is central to his theory (Zavershinskaia, 2023a). Girard (1978/2016, cited in Zavershinskaia, 2023a, p. 4) associated it with the cultural coding of violence in civil society, in particular, with its symbolic attribution and substitution through the symbolic construction of a scapegoat when the existence of a society is threatened by a mimetic crisis expressed in the antagonistic desacralising activity of social actors and state institutions. According to Girard's Mimetic Theory, society should choose and sacrifice a scapegoat to overcome a mimetic crisis and regain control over violence. However, a mimetic crisis can also intensify in case of idolatry resulting in an uncontrollable search for scapegoats. This narrows solidarity representations leading to the increased exclusion of some society's members, and undermines civil power, e.g., the status of civil institutions as gate-keepers of civil solidarity and democratic incorporation. As a rule, such negative mimesis culminates with an outbreak of uncontrollable violence in society (Girard, 1978/2016).

2.2 *The Populist Right in the Civil Sphere*

Even in the most democratic civil spheres around the globe with heterogeneous discourses and institutions facilitating the inclusive construction of civil solidarity, not every society's actor strives to maintain the civil centre's heterogeneity and the autonomy of its institutions. The phenomena of the populist Right and democratic backsliding stimulated by it are concerning trends in democratic civil societies (see Wodak, 1998/2015; Karolewski & Benedikter, 2017; Mudde, 2017; Alexander, 2021), since the right-wing populist activity potentially leads to the destruction of the symbolic structures of inclusive civil solidarity inherent in the discursive centre of the democratic civil sphere (Alexander, 2021; Zavershinskaia, 2023a). In this regard, Alexander argues that:

> Backlash populism can become determinately anticivil, moving not just to the right but far to the right, reducing civil standing to core group status, polluting those who until recently were outsiders, inciting street violence, and establishing authoritarian regimes that do not just modulate but undermine civil values and institutions.
>
> (Alexander, 2021, p. 9)

In right-wing populist discourses, democracy and the representation of the civil power are reduced to a populist notion of executing the 'will of the people'. To restore this illusion of 'people's democracy', the populist Right relies on an expanded discourse of repression, countering the centre of the civil sphere and inverting the accepted figurations of civil heroism into acts of alleged 'anticivil' perpetration through antagonising officials and public figures. Additionally, right-wing populists seek to reformat the meaning of established civil institutions as 'defenders' of civil solidarity (Alexander, 2006), framing these existing institutions as 'tools of authoritarian elites' (Zavershinskaia, 2023a, 2023b). Moreover, the populist Right is focused on a sharp construction of primordial ethnic, racial or religious barriers. This means that, in addition to the standard populist discourse bifurcation into 'civil people' and 'anticivil corrupt elites', which is also an attribute of centrist and leftist populisms (Mudde & Rovira Kaltwasser, 2017; Alexander, 2021), the populist Right includes exclusionary nativist elements that also radically narrow civil solidarity. Such populist backlash antagonism undermines civil associativity by reinforcing the often-violent exclusion of the defined Other from society's symbolic structure because of their perceived inconsistency with what is defined by the populist Right as society's physical and cultural attributes (Khosrokhavar, 2019; Ostertag, 2019).

In this regard, right-wing populist discursive techniques can be considered as triggers for the uncontrolled growth of disagreements between social actors and the desacralisation of more complex practices of civil agonism (Mouffe, 2000, 2005) in the civil sphere, replacing it with exclusionary antagonism (Alexander, 2021). This potentially leads to the amplification of mimetic crises and an outbreak of violence against antagonised actors (Zavershinskaia, 2023a), which is showcased further in this chapter by illustrating the German right-wing populist discourse expressed in the construction of mimetic crises connected to the recent traumatic events of Covid-19 pandemic and the Russian invasion of Ukraine.

3. Analysis: How the German Populist Right Constructs Mimetic Crises

Relying on the discursive analysis, this section reveals how the German populist Right constructs discourses of repression while sacralising its actions in the German civil sphere. Attempting to answer the questions stated in the introduction, this section also illustrates how its radical antagonisation of the civil sphere's centre leads to the amplification of mimetic crises and violent actions against the civil centre.

The textual data for this study was collected from the (1) Dataset for the empirical analysis of the right-wing populism in the German civil sphere (March 2020–January 2022) (Zavershinskaia, 2023a) and (2) Dataset 2: Russian state discourses disseminated by the AfD from 21st February 2022 until 27th February 2023 (Zavershinskaia, 2023b). Additionally to these two datasets, I also collected the content for this study from the

Telegram accounts of Pegida (@pegidaoriginal, @lutzbachmann) and IBD (@IdentitaereDeutschland).

After that, the obtained data was analysed by means of MAXQDA software for mixed methods. Specifically, in order to investigate the right-wing populist discursive antagonisation of the civil centre and instances of violence against it linked to the populist Right, the content was categorised according to the following parameters: exclusion of (a) regulative (e.g., office representatives [various elites]; oppositional political parties, laws) and (b) communicative (e.g., media, civil associations, research institutes, opinion polls) institutions (Table 3.1). After that, by looking into scientific and journalistic literature, I attempted to find the evidence of violent actions against antagonised institutions during the Covid-19 pandemic and the Russian invasion of Ukraine, which implicitly or explicitly were supported, provoked or executed by the chosen right-wing populist actors – the AfD, Pegida and the IBD.

Table 3.1 Matrix of civil institutions

Institution	*Example*	*Type of the institution*
Regulative	*Here specific examples of antagonised institution during the Covid-19 pandemic and Russian invasion of Ukraine will be provided*	Voting, office, political parties and law
Communicative		Fiction, mass media, associations and public polls

Note: This table relies on the Alexander's (2006) distinction of civil institutions to communicative and regulative ones and their characteristics.

3.1 The Covid-19 Pandemic

On 11th March 2020, the World Health Organisation (WHO, 2020) declared the outbreak of the Covid-19 pandemic. Shortly after, countries worldwide started to close their external and internal borders and introduce measures to combat the spread of the disease. Germany was among these countries. On 22nd March 2020, the *die Bundesregierung* (German federal government, 2020) imposed the first lockdown, followed by many months of contact restrictions and other measures to counter the Covid-19 spread. *Corona-Schutzmaßnahmen* (Corona protection measures, die Bundesregierung, 2022b) such as introducing obligatory masks in public places and other rules for public gatherings, including so-called 2G and 3G rules allowing to be in public only for vaccinated, tested or/and recovered persons, were completely lifted only on 7th April 2023 (die

Bundesregierung, 2023). Disobedience to *Corona-Schutzmaßnahmen* was penalised by serious fines and official disapproval.

All above indicated that the central discourses of German civil society underpinned that the heroic actions were expressed in citizens' responsibility to remain at home to prevent the further spread of the pandemic while *Querdenken Demo(s)* (lateral thinking demonstration[s]) – protests against governmental Covid-19 measures – were condemned as anticivil, and in cases when its participants broke the law disciplinary measures were applied to them.

These discourses of liberty and repression were also echoed in the communicative institutions of the German civil sphere. German mainstream media revealed scandalous violations of governmental measures. For instance, Zeit (2021) pointed out the violation of Covid-19 measures by *Querdenker*: 'opponents of the corona measures *demonstrated in the capital without permission*'. German civil organisations and research institutes supported the governmental approach to the Covid-19 pandemic. Robert Koch Institute (RKI, 2023) monitored the development of Covid-19 and suggested measures to counter its spread. Finally, polls (Infratest dimap, 2021; Statista, 2023) also showed that the majority living in Germany regarded Covid-19 measures as appropriate.

Contrary to this, the German populist Right condemned accepted Covid-19 measures as allegedly autocratic violations of people's freedoms (Buarque & Zavershinskaia, 2022; Volk & Weisskircher, 2023; Zavershinskaia, 2023a). Each of the three analysed actors – AfD, Pegida and IBD – antagonised both German regulative and communicative institutions mentioned above, and delegitimised their discourses, the core discourses of the German civil sphere (Table 3.2).

First, all of the analysed right-wing populist actors criticised German regional and federal officials, especially the *Bundesregierung*, for allegedly appropriating the office and, by implementing restrictive measures, supposedly turning Germany into a totalitarian State. For instance, metaphors which compared Germany to the DDR (Eastern German) regime or autocratic government from Orwell's and Huxley's dystopias were detected in right-wing populist statements regarding Covid-19 pandemic. In response to the governmental prohibition of *the Querdenken Demo* in Berlin in the summer of 2021, an AfD MP stated:

> The ugly images of water cannon deployments against women, children and the elderly must not be repeated. … why rallies by so-called *Querdenkern* are now banned. This is clearly measuring with double standards. … *as soon as tones critical of the government are to be expected*, *Interior Senator Geisel strikes again in the old SED (Socialist Unity Party of Germany in the DDR) tradition*. This behaviour *massively damages our*

liberal democracy to its very foundations and must therefore be clearly condemned.

(AfD Kompakt, 2021)

Table 3.2 Civil institutions antagonised by the German populist Right during the Covid-19 pandemic

Antagonised institution	*Example*	*Type of the institution*
Regulative	German federal and regional government and officials (e.g., Angela Merkel, Karl Lauterbach, Michael Kretschmer)	Office
	Research institutions (e.g., *RKI*)	Office
	Supranational organisations (e.g., *WHO*, EU)	Office
	Medical workers	Office
	Progressive parties (e.g., SPD, *die Grune, die Linke)*	Party
	Legislation (e.g., *Infektionsschutzgesetz)*	Law
Communicative	Mainstream media (e.g., ZDF, Zeit)	Media
	Social media (e.g., Facebook, Twitter)	Media
	Progressive associations (unspecified, *'linksradikale Vereine'* [left-wing radical associations])	Association

Note: This table draws on Table 1 and relies on the information from the 'Dataset for the empirical analysis of the right-wing populism in the German civil sphere (March 2020–January 2022)' (Zavershinskaia, 2023a).

Additionally, Covid-19 rules (e.g., vaccinations) were compared by, e.g., Pegida, as tools of the alleged totalitarian government to oppress and endanger German citizens. Referring to Orwell's *1984*, in its Telegram channel (@pegidaoriginal) Pegida reposted:

> The *professional liar Karl Lauterbach* (German federal minister of health) continues to *drum up the useless poison sludge*, which *causes a blatant side effect or death* rather than being of any use. As proof of the allegedly excellent effect of this pipe burst, *Lauterbach also cites a person who was vaccinated three times, who was then infected anyway.* This is *1984 at its finest*, George Orwell would be proud of it.
>
> (Unabhängige Nachrichten, 2022, cited by PEGIDA - das Original, 2022)

Second, German communicative institutions were proclaimed by the populist Right as 'fake news' and transmitters of state propaganda. For instance, with regard to Covid-19, IBD claimed that the mainstream media are '*Lügenpresse*' (fake news) which support the 'criminal' discourses of the German State:

> *They* (media) *happily play along with the ruling ideology* and will not miss any opportunity in the future *to secure their power* of interpretation *by means of agitation and lies against patriots*.
>
> (IBD, 2020a)

Besides antagonising German mainstream media, in his Telegram channel, Lutz Bachman (@lutzbachmann), Pegida's founder, also targeted the German research institute RKI, one of the critical actors in the development of Covid-19 measures, for supposedly fabricating information regarding the effectiveness of vaccines and its influence on decreasing of infection's numbers:

> They (ZDF, media channel) show the ineffectiveness of the measures and publish *the 'censorship' of the RKI*, which no longer publishes the number of infected people since the boosted ones are present in large numbers among them. In general, you show that the alleged effectiveness of the measures is not recognisable.
>
> (Lutz Rose, 2022, cited by LUTZiges Lutz Bachmann, 2022)

This way, under the auspices of civil repair for reinstating the 'people's democracy' shuttered by the alleged State appropriation of the German civil sphere, in fact, the German populist Right exacerbated the mimetic crisis in German civil society caused by Covid-19 pandemic and legitimised anticivil violence against the civil sphere's centre. For instance, several studies (e.g., Goertz, 2022; Hartleb, 2022; Heinke, 2022; Zavershinskaia, 2023a) evidenced that a murder plot against the Prime Minister of Sachsen, Michael Kretschmer, was supported by the German populist Right. Links to the populist Right were also found during protests against governmental Covid-19 measures (Heinze & Weisskircher, 2022; Volk & Weisskircher, 2023), including the *Querdenken Demo* in summer 2020 in Berlin, which culminated with a violent *Sturm auf den Reichstag* (Storming of the Reichstag) by Corona-sceptics and other right radical groups (Volk, 2021; Goertz, 2022).

3.2 The Russian Invasion of Ukraine

In the early morning of 24th February 2022, shortly after Russia's acknowledgement of the illegitimate Donetsk and Luhansk People's Republics (DNR and LNR, illegally formed in the Eastern Ukrainian regions under the partial occupation of pro-Russian separatists since early 2014) on 21st February 2022, Russian President Vladimir Putin declared the beginning of the so-called 'special military operation' to 'protect' Russian interest and 'denazify' Ukraine (Prezident Rossii, 2022). This day marked the beginning of the unprovoked Russian invasion of Ukraine, a violent culmination in the prolonged Russian warfare in Eastern Ukraine from early 2014 onward.

Already in 2014, after Russia's occupation of the Crimean Peninsula and the beginning of Russian hybrid intervention in Eastern Ukraine, Russia's relations with Western countries, including Germany, and attitudes toward the Russian political regime in European societies significantly worsened (Cross & Karolewski, 2021). Nevertheless, Russia's acknowledgement of illegitimate DNR and LNR, and especially its invasion of and aggression in Ukraine from 2022 onward can be considered a point of no return in Russia-Germany relations and the end of Russian-Western cooperation (Zavershinskaia, 2023b).

Germany was among the over 140 countries worldwide that condemned the Russian invasion of Ukraine. As a member state of the European Union (EU), Germany responded with severe economic and political sanctions to the Russian aggression in Ukraine. This also signified German *Zeitenwende* (watershed era) expressed, *inter alia*, in restructuring German military architecture and cardinally changing its energetic policies as responses to the Russian invasion, declared by German Chancellor Olaf Scholz in his address to the *Bundestag* on 27th February 2022 (die Bundesregierung, 2022a). Despite the encouraging performance and predictions for short-term and long-term effects of sanctions against Russia, these measures also impacted the German energy sector (Bunde, 2022). This and also society's shock caused by '*Krieg in der Mitte Europas*' (war in the middle of Europe) sparked some debates in German civil society regarding, e.g., the 'energy crisis' related to the end of the German–Russian gas deals (on which, see Harris, 2022; Liadze et al., 2023; Stent, 2022; Tjon-A-Meeuw, 2022), the need to increase the defence potential of German *Bundeswehr* (see Giegerich & Schreer, 2023) and the German involvement in the conflict and military aid for Ukraine (Zavershinskaia, 2023b, p. 145).

The German social *milieu* (according to the Eurobarometer; on which, see European Commission, 2023) and communicative institutions of the German civil sphere generally supported the EU's and German aid and governmental response to the Russian invasion of Ukraine. German mainstream media and civil associations condemned the invasion (Zavershinskaia, 2023b). Many social organisations (e.g., *Deutsches Rotes Kreuz*, *Ärzte ohne Grenzen*) and funds (Bundesverband Deutscher Stiftungen, n.d.) provided aid for Ukrainian refugees, persons in the warzone and Ukrainian military, as well as the information regarding the Russian invasion and Russian crimes in Ukraine (e.g., public events of *Demokratie*

Leben). Nevertheless, some social and political actors, including the populist Right, attempted to oppose the central discourses of the German civil sphere regarding the Russian invasion and antagonise the German government, political parties and civil organisations for their disciplinary actions toward Russia.

Despite using the term *Russischer Angriffskrieg* (Russian war of aggression) commonly accepted in the German civil sphere for describing the Russian invasion of Ukraine, still, the German right-wing populist discourses were relatively close to the Russian official discourses justifying the Russian invasion than to those of the liberal democratic actors (Zavershinskaia, 2023b). Table 3.3 illustrates the antagonised civil institutions by the German populist right during the Russian invasion of Ukraine. Strikingly, the antagonisation of these particular institutions was very similar to the Kremlin's official discourse and its demonisation of Western democratic structures (on which, see Brusylovska & Maksymenko, 2022; Tolz & Hutchings, 2023; Zavershinskaia, 2023a), which also goes in line with the argument about the right-wing reproduction of the Kremlin's propaganda in Germany.

Table 3.3 Civil institutions antagonised by the German populist Right during the Russian invasion of Ukraine

Antagonised institution	*Example*	*Type of the institution*
Regulative	German federal and regional government and officials (e.g., Olaf Scholz, Annalena Baerbock)	Office
	International political officials (e.g., Joe Biden, Ursula von der Leyen, Volodymyr Zelenskyy)	Office
	Research institutions (e.g., *ISW*)	Office
	Supranational organisations (e.g., EU, UN)	Office
	Federal parties (e.g., *die Grune*, FDP, SPD)	Party
	Legislation (e.g., *Sanktionspakete)*	Law
Communicative	Mainstream media (e.g., ZDF, Zeit)	Media
	Social media (e.g., Facebook, Twitter)	Media
	Civil associations and foundations (e.g., Amadeu Antonio Foundation; Bertelsmann Foundation)	Association

Note: This table draws on Table 1 and relies on the information from the 'Dataset 2: Russian state discourses disseminated by the AfD from 21st February 2022 until 27th February 2023' (Zavershinskaia, 2023b).

First, German and EU's political officials such as Chancellor Scholz, German foreign affairs minister Annalena Baerbock, the president of the European Commission Ursula von der Leyen and political parties associated with them, especially the SPD and the Greens, were described by such metaphors as '*Öko-Diktatur*' (Eco-Dictatorship; *Freie Sachsen*, 2023, cited in LUTZiges Lutz Bachmann, 2023a) and made responsible for allegedly exacerbating the conflict with Russia and creating the difficult economic situation in Germany. For instance, the AfD claimed that, instead of opting for diplomatic solutions, with its sanctions and weapon deliveries, the German government and political parties provoked military escalation, which could potentially lead to the Third World War. In this, the AfD also reproduced nuclear blackmail often detected in Russian official discourse (Zavershinskaia, 2023b, p. 142).

A more extreme case was an action of the right-wing group *Aktion Solidarität* (Action Solidarity) in cooperation with the IBD. The protesters, among which was the Austrian IB leader, Martin Sellner, attempted to turn on with their own hands the Russian gas pipeline Nord Stream 2 before they were stopped by the police (Merz, 2022). Afterwards, in its Telegram, the IBD reposted such statements of the *Aktion Solidarität* as:

> We double down (*geben Gas*) to put pressure on the government. For Germany's interests, we go to our limits. That was just the beginning. *We won't rest until the government hands out our gas and turns on our terminal! Turn on Nord Stream 2!*
>
> (Aktion Solidarität, 2022, reposted by IBD, 2022b)

Another discourse which antagonised German regulative institutions implied the alleged geopolitical conflict between the US and Russia caused by the US eastward expansion of NATO. In this regard, the IBD (2022a) claimed that the German government acted against its political interests and that German people should not be made '*weder US-Marionette noch Kreml Sprachrohr*' (neither US puppet nor Kremlin megaphone). Interestingly, such storytelling was also close to the metaphors of the EU's 'serfdom' and 'NATO's expansion' disseminated by Russian propaganda (Zavershinskaia, 2023b).

Another common antagonisation was directed against social networks allegedly reproducing the US 'propaganda'. For instance, referring once again to the Orwellian 1984, in its Telegram channel Pegida reposted that:

> the *US government allegedly gave a free company 'Twitter' special instructions on what should be considered 'anti-Ukrainian content'* … *Orwell had no idea how it would end: At the request of the US intelligence services, the moderators deleted everything from the social networks* that went beyond the paradigm of Washington ideas.
>
> (Node of Time DE, 2023, reposted by PEGIDA - das Original, 2023)

Interestingly, in this and many other Pegida's Telegram messages, the words of Maria Zakharova, the information and press department director of the Russian Ministry of Foreign Affairs, were used as an information source, providing another link between Russian propaganda and the German populist Right.

Additionally, reports from German mass media and the sources they refer to, such as the US nonprofit Institute for the Study of War (ISW), were proclaimed as 'the one-sided and distorted reporting on the Ukraine conflict' (Identitäre Bewegung Niedersachsen 2020, reposted by IBD, 2020b). Speculating about the explosion of the Russian gas pipeline Nord Stream 2 in September 2022, in response to the article published in German media outlet *Frankfurter Rundschau* (Durach, 2023), Bachman claimed that:

> *The same 'experts' who declared Corona dangerous*, who declared 'vaccination' harmless, classified FFP2 masks against viruses as effective, considered lockdowns sensible and *wanted to blame Putin for the US terrorist action against Nord Stream* ...
>
> (LUTZiges Lutz Bachmann, 2023b)

Here, one can also observe the amplification of mimetic crises referred to both: Covid-19 pandemic and the Russian invasion of Ukraine. Interestingly, this message also reproduced the Russian propaganda, disseminating the misinformation according to which the US allegedly exploded the pipeline (found in, e.g., RIA Novosti, 2023).

Overall, in terms of the Russian invasion of Ukraine, similarly to the previously described case of the Covid-19 pandemic, it was possible to observe the right-wing populist construction of society's discontent and amplification of the mimetic crisis connected to the consequences of the Russian invasion, which led to some instances of violence in the German civil sphere. First, the so-called *Friedensdemo* (peace demonstration), initiated by activist Alice Schwarzer and German left-wing politician Sahra Wagenknecht against weapon delivery to Ukraine and applauded by the AfD (Zavershinskaia, 2023b), was an attempt to delegitimise the German support to Ukraine's legal self-defence against Russian violence.

Another instance was the right-wing exploitation of the Russian invasion of Ukraine to strengthen the discrimination of racialised Others leading to potential violence against them (Amadeu Antonio Stiftung, n.d.). This, for instance, was expressed in the AfD's discourse regarding the alleged 'illegal immigrants' who supposedly took advantage of the war in Ukraine to penetrate the EU hiding behind the 'actual refugees' – white Ukrainian nationals (AfD Kompakt, 2022).

Finally, the failed plot to overthrow the German government by the anti-state extremist organisation *Reichsbürger* (Reich Citizens) in

December 2022, among which was AfD's former Bundestag member, Birgit Malsack-Winkemann (Whittle, 2022), which suggests a link between *Reichsbürger* and the German populist Right (Hartleb, Schliefsteiner, & Schiebel, 2023), was also indicative in this regard. Scholarly literature (e.g., Kiess, Zichert, & Wetzel, 2022) argued that pro-Russian narratives influenced the *Reichsbürger* discourses. Their planned violent action against the German political officials as well as the denial of the current German government could be considered as a provocation of a mimetic crisis through their attempts to 'breach the civil order' (on the extremism in the civil sphere, see Alexander, Stack, & Khosrokhavar, 2019) in the German civil sphere.

4. Conclusion

This study suggested that the populist Right being part of the civil sphere stimulated the narrowing of civil solidarity and was essentially directed against the democratic civil centre, delegitimising its core discourses and institutions. This chapter also argued that such right-wing populist discursive activity aggravated mimetic crises and, thereby, provoked anticivil violence against its civil centre. The analysis of the German populist Right and its discourses regarding the Covid-19 pandemic and the Russian invasion of Ukraine supported these arguments.

First, the example of the populist construction of the Covid-19 crisis evidenced that each of the analysed populist actors, namely the AfD, Pegida and IBD, antagonised German regulative and communicative institutions claiming that their 'restrictive measures' against Covid-19 were acts of autocratic appropriation of 'people's democracy'. Drawing on the example of *Querdenken Demo(s)*, which were also attended by the populist Right, violence against German civil institutions and civil actors was illustrated in this study.

Second, contrary to the German civil discourses, which condemned the Russian invasion of Ukraine, discourses of the populist Right antagonised actions of German civil actors and institutions at least as short-sided, for instance claiming that German sanctions against Russia led to military escalation in Ukraine, and at most as manipulated by US interest against the 'German people's interests'. By this, the German populist Right also reproduced some Russian propaganda metaphors, for instance, by claiming that the German government was a 'marionette' of the US. This also coincided with several attempts of violence against the German civil centre as well as discrimination of racialised Others who were blamed for using the 'conflict' to enter the EU as refugees.

The right-wing populist activity in the civil sphere is an alarming trend for contemporary liberal democracy (Zavershinskaia, 2023a, p. 1). It does not only introduce discriminatory discourses that oppose the construction of inclusive civil solidarity but also may stimulate a mimetic crisis leading to violence against the civil centre and naturalisation of external discriminatory discourses, for instance, the Russian propaganda mentioned above. Cross-country studies regarding the connection between right-wing populist discourses and violence in civil society may contribute to further understanding of the populist Right breaching the civil order. Specifically, how does the populist Right contribute to the normalisation of backlash discourses in European mass media and impact EU policies? How does the European populist Right attempt to shape the public opinion about Russia; and how its dissemination of Russian propaganda contributes to the democratic backsliding? Finally, how to prevent scenarios for emerging a sort of imitative 'uncivil societies' (Umland, 2002; see also Shekhovtsov & Umland, 2009) within the EU states when a backlash actor got an access to the state power?

References

AfD Kompakt. (2021). Berlin: Erneute Demonstrationsverbote sind nicht nachvollziehbar. Retrieved from https://afdkompakt.de/2021/07/29/berlin-erneute-demonstrationsverbote-sind-nicht-nachvollziehbar/

AfD Kompakt. (2022). Illegale Merkel-Migranten abschieben - Platz für echte Flüchtlinge schaffen! Retrieved from https://afdkompakt.de/2022/03/22/illegale-merkel-migranten-abschieben-platz-fuer-echte-fluechtlinge-schaffen/

Alexander, J. C. (2006). *The civil sphere*. New York: Oxford University Press.

Alexander, J. C. (2014). *The antinomies of classical thought: Marx and Durkheim*. London: Routledge.

Alexander, J. C. (2019). Frontlash/backlash: The crisis of solidarity and the threat to civil institutions. *Contemporary Sociology: A Journal of Reviews*, *48*(1), 5–11.

Alexander, J. C. (2021). Introduction: The populist continuum from within the civil sphere to outside it. In J. C. Alexander, P. Kivisto, & G. Sciortino (Eds.), *Populism in the civil sphere* (pp. 1–16). Cambridge: Polity.

Alexander, J. C., Giesen, B., & Mast, J. L. (Eds.). (2006). *Social performance: Symbolic action, cultural pragmatics, and ritual*. Cambridge: Cambridge University Press.

Alexander, J. C., Kivisto, P., & Sciortino, G. (Eds.). (2021). *Populism in the civil sphere*. Cambridge: Polity Press.

Alexander, J. C., & Smith, P. (2003). The strong program in cultural sociology: Elements of a structural hermeneutics. In *The meanings of social life: A cultural sociology* (1st ed., pp. 11–26). Oxford: Oxford University Press.

Alexander, J. C., Stack, T., & Khosrokhavar, F. (Eds.). (2019). *Breaching the civil order: Radicalism and the civil sphere* (1st ed.). Cambridge: Cambridge University Press.

Amadeu Antonio Stiftung. (n.d.). Analyse: Rechtsextreme und Verschwörungsideologen nutzen den Krieg in der Ukraine für sich. Retrieved from https://www.amadeu-antonio-stiftung.de/analyse-wie-rechtsextreme-und-verschwoerungsideologen-den-krieg-in-der-ukraine-fuer-sich-nutzen/

Binder, W. (2021). Memory culture, the civil sphere, and right-wing populism in Germany: The resistible rise of the Alternative für Deutschland (AfD). In J. C. Alexander, P. Kivisto, & G. Sciortino (Eds.), *Populism in the civil sphere* (pp. 178–204). Cambridge: Polity.

Brusylovska, O., & Maksymenko, I. (2022). Analysis of the media discourse on the 2022 war in Ukraine: The case of Russia. *Regional Science Policy & Practice*, rsp3.12579. https://doi.org/10.1111/rsp3.12579

Buarque, B., & Zavershinskaia, P. (2022). The far-right politics of 'truth': An exploratory analysis of the 'truths' produced by AfDKompakt and Patriotic Alternative. In V. A. Bruno (Ed.), *Populism and far-right trends in Europe* (Vol. 4, pp. 25–48). Milan: EDUCatt.

Bunde, T. (2022). Lessons (to be) learned? Germany's Zeitenwende and European security after the Russian invasion of Ukraine. *Contemporary Security Policy*, *43*(3), 516–530.

Bundesverband Deutscher Stiftungen. (n.d.). Stiftungen für die Ukraine. Retrieved from https://www.stiftungen.org/aktuelles/stiftungen-fuer-die-ukraine.html

Cohen, J. L., & Arato, A. (1992). *Civil society and political theory*. Cambridge: The MIT Press.

Cross, M. K. D., & Karolewski, I. P. (2021). Introduction: Power dynamics in EU-Russian relations. In Ireneusz Paweł Karolewski & M. K. D. Cross (Eds.), *European-Russian power relations in turbulent times* (pp. 1–28). Ann Arbor: The University of Michigan Press.

de Tocqueville, A. (2002). *Democracy in America*. Chicago, IL: Univercity of Chicago Press.

die Bundesregierung. (2020). 22. März 2020: Regeln zum Corona-Virus. Retrieved from https://web.archive.org/web/20200915100517/https://www.bundesregierung.de/breg-de/leichte-sprache/22-maerz-2020-regeln-zum-corona-virus-1733310

die Bundesregierung. (2022a). Regierungserklärung von Bundeskanzler Olaf Scholz am 27. Februar 2022. Retrieved from https://www.bundesregierung.de/breg-de/suche/regierungserklaerung-von-bundeskanzler-olaf-scholz-am-27-februar-2022-2008356

die Bundesregierung. (2022b). Corona-Regelungen: Basis-Schutz und Hotspot-Maßnahmen. Retrieved from https://www.bundesregierung.de/breg-de/themen/coronavirus/corona-regeln-und-einschrankungen-1734724

die Bundesregierung. (2023). Corona-Schutzmaßnahmen sind ausgelaufen. Retrieved from https://www.bundesregierung.de/breg-de/themen/coronavirus/ende-corona-massnahmen-2068856

Durach, F. (2023). Nach mutmaßlichem Drohnen-Angriff auf Kreml: Experten gehen von Inszenierung Russlands aus. *Frankfurter Rundschau*. Retrieved from https://web.archive.org/web/20230609115151/https://www.fr.de/politik/news-ukraine-krieg-putin-attentat-moskau-kreml-drohne-reaktion-forderung-experten-russland-92253601.html

Eisenstadt, S. N., & Giesen, B. (1995). The construction of collective identity. *European Journal of Sociology*, *36*(1), 72–102.

European Commission. (2023). Eurobarometer-Umfrage: Deutsche unterstützen den Ukraine-Kurs der EU. Retrieved from https://germany.representation.ec.europa.eu/news/eurobarometer-umfrage-deutsche-unterstutzen-den-ukraine-kurs-der-eu-2023-02-23_de

Ferguson, A. (1996). *An essay on the history of civil society*. Cambridge: Cambridge University Press.

Giegerich, B., & Schreer, B. (2023). Zeitenwende: One year on. *Survival*, *65*(2), 37–42.

Giesen, B. (2004). *Triumph and trauma*. Boulder: Paradigm Publishers.

Girard, R. (1972/2013). *Violence and the sacred*. Baltimore: Hopkins University Press.

Girard, R. (1978/2016). *Things hidden since the foundation of the world*. London: Bloomsbury Academic.

Goertz, S. (2022). *"Querdenker": Ein Überblick*. Wiesbaden: Springer VS.

Habermas, J. (1962/2015). *The structural transformation of the public sphere: An inquiry into a category of bourgeois society*. Hoboken: Wiley.

Harris, J. (2022). The conflict between national and transnational power: The Russian trap. *Race & Class*, *64*(2), 3–19.

Hartleb, F. (2022). The right-wing populist disruption in the Berlin republic. Opportunity structures and success of the Alternative for Germany (AfD). In M. Oswald & J. Robertson (Eds.), *The legacy and impact of German unification* (pp. 231–247). Cham: Springer International Publishing.

Hartleb, F., Schliefsteiner, P., & Schiebel, C. (2023). From anti-measure activism to anti-state extremism? *Perspectives on Terrorism*, *17*(1), 123–143. JSTOR. Retrieved from JSTOR.

Havertz, R. (2021). *Radical right populism in Germany: AfD, Pegida, and the Identitarian Movement*. New York: Routledge.

Heinke, D. H. (2022). The security threat posed by the Corona-skeptic Querdenken movement in Germany. *CTC SENTINEL*, *15*(3), 18–24.

Heins, V. M., & Unrau, C. (2019). Anti-immigrant movements and the self-poisoning of the civil sphere: The case of Germany. In J. C. Alexander, T. Stack, & F. Khosrokhavar (Eds.), *Breaching the civil order: Radicalism and the civil sphere* (pp. 145–169). Cambridge: Cambridge University Press.

Heinze, A.-S., & Weisskircher, M. (2022). How political parties respond to pariah street protest: The case of anti-Corona mobilisation in Germany. *German Politics*, 1–22. https://doi.org/10.1080/09644008.2022.2042518

IBD. (2020a). Lügenpresse und Corona Demonstration - Statement. Retrieved from https://web.archive.org/web/20230501075123/https://www.identitaere-bewegung.de/blog/luegenpresse-und-corona-demonstration-statement/

IBD. (2020b). DEN MAINZELS REICHTS. Retrieved from https://t.me/IdentitaereDeutschland/1018

IBD. (2022a). Differenzierte Analyse zum Ukraine Konflikt. Retrieved from https://t.me/IdentitaereDeutschland/1440

IBD. (2022b). Massiver Polizeieinsatz bei Nordstream 2. Retrieved from https://t.me/IdentitaereDeutschland/1491

Infratest dimap. (2021). Corona-COMPASS. Retrieved from https://www.infratest-dimap.de/umfragen-analysen/bundesweit/coronacompass/coronacompass/

Kaltwasser, C. R. (2012). The ambivalence of populism: Threat and corrective for democracy. *Democratization*, *19*(2), 184–208.

Karolewski, I. P. (2012). Caesarean citizenship and Its anti-civic potential in the European Union. In I. P. Karolewski & V. Kaina (Eds.), *Civic resources and the future of the European Union* (pp. 196–219). London: Routledge.

Karolewski, I. P., & Benedikter, R. (2017). Europe's refugee and migrant crisis: Economic and political ambivalences. *Challenge*, *60*(3), 294–320.

Khosrokhavar, F. (2019). The civil sphere and its variants in light of the Arab revolutions and jihadism in Europe. In J. C. Alexander, T. Stack, & F. Khosrokhavar (Eds.), *Breaching the civil order: Radicalism and the civil sphere* (pp. 145–169). Cambridge: Cambridge University Press.

Kiess, J., Zichert, M., & Wetzel, G. (2022). Frieden mit Russland?! Friedensvorstellungen in der extrem rechten Telegram-Szene Sachsens. *Forschungsjournal Soziale Bewegungen*, *35*(4), 677–691.

Koschorke, A. (2012). *Wahrheit und Erfindung: Grundzüge einer allgemeinen Erzähltheorie*. Frankfurt am Main: S. Fischer.

Lévi-Strauss, C. (2001). *Introduction to the work of Marcel Mauss*. London: Routledge.

Liadze, I., Macchiarelli, C., Mortimer-Lee, P., & Sanchez Juanino, P. (2023). Economic costs of the Russia-Ukraine. *The World Economy*, *46*(4), 874–886.

Luengo, M., & Kolankowska, M. (2021). Far-right populism in Poland and the construction of a pseudocivil sphere. In J. C. Alexander, P. Kivisto, & G. Sciortino (Eds.), *Populism in the civil sphere* (pp. 96–124). Cambridge: Polity.

LUTZiges Lutz Bachmann. (2022). ZDF legt den Finger in die Wirksamkeitswunde Karl Lauterbach. Retrieved from https://t.me/lutzbachmann/18049

LUTZiges Lutz Bachmann. (2023a). Montagsproteste: Auf die Straße, Sachsen ist im Widerstand! Retrieved from https://t.me/lutzbachmann/24851

LUTZiges Lutz Bachmann. (2023b). Die selben "Experten", die Corona für gefährlich erklärten. Retrieved from https://t.me/lutzbachmann/25071

Mast, J. L. (2021). A Civil Sphere Theory of populism: American forms and templates, from the Red Scare to Donald Trump. In J. C. Alexander, P. Kivisto, & G. Sciortino (Eds.), *Populism in the civil sphere* (pp. 1–16). Cambridge: Polity.

Merz, K. (2022). Identitäre: Martin Sellner besetzt mit Aktivisten Terminal von Nord Stream 2. *Berliner Zeitung*. Retrieved from https://www.berliner-zeitung.de/news/identitaere-martin-sellner-besetzt-mit-aktivisten-nord-stream-2-terminal-li.261485

Moffitt, B. (2016). *The global rise of populism: Performance, political style, and representation*. Stanford: Stanford University Press.

Mouffe, C. (2000). *The democratic paradox*. London: Verso.

Mouffe, C. (2005). The "end of politics" and the challenge of right-wing populism. In F. Panizza (Ed.), *Populism and the mirror of democracy* (pp. 50–71). London: Verso.

Mudde, C. (2004). The populist zeitgeist. *Government and Opposition*, *39*(4), 541–563.

Mudde, C. (2007). *Populist radical right parties in Europe*. Cambridge: Cambridge University Press.

Mudde, C. (Ed.). (2017). *The populist radical right: A reader*. London: Routledge.

Mudde, C., & Rovira Kaltwasser, C. (2017). *Populism: A very short introduction*. New York: Oxford University Press.

Olick, J. K. (2016). *The sins of the fathers: Germany, memory, method*. Chicago, IL: The University of Chicago Press.

Ostertag, S. F. (2019). Antiracism movements and the US civil sphere: The case of Black Lives Matter. In J. C. Alexander, T. Stack, & F. Khosrokhavar (Eds.), *Breaching the civil order: Radicalism and the civil sphere* (pp. 145–169). Cambridge: Cambridge University Press.

PEGIDA – das Original. (2022). Der Berufslügner Karl Lauterbach rührt weiter die Werbetrommel für die nutzlose Giftplörre. Retrieved May 19, 2023, from https://t.me/pegidaoriginal/15083

PEGIDA – das Original. (2023). Der ehemalige Moskau-Korrespondent von The Moscow Times. Retrieved May 21, 2023, from https://t.me/pegidaoriginal/19683

Prezident Rossii. (2022). Obrashchenie Prezidenta Rossijskoj Federacii. Retrieved February 6, 2023, from http://www.kremlin.ru/events/president/news/67843

RIA Novosti. (2023). Hersh rasskazal, zachem SSHA vzorvali "Severnye potoki". Retrieved from https://ria.ru/20230215/khersh-1852273678.html

RKI. (2023). Empfehlungen des RKI zu Hygienemaßnahmen im Rahmen der Behandlung und Pflege von Patienten mit einer Infektion durch SARS-CoV-2. Retrieved May 19, 2023, from https://web.archive.org/web/20221210095148/https://www.rki.de/DE/Content/InfAZ/N/Neuartiges_Coronavirus/Hygiene.html

Shekhovtsov, A., & Umland, A. (2009). Is Aleksandr Dugin a traditionalist? "Neo-Eurasianism" and perennial philosophy. *The Russian Review*, *68*(4), 662–678. JSTOR. Retrieved from JSTOR.

Simko, C., & Olick, J. K. (2021). What we talk about when we talk about culture: A multi-facet approach. *American Journal of Cultural Sociology*, *9*(4), 431–459. https://doi.org/10.1057/s41290-019-00094-7

Smith, A. D. (1991). *National identity*. London: Penguin Books.

Smith, P. (2005). *Why war? The cultural logic of Iraq, the Gulf War, and Suez*. Chicago, IL: University of Chicago Press.

Statista. (2023). Sind aus Ihrer Sicht die geltenden Corona-Maßnahmen in Deutschland alles in allem angemessen, gehen sie zu weit oder gehen sie nicht weit genug? Retrieved from https://de.statista.com/statistik/daten/studie/1147567/umfrage/umfrage-zu-corona-massnahmen-und-deren-kontrollen/

Stent, A. (2022). Germany and Russia: Farewell to Ostpolitik? *Survival*, *64*(5), 27–38.

Tjon-A-Meeuw, R. L. (2022). The new Ostpolitik: Nord Stream 2 and the politics of German-Russian gas relations. In N. Cohen & A. Dootalieva (Eds.), *European integration and disintegration: Essays from the next generation of Europe's thinkers* (pp. 157–187). London: Routledge.

Tolz, V., & Hutchings, S. (2023). Truth with a Z: Disinformation, war in Ukraine, and Russia's contradictory discourse of imperial identity. *Post-Soviet Affairs*, 1–19.

Umland, A. (2002). Toward an Uncivil Society? Contextualizing the Recent Decline of Extremely Right-Wing Parties in Russia. *SSRN Electronic Journal*. https://doi.org/10.2139/ssrn.2890627

Volk, S. (2020). 'Wir sind das Volk!': Representative claim-making and populist style in the PEGIDA movement's discourse. *German Politics*, *29*(4), 599–616.
Volk, S. (2021). Die rechtspopulistische PEGIDA in der COVID-19-Pandemie: Virtueller Protest "für unsere Bürgerrechte". *Forschungsjournal Soziale Bewegungen*, *34*(2), 235–248.
Volk, S., & Weisskircher, M. (2023). The importance of subnational politics for far-right strength: The east-west divide in Germany. In K. Kondor & M. Littler (Eds.), The Routledge handbook of far-right extremism in Europe (First Edition). Routledge.
Whittle, H. (2022). Germany's far-right AfD and the "Reichsbürger" movement. *Deutsche Welle*. Retrieved from https://www.dw.com/en/germanys-far-right-afd-and-the-reichsbürger-movement/a-64079836
WHO. (2020). WHO Director-General's opening remarks at the media briefing on COVID-19—11 March 2020. Retrieved from https://www.who.int/director-general/speeches/detail/who-director-general-s-opening-remarks-at-the-media-briefing-on-covid-19—11-march-2020
Wodak, R. (1998/2015). *The politics of fear: What right-wing populist discourses mean*. London: Sage.
Wodak, R., De Cillia, R., Reisigl, M., & Liebhart, K. (2009). *The discursive construction of national identity* (2nd ed.). Edinburgh: Edinburgh University Press.
Zavershinskaia, P. (2023a). Appropriating the civil sphere: The construction of German collective identity by right-wing populist actors during the Covid-19 pandemic. *American Journal of Cultural Sociology*. https://link.springer.com/article/10.1057/s41290-023-00189-2
Zavershinskaia, P. (2023b). "Why do we need a world without Russia in it?" Discursive justifications of the Russian invasion of Ukraine in Russia and Germany. *Nationalism and Ethnic Politics*, *29*(2), 129-153.
Zeit Online. (2021). Platzverweise und Festnahmen bei "Querdenker"-Demos in Berlin. *Zeit Online*. Retrieved from https://www.zeit.de/gesellschaft/2021-08/corona-proteste-demonstrationen-berlin-versammlung-verbot?utm_referrer=https%3A%2F%2Fwww.google.com%2F

4 “Nothing but a Strategy of Satan and the Media”

How Religious Fundamentalism and Populist Leaders Took Over the Scientific Narration of the Pandemic

Michele Martini

1. Introduction

The present chapter argues that contemporary fundamentalism is both a result and an actor of the process of globalization; to highlight how this idea might cause friction with some forms of Western self-perception, I would like to begin by recounting an anecdote that happened a couple of years ago. At that time, I was attending a seminar whose focus was the relationship between religious fundamentalism and democratic states. The main speaker was rather fond of Western democracies and framed radical religious organizations as a threat to human progress, eventually depicting the two as independent and irreconcilable enemies locked into a battle for the future of humanity. Having recently spent a few days working on *Dabiq*, one of the several magazines published by ISIS, I took the freedom to point out a simple fact: the critiques pushed by fundamentalist groups to Western democracies and the process of globalization are not necessarily meaningless. On the contrary, far from being a mere expression of isolation, ignorance or religious fanaticism, these critiques demonstrated a rather clear knowledge of Western democracies and their many flaws. In other words, I concluded, that radical Islamic groups seem to propose religious fundamentalism as an alternative to what they see as a failure of the neoliberal democratic state; a state that promised prosperity, freedom, and equal opportunities for all.

Needless to say, my comment did not go down well. However, taking this episode as a starting point, the present chapter is an attempt to counter the idea that fundamentalism is a static, independent and, possibly, “primitive” set of beliefs; in other words, that fundamentalism is a way of thinking that does not belong to our times, a monster survived in some lost pockets of socio-political backwardness or the result of irreconcilable

DOI: 10.4324/9781003457381-5

cultural differences. On the contrary, this chapter will try to show how the re-emergence and popularization of fundamentalist epistemologies are deeply intertwined with the process of globalization and, along with populism, represent a reaction to it. To this aim, this chapter will investigate the newsfeed of one of the most successful and controversial evangelical groups in Brazil: The Universal Church of the Kingdom of God (hereafter, Universal Church). This religious organization is characterized by strong leader-centrism and a particular emphasis on spiritual warfare, i.e., the belief to be permanently "locked in an epic end-times battle with the demonic" (Marshall, 2016, p. 93). Accused of manipulating believers (McClenaghan, 2022) and other illegal activities (Phillips, 2009), this organization has played a key role in supporting the government of former president Bolsonaro during the pandemic crisis.

To investigate how fundamentalist religious groups have become a key ally for populist leaders on a global scale, this chapter will be composed of a theoretical and an empirical section. From a theoretical perspective, the first section of the chapter will discuss how neoliberal globalization has created the space for fundamentalist epistemologies to rise on a global level. In this section, an initial observation on the "becoming-fragile" of the rule of law will be followed by a discussion on the relationship between populism and technocracy, and a final theoretical reflection on the relationship between populism and fundamentalism. Relying on this framework, the second section will present the case study, the methodologies employed, and the empirical findings, thus enabling a data-driven analysis of the role of fundamentalist epistemologies in the global era.

2. The Hyper-Fragility of Democracy: New Spaces for Fundamentalist Epistemologies in the Global Era

"Nothing but a strategy of Satan and the media", answered Edir Macedo, leader of the Universal Church of the Kingdom of God, when asked his opinion about the COVID-19 outbreak (Bergamo, 2020). Surely, a rather peculiar framing of the pandemic, and yet a widely credited one among believers. Nothing less than the embodiment of all evils starring alongside the media system, a global conspiracy led by an unholy alliance between the powers of hell and the powers of digital communication: old enemies, new tools.

To understand how fundamentalist epistemologies have regained space in that beacon of human progress that Western democracy prides itself to be, it is important first of all to step away from such ideological spotlight. In other words, we must avoid the temptation of reading the rise of religious extremism as an incident, a mere accident in our path towards progress. On the contrary, I argue, the revamp of fundamentalist discourse needs to be understood as part of a larger systemic change; as a component, in fact, of the neoliberal globalization project.

Have the Western democracies become more fragile over the last two decades? So it seems. And yet, "fragility" is a paradoxical property. Fragility defines the condition of something which is both very hard yet at the same time easy to break. Like glass, fragile objects either remain unchanged, trapped in the timeless prison of their original shape, or shatter abruptly into a myriad of glittering splinters. Fragility is an overdramatic, defiantly intransigent, and radically binary property; it is also potentially dangerous and usually unwanted. In this chapter, I will not only claim that Western democracies have become more fragile, but also that this fragility is connected to a crisis of legitimacy of the state which, ultimately, allowed fundamentalist discourse and parties to enter the political arena. The almost simultaneous appearance of successful populist movements in very different socio-political environments, such as the USA, Venezuela, Ecuador, Austria, Greece, Hungary, Italy, Spain, or India, signals that this phenomenon does not depend primarily on local legal or political systems. What we are facing is a systemic crisis which affects simultaneously, yet unevenly, most countries around the world. In other terms, the tendency towards what we might call a "hyper-fragility" of democratic systems is a specific trait of processes of globalization. Neither a by-product nor a mistake: the power asymmetry between global and local epistemologies is a structural component of the neoliberal globalization project (Slobodian, 2018).

Fragility is a paradoxical property, and today democratic systems are perceived, at the same time, as both more rigid and more precarious. But what does this mean? A long and well-established scholarly tradition highlights how single criminal acts, either of economic or ideological nature, do not undermine democratic systems (Foucault, 1975; Giddens, 1985; Bataille, 1989); quite the opposite, in fact. Singling out specific types of action as "illegal" reinforces the normative power of the law and, through a public performance of judgement and punishment, that of its designated agents. This process helps "to define as authoritative certain ways of seeing society" (Lukes, 1975, p. 306) and has a key function; that of constantly re-tuning the collective moral compass by drawing a line, often not only institutional, between good and bad people. This flat opposition, in most cases still loudly, if not proudly insensitive to class, gender, or cultural backgrounds (Kropotkin, 1982), allows citizens to reflexively group and position themselves in relation to a moral otherness. This positioning eventually generates that "law-abiding citizen" who does not require much surveillance and is generally considered the golden standard of national states. Voluntary compliance is effective and, not less importantly, cheap. On this basis, I argue that democratic powers become fragile when this cycle of the reproduction of social norms is disrupted and, consequently, the reliability of the moral compass offered by the ruling class is put into question. Such disruption manifests itself as a widespread feeling that a tipping point is being reached; that the same types of actions that used to trigger a collective, discursive, and performative reaffirmation of the rule of law are now powerful enough to challenge its legitimacy and that of its agents (Sassen, 2008).

The crisis of the symbolic value of the law, and the democratic institutions it is embodied by, triggers an inversion; different levels of society begin to be infiltrated by a feeling that the legal ritual is somehow underperforming, i.e., that it is not able to offer reassurance about the legally defined social order (Arnold, 1935; Frank, 1936), and provide citizens with the guarantee that their collective values and objectives are being pursued (Edelman, 1971). Thus challenged, governmental authorities tend to flex their muscles in a public display of bigotry (Davies, 2018). This usually includes investing resources in eye-catching practices, such as increasing police presence in public spaces, imposing harsher punishment for minor felonies, and targeting vulnerable minorities (Manning, 1977). Through this spectacle of power, the state tries to enforce its assumingly hegemonic symbolic order by authoritarian means shifting, *de facto*, from consent to coercion (Gramsci, 1977). And yet, coercion is also a self-sabotaging dynamic, as the explicit demand for compliance implicitly fuels the idea that most citizens are not willingly respecting the rule of law (Easton, 1975), that democratic ideals are not a shared horizon, and that democratic governments lack the legitimacy to exert their authority over the population (Hollander, 1978). A crisis silently mounts and the symbolic link between state and sovereignty begins to fray.

3. Charisma or Data? Populists and Technocrats as Natives of the Global Landscape

The current hyper-fragility of democracies is here understood as the result of an inversion, akin to a magnetic pole reversal. In the same way that the authority of the law and its agents is recursively reinforced by its diffuse communal performance, an interference in this cycle of symbolic reproduction might trigger a spiral-down effect. The power of any set of norms, i.e., their capacity to influence both individual and collective behaviour through consent and not coercion, relies on a symbolic and necessarily silent bond between institutions and citizens. Accordingly, the more the rule of law is openly enforced, the more its authority seems to wobble. But what triggers this inversion? Why is this happening today on a global scale? And, ultimately, how does a fundamentalist discourse feed on this crisis?

The first decades of the new millennium have been characterized by a renewed enthusiasm for authoritarian leadership on a global level. Under the puzzled eyes of progressive neoliberal elites, an alliance of political populism and religious fundamentalism took thick and thin democracies by storm. From the USA to India, Brazil to the UK, new leaders walked on to the world stage: they were ruthless, belligerent, and illiberal. They relied on personal charisma, openly disrespected democratic institutions, and preached for a return to a national golden age (Kyle & Meyer, 2020). This wave of populism did not always entail a change of ruling class. Leaders such as Vladimir Putin, Recep Erdoğan, Benjamin Netanyahu, and Viktor Orbán progressively adopted a populist style, shifting towards more openly authoritarian forms of governance and associating themselves with extremist groups, war-enthusiasts, racist movements, and religious fundamentalists (Meyer, 2021). In what looks today like a classic reactionary paradox, the most intransigent and uncompromising political creeds found in populist leaders have a common denominator.

Despite its diverse expressions, populism has been quickly identified as a global trend recognizable by some recurrent traits, such as strong leader-centrism, unmediated leader-follower interaction, and a loosely defined opposition between "the people" and "the elite" (Cohen, 2019). While the causes leading to the emergence of populism are still under study (Hidalgo-Tenorio, Benítez-Castro, & De Cesare, 2019; Rodrik, 2020), there is a general agreement that contemporary populism is linked to some peculiar traits of globalization (Giddens, 2003), such as competition in an increasingly complex world, fast obsolescence of acquired skills, and, more generally, a sense of powerlessness experienced by large strata of the population (Cox, 2017; Imogen, 2020). In a nutshell, populism is not a nostalgic reminiscence of old-school fascism, but rather a political style typical of a globalized world which feeds on its recurrent crises (Hidalgo-Tenorio & Benítez-Castro, 2022; Ibled, 2022). Populist leaders rely on the instability generated by globalization in local contexts to simplify the political debate and reframe any issue as a polar opposition (Moffitt, 2020), an opposition between obscure worldwide powers and down-to-earth local communities.

From this perspective, it is hardly a surprise that the core rhetoric of populism was not jammed but fuelled by the pandemic crisis. Rather than the data-based bird's-eye perspective offered by technocrats, followers of populist leaders were provided with a basic tensive identity: a simple and clear orientation against a frightening event, "nothing but a strategy of Satan and the media" (Bergamo, 2020). In these terms, populist rhetoric took over a basic symbolic function of the rule of law. However, the reason populist parties are often able to weaponize cultural symbols and redraw the boundaries of the national community along the lines of their own political creed (Butler & Spivak, 2007), is that such symbols are now up for grabs. The economic, cultural, and political assault led by global forces with no democratic legitimacy against the state has emptied it of its political authority. What was left behind was an allegedly neutral bureaucratic apparatus; a technical system tasked with the construction, maintenance, and defence of the infrastructure necessary for the functioning of worldwide neoliberal economies.

In this context, technocrats rose as the engineers of global capitalism: a new type of actor whose legitimacy does not come from its political vision but by its skills. Technocrats can manage the hydraulics of the planetary market; they can expertly regulate its flows of goods, money, data, and people. The technocrat, like the globalized state it serves, becomes ideologically translucent: a mere servant of the new planetary ecosystem, a devout custodian of the worldwide level playing field. And yet, to fulfil this mission, technocrats have something to ask from the state: the law, in terms of property rights and contract regulations, needs to be enforced, and enforced everywhere in the same way. From this perspective, then, to portray the state as a passive actor, if not even as a victim of globalization, is a dangerous mistake (Slobodian, 2018). The regulatory power of states represents, in fact, the core engine of the globalization project and, as Pistor (2019, p. 10) put it, states have been "offering their coercive law powers to enforce the legal rights that have been bestowed on capital". Far from weakened, states were offered a new role in the globalized world: to shield the market from democratic interference, and to reroute democratic power towards the protection of the market and not of the citizens. And the citizens noticed.

4. Populism and the Pandemic: A Trojan Horse for Fundamentalist Epistemologies

Populists and technocrats are, eventually, two faces of the same structural transformation of the role of the state in a globalized world. For capitalism to go global, and for multinational companies to be able to profit from planetary asymmetries, the market must be placed beyond state politics. It must be placed out of the control of citizens, local communities, labour organizations and even governmental bodies. It must be placed beyond the reach of democratic ruling, and this can be achieved only through a Faustian bargain: in exchange for voluntarily giving up sovereignty, states are promised further wealth accumulation within their jurisdictions; in other terms, democratic powers are used today by democratic institutions to maintain that the global market remains "free", i.e., out of the reach of democratic control.

From this transformation of the role of the state authority, two main tendencies are raised. On the one hand, populists filled the symbolic national space now neglected by states with a highly individualized leadership reliant on charisma and conflicting narratives. On the other hand, technocrats presented the new global ecosystem as inevitable and attempted to substitute state politics with a disembodied form of decision-making based upon data. It is within this rising tension that fundamentalist epistemologies have been growing since the beginning of the new millennium. Fundamentalism is neither an irrational position nor a necessarily conservative one (Malcolm, 2023). Yet, regardless of its ideological nature, it always relies on dogmatism and authoritarianism. It is a reaction against a perceived enemy and "the enemies of fundamentalisms everywhere are relativism, pluralism, ambiguity" (Marty, 1988, p. 21).

The COVID-19 pandemic unveiled how both autocratic populisms (e.g., Brazil or the USA) and technocratic data-governance (e.g., Italy and Germany) share a fascination for intransigent epistemologies. While the former appears more familiar, to the point that has been hastily associated with historical fascism, the latter indicates the emergence of a new ontology with hegemonic vocations: data-governance bases its legitimacy on the implied existence of an almost unmediated relationship between metrics and reality. During the pandemic, for example, it was possible for governments to present restrictions as a variable directly dependent on alterations in the data. Limitations to personal freedom, citizens were told, depend on fluctuations in the metrics: the higher the number of registered cases, the lower the level of freedom. This form of technocratic decision-making was legitimized through a synergy between global organizations, multinational companies, and scientific bodies. All these different authorities pushed to make data reports the key variable upon which all state decisions, either political, economic, or social, directly depended.

Populist leaders, on the contrary, not only rejected data as a basis for governmental policies but reframed them as foes; as tools devised to cripple their power and undermine national sovereignty in favour of global elites. Through a combination of ideological vagueness, oppositional identity, and charismatic personalized leadership, populism managed to build a heterogeneous political space where data were not only disregarded but openly antagonized. Against the abstract and ever-changing reality of data, against the feelings of alienation and anomie this globalized construction of reality produced (Gudavarthy, 2021), populist leaders offered an "authentic", "unlayered", and "univocal" truth (Kohl et al., 2021). In this context, religious fundamentalism played a specific role in providing a new moral compass, a new way for citizens to group against a moral otherness beyond the limits imposed by the state. Indeed, while in populism the reaction of "the people" against "the elite" is based on feelings of victimhood and betrayal (Castanho Silva, Vegetti, & Littvay, 2017), religious fundamentalism imbued these worldly feelings with otherworldly meanings. Through the lens of spiritual warfare (Marshall, 2016), local distrust towards the ruling class morphed into a cosmic battle for the salvation of humanity, a Manichean clash between irreconcilable forces. This overlapping of worldly and otherworldly politics is embodied by the fact that, while not representing any specific religious creed, populist leaders were often backed by high-ranked members of fundamentalist religious organizations. This is the case, for example, of former vice-president Mike Pence in the USA (Whitehead, 2021) or Bishop Edir Macedo in Brazil. The endorsement of these radical religious figures endowed political charisma with spiritual legitimacy. Once blessed, the leader would finally embody the ultimate expression of fundamentalist ethos: the holy warrior.

5. Radical Enemies for Radical Leaders: Case Study and Methodology

A holy warrior needs a holy war, and a war is "holy" when it is waged against a diabolic and powerful enemy. Needless to say, a global crisis like the COVID-19 pandemic offered a perfect setting. Accordingly, to retrace how fundamentalist religious figures found in populist leaders their ideal political counterparts and how they actively supported their political action, this study analysed the official online newsfeed of the Universal Church (universal.org/todas-as-noticias). The Universal Church is currently one of the most successful and controversial evangelical organizations in Brazil, and possibly in the world. During the pandemic, the Universal Church supported the denialist positions expressed by both the Brazilian government and former president Jair Bolsonaro. Indeed, Bolsonaro openly and systematically disregarded the guidelines issued by the World Health Organization (WHO). He refused to wear a mask in public, declined to announce a national lockdown, and, as reported by Pfizer Inc., did not secure vaccine shots when offered the possibility (Fonseca, 2021). Conversely, he frequently framed the pandemic as a spiritual battle, even going so far as to declare a national day of prayer and fasting, with the aim of "freeing Brazil from this evil" (Paraguassu, 2020). In a recent report, Brazilian senators levelled several accusations against Bolsonaro in connection to his handling of the pandemic. These allegations encompassed "charlatanism, incitement to crime, falsification of documents, improper use of public funds, prevarication, crimes against humanity, violations of social rights, incompatibility with the dignity, honour, and decorum of the office, and breaches of preventive sanitary measures" (Pedroso, Pozzebon, & Soares, 2021).

Within this context, the present study intends to trace how the Universal Church presented the pandemic to its community, how this representation transformed over time and whether such transformations can be correlated to significant political events. To this aim, we collected through a customized Python script all news articles that were published during the years 2020 and 2021 on the official newsfeed of the Universal Church (universal.org). It is important to note that all information collected was publicly available and intended for public viewership. To gather this corpus, a custom web-scraping software was developed by the researcher utilizing the Python programming language, along with the following Python libraries: BeautifulSoup, Pandas, and Urllib. This software was designed to retrieve the main textual content of each news article, eliminate any HTML formatting elements, and save the content in a plain text format (.txt). Each resulting file was automatically named using the date (YYYY.MM.DD) and time (HH.MM.SS) of publication, enabling chronological ordering of the news articles.

The collected texts (7,366 unique items) were subsequently organized by month in preparation for analysis. Initially, the frequency of publication was examined to identify any variations during the pivotal years of the pandemic. Following this, AntConc (Anthony, 2022) and Excel software were employed to analyse word frequency within the texts. This analysis encompassed both individual words and word combinations, aiding in the identification of distinctive patterns. As detailed in the subsequent findings, the creation of word combinations followed an inductive approach, subsequently validated against the corpus. Finally, specific months' news production was scrutinized using Semantic Network Analysis (Martini & Robertson, 2022). Semantic networks were constructed by identifying the 20 most frequently occurring terms within selected clusters, and then tracing collocates of these terms within a range of 10 positions, both to the left and right. As these collocates were collected to trace semantic associations, it is noteworthy that the results were not lemmatized to ensure the emergence of lexical nuances. However, a stop list was implemented to exclude irrelevant terms, such as articles and pronouns. These results were then structured using Excel software and further processed using Gephi, an open-source software tool for network analysis.

6. Fundamentalism, Gatekeeping, and the Vaccine that Never Was

The long-term analysis of this religious newsfeed enables us to make several observations on the way radical religious organizations construct, employ, and secure digital spaces. More precisely, this research sheds light on the ways information is circulated (or not) within the religious community, how such information is legitimized as authentic, and how, finally, it actively concurs to reshape the infosphere in which a religious community exists and transforms. Accordingly, our hypothesis is that in the course of time the Universal Church strategically transformed its communication around the pandemic to gain advantage from the transforming political landscape.

The first observation is that, throughout the two years of the pandemic, the news production did not change much in terms of frequency. Except for the first months of the pandemic (April–July 2020), which presents an unusual growth, the posting activity always oscillates between 250 and 300 posts per month, with an average of 11 posts per day. Despite its relatively high frequency, the monthly news production rate remains regular throughout the two studied years and seems not to be influenced by external factors (Figure 4.2, grey area). This regularity is significantly mirrored by the data obtained through the semantic mapping of the news published within a single month. The mapping, obtained through network text analysis, showed a significant stability in terms of semantic structure. Regardless of the many different topics discussed in the news and, of course, of the evolution of the pandemic, all monthly sets show that the main core of the main semantic galaxies remain unchanged: Universal Church, God, Holy Spirit, Family, and Edir Macedo (see Figure 4.1). This remarkable regularity in terms of both frequency and semantic structure indicates a first, and perhaps more general, attribute of fundamentalist communication, i.e., its fundamental insensitivity to external factors. In other words, regardless of the topic or the social situation, this form of communication always reinforces the same core concepts and revolves around the same main actors.

A second observation, more directly connected to the pandemic, concerns the irregular way events concerning the COVID-19 outbreak and the vaccine were covered by the newsfeed (Figure 4.2). In the initial months of 2020, when the pandemic was still perceived mostly as a European phenomenon, the newsfeed did not give much space to these topics (less than 2% of the news). In March 2020, however, an increasing number of COVID-19 cases were registered in Brazil, quickly shifting the focus. Between April and May 2020, around 60% of the news mentioned the pandemic and 6% discussed the vaccine. This is, nevertheless, an all-time high. The newsmakers' interest towards the pandemic seems to rapidly fade and in August 2020 only 13.5% of news mentioned the pandemic and, surprisingly, none discussed the vaccine. Rather than a temporary drop, this lack of concern stabilizes into a trend: between August 2020 and February 2021, on average, the pandemic is mentioned in 16.7% of the posts while the vaccine is mentioned in only 0.6%. This is particularly relevant if we consider that in November 2020 the discovery of the vaccine was officially announced by Pfizer. This drastic change in the space the pandemic and the vaccine occupy in the religious newsfeed is reflected in a more qualitative and very significant change. In the initial months, when the newsfeed of the Universal Church followed mainstream media into reporting on the pandemic and the vaccine, there was also a significant increase in the number

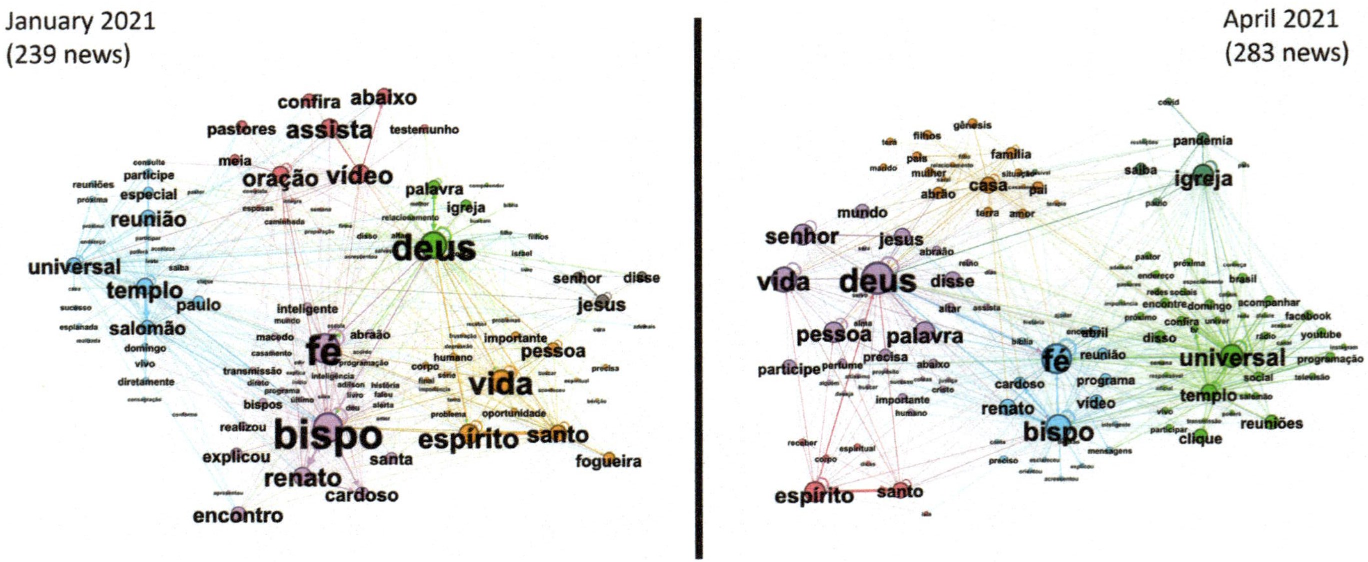

Figure 4.1 Chart demonstrates the frequency of news production during the pandemic via semantic mapping.

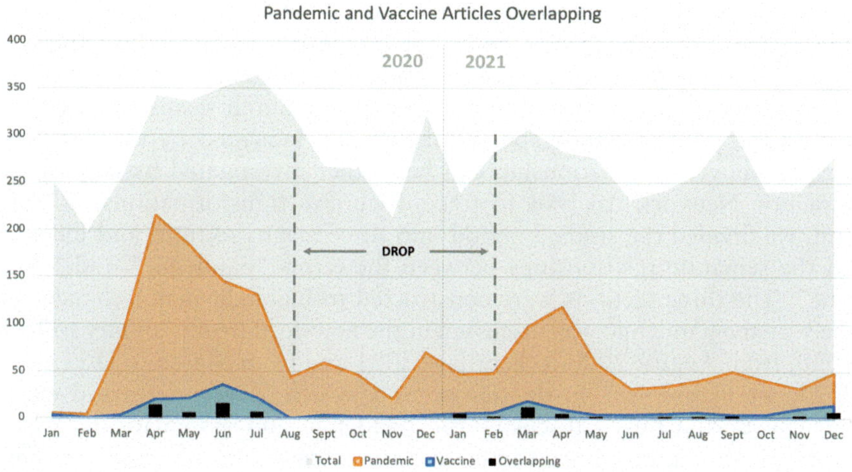

Figure 4.2 Graph that concerns the irregular way events concerning the COVID-19 outbreak and the vaccine were covered by the newsfeed.

of times scientific actors were mentioned. This included the WHO, universities, researchers and, more generally, "science" as a legitimizing authority (e.g., "science says" or "scientific research has demonstrated"). Indeed, between April and July 2020, scientific actors were mentioned almost 170 times a month, with a peak of 190 in June and 185 in July. However, following the newsfeed's attention towards the pandemic, this trend also dropped suddenly in August 2020 and has stabilized since then to about 50 mentions/month (average token/month: 103.912).

The sudden disappearance of the pandemic and the vaccine from the newsfeed, as well as the concomitant silencing of scientific authorities, seem to indicate a clear editorial decision and lead us to wonder what might have triggered such a sudden change. When correlated with a timeline describing the ways Bolsonaro's government dealt with the pandemic crisis, however, the editorial choice of the Universal Church might appear under a different light. In the month leading to August 2020, the feud between the WHO and the Brazilian government quickly escalated. Not only had the negationist positions of Bolsonaro cost him two heath ministers within a couple of months, but he eventually appointed an army general with no medical expertise (Eisenhammer & Stargardter, 2020). Following this decision, which might appear rather unconventional in the middle of a global health crisis, Bolsonaro's government tried to block the publication of data concerning COVID-19 death-toll and spread. This decision was later revoked by the Supreme Court.

Considering these events, we can see how the sudden change highlighted above does not happen in a void, but rather, it seems to reflect the political positions of the Brazilian government. This correspondence leads us to focus on the relationship the Universal Church seems to entertain within the political landscape. While already indicated by the data described above, the relationship can be further investigated by employing Semantic Network Analysis to trace discursive transformations. To this aim, we divided the studied period into three macro sections and focused on the semantic relationships between the terms "pandemic" and "vaccine". The three sections were constructed to highlight major changes in the way the pandemic was discussed in the newsfeed (from January to July 2020, from August 2020 to February 2021 and from March to December 2021, see Figure 4.2). In the first section, which covers the period when the Universal Church discusses the pandemic and systematically mentions scientific authorities, the main terms connecting the pandemic and the vaccine belong to the scientific lexicon. This includes, for example, "medication", "treatments", and "testing". In the second period, when COVID-19 is barely mentioned and scientific authorities are silenced, the limited lexicon connecting the two terms refers interestingly to the political domain and includes words such as "global", "national", and "Brazil". This semantic shift seems to suggest that, in this phase, the pandemic is not portrayed as a scientific issue but rather perceived as a matter of national positioning within the global landscape; the semantic core of a dichotomic "US vs THEM" opposition.

Finally, the third section defines a period in which, after several months of silence, the topic of the pandemic is discussed once again in the newsfeed. This renewed interest towards this issue began in March 2021, in correspondence with a significant political event: former president Lula da Silva is cleared of all charges and immediately begins his electoral campaign. From this moment on, the newsfeed of the Universal Church restarted discussing the pandemic issue and, interestingly, through a new semantic lens. Indeed, while in the first section, this issue was discussed in scientific terms and in the second section mostly as a political issue, in the third section the lexicon surrounding the vaccination campaign is primarily religious and directly refers to the Universal Church, including terms such as "temples", "church", and "bishop". This third shift suggests that the Universal Church and its leaders are now interested in associating themselves with the vaccination campaign. Despite having deliberately ignored the discovery of the vaccine in the middle of one of the most tragic moments of the pandemic, the reappearance of Bolsonaro's foe on the political scene seems to prompt a re-positioning of the Universal Church. As former president Lula da Silva began to criticize the government for the mismanagement of the pandemic crisis, they suddenly became more vocal about their institutional support to the vaccination campaign.

7. Conclusions: Fundamentalism Thinks Global and Fights Local

The present chapter discussed how the strong re-emergence of fundamentalist epistemologies, either of political, cultural, or religious nature, is not the result of a sort of inversion, of a return of part of humanity to move towards "primitive" forms of social cohesion. On the contrary, contemporary fundamentalism is a force which emerges directly from the process of globalization and feeds on its inherent and necessary structural asymmetries. More precisely, through the analysis of the case at hand, this study empirically demonstrated how the ways the Universal Church discussed the global issue of the COVID-19 pandemic altered in correspondence of significant political events on a state level. Indeed, it is in this tension between global and local powers that religious fundamentalism and populism found a common terrain.

Fundamentalism, either religious or political, "is not the same thing as conservatism, traditionalism, classicism, or orthodoxy", but "it is always reactive, reactionary" (Marty, 1988). Fundamentalism, in other words, emerges because of, and in relation to, a threat; a threat against something perceived as vital, essential, and non-negotiable. In a word: something fundamental. The creation of a global economy came at a price, and this price was a radical transformation in the role of the state. In the West, governments gain their legitimacy through popular support and yet the neoliberal globalization project demands their democratic power to be employed to maintain the market beyond the reach of citizens. Instead of a national identity constructed around cultural, religious, and linguistic elements, as well as clearly defined territorial boundaries, citizens are now offered (or forcefully imposed) a new ontology, i.e., that of the global market. In globalized societies, citizens feel personally exposed to the vagaries of a seemingly boundless environment that often materializes, in their everyday lives, in the form of colourful charts and infographics. The construction of an unmediated relationship between metrics and reality, the establishment of a new data-based social ontology, was very clear during the pandemic. Indeed, not only several governments made restrictions directly dependent on variations in the data, but compulsory data education was often evoked as a solution to people's refusal to accept such restrictions. In other words, citizens who did not accept data as a self-evident truth and questioned their value as a basis for political action were quickly framed as "ignorant", "crazy", or in need of re-education.

This chapter argues, in conclusion, that the re-emergence of fundamentalist epistemologies and their connection to populism can be better understood in relation to the hegemonic vocation of global data governance. In this chapter, we showed the ways in which a major religious organization known for its radical and often controversial practices has sided and actively supported the denialist policies of the Bolsonaro government in Brazil; polices which led, eventually, to the death of more than half a million people. Former president Bolsonaro not only rejected the guidelines issued by the WHO but even tried to prevent the publication of data concerning the pandemic and this can be seen, with hindsight, as a stern opposition to both the normative and symbolic power of the "global". In these terms, then, the alliance between religious fundamentalist and populist leaders can be understood as functional: an attempt by local authorities to protect their power, to maintain their influence over the population, and to resist the hegemonic pressure of international organizations.

This analysis showed also that such an alliance is not unshakable. Far from being what they claim to be, i.e., intransigent defenders of immutable truths and unbendable fighters of hellish enemies, fundamentalist organizations seem to be ready to silently shift their position according to the transforming landscape. In the studied case, the Universal Church first aligned with the scientific values of the international community but, in a sharp turn, quickly dropped this approach once the Bolsonaro government entered in a row with it, thus preferring an alliance with local powers rather than with global ones. However, when in March 2021 former president Lula de Silva began his political campaign and attacked Bolsonaro for his management of the pandemic, the Universal Church changed its approach once again: while not opposing the government, it began to openly associate itself with the vaccination campaign promoted by international organizations. Accordingly, this case shows that fundamentalism should not be understood as an anachronistic phenomenon, a sort of curious relic of more "primitive" societies. On the contrary, fundamentalism is a contemporary epistemology actively involved in the process of globalization; an epistemology which emerges from the global neoliberal project and the new role states play in it.

References

Anthony, L. (2022). AntConc (Version 4.1.3) [Computer Software]. Tokyo, Japan: Waseda University. Available from https://www.laurenceanthony.net/software.

Arnold, T. (1935). *The symbols of government*. New Haven, CT: Yale University Press.

Bataille, G. (1989). *The tears of Eros*. City Lights Books.

Bergamo, M. (2020, April 23). Edir Macedo apaga vídeo em que diz que coronavírus não passa de estratégia de Satanás e da mídia. Folha De S.Paulo. Retrieved October 25, 2022, from https://www1.folha.uol.com.br/colunas/monicabergamo/2020/03/edir-macedo-apaga-video-em-que-diz-que-coronavirus-nao-passa-de-estrategia-de-satanas-e-da-midia.shtml.

Butler, J., & Spivak, G. C. (2007). *Who sings the nation-state? Language, politics, belonging*. Oxford: Seagull Books.

Castanho Silva, B., Vegetti, F., & Littvay, L. (2017). The elite is up to something: Exploring the relation between populism and belief in conspiracy theories. *Swiss Political Science Review, 23*(4), 423–443.

Cohen, J. L. (2019). Populism and the politics of resentment. *Jus Cogens, 1*(1), 5–39.

Cox, M. (2017). The rise of populism and the crisis of globalisation: Brexit, Trump and beyond. *Irish Studies in International Affairs, 28*, 9–17.

Davies, W. (2018). *Nervous states: How feeling took over the world*. London: Random House.

Easton, D. (1975). A re-assessment of the concept of political support. *British Journal of Political Sience, 5*(4), 435–457.

Edelman, M. (1971 [2013]). Politics as symbolic action: Mass arousal and quiescence. Elsevier.

Eisenhammer, S. and Stargardter, G. (2020). Special Report: Bolsonaro brought in his generals to fight coronavirus. Brazil is losing the battle. Reuters. Retrieved on Cotober 25, 2022 form https://www.reuters.com/ article/idUSKBN2321DT/

Fonseca, P. (2021, April 15). Brazil's hospitals running out of sedatives as covid-19 rages. Reuters. Retrieved October 25, 2022, from https://www.reuters.com/world/americas/brazils-covid-19-response-cost-thousands-lives-says-humanitarian-group-2021-04-15/

Foucault, M. (1975 [2012]). *Discipline and punish: The birth of the prison*. London: Vintage.

Frank, J. (1936). *Law and the modern mind*. New York: Tudor.

Giddens, A. (1985). *The nation-state and violence*. Cambridge: Polity Press.

Giddens, A. (2003). *Runaway world: How globalization is reshaping our lives*. New York: Routledge.

Gramsci, A. (1977). *Quaderni del carcere*. Torino: Einaudi.

Gudavarthy, A. (2021). Theorizing populism: Lessons Learned from the Indian example. In C. Kohl, B. Christophe, H. Liebau, & A. Saupe (Eds.), *The politics of authenticity and populist discourses* (pp. 53–71). Cham: Palgrave Macmillan.

Hidalgo-Tenorio, E., & Benítez-Castro, M. Á. (2022). Trump's populist discourse and affective politics, or on how to move 'the People' through emotion. *Globalisation, Societies and Education, 20*(2), 86–109.

Hidalgo-Tenorio, E., Benítez-Castro, M. Á., & De Cesare, F. (Eds.). (2019). *Populist discourse: Critical approaches to contemporary politics*. London: Routledge.

Hollander, E. (1978). *Leadership dynamics*. New York: Free Press.

Ibled, C. (2022). The 'optimistic cruelty' of Hayek's market order: Neoliberalism, pain and social selection. *Theory, Culture & Society, 40*(3), 81–101.

Imogen, T. (2020). *Stigma: The machinery of inequality*. London: Zed Books

Kohl, C., Christophe, B., Liebau, H., & Saupe, A. (2021). *Politics of authenticity and populist discourses. Media and education in Brazil, India and Ukraine*. London: Palgrave Macmillan.

Kropotkin, P. A. (1892 [2020]). *Law and authority*. Glasgow: Good Press.

Kyle, J., & Meyer, B. (2020). High tide? Populism in power, 1990–2020. Available here: https://www.institute.global/insights/geopolitics-and-security/high-tide-populism-power-1990-2020. Retrieved: December, 14, 2022.

Lukes, S. (1975). Political ritual and social integration. *Sociology, 9*(2), 289–308.

Malcolm, F. (2023). The rationality of fundamentalist belief. *Journal of Social Philosophy*. https://doi.org/10.1111/josp.12440.
Manning, P. K. (1977). *Police work: The social organization of policing*. Cambridge, MA: MIT Press.
Marshall, R. (2016). Destroying arguments and captivating thoughts: Spiritual warfare prayer as global praxis. *Journal of Religious and Political Practice*, 2(1), 92–113.
Martini, M., & Robertson, S. L. (2022). Erasures and equivalences: Negotiating the politics of culture in the OECD's global competence project. *Compare: A Journal of Comparative and International Education*, 1–18.
Marty, M. E. (1988). Fundamentalism as a social phenomenon. *Bulletin of the American Academy of Arts and Sciences*, *42*(2), 15–29.
McClenaghan, Maeve. "'Exposed to horrendous things': Young people in UK speak out against Evangelical Church". *The Guardian*, Guardian News and Media, 29 November 2022, www.theguardian.com/world/2022/nov/29/young-uk-people-speak-out-against-evangelical-church-universal-kingdom-god.
Meyer, B. (2021). Populists in power: Perils and prospects in 2021. *Tony Blair Institute for Global Change*.
Moffitt, B. (2020). *The global rise of populism: Performance, political style, and representation*. Palo Alto: Stanford University Press.
Paraguassu, L. (2020, April 4). Brazil's Bolsonaro turns to prayer in coronavirus crisis. https://www.reuters.com/article/us-health-coronavirus-brazil-bolsonaro-idUSKBN21L3DL/?taid=5e880c4053c773000108dfaf&utm_campaign=trueAnthem:+Trending+Content&utm_medium=trueAnthem&utm_source=twitter.
Pedroso, R., Pozzebon, S., & Soares, I. (2021, October). Brazilian senators recommend Bolsonaro be charged with crimes against humanity over pandemic. *CNN*. https://edition.cnn.com/2021 /10/20/americas/brazil-bolsonaro-covid-19-intl-hnk/index.html. Retrieved on: 21 March 2023.
Phillips, Tom. "Brazilian Evangelical leader Bishop Edir Macedo charged with fraud". *The Guardian*, Guardian News and Media, 13 August 2009, www.theguardian.com/world/2009/aug/13/brazil-evangelical-leader-charged-fraud.
Pistor, K. (2019). *The code of capital*. Princeton, NJ: Princeton University Press.
Rodrik, D. (2020). Why does globalization fuel populism? Economics, culture, and the rise of right-wing populism. *Annual Review of Economics*, *13*, 133–170.
Sassen, S. (2008). *Territory, authority, rights*. Princeton, NJ: Princeton University Press.
Slobodian, Q. (2018). *Globalists*. Cambridge, MA: Harvard University Press.
Whitehead, D. (2021). "In Mike Pence, US Evangelicals had their '24-karat-gold' man in the White House. Loyalty may tarnish that legacy". *Colorado Arts and Sciences Magazine*, University of Colorado Boulder, 7 January 2021, www. colorado.edu/asmagazine/2021/01/06/mike-pence-us-evangelicals-had-their-24-karat-gold-man-white-house-loyalty-may-tarnish.

5 “Stirring Up the Hornet’s Nest”. Radicalization Strategies of the Spanish Far-Right Twitter Followers

Francisco José Sánchez-García

1. Introduction

In the digital era, it is not possible to study political communication without an in-depth knowledge of the role played by social networks. Since its earliest days, the microblogging network Twitter (renamed in 2023 by Elon Musk as “X”) has stood out as the most powerful and effective platform for disseminating information and opinion, and this, of course, has made it an indispensable tool for political communication and social activism (Camargo, 2021).

However, there is recurrent criticism of Twitter’s role as a network that encourages the polarization of opinions, and radical and hate speech (Herrero Izquierdo et al., 2022). Among other reasons, the very logic of Twitter’s algorithm tends to give greater visibility to the most popular messages (which tend to be, incidentally, the most controversial and emotional); the latter, can generate an echo chamber in which users only see opinions that are similar or contrary to their own, without nuance or diversity. Added to this is users’ lack of interest in verifying the information circulating on the Internet, which contributes to the transmission of hoaxes, rumours or deliberately false news to influence public opinion at very specific times. What is most worrying though is the potential of the web for some radical groups to discredit, harass or intimidate certain individuals or groups on the grounds of their ethnicity, gender or sexual orientation, to name but a few.

Not surprisingly, Twitter/X is the social network par excellence for transmitting inflammatory proclamations and hate messages. As Pereira-Kohatsu et al. (2019) point out, hate tweets linked to the extreme right find in this social network their ideal springboard for attacking minorities, especially migrants. These messages tend to multiply during sensitive periods, such as election campaigns, when it is crucial to generate tension to mobilize the electorate.

DOI: 10.4324/9781003457381-6

It has even been found that the platform amplifies more tweets from right-wing politicians and media than content from left-wing sources, as Dan Milmo (2021) shows in an article in The Guardian, in which he analyses tweets from elected officials in seven countries (the UK, the US, Canada, France, Germany, Japan and Spain). In Spain, the network itself published an internal report on the impact and reach of the messages of political parties (Ollero, 2021), and concluded that PP (the People's Party) is the one that most benefits from the microblogging network's algorithm, followed by Spanish Socialist Workers' Party (PSOE), Unidas Podemos and Vox. In other words, the right is overrepresented on Twitter, although not necessarily Vox. It has been pointed out that populist parties (the case of Vox and Podemos in Spain) are the ones that make the most intense use of social networks (Aparicio, 2022). In any case, regardless of the biases of the networks towards certain user niches, everything seems to indicate that it is the followers of the extreme right who consume the most unverified news, as determined by a recent study on fake news on Facebook (Pérez Colomé, 2023).

In previous research (Sánchez-García, 2022; Sosinski & Sánchez-García, 2022), we studied the populist frameworks used by Vox to construct its exclusionary narrative on migrants and revealed some clues about the nativism, authoritarianism and discriminatory drift of its discourse. In this article we will focus on the extreme right-wing messages that express opinions unambiguously and unrestrainedly, and which set the tone for the slogans that resonate among Vox supporters. Unlike the approach explored previously, here we are not interested in studying what the leaders say, but rather in examining their supporters' reactions (without the filters or self-imposed limits operating in the political sphere), in which prejudices emerge that lead to misogynist, racist, offensive messages against LGTBIQ+ minorities, or Covid and climate-change related conspiratorial messages. In short, we aim to look at the strategies used by Vox in networks to "stir up the hornet's nest" and make its slogans take hold among a large group of followers on the microblogging network.

2. Theoretical Framework. The Radical Discourse of the Far Right in Spain: The Case of Vox

2.1 *Vox's Radical Discourse: Extreme Right or Radical Right?*

Vox is usually categorized within the Spanish ideological spectrum as a "far right" party, but its leaders are also commonly referred to as members of the "extreme right" or "radical right". To begin with, it is necessary to distinguish between the two concepts, since they are not strictly equivalent. The fundamental difference, according to Mudde (2021, p. 25), is that the "radical right" accepts the rules of the democratic game and becomes part of the mainstream political scene, but "opposes fundamental elements of liberal democracy, most notably minority rights, the rule of law and the separation of powers". In contrast, the "extreme right" designates groups that reject the democratic system and support the use of violence to achieve their political purposes (Norris, 2005). Thus, we agree with Ferreira (2019, p. 79):

> It seems to me that the expression "radical right" is more neutral and better captures the ideological core of these parties than other denominations that emphasize a single specific component such as "anti-immigration parties", "anti-establishment parties" o "national-populist parties".

The Vox party, founded in 2013 by former members of PP dissatisfied with Rajoy's leadership, remained for a time a marginal formation (to the right of the PP), but has experienced rapid growth since its first electoral success in the 2018 Andalusian elections, and especially the 2019 general elections, in which it won 52 seats.

There is no doubt that Vox is a radical party and it also produces radical discourse, in the terms outlined above. But, what are the recognizable attributes of a "radical discourse" to mobilize its followers and delegitimize its opponents? (Sánchez-García, 2022). In essence, there are three main attributes:

- Polarization: Political reality is presented as a struggle between two irreconcilable camps, "us" and "them", which embody opposing and excluding values. "Us" is often defined in nativist terms (i.e., as the genuine members of the nation); "them" usually includes immigrants, minorities, traditional parties, the European Union or progressive social movements.
- Antagonism: This involves attacking the political opponent with arguments that question their legitimacy, morality, or competence. Disqualification, insult, irony, or sarcasm are used to ridicule or denigrate the opponent; moreover, dysphemisms are often employed to refer to the opponent or their ideas.
- The use of fallacies, like hasty generalization (i.e., extrapolating a conclusion from a few cases), false dichotomy (i.e., reducing options to only two extremes), straw man (i.e. distorting the opponent's position to attack it more easily) or *ad hominem* fallacy (attacking the person rather than their arguments).

2.2 *Populist Features in Vox's Discourse*

Is Vox's discourse populist? According to Rydren (2017, p. 493), populism per se is not the defining characteristic of radical right parties, as it "appeals to the general will of the people, mobilizes against elites and is anti-pluralist", traits it shares with far-left parties. Populism is, by itself, an ideology, but not a complete ideology (not at least in the same terms established by Van Dijk, 2003), because as Mudde and Kaltwasser (2012, p. 8) remind us, it would be a "thin-centred ideology that considers society to be ultimately separated into two homogeneous and antagonistic groups, the 'pure people' and the 'corrupt elite' and which argues that politics should be an expression of the general will of the people". Ferreira (2019, p. 79) prefers to avoid the label "populist" for the "radical right", insofar as "it is not central to the ideology of these parties". According to Ferreira (2019, pp. 89–90), populism is present, although it is not so explicit in the case of Vox (Ferreira, 2019), as "the word 'people' is never mentioned, compared to constant appeals to 'Spain' (¼) Its rhetoric is much more nationalist than populist".

However, we consider that Vox's usual frames in networks tend to coincide with those deployed by radical right-wing populist parties,[1] along the lines marked by other European populist parties such as Lega in Italy, Fidesz in Hungary, or Alternative for Germany (AfD), and the Freedom Party (PVV) in the Netherlands. Essentially, Wodak (2019) classifies these populist parties on the grounds of four dimensions: (1) *nativism*, (2) *anti-elitism*, (3) *authoritarianism* and (4) *conservatism*.

In line with the above and as already described in previous works (Sánchez-García, 2022; Sosinski & Sánchez-García, 2022), Vox seems to meet a series of basic requirements, that help to define the party and its discourse as distinctly populist: It uses conceptual frameworks that emphasize the difference between us (Spaniards) and them (foreigners); it appeals to nativism (i.e., exacerbated patriotism and vindication of the genuine identity symbols of the Spanish nation), to authoritarianism (i.e., the assumption that most problems must be solved with leadership and an "iron fist"), and to the defence of the nation against external and internal threats; Vox also resorts to simple and gimmicky language that simplifies complex problems; and, finally, it takes advantage of social networks to spread its message without intermediaries.

In other words, the party's populism is based, above all, on its insistence on fighting the 'corrupt' elites, sustained by the two-party system of the PP and PSOE, a manipulative media and supranational lobbies (including the EU) that leave the Spanish people and their institutions without effective power (Rama et al., 2021). Theirs is, moreover, an ultra-nationalist discourse that denies the diversity of cultures and identities in the Spanish State, while deploring multiculturalism and so-called 'illegal' migration. It also possesses some of its own traits, not necessarily present in all European radical right-wing parties: marked Anti-feminism (embodied by a supposed "gender ideology" that threatens equality between men and women), revisionism of Spain's past (apology for national Catholic values, commonly associated with Franco's dictatorship) and the demand for the recentralization of powers and putting an end to the "state of the autonomous regions" (Sánchez-García, 2022).

2.3 *Vox's Communication Strategy in Social Networks. The Case of Twitter/X*

Twitter allows direct communication between the party and its potential audience without intermediaries, which represents a challenge for mainstream media and political elites. Indeed, Vox has opted to professionalize its digital communication strategy, thus achieving greater participation and interaction from its supporters, along the lines of other extreme right-wing populist parties such as Lega in Italy (Tuñón-Navarro & Bouzas-Blanco, 2023). In its *Communication Manual*, Vox acknowledges that social networks are its main means of communication, thus feeling free from the constraints of the conventional press (Camargo 2021, p. 65). Not in vain,

> Vox, a formation that, when it burst into the public space in 2013, already carried in its genetic code new forms of political communication on social networks. Moreover, although the intense use of social media to amplify their messages is a constant feature of new political formations in general, Vox is part of a global history of digital campaign strategies developed by the European extreme right and the US alt-right.
> (Oleaque & Pelliser 2021, p. 24)

Vox's official Twitter account (@vox_es), which has more than 542,000 followers, functions as the central node of the party's media network on social networks, although Facebook, its YouTube channel, Instagram profile and WhatsApp distribution lists also have great weight. In January 2020, the social network Twitter silenced their account for 24 hours for breaching the rules prohibiting hate speech. PSOE denounced having been accused of "promoting pedophilia with public money" (regarding sex education in schools) from the party's official account. Naturally, the leaders of the far-right political party reacted angrily against the "censorship" to which they had been subjected, claiming to represent "more than 3.6 million voters" (Manuel Mariscal, tweet of 23 January 2020).

Vox leaders tend to tweet about a selection of fixed topics, namely Muslim immigration, gender policies (male violence against women and sexual identity), Spanish nationalism, Western traditions and cultural values, and, to a lesser extent, the usual topics on the political agenda (finance, education, health, etc.). Naturally, Vox also tweets positively (e.g. it vindicates victims of squatting, public figures close to the extreme right like Ortega Lara or even its own leaders), although its role in the opposition to the government normally requires it to counter or criticize contrary information (Oleaque-Moreno 2020). Nevertheless, the most important thing in any communication strategy through the new media is to transcend the leaders' own discourse and "create community", handing thus over the baton to individual users, sympathizers or followers (whether real or fictitious, in the case of bots created for this purpose to multiply the message) who are the ones who consolidate and give definitive form to the discursive frameworks that shape the climate of opinion setting the political agenda. Thus, the "retweeting" of messages and "replies" are crucial to amplify certain slogans. As Urmeneta Arbusà (2022, p. 167) rightly points out,

> In addition to revealing different dynamics among users, retweets have a major impact on the distribution of content on the platform. In fact, different research concludes that networks of retweets are more important than networks of followers and followees. The latter are compared by Murthy (2018) to television channels, an analogy that seems apt: "Twitter is broadcast" (G. R. Boynton & Richardson, 2016). However, as mentioned above, the networked digital hypertext of which Castells (2009) speaks also allows for many-to-many communication.

The key to Vox's communicative success on Twitter rests in these replies, and above all, in the type of users who are responsible for disseminating the messages. Vox's followers on social networks are a heterogeneous group that shares a radical right-wing, populist and nationalist ideology (Velázquez García-Talavera, 2019). Some of their characteristics, described in Rama et al. (2021), are the following:

- Their profile tends to be mostly male, young or middle-aged, with medium or higher education and living in urban or peri-urban areas.
- Their topics of interest usually revolve around the defence of the unity of Spain, criticism of immigration, Islam, feminism, Catalan independence, the policies of the coalition government, or the lack of freedom during the COVID-19 pandemic. They also support international leaders such as Donald Trump or Jair Bolsonaro.
- Vox's official account has more than 542,000 followers and its publications usually exceed thousands of retweets and likes. The Vox News account has more than 47,000 followers and generates a lot of interaction. But, above all, what is striking is the large number of followers that some individual users have, who from anonymous accounts are responsible for amplifying the conceptual frameworks of Vox's arguments.
- Their communicative style is aggressive, provocative, ironic, and defiant. They tend to use colloquial, emotive language loaded with patriotic

symbols. In order to support their arguments, they also resort to fallacies, disinformation, fake news, or conspiracy theories.

In general, among Vox's followers, a communicative style of "guerrilla warfare" and permanent confrontation with the political adversary stands out, normally embodied in any person or leader who does not share their ideology (including PP politicians and supporters, whom they refer to as the "cowardly right-wing"). As tends to happen in most radical ideological groups, the persecution of dissidents is commonplace. Precisely, Macarena Olona, one of Vox's best-known leaders, who resigned from political activity after her defeat as a candidate in the 2022 Andalusian regional elections, denounced a campaign of harassment via Twitter by anonymous accounts which, according to her, were linked to the party or were indirectly financed by it. Vox responded by disassociating itself from these messages, but it seems clear that there is a feedback relationship between the party's official account and these anonymous profiles, which also have numerous followers, to generate currents of opinion and publicize the argument that strategically suits Vox at any given moment (Figure 5.1).

In fact, a much-commented issue regarding Vox's communication policy has to do with the party's alleged use of fake accounts (bots). As Viejo (2021) points out in the Spanish newspaper *El País*, an investigation by the Institute for Strategic Dialogue (ISD, a British think tank that fights extremism), discovered that, during the 2019 election campaign, a network of almost 3,000 Twitter bots originating in Venezuela spread messages of hatred of Islam and in favour of Vox. According to the ISD, this network sought to influence public debate and polarize Spanish society.

In any case, if Vox uses bots to poison political debate, is this an exception or the rule? Pérez Colomé's (2020) research could reveal the existence of more than 40,000 bots that tweeted about prominent political events during the 2019 election campaign. According to this study, these bots supported all parties with little difference, with Unidas Podemos benefiting the most and PSOE the least. In this ranking, Vox occupied third place in the support of these automated profiles.

Consequently, it would perhaps be an exaggeration to say that there is an "army of bots" at the service of the extreme right in networks; nonetheless, the importance of certain users who play the role of a transmission belt between the party's postulates and its grassroots supporters is indisputable, and they have in common that they are mostly anonymous and have thousands of followers.

Naturally, it would be almost impossible to prove a direct link between these accounts and the radical right-wing party; but, to use the simile of the "tree and the nuts", the invaluable work of these profiles is crucial to the effectiveness of Vox's communication strategy.

Figure 5.1 Screenshot from Twitter where Macarena Olona denounced a campaign of harassment via Twitter by anonymous accounts.

3. Corpus and Methodology

As indicated above, the discourse of political leaders on the Internet has already been addressed in valuable works, such as Camargo (2021) or Tuñón-Navarro and Bouzas-Blanco (2023). In this chapter, we have set out to advance our knowledge of Spanish populist discourse on networks, but on this occasion we will not focus on the "official" messages of the party and its main leaders, but rather on those of its followers, and especially on a series of well-known Twitter users on the networks, who are responsible for viralising the party's most radical messages by intensifying their content, leaving them devoid of any hint of politically correct language. One of the keys to the success of Vox's communication strategy is the dissemination of its messages through anonymous accounts (a priori, in this way the party does not have to take responsibility for sensitive issues), such as @Democracia, Justicia y Libertad, @Grupo Libre, @No habrá Paz, @El aullido de España, @Adn Vox, @España Siempre, @El ciudadano español, @Team Facha, @Españabola, @InfoVlogger, @Vito Quiles and @Eugenio D'Ors, among others.

In line with previous work (Sánchez-García 2022; Sosinski & Sánchez-García, 2022), here we will rely on the methodological perspective of Critical Discourse Analysis. Regarding the linguistic characterization of the discourse on Twitter, we will start from the epistemological assumptions established in Ávila Martín (2018).

Our corpus is composed of a selection of responses from Twitter users to posts from the official account of the Vox party, in a period between 1 July 2022 and 23 July 2023, coinciding with the last year of the first legislature of the PSOE-Unidas Podemos coalition government. These users have been chosen according to a criterion of influence (large number of followers) and impact and viralisation of their messages. Recently, Twitter (now known as "X"), has changed its third-party use policy, which makes it very difficult for specialized software or the application's own search engine to process corpora of tweets. In any case, as our work has a qualitative exploratory orientation, we limit ourselves here to a selection of 100 random tweets for each of the themes (gender equality, migration and climate change policies).

After cataloguing and tagging them, the texts were processed using AntConc v.4.0.5 software to extract a list of the most frequent lexical units by profile. From the obtained tables, we disregarded function words (i.e., prepositions, articles, subordinators, coordinators, modal verbs), and kept only content words (nouns, verbs, adjectives and adverbs).

Subsequently, we analysed the tweets to identify and describe the most prominent conceptual frameworks that underpin the discourse of these network users, and which are directly linked, albeit in a more exaggerated way, in the style of the grotesque reflection of a distorting mirror, to the slogans set out by Vox from its official accounts.

4. The Conceptual Frameworks of Radical Discourse on Twitter

In the analysis section, we will examine three fundamental issues: (1) The reactions of the far right to the Law of Guarantees of Sexual Freedom, which legally protects the consent of women to sexual intercourse; (2) the migration issue (borders, arrival of immigrants and its correlation for the right with organized crime), and (3) the environmental policies implemented by the government to combat climate change. We are primarily interested in describing the starting frameworks in which the party's arguments are constructed, and then in tracing their impact on the accounts of high-impact users on Twitter.

4.1 Gender Equality Policies: The "Only Yes is Yes" ("Solo Sí es Sí") Law

Vox's appeal to the "Law of Guarantees of Sexual Freedom", popularly known as the "'Only yes is yes' Law", presented in December 2022 by Vox vice-president Javier Ortega Smith, legal vice-president Marta Castro and the spokesperson for Equality in the Congress of Deputies, Carla Toscano, includes three main frameworks:

- The law is a legal aberration that criminalizes men and undermines the presumption of innocence.
- The law does not really protect women, nor will it solve the problem of sexual assault. It is designed to make it easier for rapists and paedophiles to go out on the streets.
- It is an ideological law of the left that seeks to impose the single thinking of gender ideology and radical feminism.

As Alcaide Lara (2022, p. 287) points out, it is on social networks such as this one that

> They [Vox leaders] deploy their battery of discourteous activities against feminism, which they turn into fallacious arguments to manipulate by presenting a society that is made up of feminists (*radicals, supremacists* and *feminazis*) and women. To do so, they use *ad personam* fallacies, based on physical traits, subjectively valued behaviours, etc., identifiable with those made against the suffragettes of the late 19th and early 20th centuries.

In this breeding ground, an even more radical turn in the Twitter messages of the accounts that make up our sample was to be expected. In the following examples, we see how the selected profiles address the issue along the same lines as the frameworks defended by Vox, although on this occasion without euphemisms, directly insulting the Government (Ex. 1) for promoting the Law; and especially (in a serious and explicit way) the Minister Irene Montero (partner of former Podemos leader Pablo Iglesias, nicknamed "el coletas"), by resorting to the *ad personam* fallacy, as we see in Ex. 2.

1 Bueno pues mañana tengo cita en el Notario para firmar el papelito del #SoloSiesSi para que ninguna #feminazi me acuse de violador por meterla. #LeySoloSiesSi #StopFeminazis #DisfrutenLoVotado #GobiernoProgresista (@PerroFlauta81, 25/08/2022)

[Well, tomorrow I have an appointment at the Notary to sign the #SoloSiesSi paper so that no #feminazi accuses me of being a rapist for putting her in. #LeySoloSiesSi #StopFeminazis #EnjoyYourVote #ProgressiveGov (@PerroFlauta81, 25/08/2022)]

2 Esta cerda, desde que se la folló el coletas y luego la dejó por la concubina Montero, ha ido dando tumbos vomitando toda su basura de feminazi despechada. A esta asquerosa le gusta que a los niños se les toque en los colegios. Es una pervertida. Y fea (@VAlegrame, 20/6/2023, 23,3k followers, 1048 likes)

[This sow, ever since she was fucked by pigtails and then dumped by the concubine Montero, has been stumbling around spewing all her scorned feminazi rubbish. This filthy bitch likes children to be touched in schools. She's a pervert. And ugly (@VAlegrame, 20/6/2023, 23.3k followers, 1048 likes)]

3 "La ley del 'solo sí es sí' es una aberración jurídica que atenta contra la presunción de inocencia y la igualdad ante la ley. La izquierda radical quiere imponer su ideología a costa de los derechos fundamentales de los ciudadanos. #LeyDelSíEsSí #LibertadSexual #Justicia" (@TeamFacha, 16/11/2022)

4 [The 'only yes is yes' law is a legal aberration that undermines the presumption of innocence and equality before the law. The radical left wants to impose its ideology at the expense of the fundamental rights of citizens. #OnlyYesIsYes #SexualLiberty #Justice" (@TeamFacha, 16/11/2022).]

El mismo día que se aprueba la ley del #SoloSiesSi conocemos otra denuncia falsa por parte de una mujer, que llevó a la detención de un hombre inocente (@pfbarbadillo, 26/8/2022)

[On the same day that the #OnlyYesIsYes law is passed we learn of another false report by a woman, which led to the arrest of an innocent man (@pfbarbadillo, 26/8/2022)]

5 Las mujeres en España nunca han vivido más inseguras. Más de 400 rebajas de condena y decenas de delincuentes excarcelados por la chapuza legislativa del #SoloSíEsSí. @vox_es lo advirtió, y ahora nos vienen con que no se podía saber. @IreneMontero, cierre al salir. #SoloQuedaVox

[Women in Spain have never been more insecure. More than 400 sentence reductions and dozens of criminals released from prison due to the legislative botch-up of #SoloSíEsSí. @vox_es warned about it, and now they're telling us that we couldn't know. @IreneMontero, closing on the way out. #OnlyVoxRemains]

These results show that the most frequent words in the text are the proper names of Vox (4.25%, 17 occurrences) and Irene Montero (the government's minister for Equality, 2.25%), as well as the hashtag #SoloSiEsSi (3%, 12 occurrences), which refers to the law that is criticized in the messages. It is also observed that there are many words related to sexual offences, such as *aggressors*, *sexual* or *abuse*, which indicates that it is a sensitive and controversial topic. In addition, there are some pejorative or insulting terms, such as *feminazi*, *traitor* or *trash*, which denote a hostile and offensive attitude towards the government and its allies.

Among the hashtags most frequently mentioned by the users in the sample, the descriptive #SoloSoloSíesSí stands out, but also other clearly critical hashtags such as #IreneMonteroDimisión, #HayQueEcharlos, #QueTeVoteTxapote, #GobiernodeInútiles, #ElPeorGobiernoDeLaHistoria, #LeyDeLaCensura, #LeyDeLaVergüenza, #feminazi(s), #LeyDeLaInquisiciónFeminista and #SoloQuedaVox.

4.2 *Immigration Policies*

We have already had the opportunity to analyse this issue in previous works, focusing on the treatment of unaccompanied immigrant minors (Sánchez-García, 2022). The most recurrent conceptual frameworks were:

- Immigrant minors are criminals;
- Immigrant minors are violent;
- Immigrant minors are illegal and should be expelled;
- There are too many Muslims in Spain (Muslims are invading Spain);
- Immigrant minors are subsidized by the Government;
- An "iron fist" is needed/Only Vox can solve the problem.

In a similar way, in another article on the reception treatment of Afghan refugees in Vox networks (Sosinski & Sánchez-García, 2022), the strategic cleavage that portrays migrants as a "threat to freedoms" was repeated, highlighting Christians, and using the slogan "There is not enough room for everyone". The most important thing is that already then, we could detect a more aggressive and stark tone in the tweets of the supporters with respect to the official accounts.

6 Condenado a 1 año de prisión un gambiano por seguir a una joven hasta su casa en Zaragoza y manosearla en el portal. Esta es la basura con la que están inundando España. A estos salvajes habría que encerrarlos de por vida, pero en su país de origen. @edgar__es (27/7/2023).

[A Gambian sentenced to 1 year in prison for following a young woman to her home in Zaragoza and groping her in the doorway. This is the garbage with which they are flooding Spain. These savages should be locked up for life, but in their country of origin. @edgar__es (27/7/2023).]

7 Francia expulsa a inmigrantes nacionalizados delincuentes … y no pasa nada. VOX propone expulsar a los nacionalizados que delincan y todos se escandalizan y nos llaman xenófobos. Que no te intimiden … vota sentido común, vota VOX el voto seguro. (@GrouchoMarcos, 23/5/2023).

[France expels criminal nationalized immigrants¼ and nothing happens. VOX proposes to expel the nationalized who commit crimes and everyone is scandalized and calls us xenophobic. Don't be intimidated¼ vote common sense, vote VOX the safe vote. (@GrouchoMarcos, 23/5/2023).]

8 Las medidas que tomaría VOX, si gobiernan, con las bandas latinas que actuaron ayer en el metro de Madrid (@VitoQuiles, 27/3/2023).

[The measures that VOX would take, if they govern, with the Latino gangs that performed yesterday in the Madrid metro (@VitoQuiles, 27/3/2023).]

9 Ayuso y los progres niegan la realidad que denuncia Vox sobre la falta de seguridad en muchas ciudades por la proliferación de bandas y mafias de origen extranjero. Sino mirad esta pelea entre bandas latinas que hubo ayer en el Metro de Madrid. (@capTercio, 27/3/2023).

[Ayuso and the 'lefties' deny the reality that Vox denounces about the lack of security in many cities due to the proliferation of gangs and mafias of foreign origin. If not, look at this fight between Latino gangs that took place yesterday in the Madrid Metro. (@capTercio, 27/3/2023).]

10 Después de meses vertiendo mentiras sobre Vox, sacando un libro acusándolos de ser una secta, de pedir el voto para el PP y que no voten a Vox, el se va a Miami un mes [imagen del periodista Federico Jiménez Losantos] porque está forrado de millones de euros y tu pepero te quedas con los menas en tu barrio. Imbécil. (@JavierO66080535 26/7/2023)

[After months spreading lies about Vox, taking out a book accusing them of being a sect, asking for a vote for the PP and not voting for Vox, he is going to Miami for a month [image by journalist Federico Jiménez Losantos] because It is lined with millions of euros and you, *pepero,* stays with the *menas* [immigrant minors] in your neighborhood. Fool. (@JavierO66080535 26/7/2023)]

As we can see, the focus here is not only on unaccompanied minors, but the question of alleged violence in the neighbourhoods of large cities is emerging due to the proliferation of Latino gangs, which, according to the users studied, only Vox can cope with. In addition, immigration is also linked to the threat against women's sexual freedom, and very harsh disqualifiers are used to refer to foreigners, such as "savages" or "garbage".

On a purely quantitative level, it is curious that these supposed private users so openly show their sympathy for Vox, to the point of being the most frequent word in our corpus (5.83%, 12 occurrences), followed by Spain (3.88%), borders (3.40%), Moors (2.91%), illegals (2.43%) and immigrants (2.43%).

4.3 Environmental Conspiracy: The "Climate Scam"

The selection of tweets coincides with the same frameworks in defending a position directly contrary to the scientific evidence of climate change and the measures proposed by the UN 2030 Agenda. This is also an evident ideological affinity with the Vox party, which defines itself as nativist, conservative and anti-communist. The text therefore reflects an anti-globalist and denialist vision of climate change, considered as a fraud or scam, and in turn, a threat to the sovereignty and development of Spain. Also noteworthy are the fallacious arguments, misinformation inputs and disqualifications to delegitimize the defenders of climate action and the media in favour of the "official line" of "single thought". In sum, the underlying conceptual frameworks for this topic are:

- Climate change is a hoax of the Government and supranational organizations;
- The defenders of policies against climate change are a sect that threatens freedoms;
- Environmental policies only bring misery for companies and workers.

From our corpus, we selected the following extremely enlightening tweets:

11 Empieza el tráfico de agua!! No les funcionó el timo COVID, ni el timo climático. Ahora sí les va a funcionar! Solo VOX va contra la agenda satánica y el demoníaco globalismo. Solo queda VOX!!! (@DoloresVaquero, 15/6/2023)

[The water traffic begins!! The COVID scam did not work for them, nor did the climate scam. Now it will work for you! Only VOX goes against the satanic agenda and the demonic globalism. We only have Vox!!! (@DoloresVaquero, 15/6/2023)]

12 Y en esto también estoy de acuerdo con Vox: el timo del cambio climático, que ha empobrecido a los españoles con impuestos innecesarios (@ramonarcusa, 10/7/2023).

[And in this I also agree with Vox: the scam of climate change, which has impoverished the Spanish with unnecessary taxes (@ramonarcusa, 10/7/2023).]

13 La niña del exorcista y portavoz del timo del cambio climático ... nos implora salvar ... a los bancos... ver para creer 😅 [enlaza video con declaraciones descontextualizadas de Greta Thunberg] (@Baba_vox, 25/4/2023).

[The exorcist's girl and spokesperson for the climate change scam¼ implores us to save¼ the banks¼ seeing is believing 😅 [link video with decontextualized statements by Greta Thunberg] (@Baba_vox, 25/4/2023).]

14 Los chorizos de Bruselas que se están llenando los bolsillos con el timo del clima climático. Espero que VOX @juan_ggallardo no ceda ni medio mm. (BECAES_, 11/7/2023).

[The crooks of Brussels that are filling their pockets with the scam of the climatic climate. I hope VOX @juan_ggallardo doesn't give in even half an inch. (BECAES_, 11/7/2023).]

15 El PP se une a VOX en Andalucía para pedir la derogación de leyes rurales sobre el cambio climático. El PP se une a VOX en el Parlamento de Andalucía para pedir la derogación de leyes rurales sobre el cambio climático. Por fin abren los ojos #PrimeroEspaña

[PP joins VOX in Andalusia to request the repeal of rural laws on climate change. The PP joins VOX in the Andalusian Parliament to request the repeal of rural laws on climate change. Finally open their eyes #SpainFirst]

The statistics are especially revealing; applying a ranking of the most frequent words, the most prominent in our selection is *scam*, with a percentage of 10.05% and 19 occurrences, followed by Vox (9.52%, 16 occurrences), *agenda* (3.17%, 6 occurrences), and to a lesser extent (less than 2%): *millions, experiment, temperature, change, globalism*. Among the hashtags, apart from the recurring call to vote for Vox, #PrimeroEspaña (#SpainFirst) stands out, and it is no coincidence: it seeks to correlate the abandonment of environmental policies with an improvement in expectations for companies that will be able to exploit natural resources without restrictions (for them it is, of course, a matter of priorities).

5. Conclusion

The results obtained show that the radical discourse of Vox supporters is based on a series of conceptual frameworks that emphasize polarization, antagonism, and the use of fallacies to mobilize its followers and delegitimize its adversaries. These frameworks mainly refer to three themes: (1)

Gender equality policies, (2) immigration policies and (3) environmental policies. In all of them, Vox is positioned as the sole defender of the sovereignty, identity, and development of Spain in the face of external and internal threats represented by corrupt elites, immigrants, Muslims, feminists, environmentalists, or the mass media. Vox's followers also present an aggressive, provocative, ironic and defiant communication style on Twitter/X, which uses misinformation, fake news, conspiracy theories or disqualifications to delegitimize defenders of climate action and the media communication supporters of the "official line" of "monolithic thinking".

Based on what has been discussed here, we can conclude that the messages from the users examined fully coincide with Vox's argument, although they are significantly more radical and harsher than the originals from the party's accounts. For example, *ad personam* fallacies and personal disqualifications predominate (especially harsh if the political opponent is a woman, such as Minister Irene Montero, the Secretary of State for Equality or Vice President Yolanda Díaz, for example), which are manifested above all in cruel contempt towards minorities, especially the proclamations against unaccompanied immigrant minors and the LGTBI collective. Although Vox, through the party's official accounts, launches more subtle messages, they automatically become hate speech in the tweets of its supporters.

One might think that perhaps it is the party that tries to accommodate its tweets to the majority opinion or feeling of its militants or followers regarding certain issues, but it seems to be the opposite: The party elaborates its electoral program or publishes a message on the networks and, immediately afterwards, their followers replicate the argument very "opportunely", to give it greater reach and impact.

Such an explosive cocktail, in the hands of intermediaries with many followers, ends up leading to harsh messages from private users, most of them very young, probably victims of misinformation:

> I just voted for Vox! Sanchismo is over, goodbye to chemtrails and the 2030 agenda. Muslims to their country and menas too. Goodbye to the inverts and the squatters. At last it will be possible to compliment women and the family returns.
>
> (@adrianxdd_, 23/7/2023)

As we can see, a single tweet summarizes the main features of the hate speech that Vox spreads, through hundreds of supporters who are especially mobilized (for whatever reasons, whether ideological or economic), until reaching the common voters. As we have already defended in a previous work (Sánchez-García, 2021), it is urgent to develop educational and media strategies to promote critical thinking, respect for diversity and dialogue between citizens in the face of hate speech and polarization.

With this first analysis, we have tried to contribute to the knowledge of the phenomenon of European radical right-wing populism in Spain, as well as to the study of the role of social networks as a tool for political communication and social activism. We consider it essential to continue advancing in the investigation of the discursive dynamics that are generated on Twitter between political leaders and their followers, as well as the social and political effects that this can have on public opinion and democracy.

Note

1 In 2021, Vox presented the text *Agenda España*, in which it reformulated its previous program to focus on 20 points, including "equality among Spaniards", "the unity of Spain", the fight against the "globalist Agenda" and "ideological indoctrination of separatism and globalism". As Sales Gelabert (2023, p. 112) points out: "The ideological framework remains centered on a combination of neoliberalism with its defense of property as the basis of freedom, nativism and conservative values. The presence of nativism, the identification of immigration with delinquency, authoritarianism and neoliberal economic proposals continues".

References

Alcaide Lara, E. R. (2022). La imagen de la mujer en Vox: El discurso antifeminista de la "derecha radical" en España. *Discurso & Sociedad*, *16*(2), 275–302.

Aparicio, M. F. (2022). Interpretable and effortless techniques for social network analysis. Doctoral Thesis. University of Granada. Retrieved from https://digibug.ugr.es/bitstream/handle/10481/79151/82061%281%29.pdf?sequence=4&isAllowed=y.

Ávila Martín, M. C. (2018). La caracterización lingüística del discurso en Twitter: #TAT Granada 2017. In A. García Manso (Coord.). *Aportaciones de vanguardia en la investigación actual* (pp. 31–40). Madrid: Tecnos.

Camargo Fernández, L. (2021). El nuevo orden discursivo de la extrema derecha española: de la deshumanización a los bulos en un corpus de tuits de Vox sobre la inmigración. *Cultura, Lenguaje y Representación*, *26*, 63–82.

Ferreira, C. (2019). Vox como representante de la derecha radical en España: Un estudio sobre su ideología. *Revista Española de Ciencia Política*, *51*, 73–98.

Herrero Izquierdo, J., Reguero Sanz, I., Berdón Prieto, P., & Martín Jiménez, V. (2022). La estrategia del odio: Polarización y enfrentamiento partidista en Twitter durante las elecciones a la Asamblea de Madrid de 2021. *Prisma Social*, *39*, 183–212.

Milmo, D. (2021). Twitter admits bias in algorithm for rightwing politicians and news outlets. *The Guardian*, 22/10/2021. Retrieved from https://www.theguardian.com/technology/2021/oct/22/twitter-admits-bias-in-algorithm-for-rightwing-politicians-and-news-outlets.

Mudde, C. (2021). *La ultraderecha hoy*. Barcelona: Paidós.

Mudde, C., & Kaltwasser, C. R. (2012). Populism and (liberal) democracy: A framework for analysis. In C. Mudde & C. Rovira Kaltwasser (Eds.), *Populism in Europe and the Americas: Threat or corrective for democracy?* (pp. 1–26). Cambridge: Cambridge University Press.

Norris, P. (2005). *Radical right: Voters and parties in the electoral market*. Cambridge: Cambridge University Press.

Oleaque-Moreno, J. M. (2020). El discurso en positivo de Vox: Los medios difundidos en Twitter por la extrema derecha, *Cuadernos AISPI*, *16*, 45–62

Oleaque Moreno, J., & Pelliser Rosell, N. (2021). Vox frente a Europa: La derecha radical en Twitter durante las Elecciones Europeas de 2019. *Revista de Investigación Lingüística*, *24*, 23–46.

Ollero, D. (2021): Twitter califica a Vox de "ideología extrema" y dice que "amplifica más a la derecha" en un estudio interno. *El Mundo*. 22/10/2021. Retrieved from https://www.elmundo.es/tecnologia/2021/10/23/6172ddede4d4d8c0328b459f.html.

Pérez Colomé, J. (2020). De Vox a Unidas Podemos: Las cuentas de "bots" se reparten entre todos los partidos. *El País*. 4/5/2020. Retrieved from https://elpais.com/tecnologia/2020-05-03/de-vox-a-unidas-podemos-las-cuentas-de-bots-se-reparten-entre-todos-los-partidos.html.

Pérez Colomé, J. (2023). "Inclinación de derechas": Un macroestudio confirma que la desinformación de Facebook la consumen los conservadores". *El País*. 27/7/2023. Retrieved from https://elpais.com/tecnologia/2023-07-27/inclinacion-de-derechas-un-macroestudio-confirma-que-la-desinformacion-de-facebook-la-consumen-los-conservadores.html?ssm=TW_CM.

Pereira-Kohatsu, J. C., Quijano-Sánchez, L., Liberatore, F., & Camacho-Collados, M. (2019). Detecting and monitoring hate speech in Twitter. *Sensors*, *19*. https://doi.org/10.3390/s19214654.

Rama, J., Zanotti, L, Turnbull-Dugarte, S., & Santana, A. (2021). *Vox. The rise of the Spanish populist radical right*. London: Routledge.

Rydren, J. (2017). Radical right-wing parties in Europe. What's populism got to do with it? *Journal of Language and Politics*, *16*(4), 485–496.

Sales Gelabert, T. (2023). Reproducción, campo de batalla en la esfera pública: El discurso antifeminista de la nueva derecha radical neoliberal española. *Revista de Estudios Políticos*, *199*, 101–131.

Sánchez-García, F. J. (2021). El lenguaje xenófobo en el discurso de los adolescentes en redes sociales. Análisis y propuestas de trabajo en el aula. *Didáctica. Lengua y Literatura*, *33*, 121–131.

Sánchez-García, F. J. (2022). Prender la mecha del odio. El discurso sobre inmigración de los seguidores de Vox en Twitter. In L. R. Romero Domínguez & N. Sánchez Gey Valenzuela (Eds.), *Sociedad digital, comunicación y conocimiento: Retos para la ciudadanía en un mundo global* (pp. 339–358). Madrid: Dykinson.

Sosinski, M., & Sánchez-García, F. J. (2022). Efecto invasión. Populismo e ideología en el discurso político español sobre los refugiados. El caso de Vox. *Discurso & Sociedad*, *16*(1), 149–172.

Tuñón-Navarro, J., & Bouzas-Blanco, A. (2023). Extrema derecha europea en Twitter. Análisis de la estrategia digital comunicativa de Vox y Lega durante las elecciones europeas de 2014 y 2019. *Revista Mediterránea de Comunicación/Mediterranean Journal of Communication*, *14*(1), 241–262.

Urmeneta Arbusà, M. (2022). *Corrientes de opinión en Twitter durante el 'procés': agenda, actores, polarización y desinformación alrededor de las elecciones catalanas de 2017. Tesis doctoral*. Barcelona: Universitat Autònoma de Barcelona. http://hdl.handle.net/10803/674513.

Van Dijk, T. A. (2003). *Ideología y discurso*. Barcelona: Ariel.

Velázquez García-Talavera, T. (2019). El populismo radical de derecha en Europa: discurso, apropiación de significantes y desplazamiento de significados. *DeSignis. Publicación de la Federación Latinoamericana de Semiótica*, *31*, 137–155.

Viejo, M. (2021). Lo de Ponzano y el PP y lo de los 'bots' de apoyo a Vox. *El País*. 26/4/2021. Retrieved from https://elpais.com/espana/elecciones-madrid/2021-04-26/lo-de-ponzano-y-el-pp-y-lo-de-los-bots-de-apoyo-a-vox.html.

Wodak, R. (2019). The boundaries of what can be said have shifted: An expert interview with Ruth Wodak. *Discourse & Society*, *31*(2), 235–244.

6 Hijab Controversy in Iran

Sentiment Analysis of #MahsaAmini Tweets

Ruth Breeze and Saqlain Hassan

1. Introduction

The hijab plays a key role in Muslim women's dress around the world. However, the question of the freedom to wear it tends to spark fierce controversy. In some western countries, the debate has centred on the extent to which women should be permitted to wear the hijab (Syed, 2013; Breeze, 2014; González Ruiz & Izquierdo Alegría, 2014), while in countries with Muslim majorities clashes often arise between groups opposing the hijab and conservative groups wishing to enforce it. One such case in which this issue came to the attention of public opinion worldwide is the recent incident in which 22-year-old Iranian Mahsa Amini was arrested for wearing the hijab in an inappropriate way and subsequently died in custody. This, and the protests that followed, generated a huge response in social media, often involving direct antagonism between campaigners for women's rights and supporters of the Iranian government and leaders. It thus provides an interesting case for researching polarisation in social media in a non-western context. In what follows, we provide some essential background to the incident itself, before describing the study design, data sample and analysis.

2. Background

2.1 The Hijab in Iran

Iran is home to one of the world's oldest civilisations, dating back to 7,000 B.C.; its strategic position and natural resources give it an important position on the world stage (Sabine, 2017). However, its recent history has been marred by conflict, as its rulers veered between westernising and traditional Islamic tendencies. Back in 1930, the then Shah of Iran Muhammad Reza Pahlavi launched a series of policies to modernise the country, including measures to ban women from wearing hijabs, since these were

DOI: 10.4324/9781003457381-7

understood in western culture to signify women's oppression (Hoodfar, 1999, pp. 15–16). Women who were reluctant to comply were forced to remove their hijabs or ordered to stay at home (Hamzehei, 2014). Reza's ambition to modernise his country's image in this way was welcomed by more modern women, but also opposed by many more traditional women, who felt ashamed of leaving their houses without a veil on their heads (Zahedi, 2007, pp. 75–78). This trend continued under the Pahlavi dynasty in the 1950s–1970s, when Iranian policies appeared to lean towards the West. However, since the Iranian revolution of 1979, Iran has adopted anti-western attitudes and become increasingly conservative towards female dress and women's rights, restricting women's participation mainly to the domestic sphere. From that moment on, the hijab has been a mandatory part of Iranian women's clothing for all types of occasions. The Islamic Republic of Ian banned all freedom given to women in terms of veiling and imposed strict rules according to Sharia law; the rules described in the Holy Quran and the books of Hadith were used as a justification for these restrictions, with strict punishments for those who disobeyed. The hijab law was subsequently enshrined in Iranian legislation in 1984 (Afshar, 1996; Hoodfar, 1999; Bahramitash, 2013; Azadeh, 2010).

2.2 *Events Surrounding the Death of Mahsa Amini*

Mahsa Amini was a 22-year-old Iranian university student of Kurdish ethnicity who was arrested for not wearing her hijab correctly while visiting her brother in Teheran. According to news reports, the Iranian police's Guidance Patrol, generally known as the "Morality Police", who are responsible for checking on women's clothing to ensure that they follow the prescribed rules, took Mahsa Amini into custody on 13th September 2022, on the grounds that she was not wearing her hijab in accordance with government standards (Rogg, 2022). According to her family, in the detention centre, she was beaten and later taken to hospital in an ambulance, where she was declared dead on 16th September 2022 (Askew, 2022). The Ministry for Internal Affairs denied all the allegations and declared it a case of a heart attack (Ministry of Foreign Affairs, Iran, 2022).

Protests began in Iran shortly after the news of her death broke, starting at the hospital in Teheran and soon spreading to other parts of the country. According to Iran Human Rights (2022), at least 185 people were killed in the subsequent rioting. The print and broadcasting media gave the event wide coverage in Iran and beyond, and social media users joined in on Twitter by trending #MahsaAmini. The Ayatollah's Regime thus became a focus for criticism worldwide; as one reporter stated, "The death of Mahsa Amini is a wake-up call for Iranian people" (Abdelghany, 21st September 2022). However, social media are open to all, and supporters of the regime soon started to join in, with the result that the online debate became increasingly polarised.

3. Design of Study

For the reasons outlined above, the Mahsa Amini incident presents an interesting test case for analysing polarisation in social media. In particular, it presents an opportunity to investigate the dominant patterns of sentiment and different logics operating within the pro- and anti-protest groups. In what follows, we first provide a brief outline of methodologies for researching sentiment in Twitter, and then an overview of research on polarisation in the same medium.

3.1 Researching Sentiment and Emotion in Twitter: Methodological Issues

Automated analysis of social media data generally either relies on lexicon-based approaches or machine learning. Lexicon-based sentiment analysis approaches are based on a previously constructed list of words that can be used to identify words in the dataset with a positive, negative or neutral valence or axiology (Peker, Ozkaraca, & Sasar, 2018). Machine learning sentiment analysis approaches, on the other hand, broadly involve the application of a classifier trained to recognise positivity, negativity or neutrality on a dataset that has previously been classified (Giachanou & Crestani, 2016; Ishak et al., 2020); the software computes the semantic relatedness between the words in the test text, and generates a set of labels using various models, vector space or neural net models (Jacobs, 2019).

Similar approaches have also been adopted to conduct more detailed analyses in which specific emotions are identified in the dataset, again through lexicon-based or machine learning approaches or the combination of both (Sintsova, Musat, & Pu, 2014). Where specific emotions are sought, it is usual to work with broad classifications such as Ekman's (1992) six basic emotions (i.e., joy, anger, fear, sadness, surprise and disgust).

When addressing Twitter in particular, previous authors have discussed a number of problems with the application of automated analysis (Giachanou & Crestani, 2016). The first is the nature of the tweet: as very short texts, they do not follow the same patterns as found in longer pieces of writing and require special treatment. Nevertheless, some authors argue that it proves easier to identify sentiment or emotion in tweets than in longer texts (Bermingham & Smeaton, 2010), perhaps because a single valence or emotion can be assigned to a very short text, while teasing out the different valuations or emotions occurring in longer samples of language is more complex. Other salient issues when handling Twitter data include the frequent presence of unorthodox spelling (either typos, or words deliberately misspelled to create special effects, such as through emphatic lengthening), and the considerable presence of noise (e.g., web addresses, hashtags or emoticons). However, automated data cleaning and the use of some machine learning techniques enable the current generation of sentiment analysis programs to overcome some of these difficulties.

Finally, both lexicon-based and Machine Learning approaches are still subject to limitations: The former depend on the appropriacy and comprehensiveness of the lexicon used; the latter depend on the features selected as important and the relevance of the training they receive (Giachanou & Crestani, 2016). Issues common to both that remain to be resolved are the difficulty of detecting irony or sarcasm, and the related problem of decontextualisation (Hernández Farías & Rosso, 2017).

3.2 Researching Sentiment in Twitter: Polarisation

Twitter has long been regarded as a place for public debate. However, across its 17-year lifespan there has been an increasing realisation that its inherent dynamics also tends to further polarisation and social division. Within Twitter, communities arise through processes of adequation and discursive alignment, leading to the emergence of distinct collective identities (Bucholtz & Hall, 2005). Such social media groups are often bound together informally by particular hashtags (Darius & Urquhart, 2021; Breeze & Gintsburg, 2023). In many cases, the group behaviours they develop take on the characteristics of tribalism (North, Piwek, & Joinson, 2020), in which collective identities are reinforced by ritual exchange of slurs and insults, and by strong in-group solidarity (Breeze, 2019).

However, not all issues spark the same kind of response on Twitter. Recent research on polarisation in Twitter has shown that different types of controversy or social debate trigger different patterns of response in terms of both the types, valence and intensity of the emotive language used (Banks et al., 2022). Where issues related to gender and/or ethnicity are at stake, particular intensity is typical when both attacking and defending the protagonists (Esposito & Breeze, 2022). In different countries, similar social controversies may give rise to different patterns of polarised response (de Rosa et al., 2021). Although some of these claims may seem rather unoriginal, some research on polarisation in Twitter has brought more subtle patterns to light. For example, in the case of Covid-related Twitter controversies in Australia, Graham et al. (2021) found different logics underlying tweeting tendencies on the right and the left of the political spectrum:

whilst right-wing activists tended to work with sympathetic politicians and media, left-wing activists mainly criticised the coverage provided by news media.

4. Corpus and Methodology

The current study is a corpus-based sentiment analysis of tweets posted after the death of Mahsa Amini (trending as #MahsaAmini). The researchers used #MahsaAmini as a search term to use the Twitter API key to retrieve the trending tweets posted after Amini's arrest and death and then repeated the process several weeks after this incident to obtain more tweets and responses. Our final corpus comprised 5,000 tweets (106,781 tokens) to be analysed using Orange Software (Demsar et al., 2013). These were separated manually into two corpora: pro-protest tweets (the overwhelming majority) and anti-protest tweets (121 tweets identified as opposing the protests and defending the regime). Although the tweets were all in English, the manual analysis of the account names, hashtags and references suggests that almost all were from Muslim countries, particularly Iran itself. Twitter is an important social medium in countries where government bans on social media are frequent. In 2022, Twitter use rose in Iran from 0.45% to 10.49% of social media consumption after Instagram was banned during the protests in September 2022, falling from 89.22% to 18.4% (Statcounter, 2023). Twitter is also important in the neighbouring countries of Pakistan (where Twitter regularly accounts for around 15% of use) and Afghanistan (where Twitter rose to 15.4% in October 2022); in both cases, for the whole of 2022, Twitter was the second largest social medium after Facebook.

For the present study, Orange software was selected.[1] This is classified as a hybrid system combining lexicon-based analysis and machine learning, which has proven reasonably accurate at identifying sentiment and emotion in social media. Various other affordances are available within this software package: (1) data-mining, which enables users to generate the corpus easily by retrieving recent data from online sources such as Twitter or news media once appropriate human input is provided; (2) options for data visualisation; and (3) easy reference access back into the dataset to view tweets classified into a particular category.

The current study was conducted with Orange 3.34.0, which uses Python as its main programming language. To obtain an initial overview, we used the Word Cloud function, which cleans the data (by removing numbers and special characters such as hashtags) and displays tokens based on frequencies in the dataset. We then used the Tweet Profiler function, which offers both emotion analysis and sentiment analysis. For emotion analysis, it applies three possible filters, which correspond to different psychological models of basic emotions, namely the Ekman model (based on the six basic emotions: anger, fear, happiness, surprise, disgust and sadness) (Ekman, 1992), the Plutchik model (based on eight emotions: anger, disgust, fear, joy, sadness, surprise, trust and anticipation) (Plutchik, 1980), and the POMS model (based on six different dimensions characterising negative mood swings: Tension-Anxiety, Depression-Dejection, Anger-Hostility, Vigor-Activity, Fatigue-Inertia and Confusion-Bewilderment) (McNair, Lorr, & Droppleman, 1971). Since the POMS model is primarily intended as a measure of psychological distress in clinical situations, it is not generally used for social media analysis and was not to our present purpose. For sentiment analysis, Orange relies on sentiment lexicons and machine learning (Jacobs, 2019) to attribute negative, neutral and positive scores (a negative value would be assigned to tweets with negatively connoted elements, such as "so heartbreaking", while a positive value indicates an upbeat tone, such as "salute to all courageous Iranian people") to the tweets in a given dataset. We used this in combination with the emotion analysis based on the Ekman model to obtain an overview of the positivity and negativity in the tweets containing each of the six basic emotions.

Finally, for qualitative analysis, we used the Data Table feature, which allows us to access the exact contents of tweets, with author names, dates, as well as positive and negative scores and emotion classification.

5. Results and Discussion

In what follows, we present an overview of the data, followed by sentiment and emotion analysis using the different functions in *Tweet Profiler* and *Data Tables*.

5.1 *Pro-protest Tweets: Overview of Data*

The most frequent tokens and n-grams that appeared with the node word *MahsaAmini* (which appeared 5,035 times in the corpus) included *Iranprotest2022* (1,005), *kill* (692), *Iran revolt* (462), *regime* (275), *fight* (241), *death* (229), *massacre* (193), *murder* (161), and *kill Mahsa* (146) which provide an indication of the negatively connoted lexical content. At the same time, words such as *freedom* (477), *Iranian-lives-matter* (129) and *Iranian-women* (122) appear frequently, indicating solidarity with the women protestors in Iran.

5.2 *Pro-protest Tweets: Emotion Analysis*

Here we present the results of the emotion analysis of the pro-protest tweets using the two potentially relevant filters: Ekman and Plutchik.

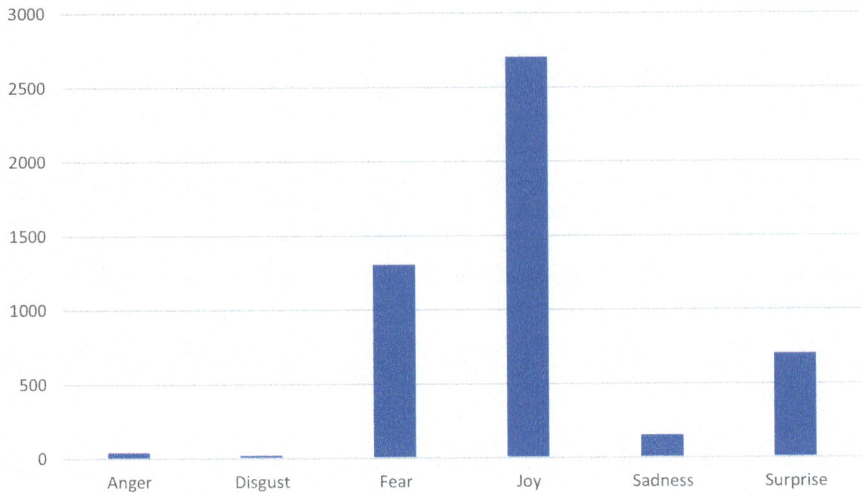

Figure 6.1 Profiles of emotion in the pro-protest tweets using the Ekman filter.

5.3 Ekman Model

Figure 6.1 displays the results using the six-emotion Ekman (multiclass) filter in both variables and subgroups categories. The prevailing emotion detected is joy, with praise of the women's protest against the regime or the Morality Police. On the other hand, the tweets were also classified as containing anger, surprise, disgust and sadness.

Twitter users expressed their solidarity with Iranian women in different ways, such as by cutting their hair and posting their videos, or by taking off their hijabs. These acts spurred outpourings of praise and solidarity from other users (example 1):

1 "Let go off my hijab in 2014. Happy to see more and more women do it in 2022. Power to all the women in #iran. Nothing angers middle eastern patriarchy more than a woman comfy in her own skin". (03/10/2022)

5.4 Plutchik Model

When the Plutchik model was used, we obtained the results displayed in Figure 6.2.

This proves an interesting contrast to Figure 6.1, since the "sadness" dimension is much greater, while "fear" is reduced. The addition of the "trust" dimension may account for the relative reduction in the category of "joy" (see conclusions, and Benítez-Castro & Hidalgo-Tenorio, 2019).

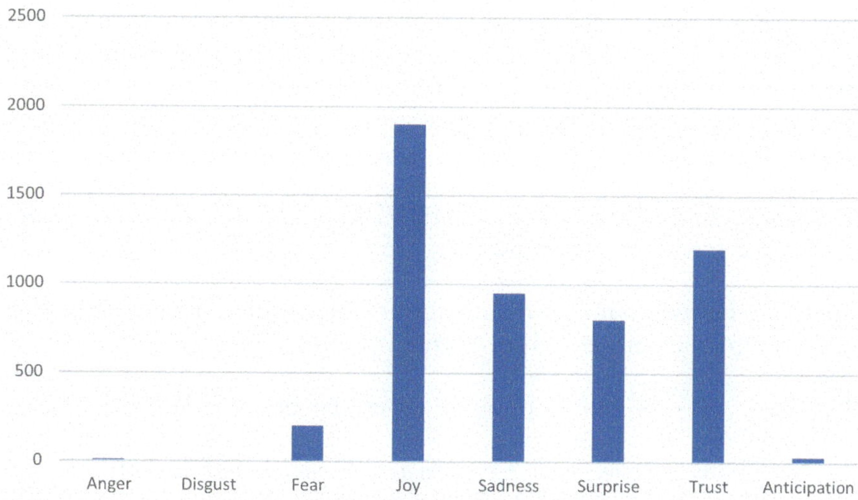

Figure 6.2 Profiles of emotion in the pro-protest tweets using the Plutchik filter.

5.5 *Pro-protest Tweets: Sentiment Analysis*

The Tweet Profiler feature also enables us to use the Analysis of Variance tool to split statistically all the occurrences of the negative, positive and neutral valued tweets. The Profiler provides the statistics for all the negative and positive tweets and their emotions classified by the Ekman filter, on a graph on which the left shade from the middle of each category represents the negative-valued tweets while the right shade from the middle represents the positive-valued tweets. All the neutral-values tweets fall in the middle (0) of the graph. Interestingly, in this dataset the emotion categories "disgust", "anger" and "sadness" account for the most negative-valued tweets, whereas "fear" appears to be associated with positive valence.

5.6 *Pro-protest Tweets: Qualitative Analysis*

Using the *Data Table* feature, we retrieved the tweet dataset in one Excel file including a column with the findings of the sentiment analysis, which contains the scores assigned to each tweet ranging from negative (highlighted by negative value –) to neutral (represented by 0 values) and positive, which are represented by simple values. In this section, we examine examples of negative-valued, neutral and positive-valued tweets.

The most negative-valued tweet scored –21.05. It contains words such as *rape* and *murder*. Furthermore, in most of the negative-valued tweets, words such as *die*, *inhumane*, *heartbreaking*, *oppression*, *cruelty*, *violent*, *brutal*, *dead*, *dangerous*, *dictator*, *hate* and *regime* frequently appeared, which added negativity to the contents of the tweets against the regime. Twitter users consider Mahsa Amini's death, widely understood to have been a murder, as either tragic, senseless or barbaric (2), or a combination of these (3):

2 "A needless barbaric murder" (23/09/2022)
3 "So heartbreaking" (22/09/2022)

Many of the tweets included calls for action, which tended to be rather general ("public outrage" (4) or "bring you down" (5)):

4 "There must be public outrage about the brutal murder of Mahsa Amini"
5 "No phony sorrow here, I mourn the senseless and barbaric murder of Mahsa Amini at the hands of your goons. You are despicable and I hope/pray that the Iranian people on the streets bring you down" (03/10/2022)

Some tweets expressed anger by criticising the regime's extremism, often using religious stereotypes, such as "*Mullahs* are clowns" or "the regime is her murderer", thereby conflating religion with the political system (6)–(8).

6 "It's time to expel #Khamenis cheap Mullahs Hyenas" (01/10/2022)
7 "If I refused to be scared of you, you will fear me more" (29/09/2022)
8 "Punish this heinous regime" (04/10/2022)

A particular target was Ali Khamenei; the supreme leader of Iran is labelled as a *Devil* or *Terrorist*, and is accused of hypocrisy and held responsible for Mahsa's murder (9). Example (9) appears to assert that this event is the tipping point, and that "the Iranian people" will take revenge on him and his family.

9 "Oh, my god, he murders an innocent Iranian girl and then shows fake sorrow. What a dark nasty terrorist you are. But it's too late Khamenei and the Iranian people will make you and your family pay" (03/10/2022).

Interestingly, Twitter users swiftly come to articulate the current protests against the regime with the experiences of the foregoing years. In the following tweet, we see how the protests are placed in the historical context of the Iranian revolutionary regime, described here as 44 years of abuses and oppression of women (10):

10 "This movement is the result of decades of abuse and oppression; it has been 44 years that our bodies have been the battlefields for abusive rootless people in power. 44 years of resistance with our existence, our bodies, our skin, our hair, our lives" (30/09/2022)

The neutral-valued tweets are those assigned by the platform to neither category, some of which contain terms that are both positive and negative and some of which appear to contain no emotion-laden terms. In fact, a qualitative reading of the "neutral" tweets suggests that they are far from neutral (e.g., "say her name" became a slogan for the protesters, but these tweets are assigned a neutral value because they contain no lexical cues that suggest emotion). Many of the "neutral" tweets are appeals by Twitter users asking others to share #MahsaAmini in their posts on Twitter, in order to further the social reach of the protest campaign and show solidarity. In addition to expressions of support ("sending my heart to the women of Iran", "our sisters need us"), these appeals also include political claims such as that Mahsa Amini "united a nation" and that her death has brought the situation of Iranian women to a wider audience ("we are not alone anymore"). Many tweets implicitly call for action: there are predictions that "the Iranian regime will be brought down by women" or that "another Iranian revolution is on the cards". We should emphasise that these tweets are classed as neutral by the software because they do not contain direct threats or negatively loaded lexis. However, they reflect the same political ambitions as the negatively valued tweets discussed above.

Among the positive-valued contents/tweets comprising positive words used in favour of Mahsa Amini and the Iranians' protest, we note that terms such as *strong*, *wonderful*, *brave*, *fight for freedom*, *happy*, *love*, *courageous Iranian People*, *salute*, *beautiful*, *equality* and *appreciate* are being used to show solidarity with, and support for, the protesters against the Iranian regime. In the positive tweets, the "Iranian people" is often conflated with the notion of "the protesters", to build a classic dichotomy between "the people", who seek "freedom and equality", and "the regime", which oppresses its people.

5.7 Anti-protest Tweets: Overview of Data

Researchers found 121 tweets presenting the other side of the story, or putting forward the position of Iran's leaders and justifying the acts of the Morality Police.

5.8 Anti-protest Tweets: Emotion Analysis

This anti-protest dataset showed less internal variety regarding emotion. Figure 6.3 shows the results when the Ekman filter was used. The main

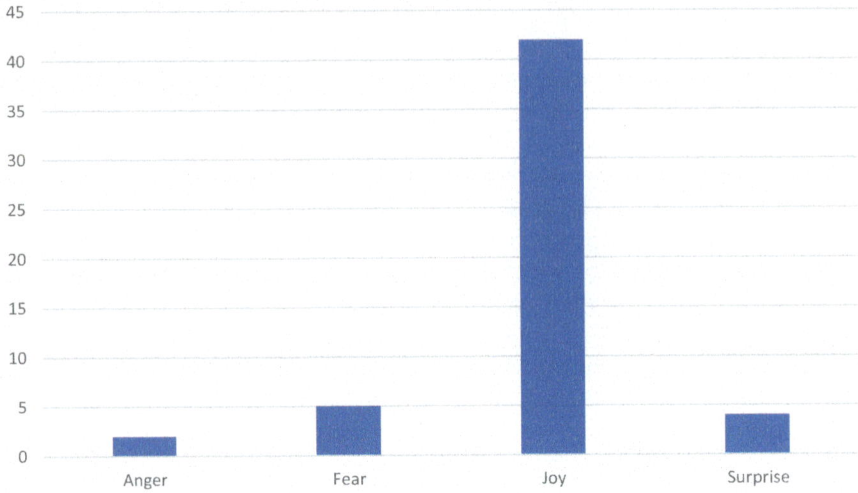

Figure 6.3 Profiles of emotion in the anti-protest tweets using the Ekman filter.

emotion identified is joy, followed by fear, surprise and anger, in that order. This surprising result can be attributed to the high frequency of words like "support" and "solidarity" in the anti-protest tweets, as well as to claims such as that women "love" to wear the hijab. It also points to the inherent problem caused by irony and sarcasm for lexically based filters: tweets such as "the CIA admits it does false flag terrorism, blowing up civilians for fun and profit" are classified under the heading "joy".

Figure 6.4 shows the results of the emotion analysis (using the Plutchik filter) of the tweets posted against the protests, in which the main emotion identified by the algorithm is "sadness". This sadness reflects negative emotions expressed by the tweeters about the protests and the protesters' attitude, with the stress on "lies", "hypocrisy" and "fake propaganda". Curiously, the Ekman filter seems to show little sensitivity to this aspect. The element of "joy" identified by the Plutchik filter can be explained using the same logic as for the Ekman filter.

The seemingly inconsistent results generated by the Ekman and Plutchik filters are examined in more detail below.

5.9 Anti-protest Tweets: Qualitative Analysis

Qualitative analysis of the anti-protest tweets revealed several recurring themes. Emergent arguments against the protests were developed in two main ways. The first relied on a range of arguments suggesting that the protests were not a genuine expression of Iranian public opinion. In these

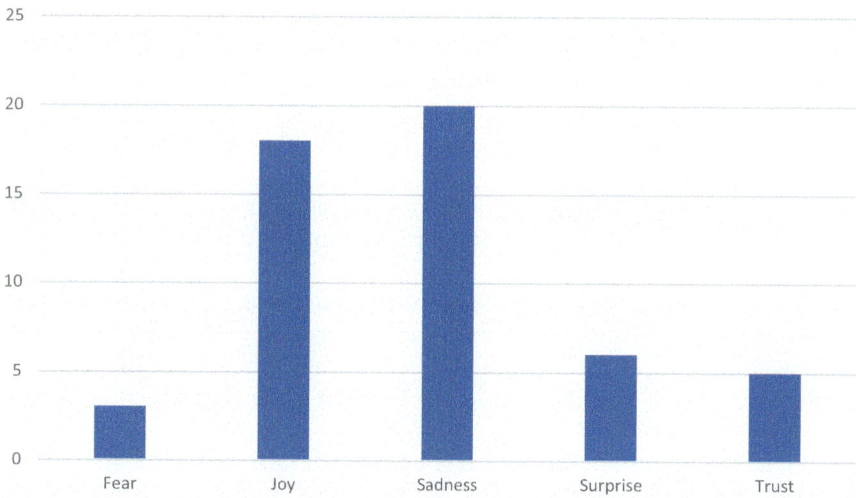

Figure 6.4 Profiles of emotion in the anti-protest tweets using the Plutchik filter.

views, the protests were being provoked as part of an anti-Iranian, or anti-Islamic conspiracy, or were simply being exaggerated through western propaganda. The motivation was variously understood to be about seizing geopolitical power, or about waging a culture war, or both.

Regarding power, Twitter users criticising the protests were swift to blame the West and the USA for backing the protestors, alluding to the US bid for power in the region. In the following example, an anti-protest Twitter user blames America and Britain for meddling in Iranian politics, and thus bearing responsibility for Islamic radicalisation in Iran. This tweet is ambiguously phrased, and appears ambivalent towards the "radicals", but its anti-western slant is clear:

11 "America and the Brits overthrew Mosedegh and install the shah for oil; that is how the radicals came back in power" (27/09/2022)

At the same time, other users framed the protests themselves as provoked by the CIA or Mossad, or their media visibility as being attributable to these (to their eye) hostile foreign intelligence services. This theme of the "fake protests" organised or hyped by Iran's enemies emerged as important in the anti-protest dataset, as embodied in examples like: *Fake protest* (6), *Agent behind* (5), *western world* (5), *Wahhabism* (3) and *USA* (9) commonly occur in clusters in tweets by different users pointing towards a group consensus concerning the involvement of foreign influence in protests against the Iranian government after the incident. In particular, some claim that this whole drama of protests was either fake (12) or planted by westerners as propaganda (13):

12 "Fake islamophobia propagated by fake liberals and Westerners" (05/10/2022)
13 "How dare you lie this obviously, what do you mean by there is no internet in Iran. #fakenews #fake propaganda" (09/10/2022)

Items such as *Israeli terror* associate the protests, or even the orchestration of the incident itself, with the notion of a conspiracy against Iran, whose organisation is variously attributed to traditional "enemies of the regime", namely the Israelis (or Mossad) or the USA (or CIA) (14).

14 "The #Mahsaamini incident is a lie, I smell CIA and Mossad all over this revolution" (28/09/2022)

The clashes between the regime and protesters were also commonly construed as part of a culture war, framed as "the will of real Iran vs CIA". On this theme, several anti-protest comments appeal to a radical Islamic identity, for example, by drawing on a different reading of recent history from that used by protesters or by the western media, offering the notion that "'Iran was progressive before 1979' is a big lie spread by the CIA" because "Iran was always veiled".

Noticeably, conspiratorial activities are also attributed to Wahhabism, Saudi Wahhabism, Wahhabis or Saudis. This last conspiracy theory is comprehensible in view of the extremely strained relations between Iran and Saudi Arabia, which have both a political and a religious dimension. The countries have long been rivals for power over the area, as well as competing over oil interests. In religious terms, they are also opposed: most Iranians are Shiites and the Iranian republic is opposed to monarchy, adhering to the view that an Islamic Faqih (jurist) should have custodianship over all Muslim followers. Saudi Arabia is a kingdom and the official version of Islam is Wahhabi (i.e., a different sect in Islam like Shia, Sunni, and Deboandi, etc.) (Blanchard, 2008; Dillion, 2009). Iran's Shiite leadership and Saudi Wahhabism have been in continuous cold conflict for decades. Diplomatic relations between the two countries have been broken off several times in recent years, the last being a seven-year suspension after the execution of Shia cleric Nimr al-Nimr by the Saudi authorities in 2016. At the time of the protests they were still in conflict.[2]

The second major kind of argument emerging from the anti-protest tweets consisted of elaborating on the theme of western hypocrisy, that is, the West supports women's rights not to wear the hijab, but fails to support the women in Europe who are not allowed to wear the hijab (15)–(16):

15 "Height of Hypocrisy, when Iranian women cut their hair, remove hijab, west gives all support coz they call it women's right when same women wear hijab in west why they call it oppression?" (05/10/2022)
16 "A lot of Celebrities and tv anchors cut their hairs in solidarity with Iran, GOOD! But not one of those wore Hijab in solidarity with those who love to wear hijab" (09/10/2022)

Other western countries, particularly France, were also criticised for having double standards: Europeans show solidarity towards protesters but do not support women's right to wear the hijab in Europe (17)–(19):

17 "These people are the biggest hypocrite, France has snatched the rights of Muslim women who wants to wear hijab or Burqa and now they are supporting women of Iran. Fake solidarity" (27/09/2022).
18 "It would be good to see the same solidarity for women who want to wear hijab. What happened to your solidarity when France banned the hijab" (09/10/2022)
19 "You should host some French women who are not allowed to wear Hijab, Hypocrisy is unlimited in Western Media" (09/10/2022)

These anti-protest tweets thus undermine the pro-protest campaigns in various ways, rejecting the idea that they are a spontaneous reaction by the Iranian people, and attributing negative roles to the western media and to particular western governments.

Regarding the two filters, the use of the Ekman filter (Figure 6.3) gives a surprising result that may be triggered by the prevalence of expressions of solidarity, and by the inaccurate classification of tweets that include sarcasm. On the other hand, the Plutchik filter (Figure 6.4) brings out the idea of fakeness and hypocrisy, with notions of "cowardice", "fake activists", "lies", etc., and appears slightly more sensitive to lexis related to violence. However, despite the different labels, there is a significant overlap between the tweets identified as negative by these two filters.

6. Conclusions

This study was designed to analyse polarised discourse in Twitter about the protests in Iran after the death of Mahsa Amini whilst in police custody. This incident may offer a relevant case for researching polarisation in social media in a non-western culture, and for profiling the social media "tribes" (North et al., 2020) that emerge in this context. In what follows, we begin by assessing our methodological approach and the tools used. We then go on to review the logics underlying the different social media trends observed.

First, concerning the mixed methodology employed in the present study, we can say that the Word Cloud tool was useful to obtain an initial overview of lexical patterns and frequencies. The Tweet Profiler sentiment analysis for classifying tweets into negative/neutral/positive also contributed to the preliminary organisation of the dataset for qualitative analysis, although its accuracy could be improved. However, the use of the Tweet Profiler emotion analysis proved less productive, since its very wide six- or eight-emotion categories organised the data according to very broad classes (i.e., "sadness", "joy") that covered too many shades of meaning to be useful as a guide for qualitative exploration. Its lack of sensitivity to ironic or sarcastic uses of lexis also proved problematic (Hernández Farías & Rosso, 2017). Moreover, although the categories used are based on psychological theory, they have not been updated to take more recent work into account, and they lack a robust grounding in the lexical instantiation of the emotions (e.g., see Gillioz et al., 2016). In fact, as Benítez-Castro and Hidalgo-Tenorio (2019, p. 326) argue, systematic analysis of the language of emotional reactions (i.e., the Appraisal system, see Martin & White, 2005) has tended to be complementary to, rather than built on, a solid psychological approach to the emotions. The accuracy of future algorithms will doubtless be enhanced by multilayered approaches that account (for example) for the affinity between sadness and anger in terms of goal-orientedness (Benítez-Castro & Hidalgo-Tenorio, 2019, p. 322) while also acknowledging their essential difference in terms of power and arousal (Breeze, 2020, p. 123). Nonetheless, although future algorithms may yield high accuracy, we consider that qualitative analysis will always be needed, not least because phenomena related to social conflict are generally embedded in a complex cultural background.

Regarding our findings, the analysis of this dataset has brought to light at least two different logics at work in this controversy, which cannot be reduced to a simple "for and against" polemic about the protests or the actions of the Iranian regime (Graham et al., 2021). First, we found that the Twitter response mostly offered outspoken criticism of the Iranian leadership and police, combined with solidarity with the victim and with Iranian women in general. Strongly emotive terms expressing anger, sadness and fear were used to condemn the Morality Police and the Iranian regime as a whole, while solidarity with the protesters was conveyed, using emotions associated with joy and appeals to values such as freedom and equality. The strong similarity within the discourses offered in support of the protests suggests that there is an expressive community of social media users, mainly situated in Iran and neighbouring countries, who back campaigns for women's freedom and launch vehement criticism against police oppression, and, by extension, against the Iranian regime and its version of strict Islam. One can imagine that the relative freedom and anonymity of Twitter encourages more outspoken participation in this regard (Breeze, 2022).

However, a smaller group of users was also identified which blamed the USA, Britain, Saudi Wahhabis and Israel for provoking or hyping this incident, and accused these actors variously of attacking Islam, plotting to defame Iran and the Iranian government, and conspiring to grab power in the region. The underlying claim that there is a culture war between "the West" and Islam, or that Islam is "under attack" is frequently found in discourses associated with radical Islamic ideology (Holbrook 2015; Baker, Vessey, & McEnery, 2021; Benítez-Castro & Hidalgo-Tenorio, 2022). Within this, the representation of Muslims as victims, which is usually generic and associated with large numbers, is particularly characteristic of extremist groups (Baker et al., 2021, p. 82). As Benítez-Castro and Hidalgo-Tenorio (2022) show, by drawing on the pain caused by perceived injustices, some Islamic groups create a strong sense of victimhood that may spur people on to violent action. In the present case, however, the depiction of Muslim women as oppressed in the West is mainly associated with attempts to undermine support for the protests, rather than specifically framed as a call to violence. The prevailing logic here is that since western countries tend to oppress women who wish to wear the hijab, the solidarity shown by westerners is simply a manifestation of sheer hypocrisy; their supposed support for women's rights may be merely yet another expression of anti-Islamic prejudice. Within the parameters of moderate, fringe and extremist radical discourses analysed by Baker et al. (2021), the anti-protest tweets are relatively mild, tending towards undermining the protesters' cause rather than spurring violent action against them.

In short, the analysis presented in this chapter sheds light on a particular case in which different logics clearly emerge to motivate strongly antagonistic social movements. It has documented the emotional force used to build community and reaffirm identity, and the particular role of victimhood in stoking resentment and inspiring solidarity. Social media analysis provides a unique window onto social conflict in areas of the world where other sociological or discursive approaches might prove impractical. Although automated sentiment analysis holds some promise, it is clear that qualitative approaches are essential to unpack the dynamics of social conflict in such contexts. Further research is needed to determine how far the logics uncovered here are typical of clashes involving radical positions in different areas of the world.

Notes

1 Orange is one of the modern data visualisation and data analysis software that works on the application of modern programming languages such as Python and C++. This software was developed in 1996 by the University of Ljubljana. https://orangedatamining.com/

2 Iran and Saudi Arabia agreed to reestablish diplomatic relations in March 2023, after negotiations brokered by China.

References

Abdelghany, M. K. (2022, September 22). The death of Mahsa Amini is a wake-up call for the Iranian people. *Daily Orange*. https://dailyorange.com/2022/09/death-Mahsa-amini-wake-call-iranian-people/

Afshar, H. (1996). *Women and politics*. London: Routledge.

Askew, J. (2022, September 15). Explained: Why is the hijab significant in Iranian society? *Euronews*. https://www.euronews.com/culture/2022/09/21/explained-why-is-the-hijab-significant-in-iranian-society

Azadeh, F. (2010). *Hijab, image, and post-revolutionary Iran* [MA thesis, University of the Arts London]. https://eprints.kingston.ac.uk/id/eprint/38702/

Bahramitash, R. (2013). Revolution, Islamization, and women's employment in Iran. *Brown Journal of World Affairs*, *9*(2), 229–241.

Baker, P., Vessey, C., & McEnery, T. (2021). *The language of violent jihad*. Cambridge: Cambridge University Press.

Banks, C., Enright, J., Mohr, S., & Kao, R. (2022). Bovine tuberculosis in Britain: Identifying signatures of polarisation and controversy on Twitter. *ArXiv*. https://doi.org/10.48550/arXiv.2211.14234

Benítez-Castro, M. A., & Hidalgo-Tenorio, E. (2019). Rethinking Martin and White's affect taxonomy. In L. Alba-Juez & J. L. Mackenzie (Eds.), *Emotion in discourse* (pp. 301–331). Amsterdam: John Benjamins.

Benítez-Castro, M. A., & Hidalgo-Tenorio, E. (2022). "I am proud to be a traitor": The EMOTION/OPINION interplay in jihadist magazines. *Pragmatics & Society*, *13*(3), 501–531.

Bermingham, A., & Smeaton, A. (2010). Classifying sentiment in microblogs: Is brevity an advantage? In *Proceedings of the 19th ACM international conference on Information and Knowledge Management (CIKM'10)* (pp. 1833–1836). ACM, New York. http://dx.doi.org/10.1145/1871437.1871741

Blanchard, C. M. (2008). The Islamic traditions of Wahhabism and Salafiyya. *CRS report for Congress*, RS21432. https://sgp.fas.org/crs/misc/RS21695.pdf

Breeze, R. (2014). Reporting public manifestations of religious beliefs: Sikhs, Muslims and Christians in the British press. In I. Olza, Ó. Loureda, & M. Casado Velarde (Eds.), *Language use in the public sphere* (pp. 271–307). Bern: Peter Lang. http://dx.doi.org/10.13140/2.1.5192.3205

Breeze, R. (2019). "Happy to be insulted": Offensive language in online discussions of UK radical politics. In R. Breeze, & A. M. Fernández-Vallejo (Eds.), *Populist discourse across modes and media* (pp. 259–282). Bern: Peter Lang.

Breeze, R. (2020). Angry tweets: A corpus assisted study of anger in populist political discourse. *Journal of Language Aggression and Conflict*, *8*(1), 118–145.

Breeze, R. (2022). Reinforcing right-wing political identities on reader comments pages. *Pragmatics and Society, 13*(1), 88–109.

Breeze, R., & Gintsburg, S. (2023). Exploiting the crisis: Populists, migration, minorities and Covid-19. In D. Weiss & N. Thielemann (Eds.), *Remedies against the pandemic: How politicians communicate crisis management* (pp. 276–298). Amsterdam: John Benjamins.

Bucholtz, M., & Hall, K. (2005). Identity and interaction: A sociocultural linguistic approach. *Discourse Studies, 7*(4-5), 585–614.

Darius, P., & Urquhart, M. 2021. Disinformed social movements: A large-scale mapping of conspiracy narratives as online harms during the COVID-19 pandemic. *Online Social Networks and Media, 26*, 100174. https://doi.org/10.1016/j.osnem.2021.100174

Demsar, J., Curk, T., Erjavec, A., Gorup, C., Hocevar, T., Milutinovic, M., Mozina, M., Polajnar, M., Toplak, M., Staric, A., Stajdohar, M., Umek, L., Zagar, L., Zbontar, J., Zitnik, M., & Zupan, B. (2013). Orange: Data mining toolbox in python. *Journal of Machine Learning Research, 14*(1), 2349–2353.

de Rosa, A., Bocci, E., Bonito, M., & Salvati, M. (2021). Twitter as social media arena for polarised social representations about the (im)migration: The controversial discourse in the Italian and international political frame. *Migration Studies, 9*(3), 1167–1194, https://doi.org/10.1093/migration/mnab00114

Dillion, M. R. (2009). Wahhabism: Is it a factor in the spread of global terrorism? [MA thesis submitted to the Naval Postgraduate School, California]. https://nps.edu/documents/105988371/107571254/DillonWahhabismThesis.pdf/23fc46fb-17a6-41da-83b8-8e312191b5bb

Ekman, P. (1992). An argument for basic emotions. *Cognitive Emotion, 6*(3/4), 169–200. http://dx.doi.org/10.1080/02699939208411106

Esposito, E., & Breeze, R. (2022). Gender and politics in a digitalized world: Investigating online hostility against UK MPs. *Discourse & Society, 33*(2), 303–323. https://doi.org/10.1177/09579265221076608

Giachanou, A., & Crestani, F. (2016). Like it or not: A survey of Twitter Sentiment Analysis methods. *ACM Computing Surveys, 49*(2), 28.

Gillioz, C., Fontaine, J. R. J., Soriano, C., & Scherer, K. R. (2016). Mapping emotion terms into affective space. *Swiss Journal of Psychology, 75*(3), 141–148. https://econtent.hogrefe.com/doi/10.1024/1421-0185/a000180

González Ruiz, R., & Izquierdo Alegría, D. (2014). The debate about the veil in the Spanish press. Boosting strategies and interactional metadiscourse in the editorials of ABC and El País (2002–2010). In I. Olza, Ó. Loureda, & M. Casado-Velarde (Eds.), *Language use in the public sphere* (pp. 397–444). Bern: Peter Lang.

Graham, T., Bruns, A., Angus, D., Hurcombe, E., & Hames, S. (2021). #IStandWithDan versus #DictatorDan: The polarized dynamics of Twitter discussions about Victoria's COVID-19 restrictions. *Media International Australia, 179*(1), 127–148.

Hamzehei, P. (2014). *Iranian women's experience of mandatory hijab: A case study of a campaign on Facebook* [MA thesis, Stockholm University, Department of Journalism, Media and Communication]. https://su.diva-portal.org/smash/record.jsf?pid=diva2%3A780122&dswid=9438

Hernández Farías, D., & Rosso, P. (2017). Irony, sarcasm, and sentiment analysis. In F. A. Pozzi, E. Fersini, E. Messina, & B. Liu (Eds.), *Sentiment analysis in social networks* (pp. 113–128). Amsterdam: Elsevier.

Holbrook, D. (2015). Designing and applying an 'Extremist Media Index'. *Perspectives on Terrorism, 9*(5), 56–67.

Hoodfar, H. (1999). The women's movement in Iran: Women at the crossroads of secularization and Islamization. *The Women's Movement Series, 1*(1), 1–49. https://www.iranchamber.com/society/articles/women_secularization_islamization5.ph

Iran Human Rights. (2022). *Iran protests: At least 185 killed/19 children amongst dead*. https://iranhr.net/en/articles/5515/

Ishak, A., Siregar, A., Aspriyati, Ginting, R., & Afif, M. (2020). Orange software usage in data mining classification method on the dataset lenses. *IOP Conference Series: Materials Science and Engineering, 1003*. https://iopscience.iop.org/article/10.1088/1757-899X/1003/1/012113/pdf

Jacobs, A. M. (2019). Sentiment Analysis for words and fiction characters from the perspective of computational (neuro-)poetics. *Frontiers in Robotics and AI, 6*. https://doi.org/10.3389/frobt.2019.00053

Martin, J. R., & White, P. R. R. (2005). *The language of evaluation: Appraisal in English*. Basingstoke/New York: Palgrave Macmillan.

McNair, D. M., Lorr, M., & Droppleman, L. F. (1971). *Profile of mood states*. San Diego, CA: Educational and Industrial Testing Services.

Ministry for Foreign Affairs, Iran. (2022, October 10). *Preliminary report on death of Mahsa Amini & ensuing events*. https://en.mfa.ir/portal/newsview/696057

North, S., Piwek, L., & Joinson, A. (2020). Battle for Britain: Analyzing events as drivers of political tribalism in Twitter discussions of Brexit. *Policy & Internet, 13*(2), 185–208.

Peker, M., Ozkaraca, O., & Sasar, A. (2018). Use of Orange Data Mining Toolbox for data analysis in clinical decision making: The diagnosis of diabetes disease. In P. Pattnaik, A. Swetapadma, & J. Sarraf (Eds.), *Expert system techniques in biomedical science practice* (pp. 143–167). Pennsylvania: IGI Global. http://dx.doi.org/10.4018/978-1-5225-5149-2.ch007

Plutchik, R. (1980). *Emotion: Theory, research, and experience*. New York: Academic.

Rogg, I. (2022, September 29). Who was Mahsa Amini, the face of mass protests in Iran. *Neue Zürcher Zeitung*.

Sabine, O. (2017). Iran, a cradle of civilization. https://www.dw.com/en/iran-a-cradle-of-civilization/g-38413585

Sintsova, V., Musat, C., & Pu, P. (2014). Semi-supervised method for multi-category emotion recognition in tweets. In *2014 IEEE international conference on data mining workshop (ICDM'14)* (pp. 393–402). http://dx.doi.org/10.1109/ICDMW.2014.146

Statcounter. (2023). *Social media stats Islamic republic of Iran*. https://gs.statcounter.com/social-media-stats/all/iran

Syed, I. U. B. (2013). Forced assimilation is an unhealthy policy intervention: The case of the hijab ban in France and Quebec, Canada. *International Journal of Human Rights, 17*(3), 428–440. http://dx.doi.org/10.1080/13642987.2012.724678

Zahedi, A. (2007). Contested meaning of the veil and political ideologies of Iranian regimes. *Journal of Middle East Women's Studies, 3*(3), 75–98. https://www.jstor.org/stable/10.2979/mew.2007.3.3.75

7 Exploring the Application of Computer Vision to Detect Faces and Emotions

An Analysis of Radical Right-Wing Leaders

Ignacio-Jesús Serrano-Contreras and Javier García-Marín

1. Introduction

The Internet was originally created to facilitate quick and global communication (Berners-Lee, 2000). From simple written messages to the rise of audiovisual platforms, all forms of media have undergone hybridization through this interconnection. This blending of media environments has not only democratized access to information, but has also empowered individuals to actively participate in content creation and distribution (Luengo, 2014), with social media standing out as a prominent example. The latter have played a pivotal role in shaping narratives and influencing public opinion, ultimately leading to a transformation in the dynamics between media, society and power (Maldonado, 2016). Nevertheless, there are divergent perspectives on the impact of these developments. On the one hand, they have been studied as potential catalysts for phenomena like disinformation, political polarization or populism (Gerbaudo, 2018). On the other hand, contrasting views exist (Lorenzo-Rodríguez & Torcal, 2022), and there is ongoing debate regarding the actual role of elements such as algorithms (recent contributions by García-Marín & Serrano-Contreras, 2023 or Ibrahim et al., 2023, offer insights into the role that computation can play in communication).

In the realm of politics, the digitalization of mass media has presented numerous opportunities for politicians to leverage and yield favorable outcomes. Platforms like Twitter and Facebook have been harnessed to bridge the divide between politicians and the general public effectively bypassing traditional media channels. This has allowed them to disseminate their messages, engage with their followers, mobilize their support bases and incite public action to champion their aspirations or to express discontent (Rahyadi et al., 2023; Segerberg & Bennett, 2011; Weismueller et al., 2022).

DOI: 10.4324/9781003457381-8

Today, the landscape appears to have evolved. While we have witnessed the professionalization of broadcasting, issues like the bi-directionality of communication, which shaped the digital agora, are no longer as central. However, a significant development in recent times has been the integration of audiovisual content into media campaigns alongside written messages. This shift has resulted in a transformation of the political landscape, with Twitter's prominence giving way to new strategies represented by new actors like TikTok (Zeng & Abidin, 2021). These new platforms support particular logics depending on the media (Altheide, 2020).

This digital age prompts questions about the evolution of both society and media. On the one hand, some of these questions have already been addressed, as studies exploring the scope and definition of the Internet and social networks reveal, although continuous reflection remains valuable (Sterrett et al., 2019). On the other hand, several challenges persist without robust or widespread solutions. As the Internet has undergone significant changes, scholars in the fields of social and human sciences have directed their research efforts toward comprehending the roles played by text and symbols, such as expressions and emojis (Barbieri et al., 2017; Debnath et al., 2020), as well as interactions between users. However, it is worth noting that most of these studies are yet to contribute significantly to the understanding of large-scale image and video broadcasting. Thus, there remains a need for a broad and experimental foundation to delve into complexities such as non-verbal language, the implications of color or the biases that can arise from different visual perspectives, which allow us to better connect the impact to specific social phenomena. Related to this, we wonder if using emotions in non-verbal language follows patterns we can analyze. As social networks have weakened the role of information filters represented by traditional media, it is interesting to see if the most extremist (and, therefore, populist) candidates take advantage of them to use specific strategies. Thus, our research question is whether we can detect patterns in the use of facial emotions in populist candidates.

2. Theoretical Framework

Various approaches have emerged to deal with the new drifts of mass communication. For example, text mining has equipped the social sciences and humanities with a potent tool capable of converting textual code into structured data. This process, known as "text as data" (Gentzkow et al., 2017; Grimmer et al., 2022), involves measuring sentiment in texts, assessing semantic distancing, or identifying the most frequently used verbs in a book, allowing for the transformation of qualitative information into quantitative values. Moreover, text mining represents just one of the initial phases in the broader field of Natural Language Processing (Serrano-Contreras, 2021), a discipline at the intersection of computer science, psychology and linguistics. However, the current media ecosystem necessitates methodologies that incorporate new tools capable of automatically extracting information from audio, images, or video content.

Spurred by the revolution brought about by the rise of television, streaming platforms, as well as video social media, generate an enormous amount of audiovisual content. In response to these transformations, the political arena has adapted by embracing trends of spectacularization (Gómez-García et al., 2023; Khoma & Kozma, 2022). This change places a strong emphasis on the mediatized image, surpassing text and therefore calm discourse in importance (Plazas-Olmedo & López-Rabadán, 2023). This symptom is one more factor that highlights the Americanization of politics, particularly in Europe, where visuals and audiovisual constructs can prove to be more effective in capturing citizens' attention and, in turn, mobilizing them (Durántez-Stolle & Martínez-Sanz, 2019; Tai & Turner, 2008). Thus, it becomes essential to design both descriptive and experimental analyses to empirically assess the extent to which these trends can impact audiences.

In recent years, algorithms in this field have been increasingly harnessing sophisticated developments, capitalizing on significant advances in computing. Presently, the concept of computer vision is emerging from disciplines in which machine learning models can make inferences from images and videos, including faces and objects. These new techniques bring forth fresh insights for a wide range of disciplines that were previously limited to manual analysis on a small scale. These innovations pave the way for such methodological advancements to be crucial in the understanding of contemporary societies (Schmøkel & Bossetta, 2022). Contributions in this domain help answer a wide array of questions in fields such as political communication, where content analysis can be enhanced through automation (Peng & Lu, 2023).

These advancements entail the ability to synthesize elements that were previously subject to the researchers' subjectivity. Machine classification, in particular, involves two main components. First, pre-trained models, developed largely through multidisciplinary research in which diverse fields in the social sciences and humanities establish guidelines for computerizing non-verbal cues, tones and rhetoric (Joo et al., 2019). Secondly, these automated algorithms can perform massive analyses, enabling the examination of hundreds of hours of video or thousands of images as an option. These breakthroughs enable the field of political communication to continue its exploration of theories like framing or priming, as well as to incorporate new areas of study into the analysis of political polarization and radicalization.

Our approach is specifically designed to open up new avenues for social inquiry. By analyzing large datasets, we aim to propose and explore fresh theoretical perspectives. In this pursuit, we concentrate on psychological factors to test whether these variables can detect distinct behaviors, thereby shedding light on potential theories of effects and concomitant structures within ideologies (Cichocka & Dhont, 2023). Our approach entails an analytical strategy capable of detecting sentiments in videos of politicians posted on YouTube. Our goal is to uncover, if they exist, common patterns among leaders framed as populist and radical right-wing. For this purpose, we propose the integration of computer vision techniques, specifically the sub-discipline known as FER (Face Emotion Recognition) (Khaireddin & Chen, 2021). FER employs models to detect emotions such as sadness, happiness or anger in facial expressions. Our mission is to identify possible patterns of non-verbal language among politicians, particularly among different leaders of the radical right, including figures such as Donald Trump, Giorgia Meloni, Santiago Abascal, Marine Le Pen or Javier Milei. Simultaneously, we intend to establish a control group featuring leaders from different ideological backgrounds.

3. Data and Method

In this research, we analyzed YouTube accounts belonging to political leaders and parties. Hence, our criteria are based on the video's popularity, not time or date. Our premise was that the official channels of politicians and parties are instrumental in conveying the image they wish to present to their voters. Therefore, we excluded all those audiovisual fragments shared by other profiles, as these may have edited the original samples and could have introduced biases or misunderstandings. In our endeavor to identify ideological patterns not necessarily tied to a specific society, we initiated our investigation by seeking the verified channels of several prominent leaders within the populist right. These leaders encompassed Donald Trump (USA), Giorgia Meloni (Italy), Santiago Abascal (Spain), Marine Le Pen (France) and Javier Milei (Argentina), in alignment with Pelinka's (2013) conception of populism. Although these profiles exhibit diversity, they were selected to test ideological patterns. We also aimed to include the president of El Salvador, Nayib Bukele, in our sample; still, his inclusion was discarded as he did not fit the predefined characteristics of our research design.

The final sample was compiled by selecting all those videos in order of popularity, with a maximum of 10 for each channel, provided that the duration of each was less than 5 minutes. We understood that longer videos would introduce unnecessary complexity to the research without yielding significant information. Additionally, the selected videos had to include a range of shots, from the wide cowboy shots to close-up shots, to ensure that the visibility of the faces was unambiguous and not compromised by the presence of third parties, the quality of the video or profile camera shots. The total sample size ($n = 50$) was then expanded to include leaders considered non-populist in the same countries: Joe Biden (USA), Giuseppe Conte (Italy), Pedro Sánchez (Spain), Emmanuel Macron (France) and Alberto Férnandez (Argentina). As a result, the total number of videos analyzed, comprising both the analysis sample and the control group, amounted to 100.

Subsequently, we proceeded to select one image per second from the videos, considering that they later were encoded at a rate of 25 frames per second. This resulted in a total of 6,981 images. Next, employing the Python programming language, we implemented a face detection algorithm. In our case, we opted for face-recognition due to its simplicity in Python and its effectiveness in face recognition with minimal training required. For the training of the algorithm, we gathered images online by conducting specific searches on DuckDuckGo (using the politician's name and the image search tool). We selected only those images that exclusively featured the politician's face, without any other additional images that could interfere with the detection process. Then, we designed the code to perform a series of steps; firstly, it detected the faces in the images from the videos (using OpenCV, which is practically a standard tool for this purpose); then, it recognized the detected faces using the face-recognition library; finally, it determined the emotions expressed in the faces using FER. The final output was a DataFrame (DF) containing the name of the recognized candidate, the timestamp of the detection and the video file. The entire process is outlined in Figure 7.1.

Note that the tools employed can detect several faces simultaneously, along with their associated emotions. Additionally, the algorithm can label

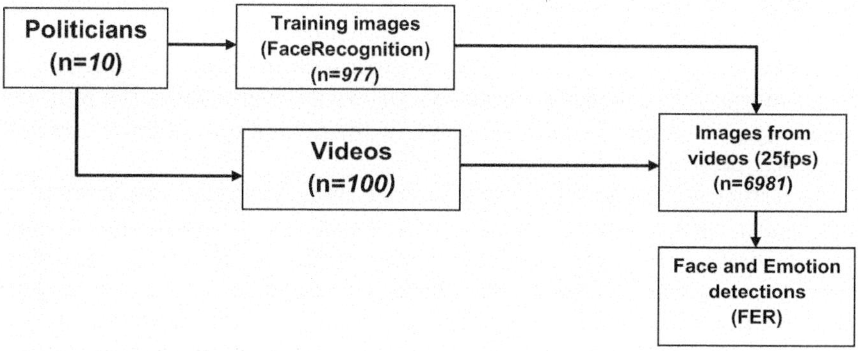

Figure 7.1 Flowchart.

a face as "unknown" when it cannot recognize a face from its training set, although it does continue to analyze its emotion. It is important to acknowledge that the algorithm can occasionally make errors, which means that some manual verification has to be carried out. Nonetheless, the incidence of errors was relatively low (only 5 out of over a 100 detections checked).

4. Results

Table 7.1 presents the raw results of the analysis, including the unknown encodings (both in the location of faces and emotions). This helps gauge the degree of effectiveness of the tools employed. The slight discrepancy between the total number of encodings (6,970) and the total number of images (6,981) represents localized errors, a small and acceptable number. As mentioned earlier, the overall effectiveness is sufficiently high for use in research settings; nevertheless, expanding the training sets, while relatively straightforward for public figures, may present challenges with other types of actors.

The data in Table 7.1 reveal several intriguing findings. First, there is a significant difference between the number of codings by name and those related to sentiment. This variance in codings by name can be attributed to two factors: the differing lengths of the videos and the prominence of the politicians features in each of them. It was also important to analyze the proportion of other faces in the videos, and the data yields some striking insights. Notably, the videos of Conte and Fernández exhibit the highest proportion of unknown faces (.17 and .16, respectively); while Trump's, Abascal and Meloni's videos feature the lowest proportion (.006, .03 and .03, respectively). On average, for politicians considered populist, the proportion of unknown faces is .04; whereas, for other candidates, the mean is .10; this represents a significant difference (with $\bar{x}$ -=.07). However, at the same time, this data also speaks to the utilization of personalism as a political strategy, and it is challenging to extrapolate broad conclusions when multiple variables may influence this relationship, from the political system (presidential or parliamentary), or the recognition of the individual and their personal style of politics.

Nevertheless, Table 7.1 reveals another remarkable finding, namely, a pronounced prevalence of feelings of sadness in the sample under analysis. Initially, one might attribute this to a poorly calibrated algorithm. However, drawing from our experience with the tool, we have reason to believe otherwise. If we exclude this possibility, we are left with the assumption that politicians have a proclivity for expressing sadness in their communications. This tendency may be due to their routinely employed communication styles, which would explain its prevalence.

Table 7.1 Coded emotions per name

Name	*Unknown*	*Anger*	*Disgust*	*Fear*	*Happiness*	*Neutral*	*Sadness*	*Surprise*	*Total*
Abascal	18	69	0	9	213	132	268	18	727
Biden	34	4	0	0	4	7	206	2	257
Conte	11	35	0	7	144	150	225	5	577
Unknown	16	79	0	7	211	257	278	15	863
Fernández	7	30	0	16	65	81	124	7	330
Le_Pen	67	113	0	124	291	301	665	72	1,633
Macron	13	73	0	8	48	43	120	26	331
Meloni	3	26	0	46	25	35	120	76	331
Milei	9	41	0	13	50	34	102	15	264
Trump	130	339	1	28	78	190	694	12	1,472
Pedro_Sánchez	3	48	0	4	22	31	75	2	185
Total	311	857	1	262	1,151	1,261	2,877	250	6,970

Figure 7.2 illustrates the sentiments assigned to each political figure, with a grouping based on populism (represented by the shaded area). The figure vividly confirms our previous observations: All politicians intensively employ facial expressions that convey sadness, which is the most common emotion among all of them. Similar trends are observed with other emotions codified in our research (i.e., neutrality, happiness and anger). Notably, disgust is absent, and there are minimal instances of surprise and fear.

The differences observed can be attributed, once again, to their individual styles of expressing ideas, as well as to shared (probably global or, perhaps, Western) communication techniques. Thus, we can discern what, in principle, appear to be different styles: Meloni uses expressions of fear or surprise more frequently than any other individual, while Trump, Macron or Sánchez exhibit a higher prevalence of anger; happiness, on the other hand, seems to be more prominent in Abascal, Conte and Fernández. Can we categorize these results based on the populism variable? Figure 7.3 shows the result of such grouping in relative values. Although we do observe variations that might suggest specific patterns, especially in the use of happiness and neutrality, it is challenging to draw scientifically valid conclusions. So, as we suspected, the results do not provide substantial information, thus reinforcing the notion that we are dealing with individual styles rather than trends that can be attributed to factors such as populism.

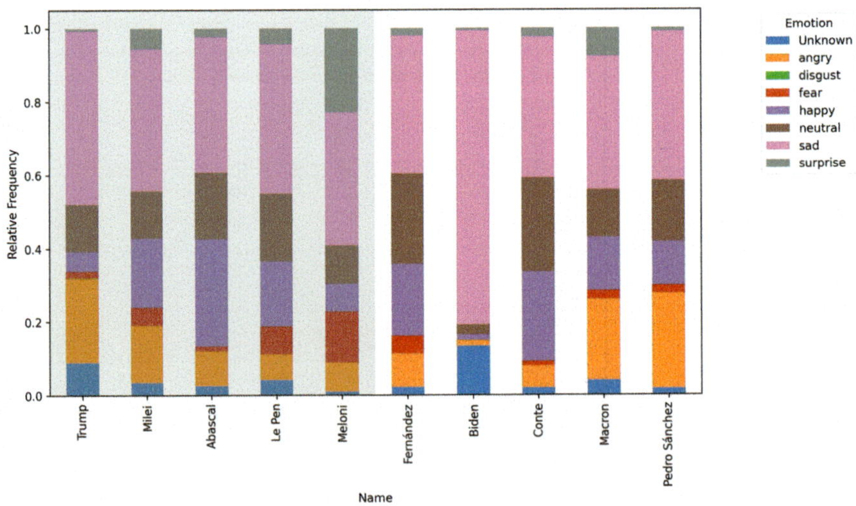

Figure 7.2 The sentiments assigned to each political figure, with a grouping based on populism (represented by the shaded area).

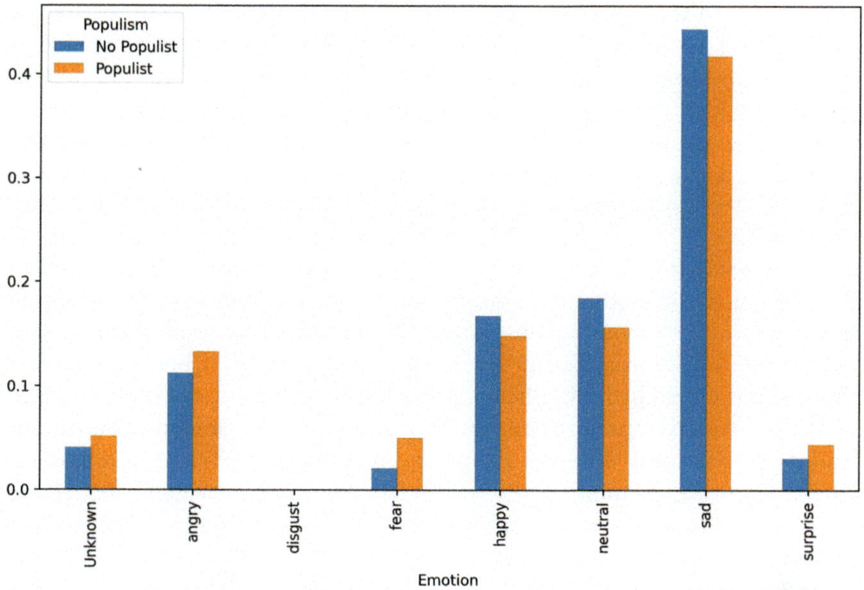

Figure 7.3 The result of such grouping in relative values.

Even so, we have endeavored to examine the relationships between the variables analyzed statistically. However, attempts to model the relationship between populism and emotions have proved to be unsuccessful. For example, logistic regression demonstrated a degree of success in predicting the presence of populism ($F_1 = .78$); nonetheless, it failed to predict the absence of populism in any instance. Consequently, we can conclude that, at least within the sample analyzed, this relationship does not appear to exist.

5. Discussion

The approaches outlined in this contribution primarily aim to expand the knowledge path paved by automated models. In this specific case, with the progress of language processing in disciplines such as humanities and social sciences, there is still a need for further research in using algorithmic models to analyze images. Conversely, this research also highlights the necessity for a broader scope, one that seamlessly integrates multidisciplinary variables into everyday practice. This starting point advocates for fields where human behavioral studies forge new drifts to extend knowledge further. Nevertheless, and in line with the preceding work, we find ourselves in the midst of a revolution that may not be all-encompassing. However, it contributes to the ongoing exploration of theories and reflections that, to date, lacked a sufficiently robust sample size to substantiate or challenge specific hypotheses. This stands as one of the central pillars for delving into this type of methodology. Reflections on topics such as the radicalization and polarization of society, as well as the rise and analysis of populist ideologies, serve as a basis for applying novel tools in an intricate social and media ecosystem. The prominence of visuals underscores the need for scientists to actively engage in the study of its massive impact (Russmann & Svensson, 2017). It is, therefore, imperative not only to continue developing these innovative computational models but also to reflect on how they can be advantageous, enhanced or effectively implemented.

Despite the systematization set out in this approach, it becomes evident that the data yield little significant value, especially when the objective is to identify distinctive patterns not merely among ideologies but also among leaders who employ different forms and techniques of expression. In such cases, certain traits might fit in with what we might anticipate from leaders who prioritize emotional appeal in their discourse, as is often seen in populist figures. Even so, as the results indicate, the differences are not as pronounced as initially expected. Thus, it is difficult, a priori, to pinpoint behaviors capable of unequivocally revealing an ideology or a particular style of politics.

However, the slight differences found elicit diverse explanations. On the one hand, we assume from the outset that both political leaders and political parties use their YouTube channels to disseminate specific, calculated information, constituting what can be termed "YouTubization of politics" (May, 2010). This approach also serves as an alternative medium for free riders or a mechanism to circumvent media authoritarianism in certain regimes (Litvinenko, 2021). While this assumption may hold true, the analyzed samples fail to show noticeable visual or non-verbal differences. Several factors may account for this, including the construction of the audiovisual narrative, which tends to be essential primarily during election campaigns, when electoral marketing takes center page, generating increased interest from supporters and the media. Hence, most of the published videos, with the exception of American leaders from both North and South America, predominantly consist of clips from rallies and parliamentary sessions. On another note, the composition of the sample itself also plays a significant role, impacting the results of data collection and analysis. Naturally, the present study only scratches the surface of possibilities for this type of analysis, revealing more questions than answers. The exploration of diverse communication styles in politics remains a viable avenue for further research, including an examination of whether different styles depend on the format (e.g. electoral debates, meetings, interviews, etc.). Furthermore, in order to target specific audiences, we could assign strategies, with election advertising serving as a control group aimed at the entire population.

This last factor reinforces the importance of embracing multidisciplinarity in our research. Such analysis affects variables that extend beyond traditional social science disciplines like sociology, psychology or political science. They necessitate the incorporation of insights and theories from the field of audiovisual communication, where a brief close-up shot can reveal distinct information compared to a long shot. Finally, we would like to highlight that automated models for image classification, like the ones discussed here, are beginning to become popular; and this, along with forthcoming contributions, should continue to raise thought-provoking questions that further our comprehension and expand our studies on topics such as populism or political polarization, and other complex social phenomena.

References

Altheide, D. L. (2020). Media logic and media psychology. In J. Bulck (Ed.), *The international encyclopedia of media psychology* (pp. 1–15). New York: Wiley.

Arias Maldonado, M. (2016). La digitalización de la conversación pública: Redes sociales, afectividad política y democracia. *Revista de Estudios Políticos*, *173*, 27–54.

Barbieri, F., Ballesteros, M., & Saggion, H. (2017). *Are emojis predictable?* arXiv. https://doi.org/10.48550/arXiv.1702.07285

Berners-Lee, T. (2000). *Tejiendo la red*. Madrid: Siglo XXI de España.

Cichocka, A., & Dhont, K. (2023). *The SAGE handbook of personality and individual differences: Applications of personality and individual differences* (pp. 323–351). Los Angeles, CA: SAGE Publications Ltd.

Debnath, A., Pinnaparaju, N., Shrivastava, M., Varma, V., & Augenstein, I. (2020). Semantic textual similarity of sentences with emojis. In *Companion Proceedings of the Web Conference 2020* (pp. 426–430). ACM, New York.

Durántez-Stolle, P., & Martínez-Sanz, R. (2019). Politainment in the transmedia construction of the image of politicians. *Communication & Society*, *32*(2), Article 2. https://doi.org/10.15581/003.32.37854

García-Marín, J., & Serrano-Contreras, I.-J. (2023). (Un)founded fear towards the algorithm: YouTube recommendations and polarisation. *Comunicar*, *31*(74). https://doi.org/10.3916/C74-2023-05

Gentzkow, M., Kelly, B., & Taddy, M. (2017). *Text as data*. Cambridge: National Bureau of Economic Research. https://doi.org/10.3386/w23276

Gerbaudo, P. (2018). Social media and populism: An elective affinity? *Media, Culture & Society*, *40*(5), 745–753.

Gómez-García, S., Zamora, R., & Berrocal, S. (2023). New frontiers for political communication in times of spectacularization. *Media and Communication*, *11*(2), 109–112.

Grimmer, J., Roberts, M. E., & Stewart, B. M. (2022). *Text as data: A new framework for machine learning and the social sciences*. Princeton, NJ: Princeton University Press.

Ibrahim, H., AlDahoul, N., Lee, S., Rahwan, T., & Zaki, Y. (2023). YouTube's recommendation algorithm is left-leaning in the United States. *PNAS Nexus*, *2*(8). https://doi.org/10.1093/pnasnexus/pgad264

Joo, J., Bucy, E. P. (TTU), & Seidel, C. (2019). *Automated coding of televised leader displays: Detecting nonverbal political behavior with computer vision and deep learning*. https://ttu-ir.tdl.org/handle/2346/90282

Khaireddin, Y., & Chen, Z. (2021). *Facial emotion recognition: State of the art performance on FER2013*. arXiv. https://doi.org/10.48550/arXiv.2105.03588

Khoma, N., & Kozma, V. (2022). Spectacularization of political activism: Subject matter and social effect. *The Greek Review of Social Research*, 3–27.

Litvinenko, A. (2021). YouTube as alternative television in Russia: Political videos during the presidential election campaign 2018. *Social Media+Society*, *7*(1). https://doi.org/10.1177/2056305120984455

Lorenzo-Rodríguez, J., & Torcal, M. (2022). Twitter and affective polarisation: Following political leaders in Spain. *South European Society and Politics*, *27*(1), 97–123.

Luengo, Ó. G. (2014). Twitter vs medios tradicionales ¿Ha implicado Twitter un espacio ciudadano real de intercambio de información? In R. Cotarelo & J.-A. Olmeda (Eds.), *La democracia del siglo XXI. Política, medios de comunicación, internet y redes sociales* (pp. 409–428). Madrid: Estudios Políticos.

May, A. L. (2010). Who Tube? How YouTube's news and politics space is going mainstream. *The International Journal of Press/Politics*, *15*(4), 499–511.

Pelinka, A. (2013). Right-wing populism: Concept and typology. In R. Wodak, M. Khosravinik, & B. Mral (Eds.), *Right-wing populism in Europe* (pp. 3–22). London: Bloomsbury Academic.

Peng, Y., & Lu, Y. (2023). Computational visual analysis in political communication. In D. Lilleker & A. Veneti (Eds.), *Research handbook on visual politics* (pp. 42–54). Cheltenham: Edward Elgar Publishing.

Plazas-Olmedo, M., & López-Rabadán, P. (2023). Selfies and Speeches of a President at War: Volodymyr Zelensky's Strategy of Spectacularization on Instagram. *Media and Communication*, *11*(2), 188–202.

Rahyadi, I., Syahraihan, A. M., Agustina, D., & Irawan, D. A. (2023). Comparison of different political figures and evaluation of Twitter utilization over time in the political communication media. In *2023 17th international conference on ubiquitous information management and communication (IMCOM)* (pp. 1–7). https://doi.org/10.1109/IMCOM56909.2023.10035586

Russmann, U., & Svensson, J. (2017). Introduction to visual communication in the age of social media: Conceptual, theoretical and methodological challenges. *Media and Communication*, *5*(4), 1–5.

Schmøkel, R., & Bossetta, M. (2022). FBAdLibrarian and Pykognition: Open science tools for the collection and emotion detection of images in Facebook political ads with computer vision. *Journal of Information Technology & Politics*, *19*(1), 118–128.

Segerberg, A., & Bennett, W. L. (2011). Social media and the organization of collective action: Using Twitter to explore the ecologies of two climate change protests. *The Communication Review*, *14*(3), 197–215.

Serrano-Contreras, I.-J. (2021). *Medios de comunicación y polarización; un análisis del feminismo en España mediante procesamiento del lenguaje natural* [Universidad de Granada]. https://digibug.ugr.es/handle/10481/71409

Sterrett, D., Malato, D., Benz, J., Kantor, L., Tompson, T., Rosenstiel, T., Sonderman, J., & Loker, K. (2019). Who shared it?: Deciding what news to trust on social media. *Digital Journalism*, *7*(6), 783–801.

Tay, J., & Turner, G. (2008). What is television? Comparing media systems in the post-broadcast era. *Media International Australia*, *126*(1), 71–81.

Weismueller, J., Harrigan, P., Coussement, K., & Tessitore, T. (2022). What makes people share political content on social media? The role of emotion, authority and ideology. *Computers in Human Behavior*, *129*, 107150. https://doi.org/10.1016/j.chb.2021.107150

Zeng, J., & Abidin, C. (2021). '#OkBoomer, time to meet the Zoomers': Studying the memefication of intergenerational politics on TikTok. *Information, Communication & Society*, *24*(16), 2459–2481.

8 Terrorism and Perception

Federico Aznar Fernández-Montesinos and Katie Jane Patterson

1. War and Perception

War is considerably more complex than its physical realization through violent action, an idea that, due to its visibility, is often presented as its centerpoint. The phenomenon of war spills over from the physical dimension in which it develops, permeating the emotional and the political spheres. As pointed out by Glucksmann (2020), war is an activity of the spirit. For this reason, von Clausewitz (1982) defined it as a clash of wills that is only resolved on the battlefield; and General Beaufre describes it as a dialectic of hostile wills.

There is also the problem of the relevance of the facts because war does not exist completely apart from them. It is even necessary to define what is 'to win' and what 'to lose'. These concepts are situated in relation to achieving one's own objectives, more than in the defeat of the opponent; and this is when, sometimes, there is no real difference between a battle either won or lost on the physical plane. In fact, during the Middle Ages, kings were often present on the battlefield to claim their victory; such a gesture assured the legitimacy of their actions and truth of the claim. If we take truth not as an autonomous reality, that is, that subsists by itself, but rather, as the result of a social consensus, winning or losing comes to be a kind of shared feeling, or not, as shown in the smiling photos of those who shortly go on to act as suicide bombers. What is important is what is believed and what is felt by those involved; that is the decisive element, and as such the truth.

Reality, in this context, becomes a variable, and conflicts, in addition to being a clash of forces and wills, also become a collision of perceptions and realities. Ultimately, war is about temporarily altering the perception of the reality in which the conflict takes place: misleading, breaking the soul of the opponent, causing him to lose initiative, depriving him of his freedom of action, and persuading him to make wrong decisions. The key is thus located in this last human feature – the will – but this is, in turn, affected by the perception of the environment in which it is integrated.

DOI: 10.4324/9781003457381-9

In the most advanced Armed Forces, globally speaking, a newly developed 'cognitive domain' is being integrated together with the traditional forces: Land, Sea and Air, alongside which others such as Cyberspace or Outer Space have in recent history also been added. Such an addition transforms truth and reality into another dimension of the battlefield; an area in which to attack and defend. Such a view removes a level of autonomy and causes the entire conflict to be disaggregated from its context, placing it in a space apart from the reality of its context.

As a social phenomenon, war infiltrates all aspects of society. Crucially, it encompasses the internet and social networks as much as the battlefield. To Glucksmann (2020), it exists as a clash of discourses, which is not won by the best, but by the one that embraces the whole battlefield. If one doesn't play this game, they run the risk of being outflanked and, so, defeated.

Thus, the population, as a creator of consensus and truth, is the object and objective of a struggle that, to a large extent, is settled in their imagination and, for this reason, it is not easy to win. In the end, it is only perception that counts in both memory and power. It is there, in the emotions and in the memory, and not in reality, where defeat is burrowed. Without winning such a battle, military victory is not possible and, furthermore, such a victory loses part of its meaning since it cannot be projected along the time, in the future. It becomes a fight for truth, as well as the need to fix the correct reference of things; and, consequently, for the results of the action and even for its justice. That is why it was not necessary to win the Vietnam War if characters like Rambo could be created a posteriori, with such dramatic force that they can capture or transform reality itself and restore the dignity of the defeat until transforming its action into victory.

Another related issue is situated in the contradiction that war embodies. The objective of all war is peace, this is its political resolution, not victory, which is its military resolution (although clearly, whoever obtains victory tries to build peace on it). However, the terms 'peace' and 'victory', are not necessarily or directly equivalent, as the case of France in Algeria or the United States in Vietnam shows us. War, by developing its actions on one plane – the military – and measuring the effectiveness of its actions on another – the political – embodies a specific logic that, far from being linear and direct, often incorporates elements of contradiction and paradox. These are the result of the translation of acts of war to the different spheres and contexts in which they take place. Such shots are endowed with a kind of refraction that significantly alters the direction and effects of military action. The same will happen with terrorism.

War is a clash of powers – the Machiavellianism of strategy often confuses force with power (Glucksmann, 2020), but it is much more than that – and, as such, it is an inherently political activity in which the military plane is very relevant (though by no means is it the only one in which the conflict is settled). Hard power – whether military or economic – is often the most visible form of power, but it is accompanied by other variants that can enable the intended purpose, sometimes in a more effective and less apparent way. Power is not action; its secret is that it is rarely used because the use of its hard forms wears it out; In addition, action incorporates tolls in terms of legitimacy. The mere image of power is also, in itself, a form of power, since it does not need to be exercised, being like all its soft forms, a halo, a way of influencing and, therefore, a sign that does not incorporate the burdens of its hard nature. As Hobbes (2010) emphasized, "the reputation of power is Power".

In asymmetric warfare, the military level continues to be important, but the weaker party, seeing its poor prospects for success, transfers its operations to other areas (economy, media, for instance), whereby the chances of achieving victory are higher, by temporarily diluting the differences in power between the parties. But above all, it can also be defined as a confrontation between two significantly different strategic models.

War and terrorism are related. War is a clash of powers. Terrorism, for its part, is a fiction of war to the extent that it is also a fiction of power and incorporates the politics paradoxical logic. Thus, what is visible in a terrorist action suggests that there is much more behind when, not infrequently, what is exhibited on the scene of an attack is all, there is not anything left. In this way, the whole is presented as a part and thus, in addition, amplified by the multiplying capacity of social media, and an extraordinary return is obtained from each action in terms of Power.

From this perspective, we can consider terrorism as an extreme case of asymmetric warfare in which the weakest party definitively abandons the military plan, replacing it with the multiplier effect of social media.

2. Terrorism as a Phenomenon of Violence

Terrorism, as a practice, has existed since the dawn of humanity. The Latin for 'terror' comes from the name Deimos, a minor god and the son of Aphrodite (Venus) and Ares (Mars). Terror, not by chance, thus appears to us as a child of Beauty and Violence; and he is also the twin brother of Phobos, or Fear. The three are accompanied in each battle by the sister of Ares, the goddess Enio, known as the 'destroyer of cities'. The combination of mythological characters is neither strange nor casual, but on the contrary, very real and human and, therefore, explanatory of reality, as all myths are. The word 'terrorism' is derived from the political regime led by Maximilian Robespierre and which in turn takes its name from the famous speech he delivered before the National Assembly: "Virtue without terror is fatal; terror without virtue is powerless" (Robespierre, 2007, p. 115).

In it, an ideology, virtue, is linked to a practice, terror, in an equation that relates both terms. Such a combination requires delicate management to prevent the ideology from being contaminated by violence, which, in addition to being dangerous, is difficult to achieve.

From this, it follows that terrorism, or rather, terror, is fundamentally a communication strategy that has its roots in morbidity. It uses what Shelley called the "tempestuous loveliness of terror".[1] The showiness of the use of violence in a world and a time in which it has become strange constitutes a powerful media attraction factor; and it even has powerful effects of legitimation for security in the very convictions that are exhibited with its use. In terrorism the media takes precedence over any other consideration, including the military element or reality itself, since with its acts, it aspires to conceptualize and to transform it. Thus, if war is basically an act of communication that incorporates a supplement of violence, terrorism is a political activity that is staged in the media through a certain amount of bloodshed. Violence is part of terrorism, but terrorism is not only violence; in fact, violence, its methodology, is not the most crucial aspect of terrorism, but, as happens in war, the discourse, is an eminently political proposal.

Terrorism is an illegitimate methodology, a strategy, put at the service of a specific political option. It is based on the provocation with which the emotional manipulation of political decision-makers is intended, either directly or implicitly; that is, through social pressure resulting from the atmosphere of alarm and fear that actions generate. It is achieved through the association of violence and media pressure, obtained through sporadic waves of terror that are prolonged over time (Münkler, 2009).

In this way, through the intentional overpoliticization of its actions, terrorism tries to alter the perception that decision-makers have of reality; and with provocation, it forces an inappropriate response to the emotional challenge posed. Not having sufficient means to defeat the State, the danger of terrorism is usually situated in the response given to the challenges it poses. In other words, it manipulates the existing cleavages of societies, its fracture lines, placing their contradictions in the firing line. It is also the case that terrorism tries to impose on the State the need for a short-term reaction that is alien to its long-term strategy so that it makes the mistake of emotionally altering the parameters and references for analyzing the situation; and thus any option adopted is inadequate. It is the old action-reaction dynamic that continues to be useful and valid for the simple reason that it works.

Terrorism can also be described as a form of theater (Hoffman, 2017), a programmed show with which it tries to exercise emotional control over the population, rather than over a territory, as is characteristic of war. These uses of homeopathic doses of violence that, applied in a custom-built scenario and amplified by the mass media, help the terrorist group to colonize the minds of the target population, both posing a problem and offering the solution simultaneously through the imaginary. In addition, and with the repetition of their actions, pedagogically, terrorists rule out any option other than the one they propose while teaching their cause; it is what Carlo Pisacane called 'propaganda by deed'.

The attacks serve to raise the debate and spread the terrorist agenda, subsequently undermining the convictions of the counterpart. The media, in their search for neutrality and equidistance, help familiarize the ideas of terrorist groups; by trivializing words and terminology, the linguistic exposure allows a group's language to be adopted, thus contributing to the risk of both indoctrination and radicalization.

As one PLO leader George Habash noted of the Munich Games massacre in 1972: "The choice of the Olympics ...it was like painting the name of Palestine on a mountain that can be seen from the four corners of the Earth" (cited in Taylor, 1993, p. 6). The simplicity of his speech associated with the use of publicity techniques ensures repercussions. Postmodern man does not think, he just informs himself; however, he looks for emotion in the news more than for truth, that is why terrorism and false news, are more viral than the trustworthy news: they adapt better to what is demanded.

In any case, the effectiveness of terrorism is not measured by the material and human damage it causes, but by the psychological impact derived from them and which is not directly related to their physical reality; from there it bleeds into the political plane. We are facing an act of communication, in which the physical dimension, violence, is not necessarily essential but simply the medium.

3. Terrorism as a Media Phenomenon

One of the fundamental elements that terrorism incorporates is an effective media strategy. Modern terrorism in fact begins at the end of the 19th century with the appearance of the mass media, whose development has been parallel. Thus, when mass media became globally reaching, so did terrorism, guaranteeing the dissemination of a group's actions and with this their impact. For this reason, both terrorism and the media maintain a quasi-symbiotic relationship: terrorism wants to be news, and the media needs news. The message is not violence itself, but rather it is conceived under the code of violence.

Terrorism thus struggles for control of the news agenda and, with it, control of the truth. In addition, the media is able to generate an anxiety by demanding a response to something that does not require it and thus preventing the implementation of one phase of the response from taking hold before moving on to the next. In this way, the emotionality of public opinion is put before rationality or, even, the resolution of the problem posed.

E.T.A.s attacks took place at 08.00, which meant that footage already dominated the news at 09.00, and later occupied the 15.00 news and ran into the evening news, winning the group the whole day's worth of media coverage for their cause. When Spain joined the EU in 1985, E.T.A. similarly murdered five people in three different attacks trying to change the news agenda of the day and in this way, to misinform.

The media give terrorism a visibility that does not correspond to its real power. Visibility and power are terms felt as equivalent. The main attribute of power is to construct a truth, so that it is exercised through its production. Only the one who has the truth has the power. And this is best understood by simplest means. The truth must be made explicit and the cheapest and most indisputable way to do it is through an image. It helps not to think beyond what is in front of you or in the proposed sense.

It is not about creating large-scale or serious damage, but about summoning a large audience. The practice of terrorism thus embodies that of a publicist; a message, the symbolism and the quality of the unexpected, as well as the surprise (inherent in the proper use of tactical intelligence), to attract the attention of the target audience. The action is converted into a perfect image and ready to be reproduced, creating and feeding its own narrative. As has been said, it is a theater in permanent search of an audience: an 'expressive violence' (Le Borgne, 1988, p. 249) which sheds light on some debates in which the victims are reified in favor of the objects and symbols that are attacked.

As a work of art and despite its appearances, the image is emotional. Images allow great results to be achieved by influencing the emotional consciousness of millions of people. An audience does not have time to make its judgments and the information with which it does so is, not infrequently, deficient. An image in this context is everything, a complete explanation of extraordinary simplicity, which, being a portion of reality, is difficult to refute. This has made the real-time media 'factories of history' and creators. Reality – what is or is not real and true – thus becomes one of the dimensions of the battlefield, of the aforementioned 'cognitive domain'. The photographer, like the painter, is an artist, a selector of reality who uses the particular to express the general. However, the image that it provides to the viewer is not complete, it is packaged; with the camera selecting the portion of truth that is intended to be transmitted and discarding the rest. This is of course artificial, since the image is a fragment of the whole; the context is missing, without which it cannot be understood. The composition focuses on some element and thus that element is stolen; moreover, the simplification allows concentration on the sustained argument, centrally situated, subsequently eliminating in the process the inconsistencies that are inherently present in human nature. With this, the camera becomes, due to its ability to create both reality and impact, an instrument of politics. Photography is primarily directed at the emotions that are directly accessible to it. It is not for scholarly and rigorous analysts whose writings and explanations are rarely of interest to public opinion. The image hides the truth, it becomes a discourse and, wars like the one in Vietnam, are transformed into a succession of images of exuberant plasticity with which sensational (and irrefutable) events are projected, even if they are not the most important ones. As such, war is seen as a succession of photographs that, due to a lack of a media strategy on one side, allows the other to choose by imposing its agenda, and with it its law.

In any case, this unwanted and diabolical concurrence of interests between terrorism and the media requires debate and management, since freedom of the press belongs to the heritage of the West. Paradoxically, any restriction on freedoms would be a victory for the terrorists, since their fight involves a struggle for legitimacy and, incidentally, their capabilities are being recognized.

4. Terrorism as a Bloody Narrative

The key element of terrorism is not, as we have said, violence, which but serves as a visible manifestation of it; rather, its central element is the political discourse that it both creates and depends on. The discourse, or narrative, surrounding terrorism is its legitimizing element in which action, message and cause are interwoven; it is a medium that is part of the message and that serves to intertwine the collective object and real objective of the struggle. Narratives are not rational but emotional; they are built on the basis of perceptions, commonplaces or stereotypes and plot leaps, aiming to express a perceived reality built on the promise of a better world.

A narrative is always a selection of facts, carried out with greater or lesser accuracy and freedom, and which leads to a pre-established imagination. It supposes a balance between reality and fiction, to the extent that it embodies a conscious act of creation, and in which rational and irrational elements predetermined by the intuited purpose are incorporated. It exists as a bridge between the implicit and the explicit. A narrative then, as a stringed set of ideas, not false but incomplete, has the potential to evolve into an ideology (a doctrine or a religion, say). Its function is to make reality intelligible through an intentionally simplified lens; it is a vision of the world no matter how biased it may be and the point of reference from which it is made extravagant, and which, most of the time, is not presented. In this sense, terrorism is nothing but a bloody narrative.

Despite the appearance of presenting itself as a formulation, narratives are characterized by the debates that they put in motion, not simply the ideas that they present. They have the power to steer the population toward a certain direction and to publicly silence certain facts or opinions that contradict them or do not support them. Thus, if a narrative, as a set of linked ideas, takes into account something unforeseen or for which it does not have an implicit internal response, it is dismantled. Hence its illustrious coherence, from which most human acts remain absent.

As Freund pointed out: "ideology does not try to know if, for example, there is a contradiction between the ideal of freedom and that of equality: it excludes as enemies those who pose a similar question... the desire for exclusion" (Freund, 1995, p. 174). Hitler, predictably, goes further claiming that political parties are prone to enter compromises; but a Weltanschauung never does this. Whilst a political party is inclined to adjust its teachings with a view to meeting those of its opponents, a Weltanschauung, instead, proclaims its own.

The truth within such a discourse is viewed not as an unattractive prose or a set of data that is not at all suggestive, but rather as the emotion of an exciting proposal or agenda, however unrealistic and biased it may be. It thus becomes a mechanism of group identity construction and socialization. That is why a narrative is not immutable in form; its premise of change to keep the background unchanged means it has the potential to evolve and adapt, incorporating elements of the present that link with its proposal for the future. Through taking control of their own narrative, terrorist groups have the ability to reinterpret the facts and even themselves in order to maintain an emotional coherence with the ends. They are romantic but not universalistic or rationally symmetrical; they always start from a happy arcade that allows explaining the future using the past; or, to be more exact, they rewrite the past in the name of the future. If a reference does not work, without hesitation, another is sought; the important thing is to preserve the mobilizing spirit, the dynamics.

Narratives do not describe reality but rather they help to create it, generating the necessary ethical space for violence. Terrorists depend on an ideology or a set of ideals, in order to be able to live with the violence they commit or threaten to commit. Without the necessary narrative, they would go from being agents of justified and necessary violence to the condition of criminals, or worse still, to that of psychopaths (Laqueur, 1981, p. 272). Through the weapon of discourse, verifiable data and stories, however interpretable, are replaced by fragmented narratives based on a diffuse plot that uses a black-and-white logic to polarize the political space while reaffirming that they are not the actual pivots of real politics and may even have nothing to do with it. These narratives, or stories, choose the photographs in relation to the imaginaries they propose. This selection of facts and perspectives comes to justify what has already been decided before; feeling precedes thought just like music precedes words.

5. Conclusions

Terrorism, as a fiction of war, embodies its characteristics and its logic. Both terrorism and war are violent activities but above all, both are politically driven acts of communication, in which physical – and apparently decisive – violence, is driven by a prevailing and inherently political discourse, operating within its own specific parameters, and its own version of reality. With discourse as its strategy, terrorism tries to alter the perception of decision-makers and educate a population that is both the object and objective of the struggle. Using online methods of communication such as social media, terrorism uses the visibility of its own actions to – simulating a power it does not have – control the media agenda and impose on the State the need for a response that, due to its emotional nature, will never be satisfactory. Rather, it will inevitably generate an action-reaction spiral, a kind of drift that will place him in front of his own internal contradictions, will show his most coercive nature and will serve to break the feeling of community. The real danger of terrorism is thus not situated in its acts but rather in the measures adopted to respond to it.

Who has the power has the truth, because, remembering Foucault, power is obtained from the production of truth. The transformation of an untrue concept into something true embodies the essence of what concerns us as a real exercise of power. The struggle for the meaning of a term and for truth is, in the end, a struggle for power. The key to terrorism lies, despite appearances, in the solidity of its narratives, and not in the violence with which it stages its aims; this is the visible element of a dramatization process that serves to summon an audience and send a message. The narratives make movements such as Salafist-jihadist terrorism exceptionally dangerous as they have appropriated an ancient philosophical tradition with which they strengthen their discourse and provide coherence to their actions.

In short, no one can hide an illuminated city on top of a mountain, unless its own inhabitants are the ones who turn off their lights; As the biblical dictum says, "Take note of the one who has integrity! Observe the godly! For the one who promotes peace has a future" (psalm 37:37).

Notes

1 Shelley, P. B. (2014). On the Medusa of Leonardo da Vinci in the Florentine Gallery. In *1819–1820* (pp. 218–223). Routledge.

References

Freund, J. (1995). *Sociología del conflicto*. Madrid: Ediciones Ejército.

Glucksmann, A. (2020). The Discourse of Hatred. *The Posen Library of Jewish culture and civilization*; Volume 10: 1973–2005, 971–972.

Hobbes, T. (2010). Leviathan-revised edition. Broadview Press.
Hoffman, B. (2017). *Inside terrorism*. Columbia University Press.
Laqueur, W. (1981). Terrorismo. Biblioteca de Ciencias Políticas, Espasa Calpe, Madrid, 1980 (Ángel Sagredo Rubio). Documentación Administrativa.
Le Borgne, C. (1988). *La guerra ha muerto*. Madrid: Ediciones Ejército.
Münkler, H. (2009). Old and new wars. In Myriam Dunn Cavelty and Victor Mauer (eds.) *The Routledge handbook of security studies* (pp. 206–215). London: Routledge.
Robespierre, M. (2007). *Virtue and terror*. London: Verso.
Taylor, P. (1993). *States of terror*. London: BBC Books (First Edition).
Von Clausewitz, C. (1982). *On War*. J.J. Graham (Tr.), Anatol Rapoport. (Ed.), London: Penguin Classics.

9 Recruiting Magnets of Jihadi Radicalization

Unity, Redemption and Manicheanism

Djallil Lounnas and Massimo Ramaioli

1. Introduction

Socio-political radicalization is the process of relative change whereby a group or individuals undergo ideological and/or behavioral transformation (Ashour, 2009, p. 5). This transformation entails the embracing of contention "outside the common routine of politics [...] oriented towards substantial change [...] using extra-institutional means" (Beck, 2015, p. 18). More specifically, radicalization often includes the rejection of liberal and democratic principles and the use of force to achieve political goals (Ashour, 2009, p. 5). From an etymological perspective, radicalization stems from the Latin word '*radix*' ('root'), which hints at a return to posited origins as a locus of truth and purpose.

Radicalization of Islamist ideologies has been the focus of much scholarly attention, in particular as manifested in Salafi-Jihadism. In this context, the return to the origins occurs via shedding undue accretions, perceived as unwarranted betrayals of an ideal attainable situation (Settoul, 2022, p. 22). For instance, formations such as Al Qaeda (AQ) and the Islamic State in Iraq and Syria (ISIS) call for a return to the period of the early days of Islam, the time under the politico-religious leadership of Prophet Muhammed and the four caliphs ('*ar-rashidun*,' 'the right-guided') that succeeded him (Haykel, 2009).[1] This era acquires in their discursive construction mythical contours and utopian features. Labeled as the age of the 'pious ancestors' ('*as-salaf as-salih*'), it represents a perfect template for the one-time religious, social and political community. As Ahmed Hashim (2018, p. 65) explains, modern-day Salafism claims the pious ancestors were able to understand and thereby live Islam in its purest and most pristine form, bereft of any unwarranted novelty (in the form of unjustified theological, jurisprudential and socio-cultural innovations) that came later. Yet, the template of the *salaf* is a utopia also in its a-historical, because largely fictional and fabricated, rendering: the hallowed beginning of Islam was not a place outside of politics and history, as contemporary Salafis

DOI: 10.4324/9781003457381-10

would have it. Their discourse is thus largely pertaining to a (historical) non-locus.

Be that as it may, Salafism maintains the perfect Islamic community emerges from the faithful and exclusive observation of two sources: the *Qur'an* and the *Sunnah*, i.e. the prophetic tradition (Hashim, 2018). What separates at this juncture Salafi-Jihadists from other Salafis is the belief that the return to the 'root' of Islam, the golden age of the *salaf*, may and ought to be accomplished by the use of violence. This process would result in the restoration of the Caliphate, in Salafi discourse the ideal religious-politico institution, a replica here-and-now of the posited there-and-then *salaf* community. Therein, the political leader would be acting as the successor of Muhammad's religious *cum* socio-political authority: mainly, implementing the *shari'ah* (Islamic law); and defending-expanding the community of the believers, i.e. the *ummah* (Guidere, 2016, pp. 17–23).

In light of these elements, Quintan Wiktorowicz (2006), Mohamed M. Hafez (2007), and Thomas Hegghammer (2009) agree in defining Salafi-Jihadism as a specific theological reading of *tawhid* ('one-ness' or 'unicity' of God), which translates and substantiates into *hakimiyyah* ('sovereignty' of God). This conceptualization of sovereignty, harking back to the template of the *salaf*, entails the rejection of any unlawful innovation (*bida'*) deemed outside the original and pure message of Islam. Crucially, and unlike other branches of Salafism,[2] Salafi-Jihadism carries out a process of excommunication (*takfir*) against those Muslims accused of engaging in *bida'* and, consequently, in unbelief: for instance, Arab regimes which do not rule according to the *shari'ah* but to 'man-made laws,' an instance of *bida'*, resulting in unacceptable violations of *hakimiyyah* and consequently of *tawhid*.[3] *Jihad*, in this reasoning, becomes the lawful and appropriate way to rectify an unacceptable state of affairs, legitimizing the deployment of violence against any (perceived) attack against Islam and its *ummah*. One further development is the targeting of non-Muslims whenever deemed harboring hostility toward Islam: Jihadis' operations against Western countries and citizens answer to this logic (Gerges, 2009).

Omar Ashour (2009, pp. 19–25) explains such Jihadis' radicalization process along three axes: first, socio-economic problems (economic deprivation, persistent poverty, social exclusion, etc.); identity issues (perceived encroachments against Muslim culture); and the institutional-political elements—chiefly, repressive authoritarian regimes, a view shared by Hafez (2003). However, albeit relevant, these structural factors fall short of fully accounting for radicalization into Jihadism, especially in relation to the Salafi-Jihadi view that we have just illustrated. This observation was shared with one of the authors by a religious leader who worked on the deradicalization of Jihadis.[4] Also in his estimation, the literature does not investigate how radicalization moves from general grievances experienced at the individual level (such as poverty, political repression, etc.) to a specific form of violent militancy that gathers disparate subjects into a shared radical religious-political project.

In what follows, we systematize insights and considerations that emerged out of two main sets of interviews and meetings: first, with psychologists who have dealt with former Jihadis, i.e. the so-called 'returnees,' who often time joined the most notorious Jihadi organizations such as AQ and ISIS; second, with a number of such returnees themselves. Given the highly sensitive nature of the identities of the individuals we contacted, we were not granted clearance to reveal names or locations, but only the time when the interview took place. The references will reflect this constraint.

With the benefit of such interactions, we argue that three 'mythical elements of Jihadism' play a crucial role in the process of radicalization. These elements act as 'magnets,' a term we use to underline their gravitational pull for individuals floating around their field. In other words, radicalization requires, "ideational constructions which will act as magnets on individuals,"[5] therefore activating the otherwise only potential radical militancy of general individual grievances.

Our argument builds on Moghadam and Fishman's insights: as an ideology, Jihadism is an instrument of opposition and contestation. It provides a cognitive map to make sense of social reality. It becomes easier to grasp, more meaningful and more coherent. Furthermore, an ideology offers a course of action to remedy the predicament a group perceives to be facing (2011, pp. 6–7). We thus propose three 'magnets' that orient Jihadism *qua* ideology and enable the transition from grievances to full-fledged radicalization: first, the template of unity-*tawhid,* positing the idealization of the Muslim community at the time of the *salaf* and the Caliphate; second, the redemptive *jihad*, a conduit to individual dignity, purity and ultimate salvation; third, Manichean reasoning, splitting neatly an otherwise confounding world into right and wrong.

2. Tawhid and *Ummah*: The Golden Age as Magnet of Unity

The scholarship on Islamism has recently addressed the issue of the relation between Salafism and Jihadism. The former is hardly ever a violent phenomenon, while the latter always and necessarily is. Adraoui maintains that "it is both true and false to say that Salafism is the ideological infrastructure of the phenomena of political violence [i.e., Jihadism] observable in several regions of the contemporary world" (2022, p. 86). It is true because Salafism and Jihadism share key discursive referents, theological contentions, and jurisprudential positions. In fact, in terms of intellectual origins, Jihadism may be considered a radical elaboration of Salafi tenets.[6] Yet, Salafism and Jihadism seem to part ways when it comes to political imagination and attendant recourse to violence. The gulf between the two may be so wide as to put under scrutiny the 'continuum thesis' (Blanc & Roy, 2021).[7] Again Adraoui (2022, p. 91) tries to square the circle: "Salafism and Jihadism have now become mutually distinct realities although the latter is empowered by the former."

In other words, Jihadists are oftentimes hyphenated Salafis ('Jihadi-Salafis') precisely because they refer to the template of *as-salaf as-salih*. Yet, we must note here two crucial differences in explaining the radicalizing power of Jihadism, which manifests in its inclination toward uncompromising posturing and overt politicization of Islamic principles.

In the first place, it is true that Salafism configures a desire, an attempt to, "going back in history to reintroduce the past in the present in anticipation of the future" (Adraoui, 2022, p. 2). However, the specific articulation of this desire under Jihadism acquires idiosyncratic features that cannot be found within Salafism at large. There is in fact an element of apocalypticism, of 'end of times,' that urgently calls the Muslim believer to appropriate History. In this sense, Jihadism shares much in common with secular radical projects of modernity unlike other Salafis, who have never adumbrated either the imminent end of times or the possibility to steer the course of history to hasten such development.

Jihadism instead offers the possible recruit the chance of partaking in such a historical endeavor. Such eminently political feature of Jihadism makes its call to action a collective one, wherein disparate individuals (indeed afflicted by a sense of Durkheimian anomie and modernity-induced alienation, as amply observed in the literature)[8] find a venue for purpose in a project they may enthusiastically join. This contention does not intend to underestimate the religious (i.e., transcendental) facet of the Jihadi discourse. Rather, it intends to highlight the merging of the religious with the political domain.

In fact, in the second place, Jihadism pivots on a radical (re)interpretation and expansion of religious concepts. First, it seizes the concept of *al-wala' wa-l-bara'*, which may be loosely translated as 'loyalty and disavowal.' Under Jihadism, it stands for utmost loyalty toward fellow Muslim companions; and total rejection of outsiders.[9] In this exclusivist and confrontational rendition, *al-wala' wa-l-bara'* re-draws the traits of the hallowed early days of the *salaf*. For most Salafis, this paradigm remains chiefly a moral and spiritual compass, its concrete attainment deferred indefinitely into the future. But for Salafi-Jihadis it embodies also a political-historical goal that may come true here and now. It would bring about a tight community, characterized by deep, mutual loyalty (because of *al-wala'*) amongst the insiders; such a feeling of brotherhood would be squarely mirrored by the rejectionist, adversarial attitude (because of *al-bara'*) toward outsiders. A former jihadist maintained that "recruitment to go to Libya and Syria-Iraq presented the areas controlled by *Da'esh* (ISIS) as paradise on Earth, where pure and true Islamic rule was applied, [where] *al-wala' wa-l-bara'* [was applied]. This played an important role in attracting recruits."[10]

Second, the return and establishment of the Caliphate, the apogee of the golden age of *salaf*, is harbinger of the restoration of God's unity in its *ummah*. We must now consider how Jihadism articulates this passage, crucial to account for its powerful magnetism to stimulate radical political action. Salafism understanding of the aforementioned concept of *tawhid* speaks of God's unity as divinity (*uluhiyyah*), worship (*rububiyyah*) and attributes (*al-asma' wa-l-sifat*). Jihadis critically add *tawhid al-hakimiyyah*, or God's earthly sovereignty: "a society can be managed only by the strict respect of religious injunctions commanded by God Himself [...] The structures of a society (political, legal, identity, cultural, etc.) must never be in conflict with the divine commands" (Adraoui, 2022, p. 89). If such a society achieves conformity to God's command and will via the application of *shari'ah*, then the jihadist must see to that with any means at his disposal. To do otherwise would be violating *tawhid al-hakimiyyah*, and thus the attendant project the true believer is called upon to fulfill. It follows that opposing the return of the Caliphate is not only futile, because ultimately divinely ordained; it is also a sign of disbelief—*kufr*.

The identity of the individual *qua* Muslim is therefore at stake when caught in the field of this magnet. A stake that could not be higher: it carries at one time the dreadful perspective of leaving the *ummah*; and the most alluring possibility to join it in its (perceived) only true embodiment. Two young Muslims express this anxiety. A young Jordanian considering moving to the territories controlled by ISIS stated that, "this [Jordan] is not Islam…there is not law [*shari'ah*] here. But the Islamic State is Islam. There I can be a true Muslim."[11] Similarly, a recruit wishing to join Jihad in Iraq in 2003–2004 on the eve of the US invasion said, "I felt that I was being made one [with the other true Muslims], that I had to stay true to my true original values, that is Islam. We were of Salafist obedience."[12]

It is thus at this juncture that the paradigm of the *salaf* acts as a powerful magnet for the radicalizing individual. Such a paradigm connects, via the expanded concepts *of al-wala' wa-l-bara'* and *tawhid*, the idea of unity in the hereafter with unity here and now, adumbrating a seducing religious-political myth that may find soon concrete realization. Again, we observe how Jihadism manifests features typical of modern radical movements, similarly capable to attract and radicalize individuals. Gentile (2005) spoke of 'sacralization of politics' in the case of radical movements in the European context of the 20th century (specifically, Fascism). Jihadism is another rendition of this dynamic, as we may speak of '(radical) politicization of religion.'

The ultimate horizon for Salafi-Jihadism configures a utopia, insofar as the template of the *salaf* and the Caliphate remain firmly the key elements accounting for its magnetic attraction. Again, from the aforementioned interview:

> the Umma was oppressed and attacked, Jihad was the right thing to do. There was *idealization* [emphasis added] of the Jihadists in Iraq and their deeds. We need to help the *ummah*: the *Qur'an* and the Sunnah were used as the main argument. We talked about *as-salaf as-salih*, the golden age, we talked about the caliphs, especially caliph 'Ummar. We felt part of the *ummah*, a brotherhood much bigger than us, we felt like the Palestinians, the Chechens, the Iraqis. [They] were our brothers, we longed toward the golden age.[13]

Hence, the era of *salaf* connects, via a specific articulation of *tawhid*, the perfection of God to the attainable perfection of its earthly community, the *ummah*, a religious-political community that rests on the strict observance of *al-wala' wa-l-bara'*. It is a utopia in that it aptly captures the two intertwined meanings of such concept: a perfect place and a non-place. The *salaf* occupy a mythical space of harmony, peace and unity, the emblem of flawless reception on the part of the community of God's message. As a mythical space, it exerts a powerful fascination on the possible recruits. This space has vacated historical time: but it can be brought back via radical political action. The individual joins a collective endeavor that promises participation, with other fellow believers, in an enterprise to restore the righteous path of History, rectifying evil, hastening the advent of *hakimiyyah*: in the words of a former Jihadi leader, "[we were expecting] the golden age of the *ummah* at the time of the Prophet and his four successors ruled by Caliph, an imaginary narrative, the perfect rule…[this ideal] creates expectation of goals to reach."[14] The Caliphate is a promise of collective —social and political —redemption. As we shall see below, this aspect readily connects with the redeeming element of the main venue to bring about the utopia, that is to say *jihad*.

However, as noted by Böker (2015, p. 92), no utopia can ever shed its non-existence when it conjures up a perfect world. It behooves also to notice how such a utopian vision is hardly specific to Jihadism, which comes instead to substantiate a mechanism eloquently illustrated by Gleave and Kristo-Nagy (2015, p. 10) in his discussion of religion and political violence:

> The unsolvable problem of suffering and death calls for a 'religious' solution: belief in what we would like to exist, in order to help ourselves to bear what we experience. *Credo quia absurdum*. [...] We believe in what we do not know, but would like to be absolutely sure we know.

3. Fighting on the Path of God: *Jihad* as Magnet of Redemption

The term was *jihad* featured prominently in the earlier section in relation to the paradigm of the *salaf*. But it has a magnetic force of its own, too. As a psychologist who dealt with jailed Jihadi returnees explains, most of those who join organizations like ISIS or AQ have "a past:" whether a criminal record or a life marked by abuse and social marginalization, they feel tainted by something for which they blame themselves.[15] Hence, a jihadi recruiter will approach such individuals with a carefully crafted message: it points toward a "way out of this otherwise unacceptable and unbearable past."[16] This message outlines to the targeted individual a ready-made solution to escape sense of guilt, inadequacy and lack of purpose; it is meant to address needs of identification, belonging or meaning for individuals who tend not to have any. The recruiter deploys a discourse that acts as a sort of, "protection against the individual troubled and shameful past, like a fortress."[17] The discourse contributing to radicalization thus primes social, political, economic, and ultimately individual fragilities. The psychologist further explains that the recruiters, often charismatic, eloquent, and confident,

> put to sleep the individual intellectual mechanisms of defense, such as alert skepticism – i.e., if and when they still exist. Then, they identify and use people's weakness, especially a sense of guilt for the shameful past; and proceed to offer solutions that want to answer immediately the needs of the possible recruit.[18]

The recruiter manages to provoke eventually a cognitive and then behavioral change by pivoting the message of personal redemption, the solution to one's existential anxiety, on the concept of *jihad*.

Originally, the word *jihad*, and cognate concepts such as *ijtihad*, indicate exerting an effort in terms of reflection, understanding and meditation. The formalization and codification of this concept correspond with the emergence of the major Islamic jurisprudential schools (the Malaki, Hanafi, Shafi and Hanbali). They tend to identify three forms of *jihad*. First, the *jihad* of conquest (or offensive *jihad*) aims at bringing Islam to the lands of Infidels (*dar al-kufr*) and converting them. Second, defensive *jihad* intends to protect the *ummah* and thus the Land of Islam (*dar al-Islam*) from external invaders and attackers. Third, internal *jihad* aims at fighting the threats from within Islam, such as those who threatens its unity: the episodes of the *kharijis* ('those who position themselves outside' [of Islam]) is an early example of this inner conflict, just like dealing with sinners (*af-fassiqin*) and the apostates (*al-murtadin*) within the community.

As Achour (2015, p. 171) explains, *jihad* is meant to protect the abode of Islam and its *ummah,* specifically its beliefs and faith (*iman*), and orthopraxis. Failing to do so could threaten the survival of Islam itself. In this sense, Filiu (2006, p. 11) argues that ultimately *jihad* becomes a question of land and territory: whether it means expanding or conversely protecting Islam from either inside or outside threats.

Jihad is not therefore simply synonymous with 'war,' although at times the term may cover that semantic space. Boukraa maintains that *jihad* means first, "an effort to understand and analyze the meaning of the Quran. The word Jihad itself appears only 35 of the over 6,000 verses in the Coran, with only 10 directly referring to the war" (Boukraa, 2009, p. 208). *Jihad* indicating holy war may be inferred however in the *surah* II (190–193: "Fight in the way of Allah those who fight against you but do not transgress. Indeed, Allah does not like transgressors"), a much-quoted passage from Jihadis when in need to justify violence. In this sense, efforts—also militant and/or military—to defend the Islamic faith become a religious obligation for Muslims. In the view of Jihadis, the enemies are clearly identifiable because openly stated in the *Qur'an*: (1) those who fight the Muslims (II, 190–193), (2) the prevaricators (II, 190–193), (3) the unbelievers (IV, 76), (4) the allies of the devil (IV, 176), (5) the Infidels who neither believe in God nor in Judgment day (II, 29), (6) the polytheists (IX, 5), (7) the people of the book (Jews, Christians) who do not pay the capitation (II, 29) (Boukraa, 2009, p. 206).

Engaging in *jihad* in this fashion earns one the honored label of *mujahid,* 'he who carries out *jihad,*' and that has become synonymous with 'Islamic fighter' in the jihadi discourse. The utmost proof of one's commitment to *jihad* is death *fi sabil-l-Allah,* 'on the path of God:' he who dies in carrying out *jihad* is referred to as *shahid,* someone 'who gives testimony' of his faith (by dying for it). It is at this point that a former jihadi explained that, "the martyr is the one who abandoned everything he has, including family and work, and fight and dies in the way of God."[19] Such ultimate sacrifice grants the individual not only salvation in the hereafter, but also a revered stature in the memories of his companions and the *ummah* at large. Again, the two domains—the earthly/political and the transcendent/religious do not manifest discontinuities in this construction.

Within Jihadism, *jihad* is then articulated around principles that outline a path, a trajectory of redemption. It is such (potential) trajectory that acts as a powerful magnet. We have discussed some of the concepts that underpin it, such as *hakimiyyah* and *al-wala' wa-l-bara'*. In addition, the idea of *hijra* or exile acquires central importance, as it enjoys leaving the lands of unbelief to go to lands of Islam (Adraoui, 2022, pp. 53–54). *Jihad* also mandates to combat *al-ta'ifah al-moumtan'iah*, 'the sect which refuses Islam.' This reasoning culminates with *nusrah al-Islam wa-l-muslimin* ('the protection of Islam and the Muslims') from aggression and oppression, the ultimate meaning of *jihad*.[20]

It is precisely at this moment, as a religious leader explains, that *jihad*, conducted often by people in distress grappling with their troubled past, informs a cognitive shift in their self-perception. They acquire a sense of dignity (*karamah*), which they feel had been lost through humiliation, oppression and past misconducts. *Jihad* has them "reborn."[21] A rebirth that, connecting with one of the central tenets of Salafism, speaks of purity, washing away a sullied, un-islamic past (Gauvain, 2013; Rock-Singer, 2020). *Jihad* therefore is an action to defend or expand *dar al-Islam* as well as an exercise in self-redemption: the two are one and the same in the eyes of the jihadi militant. The religious-political project carried out through *jihad* offers meaning and purpose, the possibility to fight for something beyond the self: purer, more worthy, away from the past lowly, selfish existence. Finally, militancy, redemption, and dignity would lead to salvation.[22]

There is one last element to consider. A psychologist who deals with returnees from ISIS, reflecting on jihadis' personal journeys, noticed how the message of *jihad* and the discourse around it pivot on "narcissist fault lines," too.[23] Narcissism decisively contributes to the feeling of redemption, which remains therefore marred by it: it fuels a sense of overbearingness, prepotency; and practices of prevarication and often heinous violence. Narcissism is a source of hubris, a handy shortcut for the recruit's move upward in terms of both social standing and self-esteem: "from zero to hero."[24] This personal history of redemption mirrors the trajectory of the age of *salaf*. The personal experience of "resurrection, where the past is abolished"[25] echoes the rebirth of the true Muslim community under the Caliphate, at last overcoming the oppression from enemies of Islam. The posited utopia of the *salaf* for the *ummah* is reflected in the posited utopia of personal redemption through *jihad* for the individual. The two magnets work together. They do so because of a third magnet, which plays the function usually attributed to ideology: the simplification of the social reality and the removal of ambiguity (Moghadam & Fishman, 2011, pp. 6–7).

4. Neat Divides: Manicheanism and the Magnet of the Simple Reasoning

Jihadi ideology attracts recruits because it provides a cognitive map to read the world. In order to sustain a sense of intellectual and ethical clarity, complex, skeptical and nuanced reasoning is foregone; straightforward, clear, and doubtless analysis is primed instead. A radical discourse precisely plays this role. It offers an overly simplified—dare we say simplistic—and binary perception of the external world, its reputed issues, and the possible solutions.

Jihadis share with Salafis of all stripes a set of core epistemological principles. As mentioned above, the *Qur'an* and the *Sunnah* of the Prophet represent the only two admitted sources for jurisprudential assessment and ethical guidance. Salafis then proceed to deem most of Islamic intellectual, philosophical, and jurisprudential history as evidence of *bida'*, therefore promptly discarding it (exceptions, such as the admiration for Ibn Taymmiyya or Abdul al-Wahhab, albeit important are far and few). This move is consonant with Salafism's idiosyncratic approach to the sources, too: its literalism and its scripturalism (Duderija, 2011). Stemming from the contention that the message of the Scriptures is *wadih* ('clear') in and of itself, Salafism does not engage in any sustained efforts of *tafsir* ('exegesis') of allegorical, let alone mystical, hidden meanings of the texts. In its search for immediacy and connection to the origins, any recourse to personal understanding and elaboration is not only discouraged, but flatly rejected. Pluralism of views is not admissible.

Again, the concept of *al-wala' wa-l-bara'* acts as a key·element: it commands, "undivided loyalty to God, Islam and their coreligionists overall all other things on the one hand, and the disavowal they must show to anything deemed unislamic on the other hand" (Wagemakers, 2008, p. 3). It crafts a world of dichotomies and pairs. Wherein, Jihadism inserts an attitude of particular animosity which comes to shape its *weltanschauung: dar al-Islam* and *dar al-Kufr*; believers and unbelievers; *karamah* and corruption; redemption and perdition. To the cognitive dynamic corresponds in fact an ethical one: 'loyalty and disavowal' compels the jihadi recruit to work with dichotomies readily portending to a Manichean view. All the good is on one side; all the evil on the other.[26] There is no nuance: it is not needed; it is to be avoided. Personal evaluations informed by independent thinking, critical assessment, alert skepticism must be relinquished by the recruit. Yet, this requirement is precisely the magnet attracting him. In a confounding, complex and whereby alienating world, Jihadism offers easy answers to complex issues, which is what the recruit is already seeking. For instance, the bewildering dynamics of international relations, to which jihadis often pay much attention, are depicted as the unfolding of the confrontation between righteous *mujahiddun* on the one hand and conniving apostates (*murtadin*) and infidels (*kuffar*) on the other:

> our goals was to support Muslims, the Afghans, the Muslims in Philippines, Kashmir, Chechens etc. to support the cause of the Muslims against hypocrisy…The Arab regimes were dictatorship and oppressive… of course, the West was hypocritical, too, and exploiting our resources.[27]

In this reading, there are no other variables beyond the binary schemata informed by *al-wala' wa-l-bara'*: no local histories and identities, no institutional dynamics, no geostrategic considerations, no economic drives—let alone overtures to cultural pluralism.

The magnetism of simplified reasoning therefore works by offering a dichotomous reading of the basic tenets of religion, which then inform the interpretation of socio-political reality at large. At the same time, this process is never purely cognitive, but also moral and ethical.[28] The connection with the magnet of *jihad* discussed earlier is clear. The universe in which the recruit is to fight on the path of God, and experience its redeeming power, is a universe of certitude of both process and outcomes: both most alluring perspectives for individuals who have often experienced socio-economic estrangement and socio-cultural alienation, thereby loosing stable cognitive and ethical references.[29] Furthermore, the recruit may enjoy a position whereby he is now in charge of extending the same treatment toward the hypocritical (even apostate) society that rejected him: blaming it and its members for his predicaments; seeking confirmation and comfort in an alternative vision that will come about thanks to his efforts (the establishment of the righteous Caliphate via *jihad*).[30]

There is one last consideration to make. As observed above, Jihadism manifests striking similarities to other radical movements that emerged in modernity. In this sense, its political trappings are just as evident as its religious and transcendental ones. The cognitive-ethical frames that inform Jihadism's Manichean reasoning clearly indicate the recruiter who is fighting alongside him and who is fighting against him. That is to say that the projects of the *salaf* and the re-establishment of the Caliphate are not individual endeavors. They are collective ones. They therefore must provide coordinates to discriminate between in-group and out-group individuals: who must be protected and who is to be repelled, who is a friend (or 'brother,' as often times Jihadis refer to one another) and who is an enemy.[31] This binary divide maps neatly onto the Schmittian distinction between 'friend' and 'enemy;' and acquires specific, and we might say even momentous, relevance.

In fact, the category of the Enemy as ontological 'other' occupies the imaginative horizon of the jihadi fighter (Ramaioli, 2023). It is against this category that the new identity of the recruit may be shaped and constructed: "[t]his enemy is imagined in the two images of the invader and the traitor (or the usurper)" (Adraoui, 2022, p. 65) allowing the jihadis to lump together as foes of Islam both the former (the infidel-*kuffar*), as well as the latter, fellow Muslims not deemed (anymore) as such (*murtad*, 'apostate'), who have thus betrayed the community. Once again, there is no nuance in this analysis. The variety of social reality is boiled down to a dichotomous variable, separating humanity as a whole in discretely identifiable groups. The political import of such a move in the process of radicalization is equally dramatic. As Schmidt contended, "[t]he distinction of friend and enemy denotes the utmost degree of intensity of a union or separation, of an association or dissociation" (Schmidt, 1996, p. 26). It is also striking how Schmidt's words closely resemble once more the concept of *al-wala' wa-l-bara'*. The intensity to which Schmidt refers famously places the stakes of the political to the highest degree: because "to the enemy concept belongs the ever present possibility of combat," then the physical annihilation of the enemy "remain[s] a real possibility for as long as the concept of the enemy remains valid" (Schmidt, 1996, p. 32). The Jihadi world is utterly political and radical in its plastic rendition of the Schmittian dichotomy of friend/enemy: "[a]n enemy exists only when, at least potentially, one fighting collectivity of people confronts a similar collectivity" (Schmidt, 1996, p. 28).

The magnet of simple reasoning ties up the loose ends of the recruit's imagination: he is now confronted by a simple world, featuring a stark recognition of friends and enemies. This recognition demands in fact the recruit to be ready—actually, willing—to deploy violence for the ultimate (political) sake of the in-group members, whose survival is predicated on the obliteration of the enemy/other. The dichotomous reasoning of Jihadism brings its starting assumptions to their most uncompromising and harrowing consequences.

5. Conclusion: Radicalization and Magnets

We have contended that three magnets contribute to the process of Islamist radicalization in the case of jihadi recruits. There are structural factors that may well predispose the individual to radicalize; however, solely focusing on such grievances falls short of considering what ultimately brings a potential recruit into the fold of formations like ISIS and AQ. Such crucial decision on a personal level is made possible—actually is encouraged—by what the jihadi recruiter, discourse and narrative offer the individual who contemplates joining a radical group. The metaphor of 'magnets' aptly captures their capacity to break a potential recruit's resistance to full commitment: having experienced either socio-economic exclusion, political repression, identity crisis or a combination thereof, the magnets finally contribute to attract the individual in a cognitive, moral, and political space where he may redress such predicaments.

In this sense, the magnets of unity, redemption and Manicheanism may be observed separately for analytical purposes, as we have done; but they act of course at the same time as they conjure up a horizon to which the recruit may well aspire and ultimately commit. The paradigm of the ancestors readily offers a political program of unity, joining efforts with like-minded individuals whose actions may now help bring about a shared political project. The communitarian unity and ethos of this project are the reflection of God's own plan for humankind and History, imbuing the laboring for the re-establishment of the Caliphate with both utopian and millenarian expectations; furthermore, as in the case with other radical political projects, endowing such efforts with a tremendous sense of purpose, capable of calling for people's ultimate dedication and sacrifice.

In order to make this project come true, fighting on the path of God via *jihad* connects the collective endeavor to a trajectory of self-redemption. Just like the advent of the Caliphate will redeem a *ummah* who went astray, so *jihad* will redeem the believer whose hitherto life has been marred by personal drifting, moral lassitude, and weak faith. The radical violence of Jihadism depends precisely on the thorough re-constitution of the subject via its deployment: abiding by God's plan, redeeming a sullied past, signaling one's own virtue by contemplating and carrying out the ultimate sacrifice.

However, such radical posturing can be articulated only within the confines of a specific cognitive, analytical, and moral map: a worldview of distinct Manichean features, the last magnet under consideration. A magnet that attracts given its (almost brutal) simplification of reality. Underpinning its functioning, as it was the case, on a close observation, for the other magnets as well, is the concept of *al-wala' wa-l-bara'*, which jihadi ideology reframes to portend an inescapable confrontation between righteous forces and evil doers. It is in fact in this stark dichotomy that utmost, relentless confrontation (and attendant violence) can truly make sense.

As argued throughout the paper, we do not consider this radical resolve as idiosyncratic to Jihadism; rather, it speaks of its ideological-political import as a modern radical phenomenon, whose dynamics, posturing and outlooks may establish clear parallels, for instance, with Schmittian concepts of friend and enemy. At the same time, it is important to recognize the specific contours and functions of these magnets. Their articulation and deployment are in fact key to the process of radicalization. Conversely, their careful dismantling—tackling, that is, their radicalizing and attractive capacity—ought not to be ignored in any program seeking instead to de-radicalize individuals. The purpose of this chapter was not to outline a thorough policy proposal for de-radicalization; however, we conclude by saying that offering to the potential recruit or returnee a different articulation, rather than the wholesale removal, of the discursive constructions analyzed here—the age of the *salaf, jihad,* and Manichean worldview—may be considered an important component of such a program. There is no need, in other words, to abandon a cherished faith and religious belief; but rather, to re-articulate some of the propositions and attendant practices with which the individual has come to associate it.

Notes

1 Contemporary Salafis regard up to the third generation of Muslims after Mohammed's revelation as 'pious ancestors.' This contention is based on the belief that the original message of his revelation was, till then, transmitted and received in its unaltered and pristine form.
2 Wiktorowicz (2006) has offered the most accepted partition of the Salafi movement: quietists, who avoid politics; politicos, who engage in institutional forms of political participation; and jihadis, the subjects of the present study, who operate outside the confines of legal and institutional politics, having rejected those as *bida'*. For a re-evaluation over Wiktorowicz's categories, see Cavatorta and Amghar (2023).
3 See for instance prominent Salafi-Jihadi thinker Abu Muhammad Al-Maqdisi, *Millat Ibrahim* (1984).
4 Interview 1 of the authors with a religious leader who worked on deradicalization programs (March 2022).
5 Ibid.
6 For works dealing with the intellectual and historical origins of Salafism and the branching out of Jihadism, see Adraoui (2022), Bishara (2022), Lauzière (2015), Wagemakers (2020).
7 The 'continuum thesis' allowed Wiktorowicz (2006) to place on the same continuum quietist/apolitical Salafis, politico Salafis and Jihadi-Salafis in his seminal work.
8 See for instance Roy (2004).
9 For an in-depth discussion of how on the concept of 'loyalty and disavowal' acquired radical political meanings, see Wagemakers (2012).
10 Interview 2 with a former ISIS member conducted by the authors (March 2022).
11 Interview 3 by the authors of a possible jihadi recruit (April 2016).
12 Interview 4 by the authors of a possible jihadi recruit (March 2015). This possible recruit eventually did not join.
13 Interview 4.
14 Interview 5 by the authors with a former jihadi leader (March 2022).
15 Interview 6 by the author with a psychologist who has treated foreign fighter returnees (October 2021).
16 Ibid.
17 Ibid.
18 Ibid.
19 Interview 7 by the authors with a former jihadist (October 2011).
20 Interview 7.
21 Interview 1.
22 Interview 1.
23 Interview 6.
24 Ibid.
25 Ibid.
26 Interview 1.
27 Interview 5.
28 Interview 6.
29 Ibid.
30 Interview 6.
31 Ibid.

References

Achour, Y. B. (2015). *Aux fondements de l'orthodoxie sunnite*. Paris: Presses Universitaires de France.

Adraoui, M. A. (2022). *Understanding salafism*. London: Springer Nature.

Al-Maqdisi, A. M. (1984). *Millat Ibrahim wa-Da'wat al-Anbiya' wa-l-Mursalin wa-Asalib al-Tughat fi Tamyu'aha wa-Sarf as-Du'at 'anha [The Religion of Abraham and the Calling of Prophets and Messengers and the Methods of the Transgressive Rulers in Dissolving it and Turning the Callers Away from It]*. Available at www.tawhed.ws/t

Ashour, O. (2009). *The de-radicalization of jihadists: Transforming armed Islamist movements*. London: Routledge.

Beck, C. J. (2015). *Radicals, revolutionaries, and terrorists*. Cambridge: Polity Press.

Blanc, T., & Roy, O. (2021). *Salafism: Challenged by radicalization?: Violence, politics, and the advent of post-Salafism*. Fiesole: European University Institute.

Böker, M. (2015). The concept of 'Realistic Utopia': Ideal theory as critique. *Constellations: An International Journal of Critical and Democratic Theory*, 24(1), 89–100.

Boukraa, L. (2009). *Le djihadism: l'Islam a l'epreuve de l'Histoire*. Alger: Les Editions APIC.

Cavatorta, F., & Amghar, S. (Eds.). (2023). Special issue: Revisiting Wiktorowicz – Salafism, politics and violence in the contemporary world. *Contemporary Islam: Dynamics of Muslim Life*, 17(2).

Duderija, A. (2011). Neo-traditional salafi Qur'an-sunna hermeneutics and its interpretational implications. *Religion Compass*, 5(7), 314–325.

Filiu, J. P. (2006). *Les frontières du jihad*. Paris: Les Editions Fayard.

Gauvain, R. (2013). *Salafi ritual purity: In the presence of God*. London: Routledge.

Gentile, E. (2005). Political religion: A concept and its critics – a critical survey. *Totalitarian Movements and Political Religions*, 6(1), 19–32.

Gerges, F. A. (2009). *The far enemy: Why jihad went global*. Cambridge: Cambridge University Press.

Gleave, R., & Kristo-Nagy, I. (2015). "Introduction: Violence, our inherent heritage." In idem (Eds.), *Violence in Islamic thought from the Qur'an to the mongols* (pp. 1–23). Edinburgh: Edinburgh University Press.

Guidere, M. (2016). *Le retour du califat*. Paris: Les Editions Gallimards.

Hafez, M. M. (2003). Why Muslims rebel: Repression and resistance in the Islamic world. Lynne Rienner Publishers.Hashim, A. (2018). *The caliphate at war: The ideological, organizational and military innovation of the Islamic state*. London: Hurst.

Haykel, B. (2009). "On the nature of salafi thought." In R. Meijer (Ed.), *Global salafism: Islam's new religious movement* (pp. 33–51). New York: Oxford University Press.

Hegghammer, T. (2009). "Jihadi salafists or revolutionaries: On religion and politics in the study of islamist militancy." In R. Meijer (Ed.), *Global salafism: Islam's new religious movement* (pp. 244–267). New York: Oxford University Press.

Lauzière, H. (2015). *The making of salafism: Islamic reform in the twentieth century*. New York: Columbia University Press.

Moghadam, A., & Fishman, B. (Eds.). (2011). *Fault lines in global jihad: Organizational, strategic, and ideological fissures*. New York: Taylor & Francis.
Ramaioli, M. (2023). Salafism as gramscian informed vanguardism. *Contemporary Islam: Dynamics of Muslim Life, 17*(2), 297–318.
Rock-Singer, A. (2020). Practices of piety: An alternative approach to the study of Islamic movements. *Religions, 11*(10), 520.
Roy, O. (2004). *Globalized Islam: The search for a new ummah*. New York: Columbia University Press.
Schmidt, C. (1996). *The concept of the political.* Chicago, IL and London: Chicago University Press.
Settoul, E. (2022). *Penser la radicalisation djihadiste: acteurs, théories, mutations.* Paris: Puf.
Wagemakers, J. (2008). Framing the "Threat to Islam": 'Al-Wala wa Al-Bara' in Salafi discourse. *Arab Studies Quarterly, 30*(4), 1–22.
Wagemakers, J. (2012). *A quietist jihadi: The ideology and influence of Abu Muhammad al-Maqdisi.* Cambridge: Cambridge University Press.
Wagemakers, J. (2020). Salafism: Generalisation, conceptualisation and categorisation. In M. Ranstorp (Ed.), *Contextualising salafism and salafi jihadism* (pp. 21–36). Copenhagen: National Center for Forebyggelse af Ekstremisme.
Wiktorowicz, Q. (2006). Anatomy of the Salafi movement. *Studies in Conflict & Terrorism, 29*(3), 207–239.

10 Representing "Muslims" in Jihadist Magazines

An Analysis of the *NUTCRACKER* Corpus Topics

Pascual Pérez-Paredes and Tony McEnery

1. Introduction

In 2023, jihadist violence remains a global issue. Jihadist violence has recently hit Mali,[1] where Al Qaeda-linked militants have killed over 60 people on an army base and a crowded passenger boat on the Niger River. In July and August 2023, the Spanish police arrested two people in Benavente (Zamora) and Cullera (Valencia) for their involvement in the largest known jihadist network in Spain. The network was involved in the recruitment of young people and minors. According to the Spanish Home Office,[2] they publicly disseminated terrorist content that allowed them to select the people most susceptible to radicalisation. These individuals became part of a private chat group, administered by the two detainees. The group comprised dozens of members dispersed across Spain. Spanish Police investigations have shown how the proselytising activities of the detainees transcended the virtual sphere; they were linked to graffiti on public roads featuring the slogans of the terrorist organisation DAESH, such as "DAWLAT AL ISLAM BAQUIYAH", which means "the Islamic State survives and expands". In late September 2023, an Ecuadorian jihadist was arrested for both preparing her four young sons to fight with Daesh and announcing that they would soon travel to Syria to join this Islamist terrorist group.[3] According to the Spanish police, she had been radicalised and used social networks to recruit prospective fighters through propaganda in Spanish, Arabic, English and Russian. In October 2023, four suspects were arrested in an anti-jihadist operation in Madrid, Barcelona and Granada.[4] They had an explosives manual. According to police sources, the most radicalised couple in the group were converts to Islam.

Violent radicalisation of Muslims depends on the internet as an identity tool (Walli, 2015). In this context, jihadist magazines are used by terrorist organisations for self-representation (Malešević, 2017) and building their membership glocally. In Europol's European Union Terrorism Situation and Trend Report 2023 (TE-SAT),[5] the most comprehensive and up-to-date

DOI: 10.4324/9781003457381-11

intelligence picture on terrorism in the EU, Member States were reported to view jihadist terrorism as the most prominent threat in the area. This perceived threat is reflected in arrest statistics; for instance, out of the 380 individuals arrested by EU Member States for terrorism-related offences in 2022, 266 were apprehended for jihadist offences. The threat is perceived to be continuing, and jihadist activities have not abated. As we write this chapter, heightened security measures are in place across the West due to a call for a "Global Day of Jihad" on October 13, 2023, issued by former Hamas leader Khaled Mashal.[6]

This chapter examines a corpus of jihadist magazines published between 2009 and 2017 (Dhiab-Hassan, Benítez-Castro, & Hidalgo-Tenorio, 2018). We bring together corpus-research methods and an analysis of (self-) representation strategies, paying special attention to the in-group representation of Muslims, and the role of youngsters, women, and the "Muslim world" in co-constructing the representation of Muslims in this crucial propaganda tool. Our aim is to exploit corpus methods to contribute to the exploration of jihadi self-identity construction, an area that has been identified as under-researched by Macdonald and Lorenzo-Dus (2021).

2. Muslims and Violence

Corpus linguists have scrutinised the representations of Muslims across diverse contexts, delving into how lexico-grammatical features unveil the role of language in the discursive construction of identity. In this section, we will examine public mass media texts and private texts found in the possession of individuals convicted of jihad-related crimes in the UK.

Research in the early years of the 21st century had already examined the portrayal of Muslims in the British media. Following the events of 9/11, Poole (2002) conducted a study on the reception of British media representations of Muslims, encompassing Muslims and non-Muslim groups. Her findings revealed that the British media perpetuate dominant discourses by framing Muslims within a context of conflict. Poole suggests that British Muslims are primarily "known to non-Muslims in the UK mostly through the media, [which] defines the meaning of the Muslim presence in Britain [and] provides us with our ways of seeing" (p. 240).

Baker, Gabrielatos and McEnery (2013a, 2013b) used corpus methods to investigate the lexico-grammatical realisations of such representations. They looked at 11 British newspapers between 1998 and 2009. Islamophobic representations of Muslims were found in some right-leaning tabloids such as the *Daily Express* or the *Daily Star*. Overall, most newspapers avoided explicit xenophobic representations, although a link between terrorism and *Muslim* and *Islam* was found. A framing of Islam with reference to violent conflict was dominant: Muslims were five times more likely to be represented in the context of conflict than other religious groups. The authors argued that there was a tendency in the British press to depersonalise Muslims in general, and British Muslims in particular. One of the main findings in Baker, Gabrielatos and McEnery (2013b, p. 256) is that the use of collective nouns such as *community* and *world* contributed to "present a picture of a monolithic Islam" where Muslims are viewed as hostile and easily angered. The use of the noun phrase *Muslim world* was found to be systematically linked to extremism. However, liberal broadsheets such as *The Guardian* and *The Independent* acknowledged the diverse branches within Islam, presenting a more balanced representation and reporting of news involving Muslims. This has been corroborated by recent qualitative research that suggests that tabloids and right-leaning newspapers represent Muslims "within a narrow and largely negative framework" (Poole & Williamson, 2023, p. 263).

Clarke, Brookes and McEnery (2022) looked at press reportage of Islam and Muslims between 2010 and 2019. Their corpus consisted of 497,523 articles and 395,930,045 words, probably the largest corpus so far of media texts that feature Muslims and Islam. The authors examined how the keywords in the data have changed since 2010. Only keywords with a log-likelihood value of >3.84, present in at least 5% of texts were retained for analysis. A list of 567 keywords was compiled and a matrix was built, to record which of the keywords were present or absent in each newspaper article. The authors found an increase in the corpus concerning themes such as war, terrorism, conflict, foreign affairs, overseas conflict, corruption, human rights, the rise of the far right, and political processes related to elections. This is a complex picture in an ever-increasing global context of widespread political change and the emergence of populism.

Other corpus-based studies have analysed extremist, pro-violence texts. In Baker and Vessey (2018), two corpora of English and French Islamist extremist texts were analysed to explore whether the authors used similar themes and linguistic strategies. The relatively small English corpus includes 27 texts categorised as extremist by UK authorities. Twenty of those texts are from two magazines, *Inspire* and *Dabiq*. The French corpus is made up of nine texts from the ISIS magazine *Dar al Islam*, also categorised as extremist by UK authorities. Using keyword and collocation analyses, the authors found that the English texts were "more focused on violence and warfare compared to the French texts" (p. 269); in the French texts, obligation and law themes predominated. Despite these differences, religion, calls for violence and othering were present in both corpora. For the authors, *Dabiq* is more formal than *Inspire* in its language, "with the latter magazine more renowned for its colloquial English, Americanisms, and popular appeal" (p. 275). Brookes and McEnery (2020) examined texts associated with people convicted of terrorist offences in the United Kingdom. They examined a corpus of texts that had been found in the possession of 11 radicalised British citizens convicted under counter-terrorism legislation of crimes or of planning crimes. The text in this English three-million-word dataset was classified as moderate, fringe or extreme. Whilst the extreme corpus contains jihadist texts which endorse violence and the dehumanisation of those who are not Muslims, the fringe corpus includes conservative and isolationist texts that are politically radical and promote the othering of non-Muslims; interestingly, the fringe texts fail to provide any justifications for or clear incitements to violence. As for the moderate corpus, it contains texts that are not linked to an encouragement to violence, radical beliefs or isolationism. The researchers used correlation analysis and found that many of the terms analysed collocate with themselves, that is, they are very likely to be used again near the original mention. This is evident in five words in the moderate texts (*jihad, kufr, shirk, sunnah, taqleed*), nine in the fringe texts (*deen, hadith, jahiliyyah, jihad, kuffaar, kufr, sunnah, tafsir, ummah*) and ten in the extreme texts (*ayah, fiqh, fitnah, hadith, jihaad, jihad, kufr, shirk, tawhid, ummah*). In the three categories, *jihad* and *kufr* self-collocate. Working on the same dataset, Baker, Vessey, and McEnery (2021) carried out what is, to date, one of the most detailed investigations into the language of jihadists using corpus methods. As in Brookes and McEnery (2020), this research studied the differences between moderate, fringe and extreme texts. The way extreme texts characterise Muslims as being under attack, and disbelievers as worthy of violence draws a line between the pro-violence and less radical texts. They also found that the use of referencing and a formal writing style seeks to establish self-representation arguments and ideas as closer to the *true* meaning of Islam.

Baker, Vessey and McEnery also noted the importance of the manipulation of metaphor in the process of radicalisation. The role of metaphor in jihadist writing was also identified by Patterson (2022), who used the *NUTCRACKER* corpus of jihadist propaganda magazines to study the use of this feature. Patterson identified key metaphors in the text such as the journey metaphor, light and dark as good and evil, and spirituality as nature. She compared this analysis with the metaphors in the Qur'an. For Patterson, these domains are dialogic and symbolise the struggles of Islam. Pragmatic associations were found in the negative prosody associated with, for example, path + of/to Allah (heresy, eternal Hellfire), or in reference to the afterlife. Patterson understands these uses are creative manipulations that draw on the metaphoric domains in the Qur'an and facilitate simple communication patterns to ensure that potential followers "are less likely to be mistaken in their understanding" (p. 497) of the implications of becoming radicalised. This smooths the path to eventually resorting to violence.

Benítez-Castro and Hidalgo-Tenorio (2022) also examined the *NUTCRACKER* corpus, this time using Appraisal Theory (Martin & White,

2003). For the authors, the magazines in this corpus "offer a vivid and poignant account of a world torn apart by a struggle between the self-anointed defenders of the true Islamic faith, and the oppressors, usurpers and detractors, allegedly bent on making the Ummah's existence a living hell" (p. 523). In their analysis, they found two distinct persuasion profiles, namely, the use of victims' affliction, and the "commendable" personal story of a good and brave jihadi fighter.

Jihadist magazines are one of the many tools that terrorist organisations exploit to spread violent ideology (Matusitz, Madrazo, & Udani, 2019). With globalisation processes, jihadism has put into place a mechanism of integration that unites people from different countries, nullifying national differences and making them less consequential (Matusitz, 2020). Jihadist magazines written in English are part of this new paradigm for reasoning and framing actions for an international audience to boost radicalisation and indoctrination (Matusitz, 2020). Watching radical videos online and reading these jihadist magazines play a key role in the radicalisation process (Macdonald & Lorenzo-Dus, 2021; Benítez-Castro & Hidalgo-Tenorio, 2022). Macdonald and Lorenzo-Dus (2021) have argued that magazines such as *Inspire* share very disturbing content using familiar visual and textual formats that use a light tone which can be seen as cool and popular. For Sivek (2019), cited by Macdonald and Lorenzo-Dus (2021), the stages of self-radicalisation are facilitated by exposure to new social norms that seem reasonable and acceptable at least in the context of radicalised Muslims.

3. Methodology

3.1 Data

In this study we use the *NUTCRACKER* corpus (Dhiab-Hassan, Benítez-Castro, & Hidalgo-Tenorio, 2018), which is a 1,231,140-token corpus of six jihadist magazines (*Azan*, *Dabiq*, *Gaidi-Mtaani*, *Inspire*, *Recollections* and *Rumiyah*) published during 2009–2017 collected from the jihadology.net website as part of the *NUTCRACKER* research project (Hidalgo-Tenorio & Castro, 2022). The corpus was POS-tagged and queried through Sketch Engine (Kilgarriff et al., 2014). Table 10.1 shows the breakdown of the magazines, the organisation or group responsible for publishing the magazine, the number of tokens as well as the average number of tokens per text in each magazine included in *NUTCRACKER*.

3.2 Data Analysis

Our methodology is informed by representation theory (Baker, 2006; Hall, 2020), and corpus-driven keyword, collocation and colligation analyses

Table 10.1 The *NUTCRACKER* corpus

Magazine	*Tokens*	*Weight in the corpus (%)*	*Average number of tokens per text*	*Period*	*Published by*
AZAN	210,384	13.4	1,878	2013–2014	The Talibanim Khurasan
DABIQ	375,182	30.8	1,465	2013–2015	Islamic State
GAIDI-MTAANI	57,152	3.9	1,786	2011–2016	al-Shabaab
INSPIRE	240,668	30.7	940		al-Qaeda
RECOLLECTIONS	105,387	8.2	1,549	2009	al-Qaeda
RUMIYAH	242,367	12.9	2,265	2016–2017	Islamic State
Total/average	1,231,140	100	1,647		

(Baker, 2006; Baker et al., 2008; Pérez-Paredes, 2020, 2024; Baker, Vessey, & McEnery, 2021). Keywords have been widely used by corpus linguists to discover the lexical items that are characteristic of a target corpus when compared to a reference corpus (McEnery & Hardie, 2012), identifying words whose use is salient "even though humans may not have noted them as especially frequent, so they can provide a relatively objective way of helping to direct attention to parts of the corpus that we wouldn't have thought to consider" (Baker, Vessey, & McEnery, 2021, p. 56). Keywords offer researchers a relatively unbiased selection of the lexical items that are salient in a corpus (Baker, 2006; Baker, Vessey, & McEnery, 2021). This is the starting point for further investigation such as collocation and colligation analyses of Muslim-related lexical items.

In this chapter, multiword keyword analysis facilitates the identification of topics, and the selection and further analysis of Muslim-related keywords. We use the 2015 EnTenTen corpus as the reference corpus and the *NUTCRACKER* corpus as the focus corpus. We have decided to use the 2015 EnTenTen to make sure that the time of production of the corpus data in both the focus and the reference corpora was as similar as possible. Following Baker, Gabrielatos and McEnery (2013b), we consider the 100 keywords with the highest keyness values for each of the corpora analysed. Only English-language keywords with a minimum frequency of 5 are considered. Keywords in Arabic script such as ىلص هللا هيلع ملسو (peace be upon him) are not considered in this analysis, though they form a well understood form of honorific used in these texts (see Baker, Vessey, & McEnery 2021, p. 43). As for the measure of keyness, Sketch Engine uses the simple math score,[7] which favours the impact of frequency on keyness. The subsequent multiword keywords are grouped in categories as in Baker, Vessey, and McEnery (2021). Within each of these categories, special attention is paid to the Muslim-related terms explored using concordances and collocations.

4. Results and Discussion

4.1 Multiword-Keyword Analysis

The top 100 most significant multiword keywords in the *NUTCRACKER* corpus of jihadist magazines can be found in Appendix 1. The keyness scores range from 97.3 for *Islamic state* to 4.7 for *fight in the cause*.[8] Using nomination strategy analysis (Wodak, 2002), and the keyword-driven topic classification guidelines in Baker, Vessey and McEnery (2021), five different topics account for the diversity of topics in our data. Nomination allows for establishing membership, creating insiders and outsiders as well as discourse objects, processes, and actions (Mansouri et al., 2017). The topics that we found in NUTCRACKER are the conflict over legitimate representation of the Islamic faith, violence and the legitimisation of violence, the use of formulaic and polite expressions, citing sources of authority, and, finally, the geopolitics of jihad. The relative importance of these topics can be seen in Figure 10.1.

Except for the use of formulaic and polite expressions, the other four topics are almost evenly spread throughout the keywords analysed. Let us examine these topics in more detail.

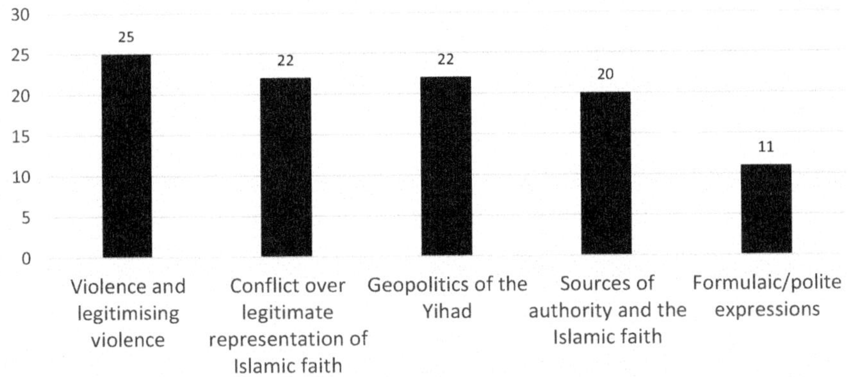

Figure 10.1 Topics of top 100 multiword keywords in the NUTCRACKER corpus.

4.2 *Violence and the Legitimisation of Violence*

This is the most important topic in the keywords analysed. Baker and Vessey (2018) have suggested that legitimation of violence and violent people are usually found in the vicinity of references to Allah, and are linked to claims that the writers are acting on His behalf. The keywords in this category corroborate this notion. The topic accounts for 25% of items in Appendix 1. It includes keywords such as *waging war* (14.2), *martyrdom operation* (9.5), *explosive vehicle* (9.4), *explosive device* (7.9), *explosive belt* (7.6), *car bomb* (6.5) or *act of worship* (6.2). The following concordance lines provide some context to this category of keywords. The name of the magazine and the title of the article/text are provided in brackets.

1 So if these people were **waging war** against Allah and His Messenger and it was obligatory to perform jihād against them. (*Dabiq. The law of Allah or the laws of men is waging war against the khilafah apostasy?).*
2 "Suicide bombing" is not suicide according to Islam because, as we will see, Islam extols the **martyrdom operation**. So martyrdom operation≠Suicide bombing. So, from now on, we will refer to these operations as "martyrdom operations" instead of "suicide bombings" which is a false term. (AZAN. *Let's understand suicide bombing*).
3 He detonated his **explosive vehicle**, destroying the headquarters, killing nearly 30 murtaddīn, and wounding several others. May Allah accept him amongst the shuhadā. (DABIQ. *A selection of military operations by the Islamic State*).

Waging war against is mostly followed by *Allah*, *Islam* or the *Islamic State*. Patterson (2022) has suggested that the war imagery in the *NUTCRACKER* corpus is directly associated with a justification of violent action for the jihadist cause. This justification is constructed using explicit references to terrorism and violence. While this explicitness is found in extreme texts in Baker, Vessey, and McEnery (2021), moderate texts show a less explicit call to action and violence. Baker and Vessey (2018) also found that, in the English texts they analysed, terms such as *explosive*, *bomb*, *army* or *operation* were more pervasive than in the French corpus. Obviously, this can only be attributed to the motivations behind the production circumstances of the texts in each of their corpora. Example (2) above leaves little room for interpretation. It is crude, direct and unsophisticated. Skillicorn and Reid (2014) have demonstrated that high levels of jihadist language in forums are associated with high sincerity and low levels of deception. They found this to be the case in *Azan*, one of the magazines in the *NUTCRAKER* corpus. Baker, Vessey, and McEnery (2021) similarly argued that extreme texts favour a direct address to the reader, usually involving extremely explicit directions and steps. In (3) we find an explicit description of a violent action which resulted in the death of so-called apostates (*murtaddīn*), that is, those people who renounce Islam. Extreme discourse constantly makes use of Islamic concepts usually seen as positive aspects of Islam, but which are manipulated to justify violence and terrorism: "Violence is cast as heroic martyrdom and justified as occurring within the context of a war" (Baker, Vessey, & McEnery, 2021, p. 169). We will come back to this idea in the following paragraphs.

4.3 Conflict over Legitimate Representation of the Islamic Faith

Together with the geopolitics of jihad, this is the second most significant topic in our data. It includes keywords such as *day of judgement* (16.3), *jihād claimant* (11.8), *Ibn taymiyyah* (10.9), *Muslim nation* (7.7), *making takfir* (6.5) or *apostate regime* (5.0). These keywords are found in contexts where there is a deliberate intention to present the magazine editorial line as representative of the true Islamic faith. This is unsurprising in extreme texts, as argued by Baker and Vessey (2018) when examining the imposition of *jiziyah*, the tax that some Islamic rulers demand from their non-Muslim subjects. They showed how this can be used, in an example from the Islamic State. The State claimed to take pride in facilitating a more rigorous and, from their perspective, true version of Islam by their imposition of jiziyah. The following concordance lines provide some further context of the use of keywords in this category.

4 And may His Peace and Blessings be upon Prophet Muhammad, his family, companions and all those who follow him till the **Day of Judgment**. Between the American withdrawals, the ongoing victories of the Mujahideen, the spread of the Jihadi manhaj all over the globe and the steady awakening of the Muslim masses to the light of faith... (AZAN. No title available).

5 Also, some of the **jihād claimants** persist on blatantly lying, claiming that the Jawlānī front did not partake in the Sahwah. (DABIQ. *The law of Allah or the laws of men is waging war against the khilafah apostasy?*).

6 They think themselves to be well-informed but the reality is that they are often as ignorant as Bedouins concerning the affairs of the mujāhidīn, with many of them relying on the slanderous kāfir media as their primary source of information on jihād. **Ibn Taymiyyah** then discusses the meaning of being truthful in one's claim to īmān. (DABIQ. *Lessons from the fitnah of the Mongols*).

7 For the one who does not **make takfir** of the mushrikin has not accepted the teachings of the Quran to be true. The Quran has made

takfir of the mushrikin and has ordered making takfir of them, taking them as enemies, and fighting against them. (RUMIYAH. *Important memorandums*)

Most of the concordance lines examined in this category are linked with the discursive efforts of these magazines to represent true believers as those that accept that jihad is more than just an internal spiritual journey for Muslims as in (4). Hence the importance of nominations such as *claimant* as in (5) or *kafir* as in (6) for those that, despite being Muslims, take a more moderate stance. Baker, Vessey and McEnery (2021) found that *kuffar* (plural for *kafir*) and *disbelievers* tended to be used interchangeably, although the former tends to be found in extreme texts. The use of these terms needs to be understood in the context of the rhetoric of jihad as embraced by the editorial lines of the jihadist magazines, which manipulate religious metaphors and concepts to draw on an association with the Qur'an (Patterson, 2022). *Making takfir* in (7) is, consequently, a form of othering Muslims who do not share the same violent take on what jihad means. These are defined as *mushrikin* and are explicitly considered as enemies. Baker, Vessey and McEnery (2021, p. 200) have suggested that this textual manipulation may be "further intensified by the use of Arabic, which allows the author to demonstrate piety not only through praising the Prophet, but also through the use of the holy language in its original Arabic script".

4.4 The Geopolitics of Jihad

This is, together with *Conflict over legitimate representation of the Islamic faith*, the second most significant topic in our data. These keywords help to frame jihadist terrorist activities in an international context characterised by infighting with political powers and a wide diversity of religious factions. It includes keywords such as *Islamic state* (97.3), *Muslim ummah* (26.1), *Arabian Peninsula* (22.1), *jawlānī front* (17.8), *Muslim land* (16.8), *new world order* (8.0) and *American people* (5.7). *Islamic State* is the most frequent multiword keyword in the data. Its most significant collocates are verb phrases that either contribute to the victimisation of the terrorist group (*fight*, *battle*, *condemn*) or to paying tribute to those that made its actions and activities possible (*join*, *establish*, *expand*, *succeed*).[9] The 1,458 *Islamic State* concordance lines examined lend testimony to one main dogmatic (Patterson, 2022) and propaganda aim, ensuring a representation of its terrorist activities that extends both geographically far beyond the Arabic-speaking headquarters (Baker & Vessey, 2018) and, emotionally, beyond standard means of propagating demagogic discourse. According to Walli (2015, p. 97), the psychological warfare found in violent Islamic propaganda is based on a self-representation that creates a unique reality that makes it "the admired and the pursued". This self-created reality evokes hyperreal feelings and overrated impressions (Walli, 2015) thanks to the text, the pictures and visuals used in the articles. Some of the keywords in this category are *Muslim ummah, Muslim land, Muslim nation* or *Muslim country*. Muslim identity is topicalised and used to increase the sense of victimisation of Muslims. A world where Muslims are the victims of a global war against them leads to the overwhelming presence of a topos that misleadingly warrants the conclusion that a violent jihad is the solution to the problems faced by the good, true Muslims (Benítez-Castro & Hidalgo-Tenorio, 2022). The following concordance lines provide some context to this category of keywords.

8 And then America invades our lands, most notably the **Arabian Peninsula**, and labels the invading force as a "peaceful army" and the purpose of the invasion as "military aid". (AZAN. *JAO-Shaykh Abu Mussab Al-Suri*)
9 When the **New World Order** emerged, and Great Britain joined the head of the axis of the American alliance, the Irish Republican Army was forced to accept a peaceful option. (INSPIRE. *The jihadi experiences (the schools of jihad)*)
10 If these two options come from the extract of America's elite minds in the field of counter Jihād, I have to say the **American people** should be ashamed, because those 'experts' know nothing about reality and history. (INSPIRE. *24/7 terrorism*)

As each of the topics uncovered in this research shows, the type of violent jihad advocated in *NUTCRACKER* is glocally situated at the crossroads between religion, extremism and violence. Keywords navigate this complexity by serving propaganda and persuasive aims (Baker, Vessey, & McEnery, 2021).

4.5 Citing Sources of Authority and the Islamic Faith

This is the third most important topic in our keywords. Baker, Vessey and McEnery (2021) observe that terrorist discourse seeks to educate readers through a selective choice of sources, which, according to Wignell, Tan and O'Halloran (2017a, 2017b) are often misrepresented. Most of the keywords within this category contribute to validating justifications for violence in the texts. The keywords in this category seem to fulfil this justification mechanism, interpreting the Islamic faith for the reader. Some of these keywords include *prophet Muhammad* (12.8), *straight path* (9.1), *wordly life* (8.7), *life of this world* (6.0) and *prophetic methodology* (5.4). Some of these keywords are linked to scholars or narrators of the life of the prophet such as Abu Hurayrah or Abu Bakr. Other sources of authority encompass figures such as Abū Dāwūd, 9th century, and Ibn Kathīr, 14th century. Jihadist magazines therefore encourage violence in part by offering a constellation of rationalisations for violence. These are frequently rooted in traditional sources of religious authority (Macdonald & Lorenzo-Dus, 2021). Some of the keywords in this category such as *worldy life* (Dunya) are framed within the argumentation that precedes or follows the cited sources of authority. The concordance lines below illustrate the use of some of the keywords.

11 And we must beware of all roads that lead us away from this pure, **straight path**. Therefore, whether it is Egypt, Syria, Afghanistan, Iraq, Pakistan or Libya – the fundamental goal of our struggle must be the uplifting of the Word of Allah, establishment of the Rule of Allah and repulsion of oppression and injustice. (AZAN. No title available.)
12 As for our time, after the Dunya was opened up before us, we began to lose that spirit – the spirit of that first generation of zuhhad, those who weren't deceived by this **worldly life** and its beautifications and comprehended that the way to be safe from it is abandoning what is in it. (RUMIYAH. *Zuhd in the Dunya is the way of the Salaf*)
13 Are you pleased with the **life of this world** rather than the hereafter? But little is the enjoyment of the life of this world as compared with the hereafter. The biggest contribution you can make to the Jihad is to do an attack in the West. (AZAN. *To the jihadis in the West*)

As Patterson (2022) shows in her analysis of metaphors in *NUTCRAKER*, the path of jihad is used as a way towards Allah, suggesting jihadism is a means to reach Allah. The *straight path* requires therefore that *worldly life* worries and the like are abandoned. Jihadist discourse is therefore not only glocally situated in geographical territories such as the Arabian Peninsula or America, but also similarly framed on a vertical spiritual axis separating earthly life from eternal life. Brookes and McEnery (2020) have suggested that these sources are a form of symbolic power that, in the context of Islamic societies, embodies political power and the legitimisation of a recourse to violence on behalf of Allah.

4.6 *Formulaic and Polite Expressions*

This is the fifth most relevant topic in the pool of keywords analysed. Previous research has shown that formulaic sequences in Arabic and English are part of the extreme jihadist discourse. Jihadist magazines are no exception. These keywords tend to occur in the context of Allah such as *alayhi wa* (52.6), *alayhi wa sallam* (52.6) or glad tidings (12.6).

14 Allah's Messenger (sallallāhu **'alayhi wa sallam**)[10] said, "Never does sexual perversion become widespread amongst a people to the point that it's openly practiced [...]". (DABIQ. *Clamping down on sexual deviance*)

15 And indeed, we give **glad tidings** to Muslims everywhere that the Battle of Raqqah will not be a picnic for the murtaddin and their supporters. (RUMIYAH. *It will be a fire that burns the cross and its people in raqqah*)

Baker and Vessey (2018) describe clusters such as (14) and (15) as honorifics. Baker, Vessey and McEnery (2021, p. 67) have noted that "positive words like glorious, peace, blessed and praise [...] describe Allah or other positively represented social actors". These clusters are found in the vicinity of keywords in the *sources* category where, as noted by Baker and Vessey (2018), jihadist English texts regularly code-switch to Arabic terms, written in the Latin alphabet with additional diacritics, as a form of legitimation.

4.7 *Representing Muslims*

Across the five topics above, nine keywords contain the lemma *Muslim*. Table 10.2 shows these keywords.

Five of these keywords were categorised as members of the *Geopolitics of jihad* topic: *Muslim Ummah*, *Muslim land*, *Muslim world*, *Muslim woman* and *Muslim youth*. These contribute to the discursive construction of Muslims' in-group representation as part of a broader system of representations afforded by the intersections of this topic with the legitimating

Table 10.2 Keywords that contain the lemma 'Muslim'

Item	*Frequency (NUTCRACKER corpus)*	*Frequency (reference)*	*Score*
Muslim Ummah	186	1,974	26.1
Muslim LAND	117	2,051	16.8
Muslim world	118	31,428	12.3
Muslim woman	65	21,914	7.8
Muslim nation	52	5,428	7.7
Muslim country	55	19,781	6.9
Muslim brother	41	2,595	6.5
Muslim youth	36	4,893	5.6
Sahīh Muslim	33	37	5.6

and justification of violence on religious grounds. The *Muslim Ummah* is presented in *NUTCRACKER* as a collectivised, victimised body. In the concordance lines we find that the Ummah is *imposed upon the new world order (Azan)*, wishes to *free from American colonialism* (*Azan*) and *is in dire need of righteous, courageous* (*Azan*) religious scholars who understand the true meaning of jihad. Some of the collocates for Ummah in *NUTCRACKER* are pre-modifiers such as *fertile* or *entire*, and verbs such as *mobilize*, *defend*, *protect* and *attack*.[11] Again, it is claimed that Muslims are first victimised and then are provided with the ideological and religious mindset to defend themselves through violence. Baker, Vessey and McEnery (2021) found that *Ummah* is more frequent in extreme and fringe texts rather than in moderate texts. In *NUTCRACKER*, the *Muslim Ummah* is key to understanding the terrorists' need to transcend geographical and national barriers. Collectivising Muslims is the way in which magazines such as *Azan* or *Dabiq* invite readers to come under a single leadership that they claim truly works for the community of what they construct as true believers (Macdonald & Lorenzo-Dus, 2021).

The *Muslim world* in *NUTCRAKER* is similarly used to collectivise Muslims and victimise them. Notably, the Muslim world is a body of people that are attacked by America and its President. There is a strong link between this keyword and claimed attacks from the US, and less frequently from European ex-colonial powers. A few examples follow:

16 In addition to their neo-colonialism in the **Muslim world**, the US has given unwavering support to Israel since 1967. (AZAN. *The rise and fall of America*)

17 All of the Mujahideen across the **Muslim world** should target US and Western interests in their respective regions. By attacking the US throughout the world, we will continue to reduce the awe that some of the Muslims still have of the US. (AZAN. *The rise and fall of America*)

18 This central issue, as I like to call it, is the pivot of what makes a Muslim begin his journey as a jihadi. No, it is not the mass slaughter of the Palestinians by the Israeli's nor the atrocious actions of America towards the **Muslim world.** (INSPIRE. *The central issue*)

As Lorenzo-Dus, Walker, and Kinzel (2018) showed in their analysis of *Dabiq* and *Inspire*, those othered are not just the West, Al Qaeda, most governments in the Middle East or apostates. An internal out group is also constructed; those that are *they-ed* in this way are the Muslims that either live in the West or that do not believe that a violent jihad is justified. They are not part of the *Muslim world*, let alone part of the *Muslim Ummah*. Baker, Gabrielatos and McEnery (2013b) found that the UK press used the sequence *Muslim world* to represent a monolithic block in contrast to Christendom. This monolithic Muslim world is represented in the press as closely linked to extremism. In *NUTCRACKER*, *Muslim world* is used together with *Muslim Ummah* to thematize both violence and victimisation. However, in our corpus these terms are not totally interchangeable. While the *Muslim Ummah* need to rise up, the *Muslim world* suffers aggression from America. The magazines specifically address the *Ummah* because they claim that the *Muslim world* is under attack.

In *NUTCRACKER*, Muslim women are systematically victimised. For example, verb collocates include *rape*, *enslave*, *target* and *oppress*. Women are given little or no agency other than *wearing* a hijab/niqab or *giving* birth. They are represented across the concordance lines examined as being raped and killed while taking care of children. Muslim women in the West are advised that they should wear the niqab as a symbol of pride and being part of the fight. As for women in Muslim countries, they are required to perform their subsidiary, family, roles as part of their contribution to jihad:

19 But because it is a right of Muslim women and because it has become a symbol of being a Muslim today, Muslims need to take a position in this battle and dig in their trenches. For this reason we promote that **Muslim women** in the West who do not view wearing niqab as being a religious duty to wear the niqab as a public sign of their rejection of forced assimilation, as a symbol of their pride at being Muslim, as a public statement that is carried as a badge. (INSPIRE. *The West should ban the niqab covering its real face*)

20 It is time to examine our duties and roles, and prioritize our concerns for the Hereafter, not the Dunya. We **Muslim women** are required to fulfill our duties attentively, and being negligent of them will only lead to our own destruction. Our mission is greater than we can imagine. Allah has honored us by choosing us to be the wives, sisters, and mothers of the mujahidin. (RUMIYAH. *Our journey to Allah*)

We argue that, contrary to the presence of different discourses around Muslim women and their representation(s) in the UK press (Baker, Gabrielatos, & McEnery, 2013b), jihadist magazines give no visibility to women's contribution to the community other than being key members in taking care of the family and related duties. However, *Muslim youth* are represented as playing an important role on the geopolitical chessboard of terrorist groups. They are both victimised, as noted by Benítez-Castro and Hidalgo-Tenorio (2022), and are represented as being much needed as part of the process of revitalising the call to fight America and the West.

Most of the concordance lines examined show that the youth represented in the corpus live in the West, although not exclusively:

21 What she was referring to, as she went on to clarify, were the countless **Muslim youth** in the West who get themselves tangled into drugs, alcohol, gangs, promiscuity, and other vices and social illnesses over which any decent Muslim family would weep for its children. (DABIQ. *O you who have believed, protect yourselves and your families from fire*)
22 We the **Muslim youth** in Kenya will work and fully corporate with any Islamic organisation that upholds the correct aqeedah, to fight the continuing aggression and crusade against Muslims specifically in East Africa. (GAIDI-MTAANI. *Leveling the scales*)
23 Opening the door for many **Muslim youth** in the West who want to seek revenge from the Crusader states that are fighting Islam. (INSPIRE. *Interview with Shaykh Abu Basir conducted by Al-Malahem staff*)

Radicalising young Muslims is an essential component of fuelling a generational revolt (Baker, Vessey & McEnery, 2021) that can increase the ranks of terrorist groups. It is unsurprising, therefore, that the use of explicit violence and online content seems to target the younger generations, who are offered "channels of expression [for], but in ISIL's manner" (Walli, 2015, p. 98).

5 Concluding Remarks

Media representations both construct and are constructed by reality "yet this is subjected to commercial and economic factors and has ideological and political implications" (De Rooij, 2023, p. 4). Jihadist magazines ignore the traditional press, constructing their own narrative. This gives them the leeway to claim the victimisation of male, female and young Muslims as part of the jihadist master narrative (Matusitz, 2020). Jihadists construct an emotionally satisfying story that explains that the world is chaotic because of the Zionist–Christian alliance that punishes and hates Muslims (Lorenzo-Dus, Walker, & Kinzel, 2018). Violent jihad is seen as the only solution as it will eradicate the impact of the West and is part of being a good Muslim (Lorenzo-Dus, Walker, & Kinzel, 2018) in an increasingly complex international context where frontiers are less important than ideologies and a sense of belonging to the *Muslim Ummah*. In *NUTCRACKER*, Muslims are both victimised and required to embrace violence. This chapter has shown how this is constructed linguistically when the magazines self-represent themselves and Muslims worldwide. Another contribution of this chapter is to replication (McEnery & Brezina, 2022). The study carried out in this chapter, that of Baker, Vessey, and McEnery (2021) and Patterson (2022) all used slightly different methods on similar, yet slightly different data sets. Yet as this study has shown, the findings from each are powerfully mutually reconfirming. The corroboration of the major findings from these studies both enhances the credibility of their findings and, consequently, acts as a powerful call to consider carefully, and where appropriate act to counter, key features of jihadist discourse.

Notes

1 See https://www.theguardian.com/world/2023/sep/08/mali-jihadists-kill-at-least-64-people-amid-growing-islamist-threat
2 See https://www.interior.gob.es/opencms/ca/detalle/articulo/La-Guardia-Civil-desarticula-la-mayor-estructura-yihadista-conocida-en-Espana-en-el-ambito-de-la-captacion-de-jovenes-y-de-menores-de-edad/
3 See https://www.elmundo.es/pais-vasco/2023/09/29/65171b43e9cf4a64638b45d6.html
4 See https://elpais.com/espana/2023-10-20/la-policia-lanza-una-operacion-antiyihadista-con-cuatro-detenidos-en-distintos-puntos-de-espana.html
5 See https://www.europol.europa.eu/publication-events/main-reports/european-union-terrorism-situation-and-trend-report-2023-te-sat
6 See https://www.reuters.com/world/middle-east/former-hamas-chief-calls-protests-neighbours-join-war-against-israel-2023-10-11/
7 Simple maths compares the frequencies in the target corpus with the frequencies in the reference corpus. A higher *N* value focuses on higher-frequency words whereas a lower *N* value focuses on low-frequency. The value should be changed in orders of magnitude, i.e., 0.1, 1, 10, 100, 1,000, 10,000 etc. Smaller changes rarely produce any noticeable effect. URL: https://www.sketchengine.eu/documentation/simple-maths/
8 All the keywords in this chapter will be in italics. Keyness score is provided in brackets.
9 Word Sketch was used to extract these collocates. All the examples display >8.0 scores.
10 May Allah honor him and grant him peace.
11 All collocates provided in this section are statistically significant (LogDice > 6.0).

References

Baker, P. (2006). *Using corpora in discourse analysis*. London: Continuum.

Baker, P., Gabrielatos, C., & McEnery, T. (2013a). Sketching Muslims: A corpus driven analysis of representations around the word 'Muslim' in the British press 1998–2009. *Applied Linguistics*, *34*(3), 255–278.

Baker, P., Gabrielatos, C., & McEnery, T. (2013b). *Discourse analysis and media attitudes: The representation of Islam in the British press*. Cambridge: Cambridge University Press.

Baker, P., Gabrielatos, C., Khosravinik, M., Krzyżanowski, M., McEnery, T., & Wodak, R. (2008). A useful methodological synergy? Combining critical discourse analysis and corpus linguistics to examine discourses of refugees and asylum seekers in the UK press. *Discourse & Society*, *19*(3), 273–306.

Baker, P., & Vessey, R. (2018). A corpus-driven comparison of English and French Islamist extremist texts. *International Journal of Corpus Linguistics*, *23*(3), 255–278. https://doi.org/10.1075/ijcl.17108.bak

Baker, P., Vessey, R., & McEnery, T. (2021). *The language of violent jihad*. Cambridge: Cambridge University Press.

Benítez-Castro, M. A., & Hidalgo-Tenorio, E. (2022). "I Am Proud to Be a Traitor": The emotion/opinion interplay in jihadist magazines. *Pragmatics and Society*, *13*(3), 501–531. https://doi.org/10.1075/ps.21029.ben

Brookes, G., & McEnery, T. (2020). Correlation, collocation and cohesion: A corpus-based critical analysis of violent jihadist discourse. *Discourse & Society*, *31*(4), 351–373. https://doi.org/10.1177/0957926520903528

Clarke, I., Brookes, G., & McEnery, T. (2022). Keywords through time: Tracking changes in press discourses of Islam. *International Journal of Corpus Linguistics*, *27*(4), 399–427. https://doi.org/10.1075/ijcl.22011.cla

De Rooij, L. (2023). *Muslims, minorities, and the Media: Discourses on Islam in the West*. London: Routledge.

Dhiab-Hassan, A., Benítez-Castro, M. Á., & Hidalgo-Tenorio, E. (2018). *Nutcracker: The JIHAD corpus*. Granada: University of Granada.

Hall, S. (2020). The work of representation. In T. Prentki & N. Abraham (Eds.), *The applied theatre reader* (pp. 74–76). London: Routledge.

Hidalgo-Tenorio, E., & Castro, J. L. (2022). Transdisciplinary approaches to the discourse of Islamist extremism. *Pragmatics and Society*, *13*(3), 353–360. https://doi.org/10.1075/ps.00058.int

Kilgarriff, A., Baisa, V., Bušta, J., Jakubíček, M., Kovář, V., Michelfeit, J., Rychlý, P., & Suchomel, V. (2014). The Sketch Engine: Ten years on. *Lexicography*, *1*(1), 7–36.

Lorenzo-Dus, N., Walker, L., & Kinzel, A. (2018). The role of discourse analysis in terrorism studies: Comparing Inspire and Dabiq. In M. Conway, L. Jarvis, & O. Lehane (Eds.), *Terrorists' use of the Internet: Assessment and response* (pp. 158–169). Amsterdam: IOS Press.

Macdonald, S., & Lorenzo-Dus, N. (2021). Visual jihad: Constructing the "good Muslim" in online jihadist magazines. *Studies in Conflict & Terrorism*, *44*(5), 363–386. https://doi.org/10.1080/1057610X.2018.1559508

Malešević, S. (2017). *The rise of organised brutality*. Cambridge: Cambridge University Press.

Mansouri, S., Biria, R., Mohammadi Najafabadi, M., & Sattar Boroujeni, S. (2017). Nomination and argumentation strategies in oratory discourse: The case of an English Sermon. *SAGE Open*, *7*(2), 1–8. https://doi.org/10.1177/2158244017702425

Martin, J. R., & White, P. R. (2003). *The language of evaluation*. London: Palgrave Macmillan.

Matusitz, J. (2020). *Communication in global jihad*. London: Routledge.

Matusitz, J., Madrazo, A., & Udani, C. (2019). *Online jihadist magazines to promote the caliphate: Communicative perspectives*. New York: Peter Lang.

McEnery, T., & Brezina, V. (2022). *Fundamental principles of corpus linguistics*. Cambridge: Cambridge University Press.

McEnery, T., & Hardie, A. (2012). *Corpus linguistics: Method, theory and practice*. Cambridge: Cambridge University Press.

Patterson, K. J. (2022). Under the shadow of swords: The Rhetoric of Jihad: A corpus-based critical analysis of religious metaphors in jihadist magazines. *Pragmatics and Society*, *13*(3), 477–500. https://doi.org/10.1075/ps.21017.pat

Pérez-Paredes, P. (2020). *Corpus linguistics for education: A guide for research*. London: Routledge.

Pérez-Paredes, P. (2024). Frequency and keyness: What are they and how can they be used to explore representation? In F. Heritage & C. Taylor (Eds.), *Analysing Representation: A corpus and discourse textbook*. London: Routledge.

Poole, E. (2002). *Reporting Islam*. London: Tauris.

Poole, E., & Williamson, M. (2023). Disrupting or reconfiguring racist narratives about Muslims? The representation of British Muslims during the Covid crisis. *Journalism*, *24*(2), 262–279. https://doi.org/10.1177/14648849211030129

Sivek, S. C. (2019). Packaging inspiration: Al Qaeda's digital magazine inspire in the self-radicalisation process. *International Journal of Communication*, *7*, 584–606.

Skillicorn, D. B., & Reid, E. F. (2014). Language use in the Jihadist magazines inspire and Azan. *Security Informatics*, *3*, 1–16.

Walli, J. (2015). *Analyzing ISILs propaganda*. Växjö: Linnaeus University. https://www.diva-portal.org/smash/get/diva2:820361/FULLTEXT01.pdf

Wignell, P., Tan, S., & O'Halloran, K. (2017a). Under the shade of AK47s: A multimodal approach to violent extremist recruitment strategies for foreign fighters. *Critical Studies on Terrorism*, *10*(3), 429–452. https://doi.org/10.1080/17539153.2017.1319319

Wignell, P., Tan, S., & O'Halloran, K. (2017b). Violent extremism and iconisation: Commanding good and forbidding evil? *Critical Discourse Studies*, 14(1), 1–22. https://doi.org/10.1080/17405904.2016.1250652

Wodak, R. (2002). Fragmented identities. In Chilton, P., & Schäffner, C. (Eds.), *Politics as text and talk: Analytic approaches to political discourse* (pp. 143–169.). Amsterdam: John Benjamins.

Appendix 1

Top 100 multiword keywords in the NUTCRACKER corpus

Topics

Conflict over legitimate representation of Islamic faith
Violence and legitimising violence
Formulaic/polite expressions
Sources of authority and the Islamic faith
Geopolitics of the jihad

Rank	*Item*	*Frequency (focus)*	*Frequency (reference)*	*Score*
1	islamic state	1,458	83,747	97.3
2	alayhi wa	376	646	52.6
3	alayhi wa sallam	377	856	52.6
4	wa sallam	375	991	52.3
5	may allah	223	5,249	29.9
6	muslim ummah	186	1,974	26.1
7	arabian peninsula	173	10,052	22.1
8	jawlānī front	121	0	17.8
9	muslim land	117	2,051	16.8
10	day of judgment	117	4,118	16.3
11	waging war	103	5,980	14.2
12	prophet muhammad	104	15,636	12.8
13	glad tidings	87	2,652	12.6
14	muslim world	118	31,428	12.3
15	jihād claimant	78	0	11.8
16	ibn taymiyyah	72	632	10.9
17	al qaeda	113	50,124	10.1
18	islamic emirate	65	1,236	9.8
19	prophet muhammad e	63	0	9.7
20	imām ahmad	63	18	9.7
21	martyrdom operation	62	451	9.5
22	explosive vehicle	61	25	9.4
23	abu dawud	60	664	9.2
24	islamic world	75	18,718	9.2
25	straight path	61	3,343	9.1

(*Continued*)

Rank	*Item*	*Frequency (focus)*	*Frequency (reference)*	*Score*
26	azza wa jall	58	79	9.0
27	worldly life	57	1,403	8.7
28	ibn kathir	56	689	8.7
29	abu hurayrah	55	387	8.6
30	ibn majah	53	531	8.3
31	dar al-harb	52	358	8.2
32	crusader coalition	51	26	8.1
33	new world order	63	16,478	8.0
34	day of resurrection	51	1,753	7.9
35	explosive device	61	15,379	7.9
36	muslim woman	65	21,914	7.8
37	good deed	62	18,290	7.8
38	muslim nation	52	5,428	7.7
39	explosive belt	48	722	7.6
40	pakistani army	50	3,884	7.5
41	waging jihad	47	278	7.5
42	abu bakr	49	3,828	7.4
43	manmade law	45	72	7.2
44	pakistan army	49	6,398	7.2
45	muslim country	55	19,781	6.9
46	nusayri army	42	0	6.8
47	āl salūl	42	0	6.8
48	jabhat an-nusrah	42	36	6.8
49	abū bakr	42	92	6.8
50	world order	54	20,015	6.7

Rank	*Item*	*Frequency (focus)*	*Frequency (reference)*	*Score*
51	car bomb	46	9,717	6.5
52	making takfir	40	0	6.5
53	muslim brother	41	2,595	6.5
54	shaykh usama	39	0	6.4
55	sahwah faction	39	0	6.4
56	crusader army	39	174	6.4
57	sahwah coalition	38	0	6.3
58	explosive vest	38	304	6.2
59	act of worship	40	4,288	6.2
60	wage war	40	4,293	6.2
61	abū dāwūd	37	29	6.1

(*Continued*)

Rank	*Item*	*Frequency (focus)*	*Frequency (reference)*	*Score*
62	shaykh anwar	36	0	6.0
63	life of this world	36	389	6.0
64	righteous deed	36	877	5.9
65	free syrian army	39	6,443	5.9
66	evil scholar	35	0	5.8
67	nusayrī regime	35	0	5.8
68	ahrār ash-shām	35	0	5.8
69	istishhadi operation	35	0	5.8
70	abū hurayrah	35	19	5.8
71	blessed operation	35	23	5.8
72	wa jall	35	61	5.8
73	azza wa	35	86	5.8
74	soldier of the caliphate	35	144	5.8
75	istishhādī operation	34	0	5.7
76	abu baseer	34	21	5.7
77	american people	71	69,466	5.7
78	muslim youth	36	4,893	5.6
79	sahīh muslim	33	37	5.6
80	ilaha illallah	33	73	5.6
81	islamic nation	34	3,095	5.5
82	number of others	34	3,662	5.5
83	abū muhārib	32	0	5.4
84	prophetic methodology	32	41	5.4
85	hand grenade	34	5,307	5.3
86	nusayri regime	31	19	5.3
87	alayhi wassallam	31	34	5.3
88	religion of truth	31	249	5.3
89	man-made laww	31	579	5.3
90	islamic front	31	1,003	5.2
91	allah the	30	25	5.2
92	armored vehicle	33	7,992	5.0
93	word of the enemy	29	24	5.0
94	apostate regime	29	46	5.0
95	abu mansur	29	47	5.0
96	my lord	30	2,991	5.0
97	wage jihad	28	308	4.9
98	war booty	28	536	4.8
99	islamic khilafah	27	18	4.7
100	fight in the cause	27	41	4.7

11 Forced Lexical Primings as Evidence of Power Relations in Jihadist Magazines

Michael T. L. Pace-Sigge

1. Introduction

This chapter presents an investigation into the evidence of fixed language use within jihadist magazines, and the extent to which forced primings appear to reflect specific power relations within that discourse community. The current investigation extends earlier research undertaken by Patterson (2022) as well as Patterson and Pace-Sigge (2022). In particular, the focus is on the use of a number of key items from a selection of jihadist magazines, namely in the *Radicals* corpus (2010–2017), referred to as RAD in the following. The use of these words is directly contrasted with language found in a general, US-American corpus of magazines, that is, a sub-corpus of COCA (Davies, 2023) covering the years 2006–2015.

The aim of this chapter is to present evidence of fixed language use within jihadist magazines; that is, to demonstrate how writers of jihadist magazines use words in a way that is unique lexically and grammatically, compared to US magazines. Approaching the corpus-based results under the hypothesis that the writers of articles in jihadist magazines have become primed to employ certain (sets of) words through their repeated usage in context, the starting point for the analysis is the theory of *lexical priming* (Hoey, 2005). Thus, lexical and grammatical associations and constructions are analysed to determine the extent to which language use is particular in the RAD corpus (Dhiab-Hassan et al., 2018). This corpus is based on editions of the following five magazines: *Azan, Dabiq, Gaida, Inspire, Guida* as well as "Recollections" of those involved. As such, an idiosyncratic discourse grammar (see Hopper, 1987) emerges from the way language is used by radicalised groups. Evidence is presented of the unique way power relationships are linguistically expressed; it is argued here that this reflects the ways in which the writers are primed for their motives or aims of recruitment. Moreover, an argument is made that the writers are also consciously priming their readers with idiosyncratic patterns (or forced primings, see Duguid, 2009). Consequently, in this research the

DOI: 10.4324/9781003457381-12

premises of *lexical priming*, indeed, *forced primings* provide the foundation: through repeat usage of words, wordings and descriptions, the writers and editors of jihadist magazines create an environment of primings which readers then absorb. For the investigation at hand, a number of words, which are fairly common in news discourse, and which are in the semantic field of power relations, have been identified as keywords in jihadist magazines. These show the level of divergence in the collocation and colligation where these are compared with occurrences in the COCA magazines sub-corpus covering the same time period.

The current paper is interested in providing the answer to the following questions:

1 Are there differences in the lexical, grammatical, semantic, pragmatic and textual patterns associated with keywords in the jihadist magazines compared to a general reference corpus?
2 What do these primings tell us about the writers and their collective ideology?

In order to address these questions, there is a twin-focus. First of all, the extent to which these fixed patterns reflect how power relations are perceived within the text community; secondly, the words which express relations that can be seen as antagonistic.

2. Background

The 21st century so far has been over two decades of radicalisation, with a clear bend towards more conservative and authoritarian forces. It can be argued that the deadly attacks of Al-Quaida in 2001 in the US helped a radicalised jihadist cause. Yet we can also see a parallel in high-income countries where, at least since the banking crisis of 2007, large sections of society also like to follow a leader who can provide easy answers (see, for example Beck et al., 2020). Indeed, Postelnicescu (2016, p. 202) points out that the "rise of extremism, radicalization and populism are facets of the same politics of fear" and she postulates that the

> psychology involved in this is simple: you turn outwards your own frustrations with the way things are as an emotional coping mechanism. In this air of tension both extremists and populist false Messiah thrive: an apparent revolutionary that will change the way things are.
>
> (p. 205)

While Brubaker (2017), might not be directly linked to the object of the research presented here, he gives a comprehensive overview of the theory of *populism*, with his focus on a "crisis of democracy" and "moves towards majoritarianism", in Europe and North America. Similarly, Robertson and Nestore (2021), focus on Higher Education, and pinpoint that "deep structural transformations" can lead to a form of regression in a society. It can be assumed that the same reasons hold true even where the Prevent strategy of the UK government is not applied as part of the Higher Education Act.[1] In their research, they describe "the ways in which understandings and experiences of class, social mobility, meritocracy, economic and social inequalities, and social justice have all been transformed to create a new common sense" (Robertson and Nestore, 2021, p. 120). While this seems to be, on the surface of it, far removed from the experience of those who aim for a jihadist overthrow of the existing order, the crucial commonality is found in the understandings and experiences of a section of society. As a result, the groundswell of disappointment and disenfranchisement are felt by certain sections in democratic and autocratic societies which make descriptions like the one given by Cohen (2019) fitting both for those who follow populist leaders and those who go one step further and actively radicalise. Cohen (2019, p. 5) links a notion of "the politics of resentment" to the concept of *populism*. He points out that, crucially "populist political entrepreneurs excel in fomenting social antagonisms by framing shifts in the forms of social pluralism in ways that foster deep political polarization, generalized distrust and a politics of resentment against "elites", "the establishment ...". A parallel between populist movements in Western countries and radical organisations can be seen when looking at descriptions like the following:

> Democratic breakdowns [can be seen as linked to] the feeling of political exclusion and loss of influence ("we do not count anymore") and the sense of economic irrelevance, dislocation and declining material, and occupational security ("we are peripheral"). It requires an examination of the experience of disdain and contempt ("no one cares or respects us") for socioeconomic groups and sociocultural forms of life that are becoming 'minoritized' in conjunction with the evisceration of their sources of social honor.
>
> (Cohen, 2019, p. 9)

Cohen gives a list of ten criteria for an ideal type of populism, most of which appear to be equally applicable to radical followers of terrorist groups who give 'Islamic Jihad' or the 'building of an Islamic Califate' as their *raison d'etre*. Roberts-Ingleson and McCann (2023), describing terrorism and radicalisation, make a similar case when it comes to their root causes. It must not be forgotten that forms of radicalisation express themselves in different ways. Clément (2023) makes the important distinction between "discourse-based" and "action-based" radicalisation. Crucially, the root causes, as described above, are similar and there is a large body of research into jihadist extremism (see below). The pathways open or chosen are very much dependent on circumstance (as, e.g., Valk et al. (2023) highlight). The important issue, which is the centre of the research shown here, is the importance of the information, the *discourse* received by a vulnerable section of society and their subsequent radicalisation. Thus, Roberts-Ingleson and McCann (2023, p. 43) say that while there appears to be an "apparent lack of empirical research on the connection between misinformation and radicalisation", their initial research found that there are "strong theoretical reasons to believe that the former may facilitate the latter". Indeed, as (for example) Evangelista and Bruno (2019) have shown, targeted misinformation using social media can be linked to radicalisation; Edsal (2023) provides a useful overview of the literature on how the 45th president of the United States of America used misinformation and a technique of relentless repetition of lies to "to mobilize a MAGA coalition that has taken on the characteristics of a religious sect, affirming its adherents' belief in Trump's false claims".[2] While the terrorist acts committed are of a different magnitude, parallels between the kind of propaganda talk and the reactions of the groups which have 'characteristics of a religious sect' are striking.

3. Prior Research

When looking at prior research, there are several approaches to radicalisation and the language of radicals which need to be taken into account. One approach is to look at what makes an audience susceptible to populist or, indeed, extremist propaganda. Looking at radicalised groups like IS, there have been a variety of studies exploring how far the descriptions by mainstream media affected these groups. For example, Yusof et al. (2013) look at how the international media describes movements like IS; Baker et al. (2012) look at the impact of jihadist groups on the portrayal of Muslims in the British press; similarly, there is also the aspect of how to spot forms of propaganda that tries to radicalise vulnerable individuals based on linguistic features. Thus, for example, Prentice, Rayson and Taylor (2012) present a discourse analysis of extremist material which centres their rhetoric on themes of morality, social proof, inspiration and appeals to religion in order to find a way to create an automated recognition system. Linked to this is the work by Marcellino et al. (2016) whose forensic linguistic approaches and corpus methods demonstrated a way to measure the spread of violent extremists' propaganda, communicated to population groups over time.

Crucially, research shows that it is linguistic features, in particular, which try to connect radical elements with a wider readership as they aim to build an inclusive, bonded group feeling. For example, O'Regan and

Betzel (2016) describe that recurrent patterns have been shown in language choices that reflect united political, social and cultural values amongst extremist groups; Matusitz and Olufowote (2016) focus on one particular linguistic aspect, namely the use of pictorial metaphors in jihadist propaganda which act as conduits for perceiving and experiencing the world and 'others'. Such features are fairly typical for all kinds of *propaganda* as Wilbur (2017) describes in his overview; Wanless and Berk (2021) give special attention to how means of propaganda are being spread in the age of social media. Simons (2018, p. 322) goes as far as calling ISIS a brand, with its leadership employing PR techniques to position and sell their 'product'. Thus "[a]spects of political marketing are used in order to create sets of relationships of attraction and avoidance with different target audiences". Simons speaks of the "politics of terrorism" with the result that "communication of meaningful and symbolic aspects of culture and history are an important factor in ISIS communications, playing the role of accumulating social capital and political legitimacy" Simons (2018, p. 331). Both Wilbur (2017) and Simons (2018) focus on the qualitative evaluation of one ISIS journal, *DABIQ*.[3] The latter describes its contents as "sets of diametrically opposed realities" (Simons, 2018, p. 343), whereas the former highlights key features, like, for example, how strongly ISIL signals literal compliance with the Qur'an (Wilbur, 2017, p. 9). While both assess the journal by looking at a range of rhetorical tools (both textual and visual), only Simons gives some quantitative insights. It must be pointed out, however, that no use of a lexical analysis based on a corpus of jihadist magazines is being made: in this, the present research differs. Wilbur, in particular, underscores his arguments with sample texts and a clear preference for visuals.

The latest research, where the RAD corpus is investigated in-depth can be found in the special issue of *Pragmatics and Society,* "Approaches to the discourse of terror".[4] The current investigation is, in a way, another, further path to analyse the material. The approach found in the *Grievance Dictionary* (van der Vegt et al., 2021) is closer to the one chosen for this chapter. Psycholinguistic dictionaries are being employed to understand and detect extreme, threatening, or hateful language on the web. They are also used to inform automatic linguistic threat assessment, according to the authors. For their dictionary, they have paid particular attention to the writings of terrorists and (online) extremists. While the research at hand focuses on one semantic field, namely *power relations*, the concept of 'seed words' employed by van der Vegt et al. is similar to the work undertaken here, where keywords found in the RAD corpus are the starting point for research into the divergence of use found where the RAD corpus material is compared to the COCA magazine material.

4. Theoretical Framework and Methodology

This investigation will employ a psycholinguistic approach for its data analysis, following Hoey's (2005) *theory of lexical priming*, which has as its main premise that each time a listener/reader comes across a term or phrases, they are being primed as to their meaning and relevance in language use. It can be said, consequently, that *power relations* are reinforced through repeated language use, driven by subconscious primings. This means that each recurrence of a lexical item facilitates its subconscious anchoring of the said lexical item in its semantic, lexical, and grammatical environments; something Hoey (2005) refers to as nesting.

The theory has been adapted to consider the (semi-) deliberate choices made by content producers, in particular political operatives by Duguid and Partington (2017), who speak of the principle of ***forced primings.*** Duguid and Partington demonstrate how the main media organisations in the USA seemingly followed the wording as presented by the then government; an example of how reporters have become primed to follow a particular choice:

Syrian Government –> Syrian Regime –> Assad Regime.

The hypothesis underlying this research is that the writers and editors of jihadist magazines take wordings and descriptions that enforce, through repeat usage, a certain framework of primings which readers then absorb.[5] The methodology to obtain relevant material consists of a number of steps:

1 To identify focal points for analysis: wordlists of the two main corpora were created with *WordSmith Tools 8* (Scott, 2023);
2 Creation of a keyword-list based on these two wordlists;
3 Focus on words that are fairly frequent in general use in English. Consequently, items like *jihad* or *caliphate* were not considered as these would naturally be expected in the RAD corpus but are rarely found in general discourses;
4 Investigation into the difference of usage where RAD is compared to the COCA magazines sub-corpus; that is, the *nestings* (cf. Hoey, 2005) of these words are directly compared.

After conducting this search, the word-field 'power relations' appeared to be amongst the most prevalent amongst the most frequent semantic groups. For the choice of reference corpus to be compared to the *Radicals* corpus of jihadist magazines (RAD), a number of criteria had to be fulfilled. First of all, the jihadist magazines are published in English, thus the need to have both corpora published in the English language Secondly, as the RAD corpus authors single out the United States of America as a frequent target

Table 11.1 Corpora used: RAD, consisting of six different publications, and COCA magazines selection

Corpus	*N tokens*	*N files*	*Notes*
RAD	1,269,749	861	Publication period: 2010–2017
COCA	37,391,960	10	Publication period: 2006–2015

of their comments, the jihadist magazines might stand in opposition to US publications and, indeed, see themselves as a kind of counterfoil to the same. It does make sense, therefore, to use US material as the point of reference. Lastly, both corpora ought to be magazines, composed of an amalgamation of texts under the umbrella of a single publication, which targets a specific audience; they cover "current affairs" rather than being driven by a daily news cycle. Consequently, the *magazines* sub-corpus of COCA has been selected as the reference corpus. Furthermore, a period starting *before* the publication of RAD has been included, in case the language choices and structures in the COCA material have, in fact, influenced the English writing in RAD. Details of the corpora are given in Table 11.1.

It must be highlighted that COCA is substantially larger than RAD. However, the need to have a varied, representative selection as well as the requirement to have frequencies of occurrence that allow for substantive comparison outweigh possible objections that differences in size might distort findings too much. Table 11.2 indicates that the reference corpus needs to have a suitably large size in order to provide relevant frequencies for a number of RAD keywords.

Table 11.2 gives a list of keywords in the field of *power* relations where RAD is compared to the COCA magazines material. The target words investigated in this chapter are highlighted here. The table points to two noteworthy idiosyncrasies of the RAD material. First of all, the apparent preoccupation in RAD with perceived enemies is displayed through keywords such as *America, Leaders, Rulers, Democracy* or *the Establishment.* Furthermore, the juxtaposition in RAD between positive propaganda (*truth, victory, truthful)* as opposed to strong negativity (*fear, falsehood, oppression, deviant, slave* and *humiliation*) appears to be a salient feature.

5. Findings and Discussion

5.1 Low-Frequency Words

This section focuses on two words, *obligatory* and *humiliation,* which are found with relatively low frequencies in both RAD and, in particular, in COCA. Furthermore, the nestings of these two items do not yield many

Table 11.2 Power Relations **keywords** in RAD; reference corpus (RC): COCA magazines

N	*Keyword*	*RAD, N*	*RAD (%)*	*COCA, N*	*COCA (%)*	*BIC*
54	STATE	2,298	0.18	18,299	0.05	2,712.21
98	VICTORY	644	0.05	2,134	0.01	1,589.68
111	TRUTH	762	0.06	3,492	0.01	1,440.39
115	ALLIES	489	0.04	1,195	0.00	1,431.35
137	FEAR	697	0.05	3,899	0.01	1,165.61
145	OBLIGATORY	205	0.02	57	0.00	1,138.29
147	FALSEHOOD	193	0.02	34	0.00	1,136.07
157	RULING	318	0.02	575	0.00	1,068.69
183	AMERICA	1,102	0.09	11,225	0.03	930.32
184	PERMISSABLE	175	0.01	63	0.00	929.26
199	TRUTHFUL	168	0.01	67	0.00	874.95
212	OPPRESSION	193	0.02	174	0.00	828.78
214	DEVIANT	142	0.01	27	0.00	823.95
228	LAND	795	0.06	7,433	0.02	754.33
240	LEADERS	547	0.04	3,966	0.01	704.17
258	RULERS	175	0.01	231	0.00	659.78
293	RULE	446	0.03	3,173	0.01	582.94
294	DEMOCRACY	317	0.02	1,561	0.00	581.27
333	SLAVE	203	0.02	633	0.00	508.09
363	TERROR	206	0.02	853	0.00	425.97
364	ESTABLISHMENT	195	0.02	759	0.00	420.81
369	NATIONS	334	0.03	2,486	0.01	410.74
371	HUMILATION	119	0.01	193	0.00	407.94

results – in this, the other relatively low-frequency term, *oppression* stands apart and it is, for this reason, discussed at length in section 6.

5.1.1 Obligatory

Obligatory stands out as one of the few adjectives amongst the most significantly overused terms in RAD. It is closely bound (denotatively) with a semantic association to power relationships as the definition given in the OED (2020) makes clear:

> 2a. "Imposing obligation or morally binding; compulsory and not merely permissive; that must be done or practised."

In RAD, the focus is, indeed, solely on this definition. In fact, the collocates in R1 and R2 position for *obligatory* are these: *deeds, prayer(s), status* as well as *fight* and *fighting*. Less frequent collocates can still be ascribed to this semantic field (and meet the "that must be done or practised" definition in the OED) as this random concordance sample line demonstrates:

"The blood of the disbelievers is obligatory to spill by default"

This stands in a marked contrast to the use of the word in COCA, which has fewer concordance lines of *obligatory,* yet these are more varied in their meaning. In the reference corpus, only 4/53 occurrences fit OED definition 2a. Instead, the majority of its occurrences fit another OED (2020) definition:

> 2b. "Frequently humorous. So customary or fashionable as to be expected of everyone or on every occasion".

In fact, this seems to be the typical form of use occurring in most concordance lines in COCA; it appears typically as a cliché in theatre or film reviews as in "I know when to break into the obligatory claps and screams"; or it reflects rituals of the "political theatre", like "after an obligatory attack against Reagan‘s irresponsible deficits". Thus, the same word seems to be employed for two diametrically opposed purposes where RAD is compared to COCA.

5.1.2 Humiliation

Of all the target words, the term *humiliation* is the least frequent in both corpora; furthermore, it has the lowest level of keyness in this selection. Both RAD and COCA have the noun phrase 'the humiliation of' as its most commonly occurring form. This appears in 12.5/100 cases in COCA and 9.2/100 cases in RAD. Yet, bi- and trigrams show a level of divergence otherwise, as is shown in Table 11.3.

Table 11.3 The grammar of *Humiliation*

COCA	*N/100*	*RAD*	*N/100*
NATIONAL HUMILATION	2.2	ISLAM **AND** HUMILATION	2.5
DOUBLE HUMILATION	1.6	HUMILATION **AND** DEGRADATION	3.3
HUMILATION **AND** DEFEAT	1.6	HUMILATION **AND** DISGRACE	3.3
PAIN **AND** HUMILATION	2.2	HUMIALTION **AND** SHAME	2.5

Table 11.3 compares the most frequently occurring bigrams and trigrams of *humiliation* in COCA with the most frequent ones found in RAD apart from the common trigram 'the humiliation of'. Unsurprisingly, both corpora use the word with strong negative prosody. An initial comparison indicates that the colligation is different. Where COCA demonstrates a preference for bigrams ('national humiliation'; 'double humiliation') which are as frequent as the most frequent trigrams, RAD tends to have meaning-making trigrams only as the typical reference to *humiliation*. In fact, this is a salient feature for RAD, which becomes particularly apparent where linked-noun-groups are concerned. Overall, *and humiliation* is (per 100 occurrences) twice as frequent; *humiliation and* is 2.5 times as frequent in RAD compared to COCA.

Furthermore, we see a clear divergence of use for this construction. While they share one collocate (i.e., *shame*), it must be highlighted that not a single linked-noun-group found in COCA can also be found in RAD trigrams. For example, in COCA there is talk of 'shame and humiliation', whereas the RAD writers tend to foreground 'humiliation' in any such linked noun group: 'humiliation and shame'. In doing so, the writers seem to create an impression that puts emphasis on the status of the victim.[6] This assessment is underlined by examples like "where you have no honor and are forced to live in *humiliation*, **subjugated** by the disbelievers" or " Muslim blood at the hands of the insolent Kuffar, *humiliation*, **violation of the Laws** of the Pure Shariah". Overall, all the RAD linked-noun-groups in Table 11.3 are inside long, often convoluted sentences, describing either victimhood or, as in the case of "humiliation and degradation" as a threat: "humiliation and degradation was made for those who oppose my command".

Furthermore, it can be said that foregrounding and end-focus of *humiliation* fall into distinct uses: On the one hand, where humiliation is foregrounded in RAD, it refers to those who have left the "right path", given up on jihad, etc.; "humiliation and degradation" is visited upon those who do not follow the alleged rules of Allah. On the other hand, 'disgrace and humiliation' is used to refer to battles that fighters have lost.

Two final points need to be noted when looking at *humiliation*. In RAD, it appears to be hyper-formulaic in the most common n-grams of this word: This is underlined by the fact that four different sources appear to use almost exactly the same wording here. Interestingly, however, the English translations of the Qur'an do not use humiliation in this particular form at all, thus supporting the view that the RAD authors and editors have created their very own, specific grammar.

5.2 High-Frequency Words

5.2.1 Establishment

The *Establishment,* according to the OED (2020) definition 10a, is "a public institution, a school, factory, house of business, etc.". In COCA, it appears 687 times (= 18.4/1 million words); in RAD, 195 times (= 153.6/1 million words), making it a markedly more frequent term in the latter. Within COCA, around one-quarter of all uses of term appear as *establishment of* (e.g., 'establishment of religion'), and premodifier_*establishment* (e.g., 'medical establishment'); by contrast, 'establishment *of*' is almost a mono-collocate in RAD (see Table 11.4).

Table 11.4 shows that, as with *humiliation*, *establishment* tends to use different grammatical structures where RAD is compared to COCA. Again, it can be said that the nesting of the word in the two discourses is divergent. Looking at *establishment* collocates, RAD appears a lot more formulaic (e.g., 'establishment of the Islamic State/Califate').

When the near collocates are compared (see Figures 11.1 and 11.2), it can be seen that RAD, grammatically and pragmatically seen, appears

Table 11.4 Establishment occurrence patterns (most frequent occurrences highlighted)

	COCA, N	*COCA, N/100*	*RAD, N*	*RAD, N/100*
ESTABLISHMENT OF	163	23.7	163	**83.6**
THE ESTABLISHMENT OF	121	17.6	142	72.8
THE ESTABLISHMENT OF THE	30	4.4	60	**30.8**
THE ESTABLISHMENT OF A (AN)	32	4.7	(11)	5.6
Adj.premodifier + ESTABLISHMENT	156	**22.7**	3	1.5
"THE ESTABLISHMENT"	78	**11.4**	1	0.5

Data in bold are the most frequently occurring ones.

L2	L1	Centre	R1	R2	R3	R4	R5
FOR	THE	ESTABLISHMENT	OF	THE	ISLAMIC	STATE	THE
THE	RE		AND	AN	RELIGION	AND	OF
OF	ITS		IS	ALLAH'S	AND	THE	AND
AND	AND			ISLAM	KHILAFAH	OF	IN
UNTIL	ISLAM'S			SHARIAH	RULE	IN	THIS
IS				KHILAFAH	HOUR	ON	KHILAFAH
WITH				JUSTICE	SHARI'AH	ISLAMIC	IT
SINCE				SHARI'AH	OF	ALLAH	HAS
AFTER					IN	AGAINST	EARTH
IN					ISLAMIC	IS	ALLAH
WAS					THE	EMIRATE	ISLAMIC
BEFORE					CALIPHATE		THAT
TO					LAW		ITS
THAT					JUST		STATE
PREVENT					PROPHETIC		
AGAINST							

Figure 11.1 Collocate pattern for *Establishment* in RAD.

more future-orientated: Moves are undertaken **towards** *the establishment of the Islamic state* (its most frequent use in a long cluster). In direct comparison, COCA tends to refer to various different elites which have been historically formed – referencing both more formal ones ('party establishment', 'Westminster establishment') and informal ones ('beltway establishment', 'art establishment'), and, indeed, oppositional ones (anti-establishment) – all of which are more metaphorical because they elude concrete definition – something that RAD uses of *establishment* appears to avoid.

5.2.2 *Democracy*

Overall, the word *democracy* presents a stark difference of use, where RAD seems to show a preference for trigrams, yet the far larger COCA-magazines sub-corpus shows a preference for bigrams. In this, a parallel to the way the word *humiliation* is employed in the two corpora can be seen. Thus, a typical example in COCA makes frequent reference to US institutions or political parties ('establishing/promoting/resembling *democracy*') whereas RAD has 'religion', 'the Qur'an' and 'jihad' plus *democracy*. RAD links *democracy* together with secularism, nationalism, socialism and also 'polytheistic religions'.

Looking at near-collocates of *democracy* (Figures 11.3 and 11.4), we see that COCA is very US-centric ("forms of democracy") whereas RAD collocates appear to be very restricted, linking *democracy* directly with 'communism', 'secularism' and 'liberalism'.

L3	L2	L1	Centre	R1	R2
THE	THE	THE	ESTABLISHMENT	OF	THE
OF	OF	MEDICAL		AND	OF
BY	AND	MILITARY		IN	RELIGION
AND	TO	AN		THE	AN
IN	FOR	POLITICAL		THAT	TO
TO	FOREIGN	PARTY		IS	IT
THAT	IN	REPUBLICAN		HAS	IN
LAW	OLD	ANTI		CLAUSE	BEEN
WITH	RESPECTING	GOP		WAS	AND
IS	BY	OF		ON	THAT
LED	NATIONAL	POLICY		HE	WAS
FIRST	THAT	RELIGIOUS		TO	ITS
FROM	BUT	DEMOCRATIC		FOR	NOT
THIS	IS	LIBERAL		WHICH	NEW
AMERICAN	WAS	SECURITY		IT	HAS
AMONG	THROUGH	DEFENSE		AS	IS
AGAINST	AS	ITS		BY	ONE
ABOUT	FROM	WASHINGTON		BUT	THIS
WAS	FRENCH	BRITISH		HAD	FOR
WITHIN	AN	RE		WITH	HE
OUT	AMENDMENT	THAT		REPUBLICANS	WITH
IT	AT	AND		WILL	YOU
FOR	OR	ART		AT	UP
HAS	FIRST	BELTWAY		THEY	WHO
CALLED	BETWEEN	NO		HAVE	EVEN
OTHER	FINE	SCIENTIFIC		ONE	BY
OLD		WESTMINISTER		WHERE	BE
AN		WHITE		AFTER	HAVE
		RESEARCH		INCLUDING	ON
		EASTERN		HIS	LONG
		DRINKING		FIGURES	ISRAEL
		CONSERVATIVE		ITSELF	
		EDUCATION		AN	
		MUSLIM		OR	
		LITERARY		MAY	
		FOR			

Figure 11.2 Collocate pattern for *Establishment in* COCA.

Possibly even more noteworthy is the colligational divergence, which is reflected in the diametrically opposed prosodies attached to the term. These tend to be positive in COCA magazines:

- Freedom and Democracy" (1/100)
- Liberal democracy" (3/100)
- American democracy" (2.8/100)

Yet, when we look at RAD, the prosodies for *democracy* are all negative:

- The religion of democracy" (3.8/100)
- Kufr[7] of democracy" (2.8/100)
- Idol of democracy" (1.5/100)

L3	L2	L1	Centre	R1	R2	R3
THE	OF	OF	DEMOCRACY	AND	THE	THE
OF	TO	FOR		IN	IS	AND
TO	THE	AND		IS	IN	TO
AND	IN	TO		THE	AND	IN
IN	AND	OUR		IT	TO	IS
IS	FOR	LIBERAL		BUT	BE	OF
WORLD	THAT	AMERICAN		TO	NOT	THAT
NOT	FREEDOM	THAT		WAS	IT	NOT
FOR	IS	PRO		AS	AS	BE
IT	NOT	IN		CAN	ITS	IT
THAT	SAFE	SOCIAL		ON	IRAQ	WAS
BE	ON	THE		WITH	OF	RIGHTS
OUR	BE	CHINESE		HAS	AN	HAVE
ON	HAVE	WITH		THAT	AMERICA	FOR
AS	WAS	ON		FOR	THAT	AN
WITH	DICTATORSHIP	ABOUT		AT	BY	PEOPLE
NATIONAL	IT	TOWARD		BY	WAS	THIS
NO	BUT	MODERN		OR	HAVE	BUT
FROM	IDEA	PROMOTE		OF	HUMAN	BY
WHO	CENTER	IS		PROMOTION	WE	ABOUT
AN	WITH	POPULIST		HE	RUSSIA	MIDDLE
HAS	OUR	IF		WILL	SAYS	ONLY
THERE	RIGHTS	WESTERN		THEY	HAS	HAS
THEIR	ARSENAL	NEW		WHICH	NEVER	WHICH
COUNTRY	AS	HAVE		WITHOUT	FREEDOM	CAN
WAR	CAN	MAKE		ACTIVISTS	WHICH	WORLD
MORE	WESTERN	DIRECT		LIKE	AT	ARE
THIS	ENDOWMENT	STYLE		COULD	WORLD	BEEN

Figure 11.3 Collocate pattern for *Democracy* in COCA.

L4	L3	L2	L1	Centre	R1	R2	R3
THE	THE	OF	OF	DEMOCRACY	AND	THE	THE
OF	OF	RELIGION	IN		IS	THAT	IS
AND	AND	THE	AND		AS	IS	OF
FOR	TO	KUFR	THAT		IN	ITS	RELIGION
THAT	IS	TO	TO		THE	AND	AND
TO	AS	THAT	FOR		TO	IT	TO
IN	ARE	NOT	WITH		OR	NOT	IN
AS	THIS	AND	SECULARISM		THAT	NATIONALISM	NOT
NO	WHO	ISLAM	THIS		ARE	ALSO	NO
THEY	FOR	IDOL	SECULAR		THIS	IN	ITS
WHICH	THEIR	SAKE	IS		BY	THEIR	AS
DESTROY	WEST	SECULARISM	AS		WAS	RELIGION	THEY
BE	FROM	THIS	USE		NATIONALISM	BE	WAS
INTO	FALSE	SHARIAH	AMERICAN		OF	ARE	ARE
SYSTEM	ISLAMIC	IS	THROUGH		SECULARISM	KUFR	ON

Figure 11.4 Collocate pattern for *Democracy* in RAD.

Of these, 'the religion of democracy' (see Figure 11.5) is the one phrase most frequently occurring in RAD, indicating that the philosophy of *democracy* is seen as a diversion which threatens Muslim brethren to divert from a true path, something which is underscored by extended descriptions of *democracy* like "courtesy of the new-age polytheistic, false religion of democracy".

1	2: Courtesy the new-age polytheistic, falsereligion of democracy: See "The Religion of Democracy" in AZAN:
2	, false religion of democracy': See "TheReligion of Democracy" in AZAN: Issue 1. NOTE 3: A flase god that
3	Abu Mus'ab AL-Zarqawi's article titled "TheReligion of Democracy" in the first issue of Azan Magazine. Ruling of
4	the Kufr of the system of Democracy and thereligion of democracy; however, applying rulings on specifc people
5	2013 has no reality. THIS is that descipablereligion of democracy that is praised openly, day and night. This is
6	by the tawaghit, such as entering into thereligion of democracy, jahili nationalism, the United Nations, and
7	and calls the Muslims in Bengal to thereligion of democracy and this is blatant shirk. Democracy is a
8	, apostatized, and participated in thereligion of democracy, demonstrating that they weren't upon the
9	the Palestinians to participate in the shirkireligion of democracy by voting for Hamas! The following
10	, how much more so is the daw'ah to the paganreligion of democracy and the battle for its cause! The "Virtue" of
11	jihad claimants apostatized and joined thereligion of democracy by entering into its system and fighting for its
12	called on his followers to participate in the kufrreligion of democracy, and also called on them to disassociate

Figure 11.5 Religion of Democracy in RAD (all concordance lines).

Another fixed phrase including the term is the bigram *democracy is....* This appears in over 1/10 of all uses of the word (10.7 occurrences per 100 in RAD), which is more than double the frequency found in COCA (4.8/100) in COCA. A direct comparison of uses highlights that, as seen already above, RAD presents *democracy* as part of an oppressive, alien power structure, as Figure 11.6 demonstrates. A further concordance line explains how democracy is seen by authors of a typical jihad magazine article: "Democracy is a religion that gives supreme authority to people rather than Allah". This stands in sharp contrast to COCA (Figure 11.7) which has, typically, positive prosodies and where critical assessment of *democracy* can be seen as well.

5.2.3 *Oppression*

The word *oppression* naturally invokes unequal power relations between the oppressed and the oppressor (whether societal, institutional or individual). The raw frequencies are similar (193 occurrences in RAD, 174 in COCA), yet even the use at the level of collocates demonstrates a striking degree of divergence. This means that there are several collocates that appear in COCA (like *women, racial, social*) which do not appear in RAD, and vice versa (words like *Muslims, evil, kufr*). In other words, frames of reference appear to be mutually exclusive.

Within RAD, collocates can be divided into two major groups. Firstly, *oppression* collocates with terms which are associated with jihadism and/or the Islamic faith ('Allah'; 'Muslims'; 'Muslim' and 'jihad'). Secondly, collocates appear to be negative words that are semantically associated with *oppression* ('aggression'; 'tyranny'; 'evil'; 'injustice'). There are, furthermore, those who appear to be seen as *agents of oppression* ('American' and 'kufr').

promises are nothing but deceptions." (Q4:120), Likewise. democracy is the religion of America, which regards itself as
in Bengal to the religion of democracy, and this is blatant shirk. Democracy is a religion that believes in giving people the
majority of your people support you. This is because democracy is a one-way highway that lands you in a position
. or refuses to make the takfir of those who are fighting to establish democracy. is himself murtadd. And whoever reads this
all those people who follow him till the Day of Judgment...The Kufr of democracy is abound in the entire world at the moment – and it
enough I enough and revolted. Getting into the debate whether democracy is not contradictory to the dictates of Islam and its
point when he said to the parliament right after that, "Turkey's democracy is your own achievement. It was not forced upon
State. We are against terrorism" they say. "maybe They think that democracy is shura and that a civil state is the opposite of a
the core objective of this discourse, but one thing for sure is that democracy is a way of life, a term which carries a bigger
Moorsi in Egypt, should be an example that the system of democracy is not a viable solution for Muslims, and that the
the fold of Islam). To put it more precisely, the new God in democracy is the desire of man, who legislates what he
as from the Shaykh Abu Basir at- Tartusi. Note 5: The question of democracy is a separate subject and has caused much
parties and does not oppose democracy. Rather the core of democracy is from the heart of Islam" (Al-Musawwir Magazine).
Bear Full faith in Democracy When it has been established that Democracy is a separate and proper Deen1, which, from its
, then in Shariah such people are called 'Mulhid' or 'Zindeeq'. Democracy is Kufr but not all people in this system are Kafir!
but not all people in this system are Kafir! There is no doubt that democracy is a proper Deen. Therefore, it is a clear rejection
opinion" Another principle that forms one of the fundamentals of democracy is the absolute acceptance of the opinion of the
and for the people What is democracy and what are its origins? Democracy is the principle of the mastership of the people:
- is in actually rather dynamic. Capatilaim is its principles and Democracy is its practice. A religion indeed is made up of both,
this is clear disbelief and polytheism. The basic fundamental of democracy is at compkete odds with the Aqeedah of Tawheed
And a few "Ulama Hre, a question will definitely be raised that if Democracy is Kufr, then why do a few "Ulama participate in this
) The satanic principle of the "Freedom of belief" The building of democracy is established on the freedom of belief. In the
to accept the decision. On the other hand, the verdict of democracy is the issue of Palestine. There is o contradiction
. One of the things that exposes the reality of the American democracy is the 'constitution of the country is the holiest
brings justice, people and honor in both this life and the next. Democracy is the polytheistic religion of the corrupt
on a Muslim environment, essentially for two reasons: Democracy is a contrary idea od Tawheed (Monotheism).

Figure 11.6 Democracy is defined as such in RAD (excerpt of concordance lines).

and building democracy across the region. Democracy is a process , not a destination, and
is an escapable irony that the cradle of American democracy is now a symbol of sports hegemony ,
" of the executive branch, it will signal that American democracy is in its death throes .# If the Capitol
thing as a free and fair election in Nigeria , where democracy is less about freedom than about
question the government every 20 years , then democracy is no longer working. That's why
evidence of forty-two years of progressive multiparty democracy is everywhere you look : an 81 percent
Darling-Hammond has written : "Right now our democracy is in trouble . Only about a one-third of
much power the Supreme court would accrue . If democracy is to remain vibrant as society ages ,
Middle East , it has become increasingly clear that if democracy is to succeed , citizenship must be
economies , and not just by redistribution , social democracy is purposeless. # The intellectual
, this is nothing less than the historic shift in how our democracy is run . The Republicans who control
. Actually , the most rock &; roll thing about Chinese democracy is he does n't care if you do . Key
everything in an innovative and scientific way ! " # 4 'Democracy is a thing of value for which we should
It is alive , breathing . # As writers from lands where democracy is still an unattained dream , we do not
revenue to fund @ @ @ @ @ @ @ @ @ @ social democracy is understanding that you need a
in building up the kingdom of God on earth . Democracy is not merely a set of empty
the New America Foundation says is essential for democracy is n't with any single technology , but @
in one country" did n't work ; pragmatic social democracy is the successful face of"
knew better . He had warned the President that democracy is " more than elections . " that Grand
, only Thailand is disintegrating . Its once vibrant democracy is now widely viewed as an
replace autocrats . The flip side of promoting liberal democracy is bolstering failing states . As we
had ! But I assume that the point of the American democracy is you can express any point of view

Figure 11.7 Democracy is defined as such in COCA (excerpt of concordance lines).

Table 11.5 *Oppression* collocates in RAD: problem-solution scheme

OPPRESSION	
AMERICAN	"THEM" The enemy
MUSLIMS	"US" The victim
JIHAD	"THE WAR" The solution

Interestingly, COCA has only five collocates which appear more than five times and these are split in the following way:

1 A general grouping ('social')
2 Negative wording ('violence')
3 Social groups ('women', 'racial', 'white')

As Table 11.5 shows, the way the term *oppression* is employed in RAD presents a neat problem-solution construction, where the 'them' (*American*) is juxtaposed with an 'us' (*Muslims).* It must be noted that *Muslims* is not further qualified, yet the concordance lines clearly indicate that the oppression by the aggressor (*American/kufr/crusader)* can be countered by violent conflict, in other words, *jihad.*

Table 11.6 describes in detail how this construction is realised at different grammatical levels. This highlights that the authors and editors of the jihadi magazines aim to make this principle all-encompassing and fully dominant. The subject (which is, the 'solution') never changes while the object *Muslims* appears always in the position of victimhood – this is underscored by the use of the passive. Meanwhile, the weight of the oppressor is magnified through the use of prepositional phrases, where the focus is on US military attacks; the adjectives chosen where it is *American* oppression which uses the possessive and is presented as factual – thus underlining how much *America* 'owns' the role as the oppressor. This stands in clear contrast to *Muslims* which are typically represented as passive, something underscored by the use of prepositions ("against" or "towards" Muslims).

5.2.4 Rule

Rule appears around 3.7 times in every 1,000 words in RAD, yet only once per 1,000 words in COCA, reflecting the importance the word appears to have for the writers in these jihadi magazines. This section will look at the

Table 11.6 Oppression: how collocates are employed in RAD

Collocate of OPPRESSION	**Grammtical realsation** + *examples*		
AMERICAN	*Adjective*	*Possessive*	*Prepositional Phrase*
"THEM" – enemy	American oppression	America's oppresion	Of the American/ Israeli coaltion against African-American of the American-allied warlords
MUSLIMS	**Prepositonal Phrase**	**Passive**	
	on Muslims	Muslims became targeted with oppression	
"US" – victim	of the Muslims against Muslims towards Muslims against Islam and Muslims alongside the Muslims!		
JIHAD	**Subject**		
"WAR" – solution	jihad are against any man made system jihad against the oppression of kufr the real jihad that will change oppression		

lemmas of the word (i.e., *rule, rules, ruling* as well as *ruler* and *rulers*). As we have seen with *oppression*, typical uses in COCA appear not at all in RAD, as the most frequent trigrams in Table 11.7 show.

Rule of is the most common bigram in both corpora, yet it is, proportionally, almost four times as frequently occurring as a construction of *rule* in RAD. It provides an instance where one article links it to its dismissal of *democracy* (see Section 5.2), and this may serve as a possible explanation. "Muslims have to a large extent realized the hypocritical disposition of the kafir west and its ever-changing selective definition of such acclaimed slogans of *democracy* as, **rule** of the people, by the people, and for the people".

Table 11.7 Occurrence patterns of *rule* in both corpora

Cluster	*RAD N*	*RAD n/100*	*COCA N*	*COCA n/100*
THE RULE OF	132	9.8	209	2.6
THE RULES OF	20	1.5	157	2.0
THE RULING OF	60	4.5	2	<1
RULE OF THE	40	3.0	29	<1
THE RULING ON	35	2.6	0	0
RULED BY THE	25	1.9	14	<1
RULE OF LAW	0	0	161	2.0
RULE OF THUMB	0	0	129	1.6
TO RULE OUT	0	0	82	1.0

It is notable that both *ruler* and *rulers* only occur in RAD as a collocate of *rule* – namely in the form of 'Muslim rulers', 'tyrannical rulers' as well as 'manmade rulers' – all of which are juxtaposed by 'ruled by Allah'. COCA, however, does not seem to record *ruler/s* as a collocate. In fact, the clearest divergence appears in the colligations of the term. Overall, RAD tends to have *nouns* as collocates, whereas COCA tends to have *adjectives*. The clusters in the US magazine data are a lot less fixed; there are also more of them (with lower frequencies), suggesting variety in both semantics and structure with the item rule(s) Therefore, in COCA idiomatic phrases appear fairly prominently: 'rule of thumb', 'as a rule' and 'to rule out' which, importantly, are not fixed in their semantic environment.

This stands in contrast to RAD, where, as Table 11.7 shows, the phrase 'the ruling on' (typically followed by 'the person who abandons their beliefs') is highly prominent. Furthermore, as is already indicated by the use of the lemmas *ruler/rulers*, there is a clear delineation between acceptable and unacceptable *rule* in RAD: *Nouns* like 'Islam', 'King', 'Law', 'Allah' and 'Shari'ah', which are dictated as the 'rules' prescribed dominate the discourse. Aside from religion and politics, there are also universal concepts such as 'earth', 'land' and 'people' emphasising Islam as the 'natural' rule on Earth ('Allah's rule of earth'; 'rule of Allah's earth'; 'rule the lands of the Muslims'). All instances of the collocate 'subjected' refer specifically to the one-fifth rule, the 'tax' levied on believers. Unsurprisingly, these uses are almost entirely absent in COCA (cf. Partington, 2014).

6. Conclusion

In conclusion, the analysis of lexical, grammatical, semantic, pragmatic and textual patterns associated with keywords in jihadist magazines (RAD) and a general reference corpus (COCA) reveals notable differences. On the surface of it, the differences described here reflect the issues that concern their readerships. Even when taking into consideration the differences in corpus size and style, the degree of divergence between the two corpora is marked, with RAD reflecting concerns surrounding religion, the Qur'an and jihad, while COCA makes frequent reference to US institutions or political parties. Unlike RAD, COCA reveals idiomatic usage ("rule of thumb") and the target words often allow a wider range of referrers than found in the RAD (though this might be partly explained by the differences in corpus sizes). This investigation also suggests that the semantic and pragmatic patterns in RAD are often very constrained and fixed, creating a different kind of discourse grammar entirely. The use of forced primings (cf. Duguid & Partington, 2017) and negatively loaded words further reinforces the writers' collective ideology. This is very much in line with findings presented by Marcellino et al. (2016), Wilbur (2017) or Milton (2020). One can draw parallels to (political) marketing campaigns where a fixed set of phrases ("sound bites") are repeated on a loop to lodge themselves in the audience's mind. There are also parallels to the (mis-) information campaigns pursued by populists where the discourse is clearly bent towards one, narrowly proscribed set of meanings, usage of which is intended to only allow one specific interpretation.

In this corpus-driven investigation, the findings indicate that the lexical, grammatical, semantic, pragmatic and textual nesting patterns in RAD reinforce these linguistic features, and present a very narrow window of possible points of reference to their readers, suggesting that the writings are very aims-driven. The reason for this ought to be clear, according to Cohen (2019, p. 14):

> [f]undamentalists embrace populist identity politics, want to take power in the name of the people, merge party and movement logics, refuse to differentiate them once elected to power, reject the legitimacy of the opposition, and thus become catalysts for the emergence of authoritarian populist regimes.

The level of repetition, the re-assigning of fairly common words for a specific purpose found here fits in with the definition Hoey (2005) gives for *lexcical priming* and can be read to be intentionally used by the authors and editors of jihadist magazines, who mirror the kind of *forced primings* that Duguid and Partington (2017) have described based on White House briefings.

As a result, COCA reflects 'civil society' according to Cohen's (IBID) definition: "[c]ivil society is open, plural with many different publics, counter publics, associations, and movements that come and go". By contrast, the language in RAD appears aims-driven, with the intent of creating a clear "us vs. them" narrative, negatively loaded words associated with the "enemy", such as *democracy*. These findings shed light on the collective ideology of the writers of jihadist magazines and offer insights into their discourse grammar.

Notes

1 Prevent Strategy 2011. Available at: https://assets.publishing.service.gov.uk/government/uploads/system/uploads/attachment_data/file/97976/prevent-strategy-review.pdf
2 See https://www.nytimes.com/2023/08/02/opinion/trump-election-lies-free-speech.html
3 *Dabiq* is one of the journals that make up the RAD corpus employed for researching this chapter.
4 Volume 13, Issue 3, July 2022.
5 Duguid (in a presentation in 2022) speaks of "flooding the discourse with a number of particular wording choices".
6 It must be noted that the term 'victim' itself appears only 25 times in the RAD. The uses and referrers of 'victim' do not seem to be fixed in any particular way, however.
7 *Kufr* = "religious wrong"; "disbeliever".

References

Baker, P., Gabrielatos, C., & McEnery, T. (2012). Sketching Muslims: A corpus driven analysis of representations around the word 'Muslim' in the British press 1998–2009. *Applied Linguistics*, *34*(3), 255–278. https://doi.org/10.1093/applin/ams048

Beck, T., Saka, O., & Volpin, P. (2020). *Financial crises and right-wing populism: How do politics and finance shape each other?* https://blogs.lse.ac.uk/businessreview/2020/07/07/financial-crises-and-right-wing-populism-how-do-politics-and-finance-shape-each-other/

Brubaker, R. (2017). Why populism? *Theory and Society*, *46*(5), 357–385. https://www.jstor.org/stable/44981871

Clément, M. (2023). Reconstructing phases of activism: Group moderation, radicalisation, and extremism. In *Collective emotions and political violence* (pp. 50–78). Manchester University Press. https://doi.org/10.7765/9781526167705.00011

Cohen, J. L. (2019). Populism and the politics of resentment. *Jus Cogens*, *1*(5), 5–39. https://doi.org/10.1007/s42439-019-00009-7

Davies, M. (2023). *The Corpus of Contemporary American English (COCA): Magazine sub-corpus 2006–2016*. Available online at https://www.english-corpora.org/coca/

Dhiab-Hassan, A., Benítez-Castro, M. Á., & Hidalgo-Tenorio, E. (2018). *Nutcracker: The JIHAD Corpus*. University of Granada.

Duguid, A. (2009). Insistent voices: Government messages. J. Morley & P. Bayley (Eds.) *Corpus-Assisted Discourse Studies on the Iraq Conflict*. New York/Oxford: Routledge, (234–260).

Duguid, A., & Partington, A. (2017). Forced lexical primings in transdiscoursive political messaging. In M. Pace-Sigge & K. Patterson (Eds.), *Lexical Priming: Applications and advances* (pp. 67–92). Amsterdam: John Benjamins. https://doi.org/10.1075/scl.79.03dug

Edsal, T. B. (2023). We are in a five-alarm Fire for democracy. *The New York Times*. https://www.nytimes.com/2023/08/02/opinion/trump-election-lies-free-speech.html

Evangelista, R., & Bruno, F. (2019). WhatsApp and political instability in Brazil: Targeted messages and political radicalisation. *Internet Policy Review*, *8*(4), 1–23. https://doi.org/10.14763/2019.4.1434

Hoey, M. (2005). *Lexical Priming: A new theory of words and language*. London: Routledge.

Hoey, M. (2017). Cohesion and coherence in a content-specific corpus. In M. Pace-Sigge & K. Patterson (Eds.), *Lexical Priming: Applications and advances* (pp. 3–40). Amsterdam: John Benjamins. https://doi.org/10.1075/scl.79.01hoe

Hopper, P. (1987). Emergent grammar. *Annual Meeting of the Berkeley Linguistics Society*, *13*, 139–157.

Marcellino, W. M., Cragin, K., Mendelsohn, J., Cady, A. M., Magnuson, M., & Reedy, K. (2016). Measuring the popular resonance of Daesh's propaganda. *Journal of Strategic Security*, *10*(1), 32–52. http://doi.org/10.5038/1944-0472.10.1.1527

Matusitz, J., & Olufowote, J. (2016). Visual motifs in Islamist terrorism: Applying conceptual metaphor theory. *Journal of Applied Security Research*, *11*(1), 18–32. https://doi.org.10.1080/19361610.2016.1104276

Milton, D. (2020). Fatal attraction: Explaining variation in the attractiveness of Islamic State propaganda. *Conflict Management and Peace Science*, *37*(4), 430–450. https://doi.org/10.1177/0738894218759

O'Regan, J. P., & Betzel, A. (2016). Critical discourse analysis: A sample study of extremism. *Research Methods in Intercultural Communication*, 281–296. https://doi.org/10.1002/9781119166283.ch19

Oxford English Dictionary (OED). (2020). https://www.oed.com

Partington, A. (2014). Mind the gaps: The role of corpus linguistics in researching absences. *International Journal of Corpus Linguistics*, *19*(1), 118–146. https://doi.org/10.1075/ijcl.19.1.05par

Patterson, K. J. (2022). Under the shadow of swords: The rhetoric of jihad. A corpus based critical analysis of religious metaphors in jihadist magazines. *Pragmatics and Society*, *13*(3), 477–500. https://doi.org/10.1075/ps.21017.pat

Patterson, K. J., & Pace-Sigge, M. T. (2022). Approaches to the discourse of terror: How power relations are represented through forced primings in jihadist magazines. *Pragmatics and Society*, *13*(3), 404–430. https://doi.org/10.1075/ps.21015.pat

Postelnicescu, C. (2016). Europe's new identity: The refugee crisis and the rise of nationalism. *Europe's Journal of Psychology*, *12*(2), 203–209. https://doi.org/10.5964/ejop.v12i2.1191

Prentice, S., Rayson, P., & Taylor, P. J. (2012). The language of Islamic extremism: Towards an automated identification of beliefs, motivations and justifications. *International Journal of Corpus Linguistics, 17*(2), 259–286. https://doi.org/10.1075/ijcl.17.2.05pre

Roberts-Ingleson, E. M., & McCann, W. S. (2023). The link between misinformation and Radicalisation. *Perspectives on Terrorism*, *17*(1), 36–49.

Robertson, S. L. & Nestore, M. (2021). Education cleavages, or market society and the rise of authoritarian populism? *Globalisation, Societies and Education.* https://doi.org/10.1080/14767724.2021.1955662

Scott, M. (2023). WordSmith Tools version 8. Stroud: Lexical Analysis Software. www.lexically.net

Simons, G. (2018). Brand ISIS: Interactions of the tangible and intangible environments. *Journal of Political Marketing*, *17*(4), 322–353. https://doi.org/10.1080/15377857.2018.1501928

Valk, F., de Jonge, L., & Nanninga, P. (2023). The regional face of extremism: A case study of the Northern Netherlands. *Journal for Deradicalization*, *35*(Summer), 76–106.

van der Vegt, I., Mozes, M., Kleinberg, B., & Gill, P. (2021). The Grievance Dictionary: Understanding threatening language use. *Behavior Research Methods*, *53*(5), 2105–2119. https://doi.org/10.3758/s13428-021-01536-2

Wanless, A., & Berk, M. (2021). Participatory propaganda: The engagement of audiences in the spread of persuasive communications. In D. Herbert & S. Fisher-Høyrem (Eds.), *Social media and social order* (pp. 111–139). Warsaw: de Gruyter Poland. https://doi.org/10.2478/9788366675612-009

Wilbur, D. (2017). Propaganda's place in strategic communication: The case of ISIL's Dabiq Magazine. *International Journal of Strategic Communication.* https://doi.org/10.1080/1553118X.2017.1317636

Yusof, S. H., Hassan, F., Hassan, M. S., & Osman, M. N. (2013). The framing of international media on Islam and terrorism. *European Scientific Journal*, *9*(8), 104–121.

12 Echoes of Extremism

Rap Music-Jihadism Dialogue and Violent Radicalization among Western Youth

Jonatan Morillo Losada

1. Introduction

When Al Qaeda's ideological roots were still in their purest form, back in their genesis, the illegitimacy of music seemed beyond question. Abdullah Azzam, who served as a mentor to Osama bin Laden and whose beliefs played a crucial role in the establishment of the first global jihadist terrorist organization, found himself compelled to prematurely withdraw from his involvement in armed struggle during his earliest experience as a violent Islamist against Israel. He came to the realization that this cause lacked religious legitimacy. In his view, his fellow combatants engaged in activities prohibited by Islamic law during their leisure time, such as playing music (Spenser, 2018).

In contemporary times, this kind of religious rigor often lacks clarity, particularly within the new generation of young jihadist terrorists characterized by limited religious knowledge and Western behaviors. Furthermore, the influence of the Internet has facilitated the emergence of evident contradictions in violent Islamist rhetoric, along with self-radicalized youth who lack a coherent discourse. Indeed, they sometimes attempt to find points of reference and legitimization for their personal contexts within various forms of extremism, thereby resulting in ideological hybridizations (Hegghammer, 2009), which extend to aesthetics and linguistic aspects. The virtual space has conditioned the increase in the development of loosely structured violent Islamist groups with an ambiguous hierarchical role. This represents an "informalization" of violent Islamist extremism where formal group affiliation is no longer as relevant; therefore, the mixing of different motives for violence becomes much more unrestricted (Hegghammer, 2009; Meleagrou-Hitchens & Ayad, 2023).

In this context, characterized by heterogeneity, contradictions and the increasingly blurred or outdated discourse of violent Islamist extremism, there is a heightened susceptibility to recruitment among one of the most vulnerable groups, namely, young individuals (Moyano, 2019a). In light of

DOI: 10.4324/9781003457381-13

this, a recent study on the shift in mobilization within the Swedish Salafi-jihadist environment after the fall of the ISIS caliphate (Nilsson & Esholdt, 2022) featured an account from a returnee from Syria; this individual asserted that today Islam[1] represents a fusion of ideas, rap, gangs and Islam. Moreover, he added that in past "you were either a Muslim or a rapper with a gang. Today you can be both" (Nilsson & Esholdt, 2022, p. 15). There is no doubt, therefore, that this militant perceives the dialogue between rap music and jihadism as an existing reality.

2. Literature Review and Research Focus

The aforementioned reality has not received the attention it deserves from researchers and analysts, and these cultural processes often outpace the scrutiny they merit. Nevertheless, some scholars and journalists have touched upon this subject, albeit tangentially. In 2014, when the Western jihadist Abdel Bary emerged in the public eye, there was a surge in writings discussing the connection between rap music and jihadism, like Khan (2014) and Smirke (2014). However, they merely provided basic descriptions of an elusive phenomenon and contributed to the popularization of the questionable term "jihadi rap". Similarly, authors like Lewis (2015) ventured to suggest, without empirical evidence, that rap could serve as a catalyzing tool for jihadism. Such a claim is highly dubious, given that violent radicalization is a multifactorial process.

Subsequently, Conti (2017) asserted that European jihadists are the result of a fusion of Western and non-Western elements (jihadist elements). He identified only a subset of these elements through a visual analysis of the propaganda created by the prominent Western jihadist, Deso Dogg. His reference to rap music, a Western element, was merely incidental, stemming from the subject's previous career as a rapper.

More recently, Larsen and Jensen (2019), along with Jensen, Larsen and Sandberg (2021), have produced the most comprehensive works to date that directly address the rap-jihadism binomial. In their studies, they diligently traced the presumed historical and cultural antecedents of the phenomenon.[2] They identified subcultural continuities between Islam and its historical presence within hip-hop, Black oppositional street culture, and the jihadist subculture. They also highlighted some of its primary "representatives". Nevertheless, there remains a significant gap in understanding the potential effects of this relationship on Western youth.

In this regard, it is crucial to focus on the analysis of song lyrics' discourses, especially considering their variability. In today's landscape, due to the efforts against jihadist propaganda, encountering lyrics with explicit jihadist symbols, as was common a decade or two ago, is no longer widespread.[3] Instead, we should shift our attention to the discursive expressions within violent rap, which is gaining significant popularity among Western youth. This encompasses a spectrum from gangsta rap to trap and drill.

Such expressions involve a manifestation of anger directed toward government indifference and a rejection of dominant structures; elements rooted in the language of Islam within hip-hop culture (Aidi, 2009). These issues are accompanied by a romanticization, not only in an aesthetic sense, of street culture, which poses a risk in terms of normalizing violence among young people; for instance, "We earn complete salaries but we never work" (Saamou Skuu & Zeu, 2021), "I was out tryna chase that money I done it", "a baby mum playing ma song", "I had a four ten before I got me a pistol" (Remz, 2023). At the same time, there are songs that incorporate religious aspects such as "I put fatwas on the heads of idiots" (Medine, 2015), and "I only trust on god big love to my clients. We don't are disbelievers, every day we pray" (Saamou Skuu & Zeu, 2021). Depending on the level of radicalization or vulnerability of a young individual, the fusion of such discourses could potentially enable both the inference of presumed Islamist radical persuasive arguments and the sensitization of violent attitudes.

3. Deconstructing the Term "Jihadi Rap": Constraints and Considerations

The attribution of the term to its originator remains obscure; however, its establishment can be traced back to "Dirty Kuffar", an Islamist extremist song released on a British digital platform managed by Mohammad al-Massari in February 2004. It is worth noting that Gartenstein-Ross (2004) might have been one of the first to use the term; he titled his article "jihadi rap", in which he defined the essence of "Dirty Kuffar" as "music that indulges in Islamist paranoia, that is anti-American in tone and substance, and that is intended to win sympathy – and perhaps recruits – for the jihadists' cause".

With the assistance of Google Ngram Viewer, we conducted a comprehensive analysis of the term's usage frequency since its inception. This approach allowed us to identify the linguistic trend of the term, enabling us to analyze the factors behind its irregular frequency and potential semantic shifts. It is necessary to point out that, in this tool, the frequencies of the searched terms are derived from printed and digital books published up to 2019. For the term under investigation, the time range of 2004–2019 is both valid and effective, as it encapsulates a significant portion of its developmental period.

There is no denying that, since the release of "Dirty Kuffar", any song with Islamic content began to face stigmatization, particularly in light of the new perspective that some Muslim rappers sought to present in response to post-9/11 islamophobia (Esposito, 2011; Swedenburg, 2009). This background is crucial in understanding the second frequency peak of the phrase "jihadi rap" that the results indicate in 2006.[4] During this year, the British Muslim hip-hop group Fun-Da-Mental released an album titled "All is war: The benefits of G-had", which raised concerns. Some voices claimed that various songs from that album contained terrorist content. Take, for example, the album "Cookbook DIY", where the latter British band allegedly appeared to reference the 2005 London bombings. Additionally, in "Che Bin Pt.2", they may have rapped expressions attributed to Osama Bin Laden himself (Swedenburg, 2010). Regardless, it is evident that at least some songs on that album could potentially be construed as containing jihadist arguments, depending on the recipient's interpretation. This type of relatively controversial or radical Islamic content had already surfaced earlier, in the year 2000, in the album "1924" by the Muslim rap group Soldiers of Allah. They seemed to endorse the establishment of an Islamic State, as well as the polarization between Muslims and non-believers (Esposito, 2011).

The third peak, slightly higher in frequency, emerged in 2010. The rationale behind this occurrence could be twofold; during that year, the Western jihadist Omar Hammami, also known as Abu Mansoor al-Amriki, released a rap-style song titled "First Stop Addis". Additionally, the former rapper turned Western jihadist, Deso Dogg, or Abou Maleeq, publicly transitioned from his music career to embrace jihadist militancy (Dantschke, 2012). At this juncture, the term "jihadi rap" acquired a dual descriptive character, namely, one pertaining to rap songs with radical Islamist/jihadist content, and the other associated with a rapper's conversion to jihadism. The latter usage, albeit simplistic in nature, would gain popularity in the years to come with the emergence of Abdel Bary.

In 2011, the frequency of the term decreased, but its usage was influenced by a series of noteworthy events. Omar Hammami, despite being reported as deceased, released two new a cappella rap songs. "Send me a cruise" seemed to be virtually an ode to his potential martyrdom, while "Make jihad with me" constituted an invitation to Western youth to partake in holy war (Mastors & Siers, 2014; Rawnsley, 2011). Despite being widely derided for their low quality, these songs had a notable impact. Even though they were produced a cappella, they exhibited a rhythmic structure inherent to rap. In fact, rap in its origins also emerged without melodic ornamentation. Meanwhile, in that same year, Deso Dogg underwent a significant transformation, changing his convert's name from Abou Maleeq to Abu Talha al-Almani, and became actively involved in substantial recruitment efforts targeting young individuals in the West. He did so by launching a T-shirt brand called "All4One", featuring the slogan "I am a Muslim, not a terrorist". His impact undeniably garnered considerable attention and proved to be genuinely influential, a fact acknowledged by Pierre Vogel, a German Salafist preacher with questionable intentions, with whom the terrorist had contact (Dantschke, 2012).

I should note that the term "jihadi rap" could also have had a completely different semantic usage during the late 2010 and 2011 timeframe, particularly in the context of the Arab Spring movements. In this context, marked by peaceful protests, rap music took on the role of a unifying agent, becoming the rhythm of resistance and the collective voice of the Arab people (Cantrall, 2013; Wright, 2011). Muslim rappers opposed violence and wielded their words as weapons. Rap music began to serve as their form of jihad, symbolizing the struggle for change, the quest for solutions, and the critical representation of their society (Esposito, 2011). The quintessential example of this particular "peaceful jihadi rap" was the Tunisian rapper known as El General. His song "Rais Lebled", which blamed President Ben Ali for all the ills of society, such as poverty, hunger, or injustice, was hailed as the official anthem of the Jasmine Revolution (Wright, 2011).

Commencing in 2011, there was a notable increase in the frequency of the term, with the peak occurring in 2015. Notably, in 2013, the term gained prominence due to the assassination of Omar Hammami at the hands of his alleged "brothers" within the Somali jihadist group al-Shabaab. This may suggest that Western jihadists had shifted their focus toward individual heroism and fame, rather than strictly adhering to the dictates of the group and its leaders (Mastors & Siers, 2014). The period spanning from 2014 to 2015 was characterized by the prominent presence of the Egyptian-British jihadist, Abdel-Majed Abdel Bary. This former rapper was mistakenly identified by MI5 as the perpetrator of the propaganda-driven beheadings disseminated by ISIS, in which some journalists such as the American James Foley were victims (Picart, 2015). The actual executioner, known as "Jihadi John", was ultimately revealed to be Mohammed Emwazi; the latter shared a highly similar jihadist profile with Abdel Bary. Emwazi, a British citizen born in Kuwait, was also deeply immersed in a lifestyle influenced by the London rap scene and gang cultures. Furthermore, he belonged to the group of British fighters known as "The Beatles", in which Abdel Bary was purportedly a member as well (Picart, 2015; Verkaik, 2016). During that period, Abdel Bary had become one of the most sought-after terrorists. This was not solely due to his association with ISIS but also because of his family background. His father, Adel Abdel Bari, was a suspected participant in the 1998 bombings of the U.S. embassies in Kenya and Tanzania, carried out by the Egyptian jihadist group al-Jihad and Al-Qaeda (Perez, 2014). Abdel Bary's case contributed to the oversimplified label of "jihadi rap", much like what happened with Deso Dogg. In this categorization, any rapper who transitioned into a jihadist was dubbed a "jihadi rapper", even if they were not primarily creating rap songs with jihadist symbols or radical Islamist themes.

Finally, from 2015 onward, there was a decrease in the frequency of the term, although its use remained relatively stable over the years. It is true that specific events did lead to minor peaks, such as the death of Deso Dogg in 2018. While this analysis does not cover the period from 2020 to the present day, it is possible that the term's frequency may have experienced fluctuations during certain intervals. For instance, in 2020, there might have been an increase in usage following the arrest of Abdel Bary by Spanish police forces. Likewise, it is conceivable that in the near future, the usage of the term may rise due to the recent and unexpected passing of Abdel Bary while in a Spanish prison.

Having explained the trend of the expression "jihadi rap", it is essential to address the limitations inherent in its usage, as well as to suggest a potentially more fitting alternative for a comprehensive examination of this phenomenon in the medium to long term. The primary challenge arises from the varying interpretations of the concept of "jihad". It is well-known that the negative connotation linked to the term represents a reinterpretation that deviates from its traditional non-violent essence. In fact, as previously discussed, during the Arab uprisings, a form of jihadi rap emerged that was not inherently tied to violence or radical Islamist ideologies. Nonetheless, the phrase "jihadi rap" can lead to ambiguity due to its potential positive or negative connotations.

Another apparent limitation is related to the narrowness of the term's scope. Just like Larsen and Jensen (2019), most authors have employed "jihadi rap" to denote musical expressions connected to the Salafist-jihadist ideology, emanating from terrorist organizations such as Al Qaeda or ISIS. In contemporary times, this definition falls somewhat short due to the informalization of violent Islamist extremism, which allows for a blending of various violent influences. Today, a young individual may adopt such an incoherent radical discourse, lending simultaneously support to the Taliban, Al Qaeda or even ISIS, despite their irreconcilable differences. This phenomenon had already occurred with "Dirty Kuffar". Interestingly, in that song, blessings were bestowed upon the efforts of Al Qaeda, Hamas and Hezbollah (Gartenstein-Ross, 2004; Golestan, 2004). In the case of Hamas, while Sunni, it does not embrace Salafist-jihadism. On the other hand, Hezbollah adheres to the Shiite branch, a significant departure from Al Qaeda's Salafist-jihadism and Sunni orientation. According to the principles of Salafist-jihadism, these "other" Shiite groups would also be considered as infidels. This inconsistency, both plausible and widespread among today's potential young jihadists, necessarily prompts the introduction of a new term. This term should encompass all forms of violent Islamist extremism expressed through rap music. Furthermore, the broader connotation of this term implies the recognition of a contemporary dimension where radical Islamist/jihadist arguments are no longer explicitly articulated in violent rap songs, but are conveyed in such a way that can be inferred.

Coining a new term that is widely accepted and accurately encapsulates the elements of the reality being defined is a complex undertaking. Nonetheless, there have been previous efforts to address the broader reality examined in this paper: rap music with radical Islamist/jihadi content, whether implicit or explicit. In addition to the widely used "jihadi rap", some authors have explored the term "terror rap" (Forest, 2006; Lombard, 2007; Nacos, 2008, 2016), which, at the very least, carried suggestive connotations. At first glance, terror rap seemed linked to the looming threat of "terror" following the 9/11 attacks. However, once again, besides its ambiguity, it proves to be rather narrow, as it would exclusively encompass Al Qaeda's involvement in the "Global War on Terror" (Wilson & Al Kamen, 2009). In a similar vein, El Difraoui and Hahn (2018) employed the term "Al-Qaeda Rap" to describe the music exemplified by "Dirty Infidels", as they called the song "Dirty Kuffar". In contrast, considering the shortcomings of all these terms mentioned earlier, I propose the concept of "Inferential Radical Islamist Rap"[5] as a more effective alternative.

4. Exploring the Connection between Violent Rap Rhetoric and Violent Islamist Radicalization

Not long ago, Mullah Ahmed Akhund, the Deputy Chief of the Taliban, was revealed to be engaged in an intimate relationship with a young bodyguard (Iyer, 2023). This is not an unusual event. In some anti-jihadist operations, law enforcement agencies have uncovered explicit homosexual content on the terrorists' electronic devices. This raises a paradox, as it is widely recognized that Sharia law imposes severe punishments for homosexuality. Furthermore, in contemporary times, we often encounter individuals who identify themselves as jihadists while concurrently embrace divergent radical and violent ideologies. This phenomenon can be exemplified in cases where terrorists display inclinations toward both neo-Nazism, White supremacism and violent Islamist extremism (Koch, Nahon, & Moghadam, 2023; Meleagrou-Hitchens & Ayad, 2023). Furthermore, some jihadists simultaneously gravitate toward distinct and irreconcilable positions within violent Islamist extremism, driven by factors such as their branch of Islam, their objectives, or their origins. These apparent inconsistencies raise one simple question: Has *jâhiliya*[6] extended to the point of encompassing even the most traditionally inclined violent Islamists? How can we place these ideological and behavioral "deviations" into context?

As a preliminary condition, we can find answers to these questions in the process of "informalization" of violent Islamist extremism. This transformation is rooted in the digitalization of jihadi propaganda and communication, dating back to the emergence of the first website, in 1996, called "Azzam.com" (El Difraoui & Hahn, 2018). After the onset of the Iraq War in 2003, the unpopular American invasion led to an exponential surge in jihadi sympathizers. Recognizing this opportunity, Al Qaeda not only re-emerged post-9/11 but also diversified through factions and alliances with other like-minded groups worldwide. Furthermore, both independent cells and individuals also proliferated, sharing a similar orientation (El Difraoui & Hahn, 2018; Reinares, 2015). These developments significantly impacted jihadi communication, particularly with the advent of interactive online forums. These novel virtual spaces facilitated the dissemination of radical ideas on a broader and more diverse scale, leading to a transformation in the nature of the jihadist internet. It shifted from a rigid hierarchical structure to evolving into a network of connections that were less formalized and more flexible. In fact, jihadi symbols and content began to be tailored to Western youth's pop culture in an effort to attract them, a concept that Sageman (2008) referred to as "Jihadi Cool". This was illustrated in the release of the rap song "Dirty Kuffar" in 2004 (El Difraoui & Hahn, 2018).

With the emergence of Web 2.0 in 2006, the informalization of violent Islamist extremism underwent rapid evolution up to the present day. Specific social networks, such as Twitter and Facebook, along with the digital platform YouTube, facilitated the dissemination of discourses that had not only become more extensive and diverse but also carried a stronger personal and emotional impact (El Difraoui & Hahn, 2018). In the Western context, this gave rise to the emergence of a global narrative that legitimized violent jihad as an identity and lifestyle. This idea was coined as "Western jihadi subculture", where active jihadi militants or sympathizers do not forsake their inherent Western customs and practices; instead, they adapt and incorporate them as a countercultural response (Cottee, 2019; Janmohamed, 2016). Unlike online forums, where discussion threads were partially moderated, the substantial influx of violent Islamist ideas disseminated through social media made them uncontrollable and often characterized by contradictions. Within these distinctive virtual environments, the jihadist terrorist profile has become highly heterogeneous, resulting in what Hegghammer (2009) termed as "ideological hybridizations".

While Hegghammer's concept specifically pertains to the nature of official jihadi groups, its framework proves highly effective in comprehending the current profile of numerous independent and informal groups, particularly individual young actors. This researcher described hybrid ideologies as "the mixing of ideal rationales for violence and the attendant blending of their associated enemy hierarchies" (Hegghammer, 2009, "Hybridization", para. 1). Another concept that aligns with the diversity amongst terrorists is what Gartenstein-Ross and Blackman (2022) called "fringe fluidity". Recently, Meleagrou-Hitchens and Ayad (2023) have chosen to describe this phenomenon as "mixed and unclear extremist ideologies". Be that as it may, Hegghammer's concept of hybrid ideology remains particularly valuable in highlighting the growing trend among young jihadists to select various violent rationales based on their individual-environment relationship. This results in the emergence of incoherent discourses that deviate further from the ideological mainstream.

In this context characterized by heterogeneity and fuzziness, it is not unreasonable to consider the potential dialogue between violent rap and its urban environment, and its relationship with jihadism. There could be even an alleged connection between these elements and narco-culture (Perlmutter, 2018). Since the release of "Dirty Kuffar", there has been ongoing speculation about jihadi rappers, such as Deso Dogg, Omar Hammami, or Abdel Bary simply because of their hip-hop background prior to their involvement in militancy. While it is true that Omar Hammami, during his membership with Al-Shabaab, produced a series of rap songs of varying quality, it seems more than coincidental that several young individuals involved in major attacks in Europe have had connections to the violent rap scene in their daily lives, either as fans or as frustrated aspirants. Some notable examples include Chérif Kouachi, who took part in the January 2015 attack on the magazine "*Charlie Hebdo* in Paris"; Hasna Aitboulahcen, who was linked to the November 2015 Paris attacks; and Moussa Oukabir, a member of the "Ripoll cell" responsible for the August 2017 attacks in Barcelona and Cambrils. Another noteworthy individual worth mentioning is the infamous Mohammed Emwazi, known as "Jihadi John", who is believed to be the executioner of American journalist James Foley; it is interesting to note that he had aspirations of becoming a rapper before his involvement in terrorism. The final example I would like to highlight concerns an alleged British jihadist named Sahayb Abu. He adopted the artistic pseudonym "Menace Masked" and aimed to establish himself as a prominent artist in the realm of violent rap music, particularly drill, using the TikTok platform (Gardham, 2021; Grierson, 2021). It is worth noting that he represents one of the early individuals to exploit such a widely popular and easily viral social media platform. In fact, contemporary songs often gather audiences primarily through this means.

Considering the young individuals mentioned earlier, a series of questions arises: How do they conceptualize violence in the first place? Could their exposure to violent rap and street culture rhetoric have influenced their attitudes and emotions toward violence? To address these inquiries, we have contemplated the introduction of violent rap (including the Inferential Radical Islamist Rap) as a potential countercultural narrative within the framework of the 3N model of radicalization, which was initially proposed by Arie Kruglanski and his colleagues (Bélanger et al., 2019; Kruglanski, Bélanger, & Gunaratna, 2019; Moyano, 2019b). This model has yielded significant empirical evidence over the last decade, proposing that the radicalization process is mainly driven by three psychosocial factors: needs, narratives and networks. Needs are lined with the theoretical concept of personal significance, while narratives encompass the ideology and culture in which individuals and groups are immersed. Finally, the social network aspect pertains to the social influence exerted by the individual's environment and group dynamics; in this sense, the network plays a crucial role in validating the narrative that incites violence through consensus among individuals who share a similar perception of reality; this validation can result from an individual's contact with friends, family, charismatic leaders and even online communities. These three psychosocial factors collectively contribute to radicalization in a dynamic and interactive manner.

In contemporary societies, music is widely perceived as a means of emotional communication, capable of inspiring, motivating and even prompting action (Gómez Escarda & Pérez Redondo, 2016). Music is also regarded as a mechanism for construing sociocultural identities. In this context, it is imperative to reflect on musical texts that present narratives embracing violence, particularly when they incorporate elements or ideas that are sensitive to the vulnerabilities of young individuals, as seen in violent rap. Additionally, it is crucial to take into account how recent jihadists seem to be acquainted with violence before entering into political-religious radicalization (Basra, Neumann, & Brunner, 2016; Crone, 2016, as cited in Ilan & Sandberg, 2019). If we adopt Pieslak's argument (2015) that emotion and reason are so intertwined that emotionally driven ideas can be readily rationalized, this raises the possibility that violent rap may contribute to the normalization of violence (as an emotion) through its seemingly "harmless" narrative.

As of today, this genre of music offers a narrative infused with elements from the culture of violence prevalent in street life and gangs. Simultaneously, it weaves in anti-systemic political ideas targeting governments and the established order, while sometimes making religious references. Essentially, a romanticized blend of materialistic, political-religious and countercultural elements is presented within a framework where violence is portrayed as something "cool". It is important to stress that the materialistic element, closely associated with hypermasculinity among rappers, finds wide acceptance within youth culture. In fact, in some ethnographic studies conducted on young militants to assess the "cool" aspect of jihad, Christine Fair observed that most of them had been drawn to the movement primarily to gain access to motorcycles, weapons and women. Religious motivation was found to be of secondary importance (Picart, 2015). Regarding the political and religious elements, as evidenced in certain song excerpts from artists like Medine (2015) or Saamou Skuu and Zeu (2021), they reflect the polarized or binary reality that is a characteristic of the violent Islamist extremism narrative: "us vs. them", "us vs. government", "believers vs. disbelievers". This narrative may have a significant impact on all young individuals, but it can be especially influential on Western second-generation Muslims who are becoming increasingly politicized and have a limited understanding of Islam. This situation may result in a greater capacity for inferring violent Islamist ideas (Dantschke, 2012).

Now, what motivational needs might Western youth have for embracing a violent rap narrative? Within the quest for significance factor, firstly, the loss of significance through feelings of marginalization and injustice, for instance, as prompted by an identity crisis. Young individuals, particularly second-generation Muslims caught between two cultures, may face challenges in establishing their place in life and finding purpose therein (Moyano, 2019b). Studies even suggest a lack of role models for these young people in the West, which may facilitate their radicalization process (Ohls et al., 2023). In response to such a need, violent rap can function as a channel for identity and sociocultural construction, even providing a sense of belonging. This process could be further reinforced, particularly through interactions with networks of followers of this narrative. Initial interactions often occur within online communities, which can range from open and more restricted, where some rap violent narratives with explicitly Islamist extremist elements may appear (Meleagrou-Hitchens & Ayad, 2023). Simultaneously, both renowned rap artists and amateur neighborhood rappers are emerging as idols and role models for young individuals. Take, for instance, the comments on certain music videos by the recently deceased Abdel Bary, known as "L Jinny" or "Lyricist Jinn". Despite his involvement in terrorism, many young people mourning his death seem to blur the lines between an activist rapper and a jihadist terrorist (Lombard, 2007). This same phenomenon can be observed in Deso Dogg's music videos. It indeed appears that gangsta rappers may be filling the role of religious leaders.

In addition to the loss of significance, the opportunity to gain substantial significance is also a motivating factor, particularly when young individuals have a rapper's lifestyle as a role model. Many of them strive to achieve fame to attain high status and social dominance, thereby attributing greater significance to their own lives compared to the lives of others.

This aspiration was shared by individuals like Chérif Kouachi, Mohamed Emwazi and Moussa Oukabir, all of whom desired to become renowned rappers (Barna, 2018). In the case of Oukabir, he eventually exhibited an antisocial attitude online, reflected in a violent rap narrative. In fact, his last video uploaded to Facebook just before the massacre on August 2nd depicted a scene typical of drill music, with young individuals on motorcycles taunting the police (Lesaca, 2017).

5. Conclusion

Violent Islamist extremism is still undergoing a significant metamorphosis even today. Heterogeneity and informalization are integral elements of many extremist profiles, rooted in the hybridization of violent ideas. As noted by Hegghammer (2009), this transformation has led to a weakening of the global jihadist movement, at least in terms of organizational structure. Nevertheless, the considerable diversity among jihadist profiles has made the identification of radicalization processes and subsequent actions increasingly complex for law enforcement. As a result, the level of uncertainty and threat is on the rise. Furthermore, in Western contexts, complexity is further heightened when we encounter young jihadists who maintain their Western customs and practices even after radicalization. This is less a matter of *taqiyya*[7] and more a consequence of informalization. It should come as no surprise, therefore, the emergence of alleged young jihadists who appear to exist at the crossroads of a dialogue between violent rap and violent Islamist extremism. Moreover, it is important to emphasize that rap can serve as a preventive tool to influence the factors postulated by the 3N model. Thus, there are experiences and intervention programs that have attempted to promote prevention using urban music as a resource (see some experiences in Moyano et al., 2018, 2022). In essence, the research subject presented in this paper, while highly specific, I believe represents an essential complement in enhancing our understanding of current radicalization processes, especially among youth.

Notes

1 Considering the interviewee's situation, he is referring to a radical and violent form of Islam.
2 They categorized "jihadi rap" as a musical genre. However, this does not much sense, as there is no clear tradition, no solid foundations, nor even a continuous progression in the development of the phenomenon. Rather, since the release of the first song with jihadist symbols "Dirty Kuffar" in 2004, the erroneously labeled "jihadi rap" consisted of intermittent, multifaceted manifestations without interconnection in terms of discourse or the channels of dissemination.

3 However, within informal violent Islamist forums, which have more restricted access, there is evidence of the existence of some violent rap music with a purely jihadist discourse, for instance, making references to Bin Laden or al-Awlaki.
4 First peak occurred in 2004, with "Dirty Kuffar".
5 I would like to clarify that the word "inferential" is intentionally meant to denote, when discussing thoughts and ideas, the potential of such rap, whether with or without explicit radical arguments, to stimulate self-construction of them by the individual.
6 This term commonly referred to the pre-Islamic period in the Arabian Peninsula, prior to the appearance of Prophet Muhammad. It was also translated as "the age of ignorance", as paganism was prevalent during that time. The most contemporary usage, adopted by extremist Islamists, relates to the deviation from traditional values and concepts of Islam by societies, whether they are Muslim or not.
7 The concealment of intentions by jihadists to avoid detection. Commonly, it has involved blending in with the Western population in everyday life.

References

Aidi, H. D. (2009). Jihadis in the hood. In M. Marable & H. D. Aidi (Eds.), *Black routes to Islam* (pp. 283–296). New York, NY: Palgrave Macmillan.

Barna, C. (2018). The role of the family in preventing the transformation of western youngsters into jihadi fighters. *International Annals of Criminology*, *56*(1–2), 157–177.

Basra, R., Neumann, P. R., & Brunner, C. (2016). *Criminal past, terrorist futures: European jihadists and the new crime-terror nexus*. Retrieved from The International Centre for the Study of Radicalisation and Political Violence: https://icsr.info/2016/10/11/new-icsr-report-criminal-pasts-terrorist-futures-european-jihadists-new-crime-terror-nexus/

Bélanger, J. J., Moyano, M., Muhammad, H., Richardson, L., Lafrenière, M.-A. K., McCaffery, P., Framand, K., & Nociti, N. (2019). Radicalization leading to violence: A test of the 3N model. *Frontiers in Psychiatry, 10*(42). https://doi.org/10.3389/fpsyt.2019.00042

Cantrall, S. (2013). The influence of rap in the Arab Spring. *Augsburg Honors Review, 6*(12), 21–32.

Conti, U. (2017). Between rap and jihad: Spectacular subcultures, terrorism and visuality. *Contemporary Social Science*, *12*(3–4), 272–284.

Cottee, S. (2019). The western jihadi subculture and subterranean values. *The British Journal of Criminology, 60*(3), 762-781.

Crone, M. (2016). Radicalization revisited: Violence, politics and the skills of the body. *International Affairs*, *92*(3), 587–604.

Dantschke, C. (2012). "Pop-jihad": History and structure of Salafism and Jihadism in Germany. *Institute for the Study of Radical Movements. Working Paper Series, 2*(13). Retrieved from https://hayat-deutschland.de/Datei-Download/23/WP_2-13_Claudia_pop_jihad.pdf

El Difraoui, A., & Hahn, O. (2018). EJihad: Behind the use of social media by ISIS. In O. Hahn & F. Stalph (Eds.), *Digital investigative journalism* (pp. 229–236). Cham, Switzerland: Palgrave Macmillan.

Esposito, J. L. (2011). *What everyone needs to know about Islam* (2nd ed.). New York, NY: Oxford University Press.

Forest, J. J. F. (2006). Training camps and other centers of learning. In J. J. F. Forest (Ed.), *Teaching terror: Strategic and tactical learning in the terrorist world* (pp. 69–109). Lanham, MD: Rowman & Littlefield Publishers.

Gardham, D. (2021, February 24). Sahayb Abu trial: Alleged terror plotter tells court he was studying Alan Titchmarsh gardening videos. *Sky News*, UK. Retrieved from https://news.sky.com/story/sahayb-abu-trial-alleged-terror-plotter-tells-court-he-was-studying-alan-titchmarsh-gardening-videos-12227781

Gartenstein-Ross, D. (2004, November 10). Jihadi rap. *FrontPage Magazine*. Retrieved from https://web.archive.org/web/20090105222239/http://daveedgr.com/publications/internet-journals/jihadi-rap/

Gartenstein-Ross, D., & Blackman, M. (2022). Fluidity of the fringes: Prior extremist involvement as a radicalization pathway. *Studies in Conflict & Terrorism, 45*(7), 555–578.

Golestan, M. (2004). Dirty Kuffar. *Index on Censorship, 33*(3), 8–10.

Gómez Escarda, M., & Pérez Redondo, R. (2016). La violencia contra las mujeres en la música: Una aproximación metodológica. *methaodos. Revista de Ciencias Sociales, 4*(1), 189–196.

Google Inc. (s.f). *Google Ngram Viewer*. Retrieved from https://books.google.com/ngrams/graph?content=jihadi+rap&year_start=1800&year_end=2019&corpus=en-2019&smoothing=0&case_insensitive=true

Grierson, J. (2021, March 12). London ISIS supporter found guilty of plotting terror attack. *The Guardian*, UK news. Retrieved from https://www.theguardian.com/uk-news/2021/mar/12/london-isis-supporter-sahayb-abu-guilty-plotting-terror-attack

Hegghammer, T. (2009). The ideological hybridization of jihadi groups. *Current Trends in Islamist Ideology*. Retrieved from https://www.hudson.org/national-security-defense/the-ideological-hybridization-of-jihadi-groups

Ilan, J., & Sandberg, S. (2019). How "gangsters" become jihadists: Bourdieu, criminology and the crime-terrorism nexus. *European Journal of Criminology, 16*(3), 278–294.

Iyer, S. (2023, August 22). Caught on tape: Alleged video of Taliban official having homosexual relationship with bodyguard sparks outrage. *Asianet Newsable*, World News. Retrieved from https://newsable.asianetnews.com/world/caught-on-tape-alleged-video-of-taliban-official-having-homosexual-relationship-with-bodyguard-sparks-outrage-snt-rzsdf9

Janmohamed, S. (2016). *Generation M: Young Muslims changing the world*. London, England: I.B. Tauris.

Jensen, S. Q., Larsen, J. F., & Sandberg, S. (2021). Rap, Islam and jihadi cool: The attractions of the western jihadi subculture. *Crime, Media, Culture, 18*(3), 430–445.

Khan, A. (2014, August 31). Al Qaeda's new front: Jihadi rap. *Politico Magazine*. Retrieved from https://www.politico.com/magazine/story/2014/08/al-qaedas-new-front-jihadi-rap-110481/

Koch, A., Nahon, K., & Moghadam, A. (2023). White jihad: How white supremacists adopt jihadi narratives, aesthetics, and tactics. *Terrorism and Political Violence*. https://doi.org/10.1080/09546553.2023.2223694

Kruglanski, A. W., Bélanger, J. J., & Gunaratna, R. (2019). *The three pillars of radicalization: Needs, narratives, and networks*. Oxford: Oxford University Press.

Larsen, J. F., & Jensen, S. Q. (2019). Jihadism from a subcultural perspective. *Critical Criminology*, *27*(3), 421–436.

Lesaca, J. (2017, Agosto 29). La pista digital de los yihadistas de Ripoll. *El Mundo*, Crónica. Retrieved from https://www.elmundo.es/cronica/2017/08/29/59a31d4bca4741eb7a8b4577.html

Lewis, M. (2015, January 17). The strange rap-jihadi connection: Straight outta Waziristan? *Daily Beast*, World. Retrieved from https://www.thedailybeast.com/the-strange-rap-jihadi-connection

Lombard, K. (2007). Gen E (Generation Extremist): The significance of youth culture and new media in youth extremism. In P. Mendis, J. Lai, E. Dawson, & H. Abbass (Eds.), *Recent advances in security technology: Proceedings of the 2007 RNSA security technology conference* (pp. 168–178). Melbourne, Australia: Australian Homeland Security Research Centre.

Mastors, E., & Siers, R. (2014). Omar al-Hammami: A case study in radicalization. *Behavioral Sciences and the Law*, *32*(3), 377–388.

Medine. (2015) Don't Laïk [Recorded by Medine]. On *Démineur* [visual album]. France: Din Records (January 1).

Meleagrou-Hitchens, A., & Ayad, M. (2023). *The age of incoherence? Understanding mixed and unclear ideology extremism* (Reports, Projects and Research 41). Retrieved from Program on Extremism, George Washington University & National Counterterrorism Innovation, Technology, and Education Center: https://digitalcommons.unomaha.edu/ncitereportsresearch/41/

Moyano, M. (2019a). *Radicalización terrorista. Gestión del riesgo y modelos de intervención*. Síntesis.

Moyano, M. (2019b). *Alienation, identity and intercultural working*. Retrieved from European Commission: Radicalisation Awareness Network: https://home-affairs.ec.europa.eu/pages/page/ran-hsc-alienation-identity-and-intercultural-working-helsinki-23-24-october-2019_en

Moyano, M., Gracia, J., Franco, A., Luna, M., Lobato, R.M., García-Coll, J., & Martín-Criado, J. M. (2022). *Programa de Mentoría Social Fénix Andalucía* [Fenix Andalusia Social Mentoring Program]. Junta de Andalucía.

Moyano, M., García, A.I., Pérez, M., Gracia, J., Mediavilla, I., & Córdoba, F. (2018). El rap como recurso para promover la convivencia y prevenir la violencia escolar: una propuesta psicosocial y educativa. En O., Nail Kroyer y C., Monereo Font (Eds), Gestión y liderazgo en el ámbito de la convivencia escolar (pp. 175–187). Santiago de Chile: RIL editores.

Nacos, B. L. (2008). The central role of media and communication in terrorism and counterterrorism. In M. J. Rozell & J. D. Mayer (Eds.), *Media power, media politics* (2nd ed., pp. 293–318). Lanham, MD: Rowman & Littlefield Publishers.

Nacos, B. L. (2016). *Mass-mediated terrorism mainstream and digital media in terrorism and counterterrorism* (3rd ed.). Lanham, MD: Rowman & Littlefield Publishers.

Nilsson, M., & Esholdt, H. F. (2022). After the caliphate: Changing mobilization in the Swedish Salafi-jihadist environment following the fall of ISIS. *Studies in Conflict & Terrorism*. https://doi.org/10.1080/1057610X.2022.2104682

Ohls, I., Hosseini, D. S., Spasojevic, A., Brandes, F., Bajwa, R., Ahmed, K., Gallinat, J., Karow, A., & Allroggen, M. (2023). A systematic review of the risk and protective factor for processes associated with Islamist radicalization and extremism. *Terrorism and Political Violence*. https://doi.org/10.1080/09546553.2023.2243349

Perez, C. (2014, August 25). Father of suspect in Foley beheading was Osama lieutenant. *New York Post*, News. Retrieved from https://nypost.com/2014/08/25/father-of-suspected-john-the-beatle-was-an-osama-lieutenant/#

Perlmutter, D. (2018, December 27). Cartel jihad rap. *FrontPage Magazine*. Retrieved from https://www.frontpagemag.com/cartel-jihad-rap-dawn-perlmutter/

Picart, C. J. S. (2015). "Jihad Cool/Jihad Chic": The roles of the internet and imagined relations in the self-radicalization of Collen Larose (Jihad Jane). *Societies, 5*(2), 354–383.

Pieslak, J. (2015). *Radicalism and music: An introduction to the music cultures of al-qa'ida, racist skinheads, Christian-affiliated radicals, and eco-animal rights militants*. Middletown, CT: Wesleyan University Press.

Rawnsley, A. (2011, April 11). American terrorist proves he still can't rap. *Wired*. Retrieved from https://www.wired.com/2011/04/american-terrorist-proves-he-still-cant-rap/

Reinares, F. (2015, Julio 1). Yihadismo global y amenaza terrorista: De al-Qaeda al Estado Islámico [Blog post]. Retrieved from https://www.realinstitutoelcano.org/analisis/yihadismo-global-y-amenaza-terrorista-de-al-qaeda-al-estado-islamico/

Remz. (2023). Grateful [Recorded by Remz]. On *Grateful* [music video]. England: Remz (September 7).

Saamou Skuu & Zeu. (2021). French Drill 5 [Recorded by Saamou Skuu]. On *French drill 5* [music video]. Paris: Th Records (November 19).

Sageman, M. (2008). *Leaderless Jihad: Terror networks in the twenty-first century*. Philadelphia, PA: University of Pennsylvania Press.

Smirke, R. (2014, October 10). Jihadi rap: Understanding the subculture. *Billboard*. Retrieved from https://www.billboard.com/music/music-news/jihadi-rap-l-jinny-abdel-majed-abdel-bary-6273809/

Spenser, R. (2018). *The history of jihad: From Muhammad to ISIS*. New York, NY: Post Hill Press.

Swedenburg, T. (2009). Fun^Da^Mental Islamophobic fears: Britain's "suicide bomb rappers". *Vis-à-Vis: Explorations in Anthropology, 9*(1), 123–132.

Swedenburg, T. (2010). Fun^Da^Mental's "jihad rap". In L. Herrera & A. Bayat (Eds.), *Being young and Muslim: New cultural politics in the global south and north* (pp. 291–308). https://doi.org/10.1093/acprof:oso/9780195369212.003.0018

Verkaik, R. (2016). *Jihadi John: The making of a terrorist*. London, England: Oneworld Publications.
Wilson, S., & Al Kamen (2009, March 25). "Global war on terror" is given new name. *Washington Post*, Politics. Retrieved from https://www.washingtonpost.com/wp-dyn/content/article/2009/03/24/AR2009032402818.html
Wright, R. (2011). *Rock the casbah: Rage and rebellion across the Islamic World*. New York, NY: Simon & Schuster Paperbacks.

13 Hate Speech under International Law and the Challenging Task of Striking a Balance between a Legitimate and a Forbidden Opinion[1]

Andrea Cocchini

1. Introduction

There is nothing new about the devastating effects of hatred and so-called "hate speech" is not a modern phenomenon. In Nazi Germany, regime media campaigns encouraged the atmosphere of hatred that later on caused the Holocaust. Since the end of the Second World War, many States have enacted domestic laws designed to curb the encouragement of hatred against minority groups. Known as "hate speech laws", these regulations began as rules to protect against anti-Semitism. Not so long ago, however, the international community witnessed the Rwandan genocide, the Srebrenica massacre and the Rohingya Muslim minority genocide, all preceded by vast campaigns of hatred.[2] So much so that the Secretary-General of the United Nations (UN), Antonio Guterres, declared that hate speech is a common "precursor to atrocity crimes, including genocide".[3] Nevertheless, the scale and impact of hate speech today appear to be magnified by new communication technologies, making hateful manifestations one of the most common ways to spread on a global scale divisive rhetoric and ideologies.

As the then UN Special Rapporteur on the promotion and protection of the right to freedom of opinion and expression, David Kaye, noted in his 2019 Report, the notion of hate speech presents two main difficulties. First, the widespread idea that hate speech "it's just speech" prevents States and online corporations from seriously tackling hateful expressions and the brutalities against helpless minorities deriving from them. Second, the absence of an internationally accepted interpretation of its precise meaning; something which may cause certain ambiguity on its concrete contours which States can exploit to restrict legitimate expressions.[4] The freedoms of opinion and expression are core elements of every democratic society, as they reinforce other basic human rights, such as the freedom of thought, conscience and religion or the freedom of peaceful assembly and association. It is then clear that government initiatives to legislate on these freedoms may cause some disquiet.[5] States must always try to reconcile the permanent tension

DOI: 10.4324/9781003457381-14

between ensuring freedoms of opinion and expression to anyone, on one side, while safeguarding individuals and minority groups and their rights to reputation or non-discrimination from hateful speech, on the other one. To reduce this friction that permeates any legal discussion on the prohibition of hate speech, it is important to shed some light on the terms in question. Mindful of the absence of an international legal definition of hate speech (Section 2), this contribution recalls the relevant international legal material dealing with hate speech, consisting of "hard law", compulsory instruments (Section 2.1) and "soft law", recommendatory tools (Section 2.2). The conclusion it reaches is that the contemporary international legal framework on this topic seems to be sufficiently mature to be incorporated by States in their domestic legislations to palliate the tension between free speech and prohibited hate speech, if only they really would like to (Section 3).

2. The International Legal Framework on Hate Speech

With the remarkable exception of the United States,[6] several States[7] have adopted domestic legal norms to fight against hate speech as a violation of the right to dignity of every human being,[8] so that a prosecutor, a judge, or a jury can determine which manifestations of hatred constitute an offence. Nevertheless, many forms of speech in very different contexts have been subsumed under the expression of hate speech. The broad terminology related to offences of incitement to national, racial or religious hatred diverges from one State to another allowing them (potentially) to incorporate in national legislation new categories of restrictions to freedom of expression. The wider the meaning of incitement to hatred is in national legislation, the more it will tolerate the discretionary enforcement of domestic laws, causing possible misconception of the relevant international legal framework.[9]

The notion of "hate speech" is commonly used to indicate odious speeches that may threaten social peace, as they target groups or individuals because of their inherent features, such as race, religion or gender. However, international law does not provide a legal definition of hate speech, as the concept is still disputed, particularly in relation to the freedoms of opinion and expression, non-discrimination and equality. To deliver a common legal frame for the United Nations system to tackle hate speech at an international level, the *UN Strategy and Plan of Action on Hate Speech* – the first UN system-wide initiative intended to challenge hate speech – describes it as:

> [A]ny kind of communication in speech, writing or behaviour, that attacks or uses pejorative or discriminatory language with reference to a person or a group on the basis of who they are, in other words, based on their religion, ethnicity, nationality, race, colour, descent, gender or other identity factor.[10]

Yet, this broad definition begs the question of what concrete conduct it covers and the standards a speech must comply with in order to be considered as hateful by States. Determining a systematic catalogue of all the forms a hate speech may take is not possible in these few pages. However, the UN Strategy's definition builds upon different international human rights instruments that offer a suitable basis for a more precise identification of hate speech, allowing States, private companies and individuals to recognise those behaviours they should consider as hateful. The following Section 2.1 will examine those instruments of "hard law" nature, i.e., those agreements that impose legal obligations on States. Subsequently, Section 2.2 will focus on one of the many "soft law" instruments, i.e., those reports, declarations, or principles that are not legally binding on States but that are useful to guide public authorities as well as private actors in understanding what is an illegal or a legal (even if detestable) speech.

2.1 *International Hard Law Tools Related to Hate Speech*

The first of such international instruments is the 1948 *Convention on the Prevention and Punishment of the Crime of Genocide*, ratified or acceded to by 152 out of 193 UN Member States. The Convention against Genocide is relevant for the problem of hate speech since it is the first UN General Assembly's treaty on human rights where States' Parties agreed to take measures to prevent and punish the crime of genocide as well as direct and public *incitement* to commit it.[11] Since genocides do not come out of the blue but involve meticulous planning, there are normally warning signals and widespread risk factors that can precede a genocide, one of them being hate speech.[12] In this regard, article 25 of the 1998 *Rome Statute of the International Criminal Court* (ICC) – the judicial body responsible for also judging the crime of genocide[13] – establishes that anyone who commits a crime within the jurisdiction of the ICC shall be individually responsible and liable for punishment. Referring specifically to the crime of genocide article 25, paragraph (e), adds that there will be a personal liability to anyone who directly and publicly *incites* others to commit genocide, stressing the importance of preventing genocide by prohibiting all those manifestations of hatred that could lead to this crime.[14]

During the same year, the UN General Assembly also proclaimed the seminal 1948 *Universal Declaration of Human Rights* (UDHR) whose article 2 declares the following:

> Everyone is entitled to all the rights and freedoms set forth in this Declaration, without distinction of any kind, such as race, colour, sex, language, religion, political or other opinion, national or social origin, property, birth or other status. Furthermore, no distinction shall be

> made on the basis of the political, jurisdictional or international status of the country or territory to which a person belongs, whether it be independent, trust, non-self-governing or under any other limitation of sovereignty.[15]

In view of the fact that hateful speech may comprise behaviours that do discriminate for reasons related to "race, colour, sex, language, religion, political or other opinion, national or social origin, property, birth or other status" it can also breach the fundamental principle enshrined in article 2 of the UDHR.[16]

However, it was in 1965 that States agreed on the first international treaty addressing specific types of expression, generally considered as hate speech, by signing the *International Convention on the Elimination of all Forms of Racial Discrimination* (ICERD). Its article 4 declares that:

> States Parties condemn all propaganda and all organizations which are based on ideas or theories of superiority of one race or group of persons of one colour or ethnic origin, or which attempt to justify or promote racial hatred and discrimination in any form [...].[17]

For that purpose, States must take immediate and active steps to eliminate and interdict all incitements and acts of such discrimination, with due regard to the principles of the UDHR and the rights set forth in article 5 of the ICERD. These measures include: (1) declaring "all dissemination of ideas based on racial superiority or hatred, incitement to racial discrimination, as well as all acts of violence or incitement to such acts against any race or group of persons of another colour or ethnic origin, and also the provision of any assistance to racist activities, including the financing thereof" as offences punishable by law; (2) prohibiting organisations and propaganda activities that promote and incite racial discrimination, and establishing that the participation in such organisations or activities are offences punishable by law; and (3) preventing public authorities or public institutions, national or local, to promote or incite racial discrimination.[18]

The rationale of article 4 of the ICERD is to avoid any behaviour that could breach individual basic human rights, such as the right to life or non-discrimination, particularly of vulnerable individuals or groups.[19] Although the Convention only deals with race-motivated discrimination, its provisions match with other manifestations of discrimination not necessarily based on race. In particular, it seems that article 4 recognises four distinct forms of hateful expression, which are: (1) the dissemination of ideas based on racial superiority; (2) the dissemination of ideas based on racial hatred; (3) the incitement to racial discrimination; and (4) the incitement to acts of racially motivated violence.[20] As Doctor Joshua Vivian explains, those four types of hate speech can be summarised into two broader categories, one related to the dissemination of ideas and the other one to the incitement to action. The "dissemination" of hate speech can be either the promotion of hatred or the spreading of the idea of the targeted group's inferiority, while "incitement" refers not just to statements but to the active encouragement to commit acts of discrimination against the members of a specific group.[21]

In the same vein, the 1966 *International Covenant on Civil and Political Rights* (ICCPR), ratified by 173 States Parties, is especially important for the purpose of this contribution, because it provides States' Parties and private actors with a global legal framework and a universal language to combat hate speech, particularly useful in today's borderless environment of the Internet.[22] There are, in particular, two articles that are important for this analysis. Article 19, in its paragraphs 1 and 2, declares that:

1 Everyone shall have the right to hold opinions without interference.
2 Everyone shall have the right to freedom of expression; this right shall include freedom to seek, receive and impart information and ideas of all kinds, regardless of frontiers, either orally, in writing or in print, in the form of art, or through any other media of his choice.

The freedom of expression outlined in this norm comprises far-reaching rights as the verbs "seek, receive, impart" show as well as the broadest possible scope as the sentence "ideas of all kinds, regardless of frontiers, through any other media" demonstrates.[23] In other terms, article 19 recognises a right "to think, speak freely and spread thoughts, ideas and opinions, whether good or bad, in writing or by any other means of expression".[24] Though, article 19, paragraph 3, limits this wide-ranging right as it acknowledges that:

3 The exercise of the rights provided for in paragraph 2 of this article carries with it special duties and responsibilities. It may therefore be subject to certain restrictions, but these shall only be such as are provided by law and are necessary:

   a For respect of the rights or reputations of others;
   b For the protection of national security or of public order (*ordre public*), or of public health or morals.

Consequently, there is no absolute freedom of expression, although any restrictions to free speech need to fulfil three conditions under article 19, paragraph 3. First, the condition of legality, which implies that limitations to free speech need to be established by law. This national law must be precise, public and transparent; it should preclude public authorities from exercising their legislative, executive or judicial powers without any limits, and it has to provide those whose speech has been limited with an appropriate notification. Domestic provisions should be under constant public scrutiny and regular legislative or administrative procedures. Procedural safeguards must be in place for the protection of rights, particularly those safeguards granted by independent tribunals. Second, limits to the freedom of expression must comply with the condition of legitimacy. This means that any restriction ought to be established with the sole purpose of protecting at least one of the legitimate interests detailed in article 19.3 (to respect the rights or reputations of others or to protect national security, public order, public health or morals). Third, restrictions to this freedom should observe the principles of necessity and proportionality. Governments imposing any limitations on free speech must prove that they are necessary to safeguard a legitimate interest and that they are the least intrusive measure available in order to reach the desired goal.[25] It follows that limits to the freedom of expression must be narrowly defined to avoid untargeted restrictions of free speech. Likewise, they must be proportionate so that the advantage to the protected interests can compensate for the disadvantages of free speech.[26]

The second relevant provision is article 20, paragraphs 1 and 2, of the ICCPR which establishes the following:

1 Any propaganda for war shall be prohibited by law.
2 Any advocacy of national, racial or religious hatred that constitutes incitement to discrimination, hostility or violence shall be prohibited by law.

States' obligation to prohibit war propaganda and incitement to hatred is a twofold duty, since countries ought, first of all, to abstain from breaching the freedoms of opinion and expression through their public authorities. As a primary principle, States must not use media companies, including online social media platforms, as instruments to curb the freedom of expression that they themselves would be prohibited from restraining under the international rules just recalled. Thus, governmental measures like Internet shutdowns or the outlawing of online political dissent or government criticism are undoubtedly contrary to article 19.3 of the ICCPR.[27] Secondly, States have also to employ their best efforts to warrant the fulfilment of international human rights law by third countries, individuals and tech companies.[28] In this sense, the ICCPR can be a formidable device for social media companies too in at least three cases, according to Doctor Talita Dias. First, when State public authorities themselves perpetrate hateful speech actions, such as in Myanmar,[29] Brazil,[30] and the United States.[31] Second, when States attack online users' freedom of expression by silencing political opponents claiming a need to fight online hate speech, as has happened recently in Russia, Iran or Tunisia.[32] Third, there are States with inadequate rules on hate speech, causing social media corporations and their users to not know exactly what are their rights and duties under human rights content moderation policies.[33]

Unlike the circumstances that may trigger the restrictions of article 19.3, article 20 specifies how States must react, i.e., prohibiting through national laws all the behaviours that it mentions.[34] Still, as the previous Special Rapporteur David Kaye underlined, under article 20, States are obliged to prohibit by law those conducts *but* they are not compelled to *criminalise* them,[35] because criminal sanctions against illegal expressions must be considered as last resort means to be enforced only in strictly justifiable situations.[36] Civil or administrative sanctions and remedies, such as pecuniary/non-pecuniary damages or those put in force by different professional and regulatory bodies, as well as the right of correction and the right of reply, should be preferred.[37] In the same vein, the Committee on the Elimination of Racial Discrimination – the expert monitoring body for the ICERD – highlights that criminalisation under its article 4 must be applied according to the principles of legality, proportionality and necessity only for very serious cases, to be proven beyond reasonable doubt, while minor situations should be tackled through mechanisms other than criminal law.[38]

From all the above it is possible to conclude that both the ICERD and the ICCPR handle three common requirements according to which it is possible to identify a hate speech: (1) offenders express themselves publicly; (2) offenders' targets belong to a minority group; and (3) offenders act with malice. Both treaties give special importance to the *intention* with whom individuals operate, even if their focus on hate speech is different. While the ICCPR concentrates on the intention to incite any act of "discrimination, hostility or violence" based on "national, racial or religious hatred" (article 20.2), the ICERD focuses on a broader variety of hateful speeches consisting of the dissemination, promotion, justification, incitement or assistance based on "racial superiority or hatred".[39]

Though, both agreements remain rather unclear for they involve concepts related to emotions, such as "hatred" or "hostility", and the provision on the advocacy of incitement that depends greatly on factual circumstances.[40] Attempts to clarify their meaning exist. For instance, according to Professor Victoria Guillén-Nieto, it is possible to enucleate from article 20 three complementary features that characterise any hate speech. First, "advocacy" which means that there must be a precise intention to publicly encourage hatred towards the targeted right-holders, so there must be some public forms of expression that are aimed at provoking an action or a reaction. Second, "hatred and hostility", i.e., the presence of an intense and irrational feelings of opprobrium, enmity and detestation towards a group of individuals legally identified. Third, "incitement" implies public forms of expression on national, racial or religious features, which may incite discriminatory, hostile or violent acts against a group of people identified by attributes protected by law.[41] In this respect, it must be recalled that article 2.1 of the ICCPR recognises rights to *all* individuals "without distinction of any kind" and article 26 requires domestic laws to "prohibit any discrimination and guarantee to all persons equal and effective protection against discrimination on any ground". The extent of this protection has expanded over time, such that other groups (for example, age or albinism) must be provided with protection and the prohibition of "incitement" covers more categories than before. Today, international rules aim at protecting against discriminatory acts, not only on the grounds of "national, racial or religious hatred", but also on the basis of sex, language, political or other opinion, social origin, property, birth or other status, including indigenous origin or identity, disability, migrant or refugee status, sexual orientation, gender identity or intersex status.[42] Yet, given that free speech is essential to the exercise of other human rights, limitations on it must be permitted only under the exceptional circumstances of ICERD's article 4 and of ICCPR's articles 19 and 20 and under close supervision.[43] If a speech, however spiteful it may be, does not reach the threshold of "incitement to discrimination, hostility or violence", it should not be criminalised as hate speech, and other measures should be applied so as to avoid unjustified restriction to the freedom of expression, including of odious ideas.[44]

2.2 *International Instruments of Soft Law Related to Hate Speech*

Restricting hateful speech requires reconciling two conflicting values: the need for a democratic society to admit open debate, on the one hand, and the equally imperative duty to avoid targeting weak groups and to guarantee equal involvement of everyone in public life without any discrimination, on the other hand.[45] Due to this necessity, international human rights law seems to be in a deadlock, as national legislative authorities are asked to forbid an unspecified type of hate speech, whereas individuals, such as social media users, want to be free to express even their heinous ideas.[46] The absence of a common definition of hate speech exacerbates the challenge of determining when a particular communication can be deemed as "incitement to discrimination, hostility or violence" (article 20.2 of the ICCPR) and so sanctionable or punishable. In order to find where the line between hate speech and free speech exactly lies, additional assistance is thus required.[47] This further help comes from different international soft law instruments that, as such, are discretionary standards of conduct but that potentially bestow wider protection against discrimination than those of international compulsory treaties.[48] Due to space limitations, this contribution considers just one of these soft law tools that seems to be the most significant for the problem at stake: the UN *Rabat Plan of Action on the prohibition of advocacy of national, racial or religious hatred that constitutes incitement to discrimination, hostility or violence*, adopted in October 2012. It is the product of a sequence of national specialists' consultations organised by the Office of the High Commissioner for Human Rights (OHCHR), where the experts analyse the collective accountability of States' officials, religious and community leaders, the media, civil society and all individuals, on the necessity of fostering social cohesion, tolerance and dialogue to avert incitement to hatred.[49] As will be discussed below, the *Rabat Plan of Action* supplements international human rights rules by establishing a set of six standards thanks to which States can evaluate, on a case-by-case basis, specific manifestations of free speech. In this way, States must be able to distinguish between demonstrations of the freedom of expression and expressions that reflect an incitement to discrimination, hostility or violence prohibited under international law.

But, first, it is important to stress that the *Rabat Plan of Action* makes a clear distinction between three different types of expression: (1) those constituting a criminal offence, such as propaganda for war and incitement to discrimination, hostility, or violence under article 20 of the ICCPR; (2) those not criminally punishable, but sanctionable under civil or administrative rules, in order to protect the rights or reputations of others, national security, public order, or morals, according to article 19.3 of the ICCPR; and (3) those that do not justify any criminal, civil or administrative sanction, but that are still concerning in terms of tolerance, civility and respect for the rights of others. In other terms, this last category comprises hateful *but* free speech, thus any heinous expression whose free manifestation prevails on any other protected interest. As the UN Human Rights Committee recalls in its *General Comment No. 34* on ICCPR's article 19, restrictions on the freedom of expression are legitimate only under the conditions and on the grounds of article 19.3. This means that limits to free speech must be established by a national law and they must be strictly necessary to protect the rights or reputations of others, or national security, public order, public health or morals.[50] Accordingly, the UN Human Rights Committee concludes that the ICCPR threshold to allow States' bans of malicious declarations, expressed in a public debate about public figures of the political domain or public institutions, is particularly high. Put differently, the mere fact that some forms of expression can be considered to be insulting to a public figure is not sufficient to explain States imposing penalties on the offenders.[51] The Committee extends this appreciation also to exhibitions of disregard for a religion or other belief system, including blasphemy laws, considered to be incompatible with the ICCPR (saving the particular circumstances of its article 20.2).[52] These sorts of provocative manifestations are not normally directed against a *specific* individual or group, but rather against an institution, such as a particular religion and its doctrines, or against a State and its government. As there is no direct expression of hate towards rights-holders, these kinds of hateful speech should be allowed as a general rule.[53] In other words, it seems that in International law there exists a right to offend and mock.[54] So much so that even the so-called "memory laws" that criminalise fraudulent public opinions about historical facts (for instance, the denial of the Holocaust) are considered to be incompatible with article 19 of the ICCPR. The Committee subsequently declares that the ICCPR "does not permit general prohibition of expressions of an erroneous opinion or an incorrect interpretation of past events", and any restrictions on the expression of such opinions "should not go beyond what is permitted" under article 19.3 or "required under article 20" of the ICCPR.[55]

Accordingly, the former Special Rapporteur David Kaye concludes in his 2019 Report on online hate speech that States should not criminalise or restrict the denial of the historical accuracy of atrocities without the evaluation of the six factors identified by the drafters of the *Rabat Plan of Action*.[56] Indeed, as is mentioned above, the *Rabat Plan of Action* identifies a six-part threshold test to settle the "severity" necessary to criminalise incitement to hatred. These six elements are: (1) the social and political context prevalent at the time the speech was made and circulated; (2) the speaker's position or status in the society, specifically the individual's or organisation's standing in the context of the audience to whom the speech is directed; (3) the intent, thus negligence and recklessness are not sufficient for an act to be an offence under article 20 of the ICCPR, as according to it the mere distribution of hateful material does not amount to advocacy or incitement; (4) the content and form, in particular "the degree to which the speech was provocative and direct, as well as the form, style, nature of arguments deployed"; (5) the extent or reach of the speech act, thus its public nature, its magnitude and size of its audience, including whether it was "a single leaflet or broadcast in the mainstream media or via the Internet, the frequency, the quantity and the extent of the communications, whether the audience had the means to act on the incitement"; (6) the likelihood or probability of harm occurring, including its imminence.

As the drafters of the Rabat Plan of Action explain, incitement is an inchoate act, a partial conduct that does not necessarily have to produce or contribute to the production of a specific result to hold the offender responsible, or as the experts clarify: "[T]he action advocated through incitement speech does not have to be committed for said speech to amount to a crime". Still, some degree of a "reasonable probability that the speech would succeed in inciting actual action against the target group" must be identified.[57]

Hence, under this sixfold evaluation, expressions that may be offensive and that can cause concerns of prejudice may frequently *not* meet a threshold of such severity as to justify a legal restriction. As the former Special Rapporteur remembers: "There is a range of expression of hatred, ugly as it is, that does not involve incitement or direct threat, such as declarations of prejudice against protected groups" and, consequently, it does not deserve any limitation according to the ICCPR and the ICERD. In any case, the prohibition of any prospective restriction of these unpleasant expressions does not mean that States cannot take any action. Actually, countries should take all those measures, such as government condemnation of prejudice, education, training, public service announcements and community projects, that appear to be adequate to fight against intolerance and to allow national powers to protect individuals and specific groups against these manifestations of hate.[58]

3. Final Remarks

The Holocaust did not start with the gas chambers, but with hate speech against minorities and the normalisation of atrocity crimes. Genocides and other international crimes develop gradually and, before their actual commission, it is possible to identify certain threatening clues, such as hateful speech against certain racial, ethnic, religious, gender or political groups. Recent examples include post-election violence fuelled by ethnic hatred, clashes related to extremist groups, offensive and false depictions of certain religions and their adherents online or in traditional media.[59] However, what makes hate speech particularly dangerous in our societies is its distribution throughout online platforms, as it can be easily exploited to circulate anonymous offensive material worldwide, exacerbating the harmful impact of hate speech and making societies more aggressive. All this generates unique challenges for the contemporary international community, because States and private actors – mainly social media platforms – strive to keep the pace of online haters.[60] Several States have adopted domestic legislations that compel online platforms to moderate or remove what they consider unlawful content.[61] However, these efforts to restrain hate speech lead to some concern that they could also produce the side effect of restricting political dissent and opposition, as information and communication technologies are increasingly used all over the world as instruments to spread ideas. Put differently, when domestic authorities need to adopt measures to prevent hate speech, they should strike a careful balance between this duty and the fundamental rights of opinion and expression which may provoke a supposed stalemate.

This contribution, by illustrating current "hard" and "soft" law international rules and standards on hate speech, has tried to demonstrate that if States would really want to limit hateful speech, they could already rely on a panoply of international compulsory norms and authoritative recommendatory reports that, contrary to common opinion, can help them to better delineate the exact contours of hate speech. However, as frequently happens when it comes to enforcing international law, some States do not seem to be interested in following the rules of the game, nor are they keen to include in their domestic laws clear and narrow definitions of key terms, such as hatred, discrimination, violence and hostility. As long as they prefer to tailor these concepts to their particular national interests, with the increase in the popularity and sheer number of online channels it will become increasingly more difficult to live in a world free of (online and offline) hatred. In the meanwhile, the task for international practitioners is to keep refining these notions as to deny States any excuses to disregard them.

Notes

1 This publication is the result of the Research Project I+D+i within the framework of the State programmes for the generation of knowledge and scientific and technological strengthening of the I+D+i system oriented to the Challenges of Society 2020, Project PID2020-112577RB-I00 "La búsqueda de una regulación internacional para las actividades cibernéticas (¿una ineludible necesidad?)", funded by the MCIN/AEI.
2 See https://www.un.org/en/hate-speech/understanding-hate-speech/hate-speech-and-real-harm
3 UN Meetings Coverage and Press Releases, "Secretary-General Launches United Nations Strategy and Plan of Action against Hate Speech, Designating Special Adviser on Genocide Prevention as Focal Point", PI/2264-SOC/4881, 18 June 2019, available at https://press.un.org/en/2019/pi2264.doc.htm
4 A/74/486, *Report of the Special Rapporteur on the promotion and protection of the right to freedom of opinion and expression*, 9 October 2019, pp. 1–23, p. 4, paragraph 1, available at https://www.ohchr.org/sites/default/files/Documents/Issues/Opinion/A_74_486.pdf
5 UN News, "UN expert warns combat against violent extremism could be used as 'excuse' to curb free speech", 3 May 2016, available at https://news.un.org/en/story/2016/05/528292
6 The United States considers any legal rule on it as a restriction to the freedom of expression. For an in-depth study on the United States' approach to hate speech, Strossen, Nadine, "United Nations Free Speech Standards as the Global Benchmark for Online Platforms' Hate Speech Policies", *Michigan State International Law Review*, vol. 29, no. 2, 2021, pp. 307 [xxviii], p. 307.
7 For some examples of countries' legislation regulating hate speech, Guillén-Nieto, Victoria, *Hate Speech: Linguistic Perspectives*, Foundations in Language and Law, vol. 2, De Gruyter Mouton, 2023, p. 212, pp. 14–20.
8 Article 1 of the *Universal Declaration of Human Rights*, 10 December 1948, available at https://documents-dds-ny.un.org/doc/RESOLUTION/GEN/NR0/043/88/PDF/NR004388.pdf?OpenElement
9 A/74/486, *op. cit.*, p. 8, paragraph 15.

10 *UN Strategy and Plan of Action on Hate Speech*, May 2019, available at https://www.un.org/en/genocideprevention/documents/advising-and-mobilizing/Action_plan_on_hate_speech_EN.pdf

11 Article 3, letter (c), of *the Convention on the Prevention and Punishment of the Crime of Genocide*, 9 December 1948, available at https://www.un.org/en/genocideprevention/documents/atrocity-crimes/Doc.1_Convention%20on%20the%20Prevention%20and%20Punishment%20of%20the%20Crime%20of%20Genocide.pdf

12 United Nations Office on Genocide Prevention and the Responsibility to Protect, *Framework of Analysis for Atrocity Crimes: A tool for Prevention*, 2014, pp. 1–32, p. 16, available at https://www.un.org/en/genocideprevention/documents/our-work/Doc.1_Framework%20of%20Analysis%20for%20Atrocity%20Crimes_EN.pdf

13 Article 5 of the *Rome Statute of the International Criminal Court*, 17 July 1998, available at https://www.icc-cpi.int/sites/default/files/RS-Eng.pdf

14 *Ibid.*, article 25, letter (e).

15 Resolution 217 A of the UN General Assembly, *Universal Declaration of Human Rights*, article 2.

16 Guillén-Nieto, Victoria, *op. cit.*, p. 9.

17 Article 4 of the *International Convention on the Elimination of all Form of Racial Discrimination*, 21 December 1965, available at https://www.ohchr.org/en/instruments-mechanisms/instruments/international-convention-elimination-all-forms-racial

18 *Ibid.*, paragraphs (a), (b) and (c).

19 Dias, Talita, *Tackling online hate speech through content moderation: The legal framework under the International Covenant on Civil and Political Rights*, BSG-WP-2022/047, July 2022, pp. 1–24, pp. 5–6, available at https://www.bsg.ox.ac.uk/sites/default/files/2022-07/BSG-WP-2022-047.pdf

20 Mohan, Vasu/Barnes, Catherine, "Countering Hate Speech in Elections: Strategies for Electoral Management Bodies", *IFES White Paper*, 2018, pp. 1–41, p. 6.

21 Vivian, Joshua, "Hate speech and international criminal law", *PKI Global Justice Journal*, vol. 35, 2021, available at https://globaljustice.queenslaw.ca/news/hate-speech-and-international-criminal-law

22 Dias, Talita, *op. cit.*, pp. 3–4.

23 A/74/486, *op. cit.*, p. 7, paragraph 12.

24 Guillén-Nieto, Victoria, *op. cit.*, p. 23.

25 A/74/486, *op. cit.*, pp. 5–6, paragraph 6.

26 A/HRC/22/17/Add.4, *Annual report of the United Nations High Commissioner for Human Rights, Addendum: Report of the United Nations High Commissioner for Human Rights on the expert workshops on the prohibition of incitement to national, racial or religious hatred*, 11 January 2013, pp. 1–15, p. 9, paragraph 18, available at https://www.ohchr.org/sites/default/files/Documents/Issues/Opinion/SeminarRabat/Rabat_draft_outcome.pdf

27 A/74/486, *op. cit.*, p. 12, paragraph 29.

28 Dias, Talita, *op. cit.*, pp. 1–2.

29 Human Rights Council, *Report of the independent international fact-finding mission on Myanmar*, A/HRC/39/64, 12 September 2018, pp. 1–21, paragraph 73, available at https://documents-dds-ny.un.org/doc/UNDOC/GEN/G18/274/54/PDF/G1827454.pdf?OpenElement

30 De Albuquerque, Alfonso/Alves, Marcelo, "Bolsonaro's hate network: From the fringes to the presidency", in C. Strippel, S. Paasch-Colberg, M. Emmer, &

J. Trebbe (Eds.), *Challenges and perspectives of hate speech research*, 2023, pp. 27–42, available at https://www.ssoar.info/ssoar/bitstream/handle/document/86287/ssoar-2023-de_albuquerque_et_al-Bolsonaros_hate_network_From_the.pdf?sequence=1&isAllowed=y&lnkname=ssoar-2023-de_albuquerque_et_al-Bolsonaros_hate_network_From_the.pdf

31 Pilkington, Ed., "Incitement: a timeline of Trump's inflammatory rhetoric before the Capitol riot", 7 January 2021, *The Guardian*, available at https://www.theguardian.com/us-news/2021/jan/07/trump-incitement-inflammatory-rhetoric-capitol-riot

32 Article 19, *International Annual Report 2022*, pp. 1–84, in particular pp. 8–11 (on Russia), pp. 18–25 (on Iran), and pp. 14–15 (on Tunisia). Available at https://www.article19.org/wp-content/uploads/2023/04/Article-19-Annual-Report-2022_web.pdf

33 Dias, Talita, *op. cit.*, p. 4.

34 CCPR/C/GC/34, Human Rights Committee, *General comment No. 34 on Article 19: Freedoms of opinion and expression*, 12 September 2011, pp. 1–13, pp. 5–8, paragraphs 21–36, available at https://www2.ohchr.org/english/bodies/hrc/docs/gc34.pdf; A/67/357, *Report of the Special Rapporteur on the promotion and protection of the right to freedom of opinion and expression*, 7 September 2012, pp. 1–24, p. 13, paragraph 51, available at https://documents-dds-ny.un.org/doc/UNDOC/GEN/N12/501/25/PDF/N1250125.pdf?OpenElement

35 A/74/486, *op. cit.*, p. 6, paragraph 8.

36 A/HRC/22/17/Add.4, *op. cit.*, p. 12, paragraph 34.

37 *Ibid.*

38 CERD/C/GC/35, Committee on the Elimination of Racial Discrimination, *General recommendation No. 35 on Combating racist hate speech*, 26 September 2013, pp. 1–10, p. 4, paragraph 12, available at https://www.refworld.org/docid/53f457db4.html

39 *Ibid.*, p. 10.

40 A/74/486, *op. cit.*, p. 7, paragraph 12.

41 Guillén-Nieto, Victoria, *op. cit.*, p. 9; A/HRC/22/17/Add.4, *op. cit.*, p. 10, paragraph 21, footnote 5.

42 A/74/486, *op. cit.*, p. 6, paragraph 9.

43 CCPR/C/GC/34, *op. cit.*, pp. 5–8, paragraphs 21–36; A/67/357, *Report of the Special Rapporteur on the promotion and protection of the right to freedom of opinion and expression*, 7 September 2012, pp. 11–12, paragraph 41, available at https://documents-dds-ny.un.org/doc/UNDOC/GEN/N12/501/25/PDF/N1250125.pdf?OpenElement; A/HRC/29/32, *Report of the Special Rapporteur on the promotion and protection of the right to freedom of opinion and expression*, David Kaye, 22 May 2015, pp. 1–21, pp. 11–12, paragraphs 32–35, available at https://documents-dds-ny.un.org/doc/UNDOC/GEN/G15/095/85/PDF/G1509585.pdf?OpenElement

44 Van Hout, Birgit, *Towards a comprehensive approach to counter hate speech*, Regional Information Centre for Western Europe, Office of the UN High Commissioner for Human Rights, 17 June 2022, available at https://unric.org/en/towards-a-comprehensive-approach-to-counter-hate-speech/

45 A/74/486, *op. cit.*, p. 4, paragraph 4.

46 Samples, John, *International Law and "Hate Speech" Online*, Cato Institute, 23 July 2020, available at https://www.cato.org/blog/international-law-hate-speech-online

47 A/HRC/22/17/Add.4, *op. cit.*, p. 4, paragraph 9.
48 See, as examples of these soft-law material, the Annual thematic reports to the Human Rights Committee of the Special Rapporteur on the promotion and protection of the right to freedom of opinion and expression, in particular: A/HRC/32/38, Report on freedom of expression, states and the private sector in the digital age, pp. 1–23, 11 May 2016, available at https://documents-dds-ny.un.org/doc/UNDOC/GEN/G16/095/12/PDF/G1609512.pdf?OpenElement; A/HRC/35/22, *Report on the role of digital access providers*, 20 March 2017, pp. 1–22, available at https://www.ohchr.org/en/documents/thematic-reports/ahrc3522-report-special-rapporteur-promotion-and-protection-right; A/HRC/38/35, *Report of the Special Rapporteur on the online content regulation*, 6 April 2018, pp. 1–20, available at https://documents-dds-ny.un.org/doc/UNDOC/GEN/G18/096/72/PDF/G1809672.pdf?OpenElement; or A/HRC/47/25, *Report of the Special Rapporteur* on the disinformation and freedom of opinion and expression, pp. 1–20, 13 April 2021, available at https://documents-dds-ny.un.org/doc/UNDOC/GEN/G21/085/64/PDF/G2108564.pdf?OpenElement. Another important document that it is worth mentioning is the UN Human Rights Council, *UN Guiding Principles on Business and Human Rights*, June 2011, pp. 1–35, in particular Guiding Principles n° 1, 2 and 11, available at https://www.ohchr.org/sites/default/files/documents/publications/guidingprinciplesbusinesshr_en.pdf
49 See https://www.un.org/en/hate-speech/united-nations-and-hate-speech/further-un-initiatives-to-combat-hate-speech
50 CCPR/C/GC/34, *op. cit.*, p. 6, paragraph 22.
51 *Ibid.*, p. 9, paragraph 38.
52 *Ibid.*, p. 12, paragraph 48.
53 Dias, Talita, *op. cit.*, p. 12.
54 A/74/486, *op. cit.*, p. 9, paragraph 17.
55 CCPR/C/GC/34, *op. cit.*, p. 12, paragraph 49.
56 A/74/486, *op. cit.*, p. 10, paragraph 22.
57 A/HRC/22/17/Add.4, *op. cit.*, p. 11, paragraph 29.
58 A/74/486, *op. cit.*, p. 11, paragraph 24.
59 A/HRC/22/17/Add.4, *op. cit.*, p. 3, paragraph 2.
60 See https://www.un.org/en/hate-speech/understanding-hate-speech/hate-speech-and-real-harm
61 Ibid., p. 13, paragraph 32.

References

A/67/357. (2012). *Report of the Special Rapporteur on the promotion and protection of the right to freedom of opinion and expression*, 7 September 2012, 1–24. Retrieved from https://documents-dds-ny.un.org/doc/UNDOC/GEN/N12/501/25/PDF/N1250125.pdf?OpenElement

A/74/486. (2019). *Report of the Special Rapporteur on the promotion and protection of the right to freedom of opinion and expression*, 9 October 2019, 1–23. Retrieved from https://www.ohchr.org/sites/default/files/Documents/Issues/Opinion/A_74_486.pdf

A/HRC/22/17/Add.4. (2013). *Annual report of the United Nations High Commissioner for Human Rights, Addendum: Report of the United Nations High*

Commissioner for Human Rights on the expert workshops on the prohibition of incitement to national, racial or religious hatred, 11 January 2013, 1–15. Retrieved from https://www.ohchr.org/sites/default/files/Documents/Issues/Opinion/SeminarRabat/Rabat_draft_outcome.pdf

A/HRC/29/32. (2015). *Report of the Special Rapporteur on the promotion and protection of the right to freedom of opinion and expression*, David Kaye, 22 May 2015, 1–21. Retrieved from https://documents-dds-ny.un.org/doc/UNDOC/GEN/G15/095/85/PDF/G1509585.pdf?OpenElement

A/HRC/32/38. (2016). *Report on freedom of expression, states and the private sector in the digital age*, 11 May 2016, 1–23. Retrieved from https://documents-dds-ny.un.org/doc/UNDOC/GEN/G16/095/12/PDF/G1609512.pdf?OpenElement

A/HRC/35/22. (2017). *Report on the role of digital access providers*, 20 March 2017, 1–22. Retrieved from https://www.ohchr.org/en/documents/thematic-reports/ahrc3522-report-special-rapporteur-promotion-and-protection-right

A/HRC/38/35. (2018). *Report of the Special Rapporteur on the online content regulation*, 6 April 2018, 1–20. Retrieved from https://documents-dds-ny.un.org/doc/UNDOC/GEN/G18/096/72/PDF/G1809672.pdf?OpenElement

A/HRC/39/64. (2018). *Report of the independent international fact-finding mission on Myanmar*, 12 September 2018, 1–21. Retrieved from https://documents-dds-ny.un.org/doc/UNDOC/GEN/G18/274/54/PDF/G1827454.pdf?OpenElement

A/HRC/47/25. (2021). *Report of the Special Rapporteur on the disinformation and freedom of opinion and expression*, 13 April 2021, 1–20. Retrieved from https://documents-dds-ny.un.org/doc/UNDOC/GEN/G21/085/64/PDF/G2108564.pdf?OpenElement

Article 19. (2022). *International annual report 2022* (pp. 1–84). Retrieved from https://www.article19.org/wp-content/uploads/2023/04/Article-19-Annual-Report-2022_web.pdf

CCPR/C/GC/34, Human Rights Committee. (2011). *General comment No. 34 on Article 19: Freedoms of opinion and expression*, 12 September 2011, 1–13. Retrieved from https://www2.ohchr.org/english/bodies/hrc/docs/gc34.pdf

CERD/C/GC/35, Committee on the Elimination of Racial Discrimination. (2013). *General recommendation No. 35 on Combating racist hate speech*, 26 September 2013. Retrieved from https://www.refworld.org/docid/53f457db4.html

de Albuquerque, A., & Alves, M. (2023). Bolsonaro's hate network: From the fringes to the presidency. In C. Strippel, S. Paasch-Colberg, M. Emmer, & J. Trebbe (Eds.), *Challenges and perspectives of hate speech research* (pp. 27–42). Retrieved from https://www.ssoar.info/ssoar/bitstream/handle/document/86272/ssoar-2023-strippel_et_al-Challenges_and_perspectives_of_hate.pdf?sequence=1&isAllowed=y&lnkname=ssoar-2023-strippel_et_al-Challenges_and_perspectives_of_hate.pdf.

Dias, T. (2022). Tackling online hate speech through content moderation: The legal framework under the International Covenant on Civil and Political Rights. *BSG-WP-2022/047*, 1–24. Retrieved from https://www.bsg.ox.ac.uk/sites/default/files/2022-07/BSG-WP-2022-047.pdf

Guillén-Nieto, V. (Ed.). (2023). *Hate speech: Linguistic perspectives*. Retrieved from https://www.degruyter.com/document/doi/10.1515/9783110672619/html

Mohan, V., & Barnes, C. (2018). Countering hate speech in elections: Strategies for electoral management bodies. *IFES White Paper*, 1–41.

Pilkington, E. (2021, January 7). Incitement: a timeline of Trump's inflammatory rhetoric before the Capitol riot. *The Guardian*. Retrieved from https://www.theguardian.com/us-news/2021/jan/07/trump-incitement-inflammatory-rhetoric-capitol-riot

Samples, J. (2020, July 23). International law and "hate speech" online. *Cato Institute*. Retrieved from https://www.cato.org/blog/international-law-hate-speech-online

Strossen, N. (2021). United Nations free speech standards as the global benchmark for online platforms' hate speech policies. *Michigan State International Law Review*, 29(2), 307 [xxviii].

UN Human Rights Council. (2011). *UN guiding principles on business and human rights*. Retrieved from https://www.ohchr.org/sites/default/files/documents/publications/guidingprinciplesbusinesshr_en.pdf

UN Strategy and Plan of Action on Hate Speech. (2019). Retrieved from https://www.un.org/en/genocideprevention/documents/advising-and-mobilizing/Action_plan_on_hate_speech_EN.pdf

United Nations Office on Genocide Prevention and the Responsibility to Protect. (2014). *Framework of analysis for atrocity crimes: A tool for prevention*. Retrieved from https://www.un.org/en/genocideprevention/documents/our-work/Doc.1_Framework%20of%20Analysis%20for%20Atrocity%20Crimes_EN.pdf

Van Hout, B. (2022, June 17). Towards a comprehensive approach to counter hate speech. *Regional Information Centre for Western Europe*. Retrieved from https://unric.org/en/towards-a-comprehensive-approach-to-counter-hate-speech/

Vivian, J. (2021). Hate speech and international criminal law. *PKI Global Justice Journal*, 35. Retrieved from https://globaljustice.queenslaw.ca/news/hate-speech-and-international-criminal-law

14 A Grassroots Model for Preventing Radicalisation

Fostering Belonging, Bridging Social Capital, Voice and Networking to Promote Successful Integration

Francesc Torras and Jordi Collet

1. Introduction

The terrorist attacks of August 17 and 18, 2017, in Barcelona and Cambrils (Catalonia, Spain) are still very much alive in the collective memory, especially for the population of Ripoll, a small town of 11,000 inhabitants in Girona (Catalonia, Spain). So alive that the victory of anti-Islamic "Aliança Catalana" in the 2023 local elections would have been hard to explain if these attacks had not been committed by a group of young men who had grown up in Ripoll. The 17-A terrorist cell was formed by ten men who, having been indoctrinated by imam Es-Satty, fatally ran over 14 people on the Ramblas in Barcelona, injured more than a hundred, fatally stabbed another and ran over one more person as they fled. Seven out of the ten young men were directly involved in the attacks and died handling explosives with the imam or were shot down by the police; the other three were collaborators to varying degrees and were given prison sentences. In total, 23 people were killed or shot down during those fateful days of August 2017. As Teixidor (2020) explains, once the imam and some of the young men were dead and the rest imprisoned, the issue could have seemed to be already closed. But it was later that some questions arose in this town and in Catalan society as a whole: How could these young students from the only state secondary school in the town end up becoming terrorists? How could they come up with, and devise strategies, to kill people who were their fellow citizens? How could they try to destroy key pieces of their identity such as the basilica of Sagrada Familia with truck explosives? Was the imam alone responsible for their radicalisation or did other elements contribute to this process? Could this happen there again and/or in other urban or rural towns in Spain? Under what circumstances and in relation to what processes? And, most relevantly for this chapter,

DOI: 10.4324/9781003457381-15

could it have been prevented? Can it be prevented from happening again? And, if such prevention is possible, how should it be structured and under what conditions?

Research on terrorism with an Islamic bent and radicalisation processes associated with this religion was consolidated in Spain as a result of the train bombings on March 11, 2004, in Madrid, where almost 200 were killed and thousands injured. Before, as Moyano (2010, p. 5) explains in his doctoral thesis, much less attention had been paid to this phenomenon in a country that, for decades, had its sights set on the terrorist acts of the Basque independence group ETA. Following these tragic attacks, the invasions of Iraq and Afghanistan, the escalation of the conflict between Israel and Palestine, and the emergence of Al-Qaeda after 9/11 and the subsequent creation of the Islamic State, among other events, extensive multidisciplinary research has been carried out in Spain in relation to the three key stages in the fight against terrorism: (1) The prevention of recruitment and radicalisation; (2) the fight against terrorist acts in its different forms; and (3) the reintegration process. In line with Moyano et al. (2022, p. 6), we can define radicalisation as

> a process where the commitment to an extremist ideology is gradually increased. This commitment can get to the point of legitimizing the use of violence. From a preventive point of view, it is essential to put the focus on the radicalization process.

This chapter deals with the Salam Project, which is an initiative to prevent radicalisation implemented between 2016 and 2020 in the county of Osona (Barcelona, Spain). Osona is a region adjacent to Ripollès, the county to which Ripoll belongs, and with very similar socio-demographic characteristics; here a second van was rented by the 17-A cell and abandoned during those fateful days of August 2017.

2. Theoretical Framework

2.1 *Understanding Radicalisation through the 3N Model*

Kruglanski et al. (2019) explain that one of the models most often used to understand the radicalisation process is the 3N model, which focuses on the following: (a) The individual's needs or motivations; (b) the narratives of the individual's culture; and (c) the interaction between group pressure and social influence within the individual's social network. As González et al. (2022, pp. 3–4) put it:

> The road to radicalization begins with the activation of the quest for significance, which directs attention to the means needed to achieve this

> significance. These means are found in the collective narrative (ideology) of the reference group, which the individual learns in their own milieu via contact with friends, family members, charismatic leaders, etc. If this narrative identifies political violence as a means to achieve significance, individuals will pledge to use it in order to restore their significance. Likewise, group processes join the two previous processes so that the commitment to the group which promotes extremist violence restores the significance because it is associated with different gratifying contingencies which serve as rewards (e.g., prestige, resources, feeling of belonging).

We will firstly highlight the central idea of the "radicalisation process". Until reaching the point of carrying out an attack, as the young men of Ripoll did, various changes and adaptations of their (self)perceptions, of their ethical and moral systems and of their self-concept need to have taken place. In addition to some individual needs and motivations accompanying a narrative (presumably linked to Islam) that justifies and guides violent actions within the framework of a group, there are other factors that facilitate this radicalisation. Secondly, with Moyano (2010, pp. 25–26), we will emphasise the external (or determining) factors and the internal (or disinhibiting) factors that push young people closer to terrorist violence throughout the radicalisation process. The main external factors are the following: (a) The diffusion of responsibility (i.e., the group progressively allows the individual to feel less responsible for their conduct); (b) the shifting of responsibility for the facts by acting in obedience to the group's leader; and (c) the deindividuation of the subject, which places them in a position of anonymity within the group and allows them to gradually act with fewer ties and moral barriers. The main internal factor during the radicalisation process is the dehumanisation of the victims, which turns them into a demon or animal that does not deserve to be treated humanely and with dignity, and thus deserves the violence they experience. This victim-blaming attitude makes the terrorist attack an act of restorative justice against an oppressor (an enemy), which is usually justified by a higher moral principle (in this case, religion). The last factor built during the radicalisation process that facilitates the perpetration of the violent attack is the progressive desensitisation of the consequences of the attack.

Recent research highlights the enormous difficulties and uncertainties in reversing the radicalisation process, and in safely and permanently de-radicalising people who have experienced it (reactive approach). As González et al. (2022, p. 2) explain, "Reactive approaches that attempt to deal with terrorism have been shown to be insufficient, which prompts the need to ascertain how subjects are radicalized in order to prevent these processes and their consequences". Thus, experts on radicalisation (Horgan &

Braddock, 2010; Dugdale, 2017; Bélanger et al., 2019; Kruglanski et al., 2019; Walanda, 2020, etc.) point out the great complexity and uncertainty of the processes of de-radicalisation, and, consequently, the importance of preventing radicalisation. Following this recommendation, below we present the theoretical bases of the Salam Project, which sought to prevent, avoid and/or minimise the conditions of possibility of these radicalisation processes linked to individuals' needs, narratives and networks (see Moyano, 2019; González et al., 2022), as well as the internal and external factors facilitating (see Moyano, 2010) this re-socialisation of Islamic roots in the county of Osona in Barcelona.

2.2 *Theoretical Bases of the Salam Radicalisation Prevention Project*

If, following the 3N model, radicalisation processes begin with the unresolved need to be somebody, to be recognised and valued by somebody, the ultimate goal of any prevention process using the same model (as long as there has not been a similar process before), "is to create resilient individuals, groups, and communities. That is, people who have significance and a support network within the community" (Moyano et al., 2022, p. 3). To achieve this, there are three core complementary strategies:

> First, a direct route consisting of delegitimizing violent narratives or narratives that present some components such as grievances, culprits, or violent means. Second, there would be an indirect pathway based on providing other sources of significance in order to move individuals toward more favourable contexts. Third, another indirect pathway related to reducing relationships with deviant peers who may exert a negative influence.
>
> (Moyano et al., 2022, p. 4)

In other words, especially linked to the second and third strategies, it is a matter of filling this need for significance, for a link, for support, for belonging and for meaning so that there is no space for radical discourses, people, groups, and ideas to enter. Making people, groups and communities resilient was precisely the goal of the Salam Project. Drawing on previous research (Collet & Tort, 2017; Beneyto et al., 2019; Collet, 2020), the key elements of this radicalisation prevention project, which worked *with* (and not *for* or *on*) the young Muslims of Osona, were as follows:

1 To build up a clear sense of belonging for all young Muslims in different socio-educational spaces based on Healy's (2019) three parameters (i.e., membership/formal belonging, feeling/sense of belonging and perceived belonging). Feeling that you belong to various groups linked to sports,

leisure time or informal activities can make it easier to fulfil the need for recognition, and can contribute to making individuals and communities more resilient to radicalisation processes (Moyano et al., 2022, p. 3).

2 To construct bridging social capital to prevent the process of insulation, bonding and encapsulation related to radicalisation (Putnam, 2001). By being connected with other groups, other sources of significance and various personal ties can be built. This reduces the possibilities of dehumanising and blaming the other (Moyano, 2010, p. 5).
3 To open up spaces for hearing different voices, experiences and views in all educational contexts. Having spaces where the voice of young people is heard is key to deactivating (or reducing) the power of external factors that can facilitate radicalisation. Specifically, when young people individually have a voice and are heard, the shift of responsibility to the group, their deindividuation and anonymity are reduced. Additionally, this process increases a sense of personal responsibility towards the people who have listened to, debated with and talked to them (Moyano et al., 2022, p. 3).
4 To build a strong community network to co-generate projects and knowledge that can foster belonging, bridging social capital and social polyphony; as well as to alert the institutions of any sign of isolation and indoctrination. Building a resilient community makes it possible to warn of, and prevent, possible signs of the radicalisation process. That is why it is so important that this is not an issue for "them", but rather something that affects the whole community that conceives of, and experiences, all the young people of the area as their own. In this way, they become co-responsible, together with the families and the young people themselves, for their care, well-being, integration, and opportunities.

3. The Salam Radicalisation Prevention Project

3.1 *Introduction: Context, Objectives and Methodology*

The Salam Project was created in 2016 as a joint network of different social actors. It was run primarily by the Muslim communities of Osona, as a result of the concern caused by the realisation that Europe aimed to fight Jihadist terrorism solely (or mainly) through police forces, from a reactive perspective. This intention was carried out in Catalonia via the Procedure for the Detection of Islamist Radicalisation (PRODERAI), led by the Ministry of Home Affairs of the Generalitat (Catalan Government) and the Mossos d'Esquadra (Catalan police). School teachers, who were considered trainers against radicalism and antennas for its detection, also participated. The turning point of this change of approach by European states was the terrorist attack carried out on January 7, 2015, against

French magazine Charlie Hebdo, following the publication of satirical cartoons of Muhammad that hurt the sensibilities of millions of Muslims (Gil, 2021). Here, something happened that started to occur in terrorist attacks in Europe: The terrorists were people with European passports, raised in Europe and "beneficiaries" of its welfare. For the first time, the threat did not come from "outside"; it came from "within", and possessed a phenotype frequently seen in the streets of Europe, which fostered permanent suspicion, and fueled stereotypes, rumour and racism (Pàmies & Carrasco, 2021).

In this context of a state of alert, arrests of young men of Moroccan origin in some towns in Osona,[1] in Catalonia[2] and in Spain[3] in general began to take place. These were arrests related to the promotion of jihadism, and the young men arrested were therefore treated as terrorists by the police (Reinares & García-Calvo, 2016). These facts show that any flirting with certain radical web pages by young people in Muslim communities could lead to social ruin for the young wo/man, their family and their community. Given this situation, the Muslim communities in Osona themselves decided it was necessary to prevent these incidents, by questioning, listening to, and conveying the concerns and wishes of young Muslims. The Muslim communities saw that social cohesion and inclusion were at stake. It was here that the Salam (peace in Arabic) project was created in 2016, as a result of the conversations and concerns expressed by the representatives of these Muslim communities who went to the private Foundation for social and education work *Projecte i Vida* (Project and Life) to see how these concerns could be translated into a structured project. Taking advantage of the Foundation's experience and background in working with young people, and with the desire to contribute to and generate community improvements, at the beginning of 2017 an exploratory diagnosis was realised.

The diagnostic field work began by carrying out 20 exploratory interviews with several young Muslims in the county of Osona, people selected through the communities themselves or by the technical teams of the local government seeking maximum diversity in the profiles, especially of the young Muslims (men-women; different ages; different municipalities; different life situations, etc.). This exploratory phase was important because the young Muslims valued the project positively, although they questioned it as they saw it as being ethno- and adult-centric. For example, they all said that violent radicalisation was completely foreign to them and to Islam; and that, instead, they were its collateral victims, since it directly affected them through the perception that the rest of society had of them and the daily consequences this had (i.e., ethnocentrism). This involved a growth in stereotypes and prejudices specifically against the young Muslims of Osona (see Collet, 2020). They also proposed that the project can be approached differently: They wanted the project to give them a voice to become equal actors. And, above all, several of them specified that they wanted Muslim and non-Muslim adults to remain quiet and listen to them without judging young Muslims' accounts, experiences and proposals (i.e., adult-centrism). After this exploratory phase and the 20 interviews, the objectives of the project, initially planned for four years (2017–2020), were redefined, focusing on:

- Promoting the organisation of actions for the non-criminalisation of the Muslim communities.
- Establishing strategies for the prevention of the violent radicalisation of young Muslims with the Muslim communities themselves as promotors of the actions.

From the beginning, the theoretical approach was based on community work focused on developing a sense of belonging in all young people; on building more and better bridging social capital that allows young Muslims to have access to various social spheres (Putnam, 2001); with spaces where their voice can be heard without prejudice, especially by adults; and with the involvement of the whole community on how each step is carried out (Richards-Schuster & Brisson, 2016). It was thus made clear that it would be a participatory project where young people would have a voice and a key role in every phase; and that the main protagonists were Osona's Muslim communities, which participated by co-designing the project from its inception through a design inspired in action research methodology (Lewin, 1946; McNiff, 2013; Beneyto et al., 2019). The project contacted the university of the region to accompany the whole process, and to ensure the scientific and methodological rigour of the project. Once the exploratory project had been carried out and the project had been validated by both the Muslim communities in the region and the Union of Islamic Communities in Catalonia, all community experts in the region were also contacted in order to take advantage of their knowledge and inform them about the nature of our project, and asked them to collaborate in a participatory project aimed at preventing radicalisation processes as an important element for their wellbeing, and their life journeys and opportunities.

From an organisational point of view, a network of actors was built that would be part of the project: The Muslim communities of Osona (and, in particular, their young people), those responsible for the coexistence and immigration policies of the municipalities in the region, the schools, the social services, the Socio-Educational Intervention Centres with young people, the security forces, the General Directorate of Migration and the General Directorate of Religious Affairs of the Generalitat, the Osona town councils, and the University of Vic – Central University of Catalonia. From all of these, a steering committee was formed that would be in charge of guiding the project and defining its central lines. It was made up of eight young people between 16 and 28 from different Muslim communities of Osona, the project director and a researcher from the University of Vic.

Methodologically, after the exploratory diagnosis, a participatory diagnosis was proposed with all the young Muslims in the region that would begin with three days of listening and dialogue, called "Islam and young people". Once these diagnosis sessions had been carried out, it was up to the steering committee to re-route the project, to identify the needs and proposals made, and to see what actions had started to be considered. Unfortunately, the terrorist attacks of Barcelona and Cambrils took place, after the exploratory phase, the participatory diagnosis and the three days of listening and dialogue. Faced with these circumstances, the different actors of the project decided to stop it, understanding that the context after these attacks was not conducive to developing the project.

3.2 *Actions: Participatory Diagnosis and the Days of Dialogue and Listening*

Once the exploratory phase (2016) had been completed, there were two actions of the project (2017) that stood out: The participatory diagnosis, and the three days of listening and dialogue "Islam and young people".

a Participatory Diagnosis

Within the framework of action research methodology, the most important part of the participatory dialogue was not obtaining an exhaustive knowledge of the reality of young Muslims in Osona, but the consensus on what the starting situation was and what their needs, experiences, strengths, weaknesses, opportunities and threats were, following a SWOT model (Ghazinoory et al., 2011). To carry it out, five information-gathering sessions were held that were open to all young people from the five communities where the sessions were physically held. These participatory diagnostic sessions conformed to the following model: Questions for individual reflection on the experience of being a young Muslim in Osona; strengths, weaknesses, opportunities and threats (SWOT); sharing of individual reflections in small groups; and putting together in a large group the consensus reached in the small groups. After collecting the results of the diagnosis by young people, some questions regarding this diagnosis were raised in a dialogue open to the whole group. The five participatory diagnosis sessions were attended by 237 young people from the region. In parallel, open listening sessions were held with young people from all over the region on four key themes that emerged in the participatory diagnosis sessions, namely, identity, integration, emancipation and religious liberty.

Throughout this participatory diagnosis from the general and thematic sessions, the community worker of the Project and Life Foundation assumed the role of secretary, companion and facilitator, so that there was always an atmosphere of respect, positivity and dialogue.

b Days of Listening and Dialogue "Islam and Young People"

Complementary to the general and thematic sessions of participatory diagnosis, and in line with the results of the exploratory work, the Salam Project brought together in three areas of Osona (i.e., south, centre and north) the adult representatives of the Islamic communities of Osona, police members, councillors, municipal experts, university researchers and other social actors, in order to listen and dialogue about the situation of young Muslims in the region with the young people themselves. The aim of these three days was to make several young Muslims protagonists of the projects; to enable the various adult representatives to hear their voice; and to create a space for respectful and positive dialogue about their situation in Osona in different areas (e.g., studies, work, gender, leisure activities and religion). Several groups of young Muslims were tasked with preparing a series of interventions to present them at each meeting with the different representatives of Muslim and non-Muslim adult life. About 30 people attended each of the three sessions. Half were young Muslims who explained different aspects of their experience, and the rest were adults from the Islamic communities of Osona, Catalonia and Spain, town councils (politicians and specialists), university researchers, residents of the different towns, and sports and cultural associations, among others.

Very briefly, from the two instruments of diagnostic analysis, the issues that were of recurrent concern to the young Muslims and that, had the project continued, would have been at its core, emerged. In addition, explicit questions were asked about the phenomenon of Islamic terrorism. The results, in SWOT format, were as follows.

a Strengths: What experiences, opportunities and positive relations have you had as a result of being a young Muslim in Osona?

Here the young people talked about health and educational conditions, among others, that were better than those of their parents in Morocco; the possibilities of being multilingual, of having more than one culture and of being able to act as a bridge between them (multiple identities), enriching them both; the fact of being accepted and being part of Osona society; the possibility of being able to practice their religion in freedom; the pride of being Muslim and the positive experience of being one; being able to live Ramadan, which is linked to solidarity and support of the poor, among other aspects.

b Weaknesses: What experiences, difficulties, dangers and negative relationships have you had as a result of being a young Muslim in Osona?

Here their experiences of racism, discrimination, insults, prejudices, elements of discrimination especially for women linked to the hijab (for example, in the working world) or to stereotypes about what they are (e.g., submissive, resigned) were prominent. They pointed out the double discrimination for being a woman and a Muslim in a patriarchal society, both Moroccan and Catalan; the added difficulties in accessing work; the negative expectations from the teaching staff ("I don't think you'll get a degree", "you don't need to get a degree, do vocational training", and so on); having to hide their culture and religion in order to present themselves; the difficulties in getting people to understand their culture and the difficulties in having available public holidays to celebrate their religious festivals; the fact that young Muslims are generally addressed in Spanish (not in Catalan), even though they speak Catalan; the fact that young men and women are not present at most events held by the Muslim community; and, finally, the fact that the media almost exclusively reflect a negative image of Islam.

c Opportunities: Are you satisfied with what your community is doing? What suggestions for improvement would you make?

In general, they were ambivalent about the fact that they had to justify themselves, because others carried out terrorist acts in the name of Islam that they completely rejected; and they saw it both as an opportunity to explain who they are (and what they are not) and as a threat ("we have to give explanations when there is a terrorist act"; "Negative actions are highlighted, there is no echo of good students, of acts of solidarity, etc."). They also believed that, with more support from the host community, more progress could be made in mutual knowledge and social integration and that, for this reason, mutual respect is key. Some emphasised that Osona is a good host county.

d Threats. What future threats do you see as a Muslim?

Here, the young Muslims highlighted that, socially, the duties of people of foreign origin are always talked about but not their rights (for example, to be taught Islam at school). Feelings of being discriminated against (for example, not being taught Islam at school) or of creating "fear" for being Muslim reappeared. They also emphasised as a threat the fact that the Muslim community closes in on itself and the few opportunities for participation given to it. With regard to schools, they also mentioned the importance of establishing more links with schools and family associations in those contexts, as well as the issue that some families do not allow physical education or excursions, swimming and music, especially girls, and that this had to change. In one case, it was claimed that it should not be changed since boys and girls swimming together is against Islam. Gender inequality came up once again, pointing to women as being victimised, sometimes by the Muslim community itself, sometimes by the host society, sometimes both. On the one side, from the host community, as it was collected from young Muslim women's experiences in Osona (Collet, 2020, p. 513), sometimes they receive messages like "religion always has to stop you doing things", "this is a secular country, if you don't like it go to another country" or themselves, they realise that "boys, since they are not so physically identifiable, are judged less than the girls". On the other, related to their own Muslim communities,

> the girls have brought up conflicts around possible gender discrimination both with regard to their own communities and society in general (...). For example, Muslim girl 1 said (...). It could be that even the parents think that it is more normal for a man to party than for a girl.
>
> (Collet, 2020, p. 511)

In the end, criticism of the media as a threat that distorts reality also appeared, as did episodes of discrimination by the police for being Muslim.

e Opinion on Islamic terrorism. Do you think someone could radicalise you? How and why?

The vast majority were clearly against those who use Islam for their terrorist goals. They reflected, for example, that terrorists do not differentiate between different communities and religions; that we are all targets of this reality; that a person who kills is not a Muslim ("The Qur'an says that whoever kills a soul is as if he had killed all people, and whoever revives it is as if he had given life to all humanity."); that this terrorism contradicts Islam; that placing Islam and terrorism together is an oxymoron because Islam seeks peace; that a "Muslim terrorist" is not a Muslim and that you cannot qualify terrorism.

As regards radicalisation, most answers were negative, arguing that if you know your religion you cannot be manipulated; that they cannot do it if your identity is clear and strong. But they also warned that "weak" personalities or ignorance could make it easier for someone to brainwash and radicalise you. It is a process that, in certain cases, is easier when someone is experiencing financial and emotional difficulties.

3.3 Evaluation

Both the diagnostic interviews and the two participatory diagnostic tools collected the opinions and assessments of all the people who participated in each of the sessions. In general, they were all positive, but, more specifically, the young Muslims of Osona expressed their great satisfaction regarding the start of a process that, as mentioned above, was cut short, paradoxically, due to the terrorist attacks of August 2017 in Barcelona and Cambrils. Of all the things evaluated, what the young people highlighted the most were the spaces where they could have a voice, be listened to by adults (Muslim and non-Muslim) in the area; and have meeting spaces with other young people like themselves. From the perspective of analysing the radicalisation processes of the 3N model (Kruglanski et al., 2019; González et al., 2022), these young people asked for spaces to respond to the need for personal recognition; for spaces where alternative narratives about Muslimness can be co-constructed; and, finally, meeting spaces where they can meet and recognise other young people like them with whom they can develop a personal and collective sense of being young and Muslim. In short, we believe that the limited qualitative evaluation carried out in 2016 and 2017 shows the potential of the Salam Project to help to build resilient individuals and communities against the possible threats of radicalisation based on belonging, bridging social capital, voice and community networking.

4. Conclusion

The 2017 attacks in Catalonia put an unexpected problem on the table: The possibility of young people who had been living in Spain for years or who had been born there to become terrorists using Islam as a justification. As we have seen, this wound is not yet closed and many questions regarding their radicalisation process remain open. Before this happened, the Salam Project aimed to respond to the challenge of preventing the radicalisation of young people, precisely because, due to its participatory design, it had detected signs of young people in Osona, a county next to Ripollès where the young people involved in the 2017 attacks were from, who could enter into this spiral. To do this, an initial exploration was proposed with 20 young people who questioned the ethnocentric and adult-centric assumptions of the project because they did not match their needs, narratives and points of view of their social network. The two actions that could be carried out before the project was stopped – the participatory diagnosis and the "Islam and young people" sessions – revealed the enormous interest of young people in these spaces of listening and dialogue, and the potential to prevent isolation and radicalisation. The adult representatives of the

Muslim communities and those of the host society also valued positively these spaces of listening and dialogue with the young people. This is so because the challenge of well-being, belonging and integration as key elements of prevention is a joint one, and the town councils, the police, the social services, the university and other entities must play an active role in co-constructing acceptance and well-being for each young person.

Thus, we believe that projects with a community perspective and based on action research that seek to include young Muslims and their communities in participatory processes of dialogue, diagnosis and proposals can be a useful tool to prevent radicalisation. This is especially so when they focus, as we have explained in the design, on the objectives of building a sense of belonging and recognition for all young people; on building bridging social capital that connects them with more and new social areas; if they are done by placing the direct voice of young people at the centre and as their guiding thread; and oriented to networking with each other and with other actors who also feel directly affected by the experiences and needs of these young people. If prevention is a key element of any strategy against radicalisation, the development of new regional projects based on premises underlying the Salam Project may contribute to this goal. To find this out, they will need to incorporate several assessment tools in their design to measure their impact at different levels (personal, small group, community and host society), and their degree of effectiveness in the short, medium and long term.

Notes

1 https://el9nou.cat/osona-ripolles/actualitat/societat/un-detingut-a-roda-de-ter-acusat-de-pertanyer-a-estat-islamic/
https://el9nou.cat/osona-ripolles/actualitat/expulsat-de-lestat-un-presumpte-gihadista-que-sestava-a-manlleu/
https://el9nou.cat/osona-ripolles/actualitat/societat/els-dos-veins-de-roda-relacionats-amb-el-gihadista-seran-jutjats-a-laudiencia-nacional/
2 https://elpais.com/cat/2015/04/08/catalunya/1428471781_229630.html
https://elpais.com/cat/2015/11/28/espana/1448696228_590338.html
3 https://www.dsn.gob.es/es/lucha-contra-terrorismo-yihadista-espa%C3%B1a

References

Akbarzadeh, S. (2013). Investing in mentoring and educational initiatives: The limits of de-radicalisation programmes in Australia. *Journal of Muslim Minority Affairs*, *33*(4), 451–463.

Bélanger, J. J., Moyano, M., Muhammad, H., Richardson, L., Lafrenière, M-A. K., McCaffery, P., Framand, K., & Nociti, N. (2019). Radicalization leading to violence: A test of the 3N model. *Frontiers in Psychiatry*, *10*(42), 1–12. https://doi.org/10.3389/fpsyt.2019.00042

Beneyto, M., Castillo, J., Collet-Sabé, J., & Tort, A. (2019). Can schools become an inclusive space shared by all families? Learnings and debates from an action research project in Catalonia. *Educational Action Research*, *27*(2), 210–226.

Collet, J. & Tort, A. (2017). *Escuelas, familias y comunidad. La perspectiva imprescindible para educar hoy*. Barcelona: Octaedro.

Collet, J. (2020). Religious discrimination in young Muslim assimilation in Spain: Contributions to Portes and Rumbaut's segmented assimilation theory. *Social Compass, 67*(4), 599–616.

Dugdale, W. (2017). Prison de-radicalisation: To rehabilitate or merely isolate? *Antigone, 1*, 201–221.

Ghazinoory, S., Abdi, M., & Azadegan-Mehr, M. (2011). SWOT methodology: A state-of-the-art review for the past, a framework for the future. *Journal of Business Economics and Management*, *12*(1), 24–48.

Gil, A. (2021). El fenómeno de la radicalización violenta: una aproximación multifactorial. In J. Pàmies & S. Carrasco (Eds.), *Una aproximación a los procesos de radicalización y extremismo violento*. Bellaterra: Ediciones de la Universidad Autónoma de Barcelona.

González, I., Moyano, M., Lobato, R., & Trujillo, H. (2022). Analysis of the radicalization of the 17-A terrorist cell: an empirical approach using the 3N model. *International Journal of Social Psychology*, *37*(3), 529–553.

Healy, M. (2019). Belonging, social cohesion and Fundamental British Values. *British Journal of Educational Studies*, *67*(4), 423–438.

Horgan, J., & Braddock, K. (2010). Rehabilitating the terrorists? Challenges in assessing the effectiveness of de-radicalization programs. *Terrorism and Political Violence*, *22*(2), 267–291.

Kruglanski, A. W., Bélanger, J. J., & Gunaratna, R. (2019). *The three pillars of radicalization: Needs, narratives, and networks*. Oxford: Oxford University Press.

Lewin, K. (1946). Action research and minority problems. *Journal of Social Issues, 2*(4), 34–46.

McNiff, J. (2013). *Action research: Principles and practice*. Abingdon: Routledge.

Moyano, M. (2010). *Factores psicosociales contribuyentes a la radicalización islamista de jóvenes en España. Construcción de un instrumento de evaluación* [PhD thesis]. Universidad de Córdoba (Psychosocial factors contributing to Islam radicalisation of young people in Spain).

Moyano, M. (2019). *Radicalización terrorista. Gestión del riesgo y modelos de intervención* (Terrorist radicalization. Risk management and intervention models). Madrid: Síntesis.

Moyano, M., Lobato, R., Blaya-Burgo, M., Arnal, N., Cuadrado, E., Mateu, D., Ramírez-García, A., Murga, M., & Trujillo, H. (2022). Preventing violent extremism in youth through sports: An intervention from the 3N model. *Psychology of Sport and Exercise*, *63*, 102283. https://doi.org/10.1016/j.psychsport.2022.102283

Pàmies, J. & Carrasco, S. (coords.) (2021). *Una aproximación a los procesos de radicalización y extremismo violento (predein)*. Bellaterra: Universitat Autònoma de Barcelona.

Portes, A., Aparicio, R., & Haller, W. (2016). *Spanish legacies: The coming of age of the second generation*. Oakland: University of California Press

Putnam, R. (2001). *Bowling alone*. Ney York: Simon & Shuster.

Reinares, F., & García-Calvo, C. (2016). *Estado Islámico en España*. Madrid: Real Instituto Elcano. https://media.realinstitutoelcano.org/wp-content/uploads/2016/11/informe-estado-islamico-espana.pdf

Richards-Schuster, K., & Brisson, K. G. (2016). Strengthening youth leadership in a metropolitan region: Examining lessons from a multiyear community foundation initiative. *The Foundation Review*, *8*(3). https://doi.org/10.9707/1944-5660.1310

SALAM Project. (2018). *An Action-research project with young Muslims in the county of Osona, Spain*. Osona: Projecte i Vida private foundation.

Teixidor, A. (2020). *Sense por de morir*. Barcelona: Portic.

Vincent, C. (2022). The illiberalism of liberalism: Schools and fundamental controversial values. *Journal of Ethnic and Migration Studies, 48*(9), 2073–2090.

Walanda, G. (2020). The path to sustainable deradicalization program. *Journal of Terrorism Studies*, *2*(1), 51–77.

15 Counter Terrorism in a Pre-crime Space

Safeguarding, Radicalisation and Extremism in Schools in England

Lynn Revell

1. Introduction

The notion of pre-crime and the preventative state is a criminological construct, a conceptual tool that allows legal theorists to identify trends and patterns (Zedner & Ashworth, 2019, p. 430). The same is true of the presentation of the pre-crime school and its relationship to counter terrorism in English schools in this chapter. It too is a construct crafted from an assemblage of pre-existing trends and practices within education. The value of this construct is that it allows us to understand how certain narratives and policies that are both normalised and normative are not only illiberal, but subvert relationships between teachers and pupils in ways that appear to protect and defend liberal values. The aim of this chapter is to show how the Prevent Duty (henceforth Prevent) is successfully embedded in schools precisely because schools already accommodate many of the practices associated with pre-crime environments.

Pre-crime is a term that will be familiar to fans of the science fiction writer Philip K. Dick and his short story *Minority Report*. In the story, society has the capacity to predict who will commit crimes in the future through the visions of *pre-cogs*, and social crime control agents are able to arrest and convict individuals before any crime has been committed. In the story, Philip K. Dick explores the tension between convicting an individual before the crime has been committed and the fact that, when they are convicted, they are still innocent of any crime (Dick, 2002). The story hinges on the experiences of a protagonist who is wrongly convicted of a crime he did not commit, and Dick asks how pre-crime convictions can be justified when it means that the innocent are criminalised. His answer is that even though the system is fallible and innocent people will be mistakenly convicted, arresting individuals before the crime has taken place makes society a more peaceful and safer place. It is this tension between the desire for security and the individuals' rights so brilliantly explored in fiction that frames the tensions caused by the Prevent Duty in schools.

DOI: 10.4324/9781003457381-16

The criminalisation of thought or behaviour before it happens marks Prevent and the 2015 Counter Terrorism Act as a particular type of law that is sometimes characterised as pre crime (Zedner, 2007; Rizq, 2017; Heath-Kelly & Shanaah 2023). The growth of pre crime represents a paradigm shift in law from a criminal justice system whose focus was the punishment of crimes that had already been committed to one where the possibility of forestalling risks takes precedence over responding to wrongs done (Zedner, 2007). This change in emphasis represents more than a shift of focus, it represents a new phase in the way rights are conceptualised in law that impacts on civil liberties, human rights and international law (Donkin, 2013).

There are important continuities as well as significant differences in both the execution and rationale between traditional crime prevention and pre crime. Crime prevention as opposed to pre crime is traditionally focused on non-punitive measures. Pre crime includes laws and police powers that expand the remit of criminal law beyond the extant offences of conspiracy (McCulloch & Pickering, 2009), and its focus is on privileging measures that anticipate and imagine where and how harm may take place. Typical crime prevention measures are aimed at preventing crimes that have happened in the past and they aim to stop their reoccurrence. In contrast, pre-crime measures aim to pre-empt offending altogether.

Perhaps the greatest significance of the prevalence of the pre crime are the consequences of the temporal nature of the way in which pre-criminal acts are identified and prosecuted. The definition of a criminal act refers to the past. A crime is thought to have been committed and the judgment of whether an individual committed that crime takes place in a public space, normally in a court of law. In contrast, a pre crime has yet to happen and it cannot be examined in the same way as a probable crime that has already taken place (Zedner, 2007). The temporal nature of the pre-criminal act means that not only must society anticipate when a crime may take place, but it must find a way of assessing the likelihood of whether that crime will take place, if it had not been prevented. Some legal scholars have argued that extensive use of pre crime is unworkable and impractical precisely because of the difficulties in proving intention beyond reasonable doubt (Rose & Nestorovska, 2007); yet recent counter-terrorism legislation, including Prevent means that "prosecutions that would once have been seen as beyond the temporal pale of even exceptional counter terrorism laws are now unexceptional" (McCulloch & Pickering, 2009, p. 135).

Like the citizens in Dick's story, children and young people in English schools exist in a pre-crime space where their ideas are policed before those ideas are realised or acted upon. Before the chapter explains how the pre-crime space is embedded in existing narratives of safeguarding, risk and surveillance, it examines the context in which Prevent and the definition of extremism which is at its heart emerged.

2. Context – Education and Ideology

Counter terrorism legislation and policy in the UK is a disjointed and constantly evolving mosaic of initiatives and developments (Boukalas, 2017). UK counter-terrorism legislation includes (to date) eight dedicated Parliamentary Acts and provisions within legislation that relate to finance, immigration, the prison service, social work and education. Within the field of education, the legislation and policy that relates to counter terrorism are sprawling and cover every aspect of educational life, from the professional codes of conduct for teachers, classroom practice, governance and government inspection regimes (Bryan, 2017).

CONTEST, the UK's counter-terrorism strategy, was developed by the Home Office in 2003 as a response to the 9/11 bombings, and was comprised of four strands: Prevent, Pursue, Protect and Prepare. In the earliest iterations of CONTEST, the strands dealing with the mitigation of the impact of terrorism and protection against terrorist attacks were prioritised, and Prevent, dedicated to the prevention of extremism, was dormant (Thomas, 2016). CONTEST was revised in 2006 and 2011 with an emphasis on the need to combat the causes of radicalisation rather than just responding to current threats (HAC, 2008–2009), and Prevent too has undergone several shifts in its focus and remit.

Although early iterations of Prevent included education sites as part of its overall approach to counter terrorism, the responsibilities of teachers and schools have increased as the policy has developed. CONTEST 2011 mentions education only once, but by 2015 Prevent's focus on Education had escalated so that Prevent can be best understood not as a single policy initiative but more accurately as a series of constantly evolving measures and interventions (Heath-Kelly, 2017). These interventions in education include guidance for schools and childcare providers produced by the Department for Education in 2015, which states that it is "essential" that staff are able to identify children who might be vulnerable to radicalisation and that these duties are "entirely consistent with schools' and childcares' existing responsibilities and should not be burdensome" (Department for Education, 2015, p. 5). In 2012, The Teachers Standards, the professional code for all teachers in England, established a link between the professional obligations of teachers and counter terrorism when they required teachers not to "undermine fundamental British values" and made explicit reference to Prevent (Department for Education, 2011, p. 9).

Furthermore, the Office for Standards in Education (Ofsted), the body that inspects schools, integrated the duty of schools to detect radicalisation as part of its inspection framework. As a result of changes to the inspection guidance, Ofsted inspectors now comment on whether schools make sufficient care in relation to the safety of pupils through a safeguarding process that expects teachers to identify those who are at "risk of being radicalised or exploited" (Department for Education, 2022a, p. 9).

Perhaps the single most significant development in CONTEST and Prevent was the change to the definition of extremism in 2011 when the amended version of Prevent stated that extremism was to be defined as violent and non-violent (Home Office, 2011, p. 6). Alongside most other European states, extremism was originally defined as violent extremism with a focus on Islamist ideology. The definition of terrorism, as laid out in the Terrorism Act 2006, was limited to behaviours that directly cause physical harm. The 2015 Counter Extremism Strategy consolidated the 2011 focus by Prevent on an ideological definition of extremism when it states that extremism "is the vocal or active opposition to our fundamental values" (HMG, 2015). Fundamental British values have been critiqued as ambiguous and even non-sensical (Elton-Chalcraft et al., 2017) but they are positioned by policy as the mechanism by which the beliefs of individuals are determined as extremist or as "dangerous ideology" (Skoczylis & Andrews, 2020, p. 1.)

2.1 *Prevent – Success and Critique*

Prevent is often lauded as a "pioneer in the field of counter terrorism" (Vidino & Brandon, 2012, p. 1). It is unique in counter-terrorism measures in placing expectations on health and educator sectors to play such an explicit role in detecting radicalisation and it is this aspect of Prevent that is often identified as key to its success. When Prevent is compared with CVE initiatives in other Western countries, it is often identified as comprehensive and thoroughly integrated across public service sectors; while other countries have emulated aspects of Prevent (MME, 2018), no other nation has integrated responsibilities to detect radicalisation as thoroughly as in the UK. In a review of Prevent Strategy and the lessons to be learnt by other European states, the Radicalisation Awareness Network (RAN) described UK policies as "inspiring and to some degree even guiding" (RAN, 2016, p. 1). Prevent 2011 identified integration and the capacity of individuals and organisations to make referrals as a marker of its success (Home Office, 2011); if we take the degree of integration and number of referrals as a measurement for the efficacy of Prevent, it has been extraordinarily successful both in the degree of integration and the number of referrals.

All local authorities, schools, universities and colleges, NHS Trusts and Foundation Trusts, social workers, police, youth justice services, probation services and prisons are obliged to incorporate Prevent into their structures (HMG, 2019; Department of Health and Social Care, 2022, p. 1). As part of the UK counter-terrorism strategy, Prevent has achieved significant results, including a greater understanding of radicalisation, increased referrals for the Channel Programme, increased training of professionals, more local prevent projects, a new higher education body and a new prison and probation network for CVE, exclusion of 100 hate preachers from the UK and removal of over 180,000 pieces of terrorist-related content online since 2010 (RAN, 2016, p. 6).

Another marker of the success of Prevent is the way most teachers engage positively with the duty. Research examining the ways teachers in Britain and Denmark recognise radicalisation found that, although they recognise radicalisation in similar ways, British teachers were more likely to react formally, that is, report pupils to the authorities (Parker, Lindekilde, & Gotzsche-Astrup, 2020). Figures released by the Home Office in the nine years since the 2015 Counter Terrorism Act was introduced show that teachers and educators are consistently more likely to refer pupils and students (36%) than other sectors including the Police (28%) (Home Office, 2023a). A year after schools were given a legal duty to prevent pupils from being drawn into extremism, government statistics showed that just under a third of all referrals to the counter-terrorism programme came from teachers and other professionals in education. 6,093 people were referred through the Prevent duty to the Chanel Programme, and 1,976 came from the education sector (Home Office, 2018, p. 4). The latest figures continue this trend. In the year ending 31 March 2022, of the 6,406 referrals made to Prevent 2,305 (36%) came from education (Home Office, 2023a).

Giving evidence to the House of Commons in a review of Prevent 2023, Tom Tugendhat argued that he had seen no evidence that Prevent silenced freedom of speech or that discriminated against Muslim communities; he claimed that Prevent was effective and working well:

> Some 3,800 have been referred and come out the other end. It is not only high; it is productive. This is a system that has worked. It has diverted mostly young people away from extremist ideology... In conversations with colleagues around Europe and elsewhere, it is quite clear that they are looking at the work we are doing ... to learn from it and see how they can adapt and improve it for their own circumstances.
>
> (House of Commons, 2023, p. 3)

Critiques of Prevent can be broadly categorised into three overlapping areas:

- that Prevent discriminates against Muslim communities through constructing Muslims as a “suspect community”;
- that Prevent radically transforms the traditional relationship between teachers and pupils;
- that Prevent is conceptually flawed leading to possible abuses of civil liberties.

The notion of groups as a suspect community was originally developed to describe the way Irish communities were identified and discriminated against as a result of the enactment of the 1974 Prevention Against Terrorism Act (Hillyard, 1993). In 2010, the Equality and Human Rights Commission commissioned a report to determine if the current counter-terrorist legislation was contributing to the creation of a new suspect community through its focus on Muslim communities. The report concluded that many participants believed that counter-terrorism policies were contributing towards hostility to Muslims as a suspect group (Choudhury & Fenwick, 2011). In the decade since that report, a growing body of research demonstrates a near consensus that Muslims in education as well as public sector organisations and wider society experience the hostility, disciplining and surveillance associated with a suspect community (O'Toole et al., 2016).

From its inception, critics of Prevent insisted that it radically transforms the traditional relationship between teacher and pupil (Choudhury & Fenwick, 2011; Scott-Baumann, 2017; Abbas, Awan, & Marsden, 2021). In the year following the introduction of the Counter terrorism Act 2015, members of the NUT (the largest UK Teachers Trade Union) voted to reject Prevent on the grounds that it suppressed debates in the classroom and failed to prevent extremism (Hooper, 2016). Teachers who act as the eyes and ears of the Home Office are placed in a position where they must suspect and interrogate pupils' speech in the classroom in relation to counter terrorism rather than pedagogy (Miller, 2010). The trust between teacher and pupil is not only refigured along security criteria but is potentially undermined and damaged as teachers are expected to privilege their concerns about possible radicalisation over their roles as teachers (Edwards, 2021). As informers rather than as educators, teachers and tutors could reasonably expect that their pupils will be less inclined to speak openly and ask difficult questions if they believe that their words may be reported to the Home Office (Faure-Walker, 2019; Lockley-Scott, 2020).

The third critique of Prevent is that the rationale supporting Prevent is conceptually flawed. Some critics note that the focus on ideology means that Prevent does not attend to the political and social factors that may lead to radicalisation (Hussain, 2016). The law underpinning Prevent has been identified as incoherent so that key concepts, including extremisms itself, are opaque (Scott-Baumann, 2017). One consequence of the legal opaqueness that characterises Prevent is that a space is created where the execution and interpretation of policy and legislation can lead to the abuse of civil liberties (Ramsay, 2017; Awan, Spiller, & Whiting, 2019). Some civil rights abuses directly relate to the way Muslims are targeted; nonetheless, other liberties, including freedom of expression and the right to protest, have detrimental consequences for civil society more generally.

Some critics argue that the definition of extremism at the heart of UK counter-terrorism policy and the nature of Prevent as a pre-crime legislation means that the internal logic of Prevent is inherently illiberal (Abbas, 2019; Boukalas, 2019). The decision to define extremist ideas as ideologies that undermine fundamental British values has raised similar concerns precisely because of the use of terminology that is contested and opaque (Winter, Heath-Kelly, & Mills, 2021). This focus on values and ideas that may lead to radicalisation, but which are poorly defined and vague, means that there is scope for civil rights abuses because the range of views and beliefs that can be considered potentially risky is limitless (Ramsay, 2017; Farrell, 2023).

Despite criticism that key definitions including the focus on ideology as a driver of radicalisation are flawed, the government maintains its commitment to a definition of extremism based on ideology. In 2015, the Independent Reviewer of Terrorism Legislation Group presented evidence to a House of Commons Home Affairs Committee in response to growing criticism of Prevent. The committee argued that, although Prevent was broadly useful, it lacked transparency, that aspects of the programme were ineffective, and that it sometimes operated in a manner that was discriminatory and insensitive (Anderson, 2016). The government established a review (Shawcross, 2023) that was then mired in controversy and accused of bias (Holmwood & Aitlhadj, 2023). In response, the Home Secretary, Suella Braverman warned that the government would "do more to rebut those attempting to spread fear and disinformation about Prevent", and reiterated that "Prevent's first objective will be tackling the ideological causes of terrorism" (Home Office, 2023b).

The controversial nature of Prevent appears to have had little impact on the degree to which schools have engaged with the Prevent Duty. Given the critical response to Prevent by human rights, trade unions and civil liberty groups, how can the embedded nature of Prevent in education be explained? In research on the impact of Prevent in schools, a common theme is the role of safeguarding practices in facilitating and normalising policies to do with counter terrorism, but there is less discussion about how the narratives associated with safeguarding have intertwined with so little friction with the narratives associated with the Prevent Duty (Busher et al., 2017).

What is rarely considered is how and why the duties and surveillance that teachers now routinely undertake as part of their everyday practice were so successfully subsumed within the safeguarding agenda (Ghaemmaghami & Jabbar, 2023). The following section suggests that the policy and pedagogical landscape in schools can be characterised as a pre-crime environment, and that it is the pre-crime nature of schools that provides the conceptual and professional frame that means that professional behaviour that once would have been regarded with suspicion in schools are now not only acceptable but regarded as good practice (Miller, 2010).

3. The Pre-Crime School

The key features associated with pre crime were identified at the start of this chapter as, firstly, the existence of normalised regimes of surveillance that are accepted as routine and necessary within education; secondly, a mechanism by which professionals could measure and estimate how likely it was that individuals might break the law at some future date; and lastly, a conceptual framework that legitimises intervention so that it is acceptable that individuals should be prevented through the law before a crime has been committed.

3.1 Surveillance and Regimes of Inspection and Accountability

The pre-crime school as an educational construct depends on an environment where there is an expectation that professional roles are monitored and the expectation that professionals will also monitor. The emergence of securitisation and surveillance as dominant trends in English education provides the context in which the relationship between education professionals and counter-terrorism initiatives exist. Schools in the modern period have always been sites of some form of surveillance (Taylor, 2018), but in more recent times there is a recognition that surveillance has become, at the same time, more overt and more embedded into activities and that are routine in schools (Carlile, 2018). In English schools, surveillance takes places in a number of ways including what Stephen Ball (2003, p. 1) refers too as the "terrors of performativity", a culture generated within neoliberal educational structures where teachers "live a life of calculation" in order to avoid negative scrutiny. The generation of a discourse where progress and attainment are aligned with continual monitoring, the introduction and widespread use of surveillance technologies is widely recognised (Page, 2016; Cushing & Snell, 2023) as are regimes of surveillance that legitimise the behaviours that teachers are expected to play in the monitoring and reporting of their students and pupils (Perryman et al., 2017).

For many observers, Ofsted is identified as the dominant form of surveillance in schools and the work of teachers (Page, 2016). Ofsted creates an environment where monitoring (against the criteria) becomes the norm and where an increasingly wider range of activities (including policy decisions, leadership and management and teacher performance) are scrutinised (Courtney, 2014; Perryman et al., 2017; Wood, 2019). The surveillance generated by Ofsted is an integral part of teachers' lives, and surveillance of teacher work is integrated into professional behaviour for all teachers through Ofsted inspection frameworks and teachers' professional code of practice, the Teachers' Standards (Department for Education, 2011).

English teachers train and work in a culture of surveillance but pre crime demands not only the normalisation of the surveillance of others but that teachers are willing to make judgments based on that surveillance. In a pre-crime environment, the way that calculation and judgement is made is through the use of the idea of *risk*. Risk factors, factors which are meant to help professionals calculate the probability of an event are now widely used in a number of fields including education, social work and health care (Parton, 2017). More importantly, the use of "risk" as a mechanism through which the likelihood of possible harm is judged is a key element in the construction and perpetuation of the pre crime and the successful way in which "the war on terror is now embedded in safeguarding policies of schools and colleges" (Farrell, 2016, p. 283).

3.2 Risk

The pre-criminal space relies on factors that can be evaluated as evidence of the likelihood that a crime may occur; in relation to schools, these factors are associated with signs that teachers are expected to interpret as evidence of radicalisation (Department for Education, 2022b). The notion of risk is located at the heart of security and counter-terrorism policy (Mythen & Walklate, 2006), and government policy frequently characterises the threat of terrorism as a risk; interestingly, CONTEST uses *risk* 143 times and the Prevent Duty Guidance published in 2021 outlines it strategy to prevent radicalisation as a "Risk Based Approach" (Home Office, 2021). In contemporary theory, the idea of risk is most commonly associated with the work of German sociologist Ulrich Beck, who developed the idea as part of his analysis of late modernity. In *The risk society*, Beck (2009) suggests that, rather than abating our fear of risk, science and technology accentuate and even create a hypersensitivity to risk. In the intervening 20 years, references to risk dominate social, political and economic discourses, but it has become a lens in itself, a prism through which we regard and experience changes in society, so that every new development is experienced as risky. As a cultural mindset, risk proliferates like a virus. Not only do multiple fields of inquiry use risk as a prism through which to consider everything from environmental disasters to mental health, but the idea that we can estimate risk is evident in the ubiquitous use of procedures designed to measure risk and the creation of risk registers.

The expanding milieu of risk provides the context in which the pre crime operates but there is an important relationship between the notion of pre crime and risk. Pre crime demands a mechanism by which it is possible for experts to assess how likely it is that a crime will take place at some future date. In the world of Philip K Dick, this problem was solved by the use of pre-cogs, beings with supernatural/psychic powers who, in a dream state, catch glimpses of possible futures. In the worlds of social work, education and law, possible futures are glimpsed through the analysis of risk factors. In social work, risk factors were used as a mechanism by which professionals could measure and anticipate the likelihood of future abuse or negligence. In his analysis of emerging discourses around child protection in relation to social work, Parton (2017) argues that the model of risk factors was particularly attractive to policy makers because they were able to draw on an extensive range of overlapping personal and environmental risk factors that could connect to future criminal activity in multiple areas, including violence and drug abuse. The more risk factors any individual experienced the more likely they were to suffer and the greater justification there was for early intervention.

What is sometimes called the Risk Factor Prevention Paradigm is now firmly entrenched in a number of fields, including education and counter terrorism (Parton, 2017). Prevent, CONTEST and resources for schools created by the Home Office in relation to extremism identify factors that might indicate risk as an aid to teachers. The vulnerability assessment framework (VAF) used by Channel (the government programme that supports those who may have been radicalised) is designed to support professionals in identifying adults and children from being drawn into terrorism-related activity and help them decide whether individuals need "support to address their vulnerability" (HMG, 2018, p. 2). VAF stresses that the characteristics it outlines do not "necessarily indicate that a person is either committed to terrorism or may become a terrorist", but they are all factors which professionals may take into consideration when making decisions about the likelihood of an individual becoming radicalised (HMG, 2018, p. 2). The factors include:

- A need for identity, meaning and belonging;
- A desire for political or moral change;
- A desire for excitement and adventure;
- Over-identification with a group or ideology.

Positioning vulnerability as a defining quality means that vulnerability becomes a universal characteristic and that we are all therefore potentially at risk and are potentially in need of safeguarding.

4. Safeguarding and Vulnerability

Pre-crime environments depend on mechanisms that allow the preventive function to be enacted. Pre-crime environments also depend on narratives that legitimise what would in other circumstances be considered a violation of liberal values, that is, the criminalisation of individuals before any law has been broken. In schools, the necessity of safeguarding vulnerable pupils is that narrative. The use of risk factors enables professionals to identify individuals who are likely to be susceptible to radicalisation, but it is the belief that particular pupils require safeguarding because some risk factors indicate that they may be vulnerable that legitimises the preventative function in the pre-crime school. Regimes of surveillance and the use of risk to determine the likelihood of crime are operationalised through safeguarding narratives and practices. However, it is the nature of extremism, as it is defined in Prevent, as a dangerous ideology, that enables Prevent to sit so comfortably within safeguarding structures in schools.

Policy and guidance for schools on Prevent situates radicalisation as a safeguarding issue that is essentially the same as any other safeguarding issue (McKendrick & Finch, 2019). Guidance produced by the Home Office to schools in 2015 reassured schools that their duties under Prevent should not be "burdensome; because the Prevent Duty is entirely consistent with schools' and childcare providers existing responsibilities" (Department for Education, 2015, p. 5). In 2022 guidance from the Department of Education on Safeguarding assumes that the same referral routes that are used by schools for safeguarding will be used for children and young people thought to be at risk from radicalisation. Furthermore, the guidance sets out the expectations that as part of this safeguarding all schools must be able to show evidence of cooperation with the Police and Prevent staff, as well as the capacity to work alongside multi-agency forums (Department for Education, 2022c).

A review of the existing empirical studies on Prevent in schools in the England up to 2019 suggests that teachers exercise agency in relation to the demands Prevent imposes on them, and this is true in relation to safeguarding (Jerome, Elwick, & Kaim, 2019). Not all the studies focused on safeguarding but the ones that did establish a link between the familiarity that teachers have with the language and expectations of safeguarding and their confidence in detecting radicalisation (Bryan, 2017). In the single largest piece of research on Prevent in schools to date data suggests that teachers feel confident about exercising their duties under Prevent because Prevent is positioned within a framework that they are already familiar with. One of the clearest findings from their data was that positioning Prevent as a safeguarding issue made it easier for teachers to incorporate it into their professional lives and that this was even the case among respondents who expressed scepticism about the Prevent Duty' (Busher et al., 2017, p. 24).

Why should teachers consider potential radicalisation a phenomenon that should be covered by a safeguarding agenda? Safeguarding assumes that some individuals are especially vulnerable to harm. In other contexts, the harm that people may be vulnerable to is easier to identify, for example, violence or deprivation. But in the context of radicalisation, what exactly is the nature of the harm that we are safeguarding the vulnerable from? As successive policy makes clear, the vulnerability in question is the vulnerability to radicalised ideas but the content of those ideas is rarely articulated (Heath-Kelly, 2017; Lowe, 2021; Ramsay, 2017). The vagueness that characterises risk factors and the vulnerable also characterises any understanding of what these dangerous ideas, are and even Channel Guidance does not outline the content of the religious or political ideas that could cause harm (Ramsay, 2017). The oblique nature of risk indicators around radicalisation means that every utterance may be considered potentially harmful and all students/pupils must be safeguarded because they are all potentially vulnerable to radicalising ideas. Educators are required to make decisions about the possible radicalisation of pupils that are both speculative and subjective, and which will reflect their own interpretation and relationships with their students. The irony of Prevent is that its intent is to prevent radicalisation that undermines liberal democracy but its execution in precrime schools undermines the very values it seeks to protect (Boukalas, 2017).

5. Conclusion

In her seminal work *The limits of the preventive state*, Steiker (1998) considered why so few scholars addressed the question of the appropriate limits of the preventative state. The same could be asked of pre-crime in the form of Prevent in English classrooms. Narratives of vulnerability and safeguarding mediated through the prism of pre crime generates school environments where it is expected that pupils must be endlessly monitored for their own safety and the safety of others. Children and young people are drawn into the orbit of the security forces before they have committed an offence, and teachers are not only complicit in this process but many actively support a pre-crime agenda in their classrooms because they believe it is the best way to defend liberal values. Steiker ends her article with the reminder that we should be most suspicious when our liberties are eroded by forces that present themselves as benign (Steiker, 1998, p. 807). The failure of schools to reflect on the impact of Prevent on their professionalism, their teaching and their relationship with pupils leaves the authority and power of the pre crime in education unchecked and unquestioned.

References

Abbas, M. S. (2019). Producing 'internal suspect bodies': Divisive effects of UK counter-terrorism measures on Muslim communities in Leeds and Bradford. *The British Journal of Sociology*, *70*(1), 261–282.

Abbas, T., Awan, I., & Marsden, J. (2021). Pushed to the Edge: The consequences of the 'Prevent Duty' in de-radicalising pre-crime thought among British Muslim university students. *Race, Ethnicity and Education*. Retrieved from https://www.tandfonline.com/doi/full/10.1080/13613324.2021.2019002

Anderson, D. (2016). *The Terrorism Acts in 2015 Report of the independent reviewer on the operation of the Terrorism Act 2000 and Part 1 of the Terrorism Act 2006*. Retrieved from https://assets.publishing.service.gov.uk/government/uploads/system/uploads/attachment_data/file/579233/THE_TERRORISM_ACTS_IN_2015__web_.pdf

Awan, I., Spiller, K., & Whiting, A. (2019). *Terrorism in the classroom*. Bristol: Palgrave.

Ball, S. J. (2003). The Teacher's soul and the terrors of performativity. *Journal of Education Policy, 18*(2), 215–228.

Beck, U. (2009). *The risk society*. London. Sage.

Boukalas, C. (2017). U.K. counterterrorism law, pre-emption, and politics: Toward 'authoritarian legality'? *New Criminal Law Review, 20*(3), 355–390.

Boukalas, C. (2019). The prevent paradox: Destroying liberalism in order to protect it. *Crime, Law and Social Change, 72*, 467–482.

Bryan, H. (2017). Developing the political citizen: How teachers are navigating the statutory demands of the Counter Terrorism and Security Act 2015 and the Prevent Duty. *Education, Citizenship and Social Justice, 12*(3), 197–289.

Busher, J., Choudhury, J., Thomas, P., & Harris, G. (2017). *What the Prevent duty means for schools and colleges in England: An analysis of educationalists experiences*. Research Report, Aziz Foundation.

Carlile, A. (2018). School surveillance, control, and resistance. In J. Deakin, E. Taylor, & A. Kupchik (Eds.), *The palgrave international handbook of school discipline, surveillance and social control* (pp. 17–42). Cham, Switzerland: Palgrave Macmillan.

Choudhury, T., & Fenwick, H. (2011). The impact of counter-terrorism measures on Muslim communities. *International Review of Law, Computers and Technology, 25*(3), 151–181.

Courtney, S. J. (2014). Post-panopticism and school inspection in England. *British Journal of Sociology of Education, 37*(4), 623–642.

Cushing, I., & Snell, J. (2023). The white ears of Ofsted: A raciolinguistic perspective on the listening practices of the schools' inspectorate. *Language in Society, 52*(3), 363–386.

Department for Education. (2011). *The new teachers' standards*. London: DfE.

Department for Education. (2015). *The prevent duty – Departmental advice for school and childcare providers*.

Department for Education. (2022a). *Understanding and identifying radicalisation risk in your education setting*. Retrieved from https://www.gov.uk/government/publications/the-prevent-duty-safeguarding-learners-vulnerable-to-radicalisation/understanding-and-identifying-radicalisation-risk-in-your-education-setting

Department for Education. (2022b). *The prevent duty: an introduction for those with safeguarding responsibilities*. Retrieved from https://www.gov.uk/government/publications/the-prevent-duty-safeguarding-learners-vulnerable-to-radicalisation/the-prevent-duty-an-introduction-for-those-with-safeguarding-responsibilities#:~:text=Contents&text=The%20Prevent%20

duty%20requires%20all,from%20extremist%20ideologies%20and%20radicalisation

Department for Education. (2022c). *Keeping children safe in education. Statutory guidance for schools and colleges.*

Department of Health and Social Care. (2022). *NHS prevent training and competencies framework.* Retrieved from https://www.gov.uk/government/publications/nhs-prevent-training-and-competencies-framework/nhs-prevent-training-and-competencies-framework#

Dick, P. K. (2002). *Minority report.* London: Gollancz.

Donkin, S. (2013). The preventative turn in criminal justice. In S. Donkin (Ed.), *Preventing terrorism and controlling risk: A comparative analysis of control orders in the UK and Australia* (pp. 3–9). London: Springer.

Edwards, P. (2021). Surveillance, safeguarding and beyond: the prevent duty and resilient citizenship. *Critical Studies on Terrorism, 14*(1), 47–66.

Elton-Chalcraft, S., Lander, V., Revell. L., Warner, D., & Whitworth, L. (2017). To promote, or not to promote fundamental British values? Teachers' standards, diversity and teacher education. *British Educational Research Journal, 43*(1), 29–48.

Farrell, F. (2016). 'Why all of a sudden do we need to teach fundamental British values?' A critical investigation of religious education student teacher positioning within a policy discourse of discipline and control. *Journal of Education for Teaching, 42*(3), 280–297.

Farrell, F. (2023). *Fundamental British values: Michael Foucault and religious education teacher subjectivity.* London: Palgrave McMillan.

Faure-Walker, R. (2019). Teachers as informants: countering extremism and promoting violence. *Journal of Beliefs and Values, 40*(3), 368–380.

Ghaemmaghami, A., & Jabbar, N. (2023). Delegated safeguarding or surveillance by proxy? Education: The prevent statutory duty in action. *International Journal of Law, Crime and Justice, 74*, 2–13.

HAC (Home Affairs Committee). (2008–2009). *Project CONTEST: The Government's counter-terrorism strategy.* Retrieved from https://assets.publishing.service.gov.uk/government/uploads/system/uploads/attachment_data/file/228674/7703.pdf

Heath-Kelly, C. (2017). The geography of pre-criminal space: Epidemiological imaginations of radicalisation risk in the UK Prevent Strategy. *Critical Studies on Terrorism, 10*(2), 297–319.

Heath-Kelly, C., & Shanaah, S. (2023). Rehabilitation within pre-crime interventions: The hybrid criminology of social crime prevention and countering violent extremism. *Theoretical Criminology, 27*(2), 183–203.

HMG. (2015). *Counter extremism strategy.* Retrieved from https://assets.publishing.service.gov.uk/government/uploads/system/uploads/attachment_data/file/470088/51859_Cm9148_Accessible.pdf

HMG. (2018). *CONTEST.* Retrieved from https://assets.publishing.service.gov.uk/government/uploads/system/uploads/attachment_data/file/716907/140618_CCS207_CCS0218929798-1_CONTEST_3.0_WEB.pdf

HMG. (2019). *Integrated communities strategy green paper*. Retrieved from https://www.belongnetwork.co.uk/resources/integrated-communities-action-plan/#:~:text=The%20Integrated%20Communities%20Action%20Plan,to%20promote%20the%20integration%20agenda

Hillyard, P. (1993). *Suspect community*. London: Pluto Press.

Holmwood, J., & Aitlhadj, L. (2023). *A response to the shawcross report*. Retrieved from https://peoplesreviewofprevent.org/wp-content/uploads/2023/03/A-Response-to-the-Shawcross-Report.pdf

Home Office. (2011). *Prevent strategy*. London: The Stationary Office. Retrieved from http://www.homeoffice.gov.uk/publications/counter-terrorism/prevent/prevent-strategy/

Home Office. (2018). *Individuals referred to and supported through the prevent programme*. Retrieved from https://assets.publishing.service.gov.uk/government/uploads/system/uploads/attachment_data/file/694002/individuals-referred-supported-prevent-programme-apr2016-mar2017.pdf

Home Office. (2021). *Prevent duty guidance*. Retrieved from https://www.gov.uk/government/publications/prevent-duty-guidance

Home Office. (2023a). *Individuals referred to and supported through the prevent programme*. Retrieved from https://www.gov.uk/government/statistics/individuals-referred-to-and-supported-through-the-prevent-programme-april-2021-to-march-2022/individuals-referred-to-and-supported-through-the-prevent-programme-april-2021-to-march-2022

Home Office. (2023b). *The response to the independent review of prevent*. https://www.gov.uk/government/publications/independent-review-of-prevents-report-and-government-response/the-response-to-the-independent-review-of-prevent-accessible

Hooper, R. (2016, March 16). *Teachers reject prevent anti-terrorism strategy*. Retrieved from https://www.huffingtonpost.co.uk/2016/03/28/teachers-reject-prevent-anti-terrorism-strategy_n_9559716.html

House of Commons. (2023). *Home affairs committee oral evidence prevent review*. Retrieved from https://committees.parliament.uk/oralevidence/12904/pdf/

Hussain, D. (2016). *The serious way forward to 'prevent' terror in Britain*. Retrieved from http://www.middleeasteye.net/columns/beginning-end-prevent-716599408

Jerome, L., Elwick, A., & Kaim, R. (2019). The impact of the Prevent Duty on schools: A review of the evidence. *British Educational Research Journal*, *45*(4), 821–837.

Lockley-Scott, A. (2020). *Exploring the imagined identities of Muslim pupils in the context of prevent*. Retrieved from https://wrap.warwick.ac.uk/153071/1/WRAP_Theses_Lockley-Scott_2020.pdf

Lowe, D. (2021). Determining extremist behaviour. In D. Lowe & R. Bennett (Eds.), *Prevent strategy*. (pp. 51–72). London: Routledge.

McCulloch, J., & Pickering, S. (2009). Pre crime and counter terrorism. *British Journal of Criminology*, *5*(49), 628–645.

McKendrick, D., & Finch, J. (2019). PREVENT, safeguarding and the common-sensing of social work in the United Kingdom. *AOTEAROA New Zealand Social Work*, *31*(2), 18–28.

Miller, J. (2010). The contribution of Local Authorities and their SACRES to promoting cohesion through Religious Education. In M. Grimmitt (Ed.), *Religious education and social and community cohesion* (pp. 56–77). Essex: McCrimmon.

MME. (2018). *France announces prevent like counter radicalisation programme*. Retrieved from https://www.middleeasteye.net/news/france-announces-prevent-counter-radicalisation-programme

Mythen, G., & Walklate, S. (2006). Criminology and terrorism: Which thesis? Risk society or governmentality? *The British Journal of Criminology, 46*(3), 376–398.

O'Toole, T., Meer, N., DeHanas, D., Jones, S., & Modood, T. (2016). Governing through prevent? Regulation and contested practice in state-Muslim engagement. *Sociology, 50*(1), 160–177.

Page, D. (2016). Conceptualising the surveillance of teachers. *British Journal of the Sociology of Education. 38*(7), 991–1006.

Parker, D., Lindekilde, L., & Gotzsche-Astrup, O. (2020). Recognising and responding to radicalisation at the 'frontline': Assessing the capability of school teachers to recognise and respond to radicalisation. *British Educational Research Journal*, *47*(3), 634–653.

Parton, N. (2017). Concerns about risk as a major driver of professional practice. In M. Connolly (Ed.), *Beyond the risk paradigm in child protection* (pp. 3–14). London: Bloomsbury.

Perryman, J., Maguire, M., Braun, A., & Ball, S. (2017). Surveillance, governmentality and moving the goalposts: The influence of Ofsted on the work of schools in a post-panoptic era. *British Journal of Educational Studies*, *66*(2), 145–163.

Ramsay, P. (2017). Is prevent a safe space? *Journal of Education, Citizenship and Social Justice*, *1*(2), 143–158.

RAN. (2016). *Ex post paper – UK prevent strategy*. Retrieved from https://home-affairs.ec.europa.eu/system/files/2020-09/ran_study_visit_uk_prevent_strategy_16-17_062016_en.pdf Ratcliffe 2016 https://www.theguardian.com/uk-news/2016/jul/12/teachers-made-one-third-of-referrals-to-prevent-strategy-in-2015

Rizq, R. (2017). 'Pre-crime', prevent, and the practices of exceptionalism: Psychotherapy and the new norm in the NHS. *Psychodynamic Practice, 23*(4), 336–356.

Rose, G. L., & Nestorovska, D. (2007). Australian counter-terrorism offences: Necessity and clarity in federal criminal law reforms, *Criminal Law Journal*, *31*(1), 20–55.

Scott-Baumann, A. (2017). Ideology, utopia and Islam on campus: How to free speech a little from its own terrors. *Education, Citizenship and Social Justice, 12*(2), 159–176.

Shawcross, W. (2023). *Independent review of prevent*. Retrieved from https://assets.publishing.service.gov.uk/government/uploads/system/uploads/attachment_data/file/1134986/Independent_Review_of_Prevent.pdf

Skoczylis, J., & Andrews, S. (2020). A conceptual critique of prevent: Can prevent be saved? No, but .... *Critical Social Policy, 40*(3), 350–369.

Steiker, C. (1998). The limits of the preventative state. *The Journal of Crimminal Law and Criminology*, 88 (3), 771-808.

Taylor, E. (2018). Curating risk, selling safety? Fear of crime, responsibilisation and the surveillance school economy. In M. Lee & G. Mythen (Eds.), *The Routledge international handbook on fear of crime* (1st ed., pp. 312–321). Abingdon: Routledge.

Thomas, P. (2016). Youth, terrorism and education: Britain's Prevent programme. *International Journal of Lifelong Education, 35*(2), 171–187.

Vidino, L., & Brandon, J. (2012). Europe's experience in countering radicalisation: Approaches and challenges. *Journal of Policing, Intelligence and Counter Terrorism, 7*(2), 163–179.

Winter, C., Heath-Kelly, C., & Mills, C. (2021). A moral education? British values, colour-blindness, and preventing terrorism. *Critical Social Policy*, 42(1), 85–106.

Wood, E. (2019). Unbalanced and unbalancing acts in the early years foundation stage: A critical discourse analysis of policy led evidence on teaching and play from the office for standards in education in England. *International Journal of Primary, Elementary, and early Years Education, 47*(7), 784–795.

Zedner, L. (2007). Pre crime and post criminology? *Theoretical Criminology, 11*(2), 261–281. https://doi.org/10.1177/1362480607075851

Zedner, L., & Ashworth, A. (2019). The rise and restraint of the preventative state. *The Annual Review of Criminology*, 2, 249–250.

Index

Note: **Bold** page numbers refer to tables; *italic* page numbers refer to figures and page numbers followed by "n" denote endnotes.